Almost a Family

JOHN DARNTON

Almost a Family

A Memoir

ALFRED A. KNOPF · NEW YORK · 2011

THIS IS A BORZOI BOOK
Published by Alfred A. Knopf

Copyright © 2011 by Talespin, Inc.

Grateful acknowledgment is made to Harold Ober Associates
for permission to reprint an excerpt from "Sunday: New Guinea"
by Karl Shapiro, copyright © 1943, 1970 by Karl Shapiro.
First published in *Good Housekeeping*. Reprinted by permission
of Harold Ober Associates.

Library of Congress Cataloging-in-Publication Data
Darnton, John.
   Almost a family : a memoir / by John Darnton.
       p.   cm.
   ISBN 978-0-307-26617-0
   1. Darnton, John.   2. Darnton, John—Family.   3. Authors, American—20th century—
Biography.   4. Fathers and sons—United States—Biography.   I. Title.
   PS3554.A727Z46 2010
   813'.54—dc22
   [B]   2010016835

Jacket photograph courtesy of the author
Jacket design by Carol Devine Carson

Manufactured in the United States of America
First Edition

For Nina
and

Kyra, Liza, and Jamie
and

Zachary and Ella   Asher and Adara

A man who has spent his life in newspaper work is apt to believe that in the long run the best thing to do is to tell the truth.

—Byron Darnton

And over the hill the guns bang like a door
And planes repeat their mission in the heights.
The jungle outmaneuvers creeping war
And crawls within the circle of our sacred rites.

I long for our disheveled Sundays home,
Breakfast, the comics, news of latest crimes,
Talk without reference, and palindromes,
Sleep and the Philharmonic and the ponderous *Times*.

I long for lounging in the afternoons
Of clean intelligent warmth, my brother's mind,
Books and thin plates and flowers and shining spoons,
And your love's presence, snowy, beautiful, and kind.

Karl Shapiro,
"Sunday: New Guinea"

Almost a Family

shooting at him, and when he struck shore he was dead. Windy Marshall told me about it. He saw it. He was captain of the boat.

"Years ago, the Darnells was so thinned out that the old man and his two sons concluded they'd leave the country. They started to take steamboat just above No. 10; but the Watsons got wind of it; and they arrived just as the two young Darnells was walking up the companionway with their wives on their arms. The fight begun then, and they never got no further — both of them killed. After that, old Darnell got into trouble with the man that run the ferry, and the ferry-man got the worst of it — and died. But his friends shot old Darnell through and through — filled him full of bullets, and ended him."

The country gentleman who told me these things had been reared in ease and comfort, was a man of good parts, and was college-bred. His loose grammar was the fruit of careless habit, not ignorance. This habit among educated men in the West is not universal, but it is prevalent — prevalent in the towns, certainly, if not in the cities; and to a degree which one cannot help noticing, and marveling at. I heard a Westerner, who would be accounted a highly educated man in any country, say, "Never mind, it *don't make no difference*, anyway." A life-long resident who was present heard it, but it made no impression upon her. She was able to recall the fact afterward, when reminded of it; but she confessed that the words had not grated upon her ear at the time — a confession which suggests that if educated people can hear such blasphemous grammar, from such a source, and be unconscious of the deed, the crime must be tolerably common — so common that the general ear has become dulled by familiarity with it, and is no longer alert, no longer sensitive to such affronts.

No one in the world speaks blemishless grammar; no one has ever written it — *no* one, either in the world or out of it (taking the Scriptures for evidence on the latter point); therefore it would not be fair to exact grammatical perfection from the peoples of the Valley; but they and all other peoples may justly be required to refrain from *knowingly* and *purposely* debauching their grammar.

I found the river greatly changed at Island No. 10. The island which I remembered was some three miles long and a quarter of a mile wide, heavily timbered, and lay near the Kentucky shore — within two hundred yards of it, I should say. Now, however, one had to hunt for it with a spy-glass. Nothing was left of it but an insignificant little tuft, and this was no longer near the Kentucky shore; it was clear over against the opposite shore, a mile away. In war times the island had been an important place, for it commanded the situation; and, being heavily fortified, there was no getting by it. It lay between the upper and lower divisions of the Union forces, and kept them separate, until a junction was finally effected across the Missouri neck of land; but the island being itself joined to that neck now, the wide river is without obstruction.

In this region the river passes from Kentucky into Tennessee, back into Missouri, then back into Kentucky, and thence into Tennessee again. So a mile or two of Missouri sticks over into Tennessee.

The town of New Madrid was looking very unwell; but otherwise unchanged from its former condition and aspect. Its blocks of frame houses were still grouped in the same old flat plain, and environed by the same old forests. It was as tranquil as formerly, and apparently had neither grown nor diminished in size. It was said that the recent high water had invaded it and damaged its looks. This was surprising news; for in

One of the few acknowledgments of my existence to come from my father happened in the middle of a feud between the Darnells and the Watsons on the banks of the Mississippi in the 1840s. That is, in the description of such a feud in Mark Twain's *Life on the Mississippi*. There, halfway down page 210, just as friends of the ferryman shoot old Darnell through and through—"filled him full of bullets, and ended him"—lies an X in the margin. At the page's bottom, the X is explained:

> *Nov 20, 1941—1:40 AM. As I was reading this in French Hospital, N.Y., Dr. Heaton came into the waiting room and said: "You've got another boy."—It was John.*
>
> —B. D.

I like my father's handwriting. It's in thick black pencil straight across the full width of both pages, sprawling and virile. The "B." and the "D."—for Byron Darnton—are full-bellied. No question about it: It is a declaration for history. Looking closely, I see the "20" after "November" is superimposed over a "19." A natural mistake: It's

1:40 a.m. Perhaps he's sleepy and thinks it's still the night before. Or maybe he's so excited by the news that he wants to get it down and only a moment later, rereading, realizes his error. I picture the waiting room in my imagination. It's a stuffy enclosure off the entrance to the maternity ward: two windows, grime-covered, a lineup of straight-backed metal chairs, a beaten-down couch, framed prints of British foxhunting scenes on the wall, a rack with ragged copies of *Collier's* and *The Saturday Evening Post,* two stand-up ashtrays overflowing with cigarette butts, a radiator pumping away in the corner and worn linoleum on the floor—or maybe a thin carpet. I see my father waiting there, reading. He's sitting comfortably, self-contained, right foot resting on his left knee. His eyes sparkle with amusement at a nervous young man walking in and out from the corridor. They've exchanged a few friendly words. He provides the comfort of an older man, an old hand at this. A smile is ready to break out under his bushy dark mustache. He's wearing a tweed jacket around his broad shoulders, and his dark brown trousers are beginning to lose the sharpness of their crease. His overcoat and fedora are hanging from a coatrack. Is he smoking? Surely. But what? Luckies? Camels? Is he carrying his fancy leather-bound flask, and does he offer the young man a swig of whiskey? He goes back to reading, back to the Mississippi. The door swings open and the doctor comes in to tell him about me. He stands up to take the news, beams, and pumps the doctor's hand.

But what is he feeling? Had he wanted a girl? Is he worried about his wife? Does he feel the rush of second fatherhood—another son to round out the family, another little body at the dining room table? Or is there just a smidgeon of uncertainty, regret even, the vague sensation of being trapped? Another mouth to feed on a reporter's salary, another obligation. Now he will surely have to settle down.

He would be told to wait a few minutes before seeing his wife and baby. Does he, too, pace about now and look out the window at Eighth Avenue far below, yellow headlights penetrating what appears, perhaps, as a cold rain and billows of steam rising from the manholes? Or does he sit down again and jot the note in the margin and resume reading, lulled by the companionship of Twain, who goes on to describe the great flood of 1882, which broke down the levees, destroyed the crops, washed away the houses, and turned the mighty Mississippi into a scourge seventy miles wide?

The book resurfaced after forty-three years, hidden in plain sight in my brother's bookshelf. He sent it to me with a note: "This isn't really a present, because by rights it belongs to you. . . . Happy birthday!" It had moved houses many times without being opened, testament to the immutability of a moment of supreme consequence (as far as I'm concerned)—and also to its transience.

And so I was born.

CHAPTER I

Four days old, I was taken home to a cozy white clapboard house in the backwoods of Connecticut. According to family lore, I was carried across the threshold by a nurse, so that my brother, Bob, wouldn't become instantly jealous. My mother carried a toy for him, a brand-new fire engine. But—and here the lore surely verges into the apocryphal—he pushed it aside and demanded, "Where's my brudder?"

Two weeks later, the Japanese bombed Pearl Harbor.

My father heard the news over the car radio as he drove our family off on a long-awaited vacation. He immediately spun the car around, dropped the three of us off, and headed to the headquarters of *The New York Times* on West Forty-third Street. The vast third-floor newsroom, on what was to have been a quiet Sunday afternoon, was thrown into high gear. Copyboys rushed from the agency tickers with the latest bulletins, and the switchboard was jammed with calls from a frantic public. Reporters and editors streamed in from all corners to man the phones and take up assignments. My father headed for an enclave in the city room, where eight wooden desks had been pushed together for an enterprise that had begun only six days earlier and that he headed: news broadcasts over the radio station WMCA (the forerunner to WQXR). Until well after midnight a steady stream of copy flowed out through a Teletype operator to the station, which beamed it to the city.

My father, listed as Francis Byron Darnton on his birth certificate, was known to everyone simply as "Barney." With a dry wit, cool composure, and an air of dependability and integrity, he was, at forty-four, an important figure at the *Times*. Gossiping reporters speculated he was on track to become managing editor. He had joined the paper in 1934, following a traditional stepladder of newspaper jobs that had long ago taken him from his hometown of Adrian, Michigan. At the *Times*, he had performed a number of high-level assignments, including setting up "The News of the Week in Review" section, but he had hungered for a closer contact with the news and so two years before had become a roving correspondent. Now, with war upon the country, he felt a new restlessness. For some time, he and "Tootie"—as our mother, Eleanor, was known to close friends—had taken the position that armed conflict with Adolf Hitler was inevitable. As debates raged in bars and around dinner tables, they had long since sided with the interventionists against the isolationists. After the Japanese attack, in late December or early January, as our mother told the story, our father became quietly moody. One morning, in bed with him, divining his secret, she turned to him and said, "So when do you leave for the war?" He wrapped her in his arms and replied, "Thank God. I was wondering how to tell you."

Our father left to become a war correspondent on a cold winter's day, striding purposefully down the front path of our country home in Westport. He and our mother had traveled hard and separate roads to end up together there, and in leaving the three of us, he was putting a dream on hold. Shortly before his departure, in the flurry of securing accreditations and buying uniforms and gear and getting inoculations, he had sat down to explain why in a letter to his older brother Robert, whose automobile factory back in Michigan had been converted for the manufacture of aircraft. Barney was the youngest of seven children—six boys and one girl. Most of them had stayed close to home, but when he was just out of high school, with World War I raging in 1917, he had enlisted in the

32nd "Red Arrow" Division and saw plenty of tough fighting in France. His wanderlust wasn't entirely quashed by his time in the trenches. Now, somewhat defensively in writing to his brother, he set down his reasons for going to war again, "because my decision might seem lighthearted and irresponsible to anyone who knew only the exteriors." Banging out the words quickly on a typewriter and copyediting them afterward with a black pencil, he wrote, in part:

> *In these times it is rather difficult to fix the order of one's responsibilities. The first is, of course, to my family, but it seems to me that certain actions that would be unthinkable in ordinary times are not in these times. My absence may run to a couple of years. That certainly isn't an ideal situation with a couple of young boys. But unless those boys can grow up into a decent sort of a world it won't make any difference anyway—and it seems to me that I must do something toward the end that we all pray for. You are making airplanes. I'm no good in any such field, nor in active service. But I am trained for one job, and I think it's an important job.*

His family, he said, would be taken care of if anything happened to him and, through the generosity of the paper, would be "better provided for than they ever would be if, in other circumstances, I fell off a cliff." Still, the decision to go would have been impossible if his wife had not been the woman she was:

> *Bob and Johnnie can safely be left to her. She isn't the stuff that cracks under a bit of difficulty. She, too, wants the kids to grow up in the right kind of world, and she too believes that we can bring that about only if every one of us does his utmost. This is a joint, not individual, decision.*

After a few sentences on the national need for sacrifices, he returned to the subject of his chosen profession:

> *And there is another motivation. I very much respect the business I am in, even though it falls far short of perfection in all its parts. But it is rightly given special status in the Consti-*

tution, for it is an indispensable force in the achievement of democracy. That special status must be justified by the service performed by the press. And that service can't all be easy. It can't all be privilege without any duty.

All this sounds like a sermon. And I don't like preaching them any more than I do hearing them. But I'll let it stand because I very much want you to understand. It would be most natural, in view of the different ways in which our lives have developed, for you to incline to the belief that I was going off half-cocked. Even if you disagree with my motives, I want you to respect them. And to stand advocate for me before the rest of the family. Middle life can easily be a time of the weakening of family ties. I hope that when this is over we can enjoy the strengthening of them.

I expect to start Monday. The best of things from us to you and yours, and for God's sake turn out those airplanes.

Along with a contingent of other reporters and photographers, my father shipped out of San Francisco in February 1942, and reached Australia some three weeks later. It was a low point of the war: The Germans and Italians were dominant in Europe. In Asia, the Japanese were leaping southward in a stepping-stone series of lightning conquests and besieging American forces in the Philippines. By the time the correspondents arrived in Brisbane, Japanese soldiers were digging in along the northern coast of New Guinea, the huge island just to the north, and invasion fever had struck Australia. For months it was clear the enemy had the upper hand.

Barney was older than the other correspondents, the dean of the American press corps. His dispatches were notable for their clear-eyed humor and the admiration, dosed with affection, shown for the young men doing the fighting. But over seven months he was to grow increasingly frustrated. He had volunteered to cover the war, and he had lobbied hard for the assignment at the *Times,* but so far his coverage had been heavy on human-interest features. He had pieced together accounts of the Battle of the Coral Sea in May and the Battle of Midway in June, but his war stories had been based on sources, not firsthand experience. Aside from an occasional bombing run by Japanese planes over Port Moresby, the key town on the Papuan peninsula of New Guinea, not once had he seen combat firsthand. All the major engagements so far had taken place in remote seas and skies, far from his eyes and ears. On top of that, he had had to contend with reams of red tape from the armies of both the United States and Australia and to fight tooth and nail with the U.S. Army censors. They cut any breath of news that departed from the vapid daily communiqués and excised color as if it were gristle on a steak. Worse, their main job seemed to be to burnish the warrior image of the vain supreme commander of the South West Pacific Area, Gen. Douglas MacArthur.

Then abruptly, in mid-October, things turned around. Barney was about to see some action. As luck would have it, the division he had served with in the Great War, the 32nd, had been chosen to dislodge the Japanese from their stronghold at Buna on Papua's northern shore.* Barney rarely spoke of his wartime experience a quarter of a century before, even to close colleagues, but this time he had shamelessly exploited it to argue that he should be allowed to chronicle his old outfit's exploits. He had buttonholed the division commander, Maj. Gen. Edwin F. Harding, a genial man with a soft side who composed poetry and stashed Kipling verse inside his army manual. Harding bought the argument and gave him permission to accompany the battle-green troops.

On October 16, Barney sat on the veranda of the correspondents' hut in Port Moresby. He drafted a cable to the home office: "Won't be filing for some time." It was the only hint that he was about to undertake a dangerous trip. Then he sat down to finish a letter home to Tootie. He had begun it the day before, chatting about everyday things. He had mentioned that he had broken in a heavy pair of army boots by putting them on, soaking them in a tub of water for fifteen minutes, and shining them. "It worked very well, but the spectacle of a man soaking his feet with his shoes on appealed to all gents having cameras, and the scene has been deathlessly recorded." He vowed to send home a print once he got to a place where the chief censor could pass on it.

---

* During World War II the island's eastern half was divided into North-East New Guinea and Papua. In 1949 they united into the nation of Papua New Guinea. The island's western half, which was Dutch New Guinea, is today part of Indonesia.

"Also, I've been driving a jeep," he said. He had been worried that he would veer to the right side of the road, but after a few times had gotten used to driving on the left. "After you've been passenger enough times on the left side, and have pushed down on the floor boards enough to help the driver brake, it all seems natural enough." The vehicle was heaven because it was breezy.

"We shall have a jeep when all this is over and I shall use it for getting to and from the station. It makes a lovely noise. You'll want to do me out of it. And I won't object too much." As far as his corner of the war, he said things were looking up. There'd been a change in spirit and it was going to make a difference "on the lives of you and me and all the other men and women who are separated." He added, "It's strange how often that thought recurs. You can get an almost wholly personalized view of what you see. When the bombers come back from mission and you talk to the guys and find out they've done well, you say to yourself: This job cut a piece out of the calendar. But the pieces of course are still only tiny.

"Now it's October 16, there having been an interruption. . . . My goodness, we near November and that'll be one (birthday) for Johnnie. Heigh-ho! I'm tired out and going to bed in a few moments. But not before I tell you for at least the second time that you're a damn swell gal. I shouldn't be so tired. I should write you a love letter. Will you take the wish for the act? Oh, my dear, it's going to be pretty nice under that apple tree with that Tom Collins. . . . Good night, my dearest. Some time I'll really tell you what you are and what you've done. Or maybe you know? . . . Tell Bob I hope he has a lot of fun in the snow this winter. He'll have to enjoy it for me, too, for I'm afraid I won't see any. Night, Sweet."

He wrote a large "BOB" on the last page. (He had been told that Bob poured over his letters, looking for the one word he could recognize.) He jumped in a jeep and drove along a dusty road to a tent, where he dropped off the letter and the cable for transmission to the censor. Then he drove back, packed his full field kit, and went to bed, crawling under the mosquito netting to lie on his cot. He would have to get up early in the morning to catch a flight over the Owen Stanley Mountains, the treacherous ridge that split the Papuan peninsula, to reach the northern coast.

. . .

Meanwhile, two old fishing boats requisitioned by the U.S. Army were making their way toward the north by circumnavigating the island's eastern tip. One was the *King John,* a seventy-foot wooden trawler plucked from its berth in Sydney in July. The other was a sister ship, the *Timoshenko,* a fifty-footer, also from Sydney. They were hardly impressive—not what you'd expect to spearhead MacArthur's long-awaited amphibious counteroffensive. The *King John* had a balky reverse gear, her engine wheezed, and her sun-scorched decks reeked of fish and copra. She rode low in the water, looking about to sink at any moment, and her most conspicuous feature was the hoist bar angled off the mast for hauling nets. The *Timoshenko* looked, if anything, even stranger. Someone had painted a large red hammer and sickle on her funnel, apparently in jest. Neither ship had weaponry beyond a .50-caliber machine gun mounted on a shoulder-high tripod in the prow. The two vessels belonged to the "small ships" fleet, a ragtag group of luggers, trawlers, and ketches assembled to carry troops and supplies for the army in the absence of the U.S. Navy, which was otherwise occupied in the Central Pacific. One American general, taking his first look at the rust buckets, was said to have exclaimed, "Goddamn war's gone all old-fashioned on us here!"

The ships left Port Moresby on October 12 under the fleet commander, Lt. Col. Laurence A. McKenny, the division's quartermaster, who in his prewar incarnation had been a Detroit elementary school principal. By October 14, they had made it to Milne Bay, on the island's far eastern tip. It had been the site of an attack five weeks earlier, in which Australian soldiers, the "diggers," had repulsed the Japanese in hand-to-hand combat, much of it at night during torrential rains. Enemy tanks were still mired in muddy ditches beside the road, their narrow treads splayed and the hatches on their cylindrical turrets blown open. At Gili Gili wharf, the crew loaded supplies: ammo, gasoline, medical equipment, and rations.

The next morning, the *King John* and the *Timoshenko* departed Milne Bay. On board was a handsome lieutenant, already well known at thirty-one, Bruce Fahnestock. Bruce and his brother,

Sheridan, were renowned for their prewar explorations of the South Seas. They had sailed schooners around the islands, collecting songs, cultural artifacts, and rare specimens of birds and fish for the American Museum of Natural History. Now in wartime, they had returned, scouring Australian ports for suitable vessels for the "small ships" fleet. So Lieutenant Fahnestock was riding in one of his own recruited trawlers.

The ships arrived at Wanigela just after noon on the sixteenth. Immediately, there was confusion, leading to a change in plans. McKenny, believing his mission was to bring up more supplies from the rear, had expected to turn right around and head back east to Milne Bay to load up again. But after taking a dinghy to shore to confer with Gen. Hanford MacNider, commander of MacArthur's coastal force, he was stunned to learn that instead the ships were to go in the other direction. They would push on west, farther up the coast, toward the Japanese, carrying troops. Instead of gradually building up supplies, their job was to forge ahead and stake out ground for a rapid assault. The pressure was on. Fearing that the Japanese would reinforce their stronghold at Buna, MacArthur wanted to seize it quickly and set up an air base that would push the enemy out of New Guinea. That way, he would protect Australia and begin the long island-hopping road to Tokyo.

The new route meant that the ships would round a large cape, Cape Nelson. Already, MacNider had sent two battalions on foot to cut across the neck of the peninsula, where preliminary reconnaissance indicated the trails were good. (The recon reports turned out to be wrong; the trails were inundated with seven-foot-deep fetid swamp water, and the overland crossing had to be aborted.) All the troops were to meet up at a speck on the map called Pongani, a village of a dozen or so thatched-roof huts on a half-moon bay lined with tall coconut palms. Buna, heavily fortified and surrounded by chest-high swamps and razor-sharp kunai grass, was only thirty miles to the north. The problem with the new route, MacNider realized at once, was that ships never ventured into those waters because they were treacherous. The reefs, some a mere two feet below the surface, were uncharted. Crossing one could rip the bottom of a boat and peel it back like a tin can. Getting stuck on one could mean being a sitting duck for the Japanese aircraft, plume of smoke into the air. The *King John* was the lead ship, and in her bow a young native sat on his haunches, staring intently ahead for a reef. Whenever he spotted a telltale patch of blue-green, he flicked his hand to the left or right. In the wheelhouse, the skipper, Bill Priest, yanked the wheel to port or starboard, sometimes so violently that it jolted the soldiers. At dusk the lookout pulled out a lead line and let it down every two or three minutes, softly calling out the marks over his shoulder.

At night the young soldiers were quiet and reflective, too jittery to sleep. From time to time one would stand up on deck to stretch, staring down at the sparkling phosphorescence in the water or tilting his head back to take in the brilliant, eerily unfamiliar constellations in the southern sky. Fahnestock stayed on deck to direct the course—he knew more about navigating than anyone else—and in the cramped cabin below, as a swinging lantern threw shadows around, McKenny pulled out aerial maps of Pongani. Barney watched. He felt the excitement of a newsman on a big story—the army's first ground assault, the first engagement with the enemy—and he would be the only one to write about it.

By 3:00 a.m., the ships reached their destination off Pongani. They anchored a half mile out to sea and shut off the engines. Barney slept two hours in the cabin. When he awoke he spotted Orion and waited for the sunrise. At 6:00 a.m., he wrote, "just turning light," as the sun's rays shot across the water and cast a rose-tinted hue on the hulking mountains ahead. The silhouette of the palm trees and half a dozen square huts could be seen now, and so could the beach, which was beginning to turn golden. The men "caught a mackerel and a pike for stew," he wrote. By 6:45, "the mountains had emerged" and were clearly visible. "Grenades distributed" to the troops. The two ships weighed anchor and crept toward shore, preparing to launch landing parties. The huts came into focus. He could make out the stilts that held them up six feet off the sand and the thatched roofs. But no natives. Nothing was stirring.

Then, at 8:00 a.m., the silence was broken. A plane roared out of the southeast. It was a twin-tailed, two-engine bomber, hard to identify. It could have belonged to either side. Barney stared up at it and squinted and shielded his eyes from the early-morning sun for a better look. So did all the men. He pulled out his notebook.

"Plane across course," he scribbled. "Jap or our?" The plane circled in a wide loop, apparently trying to identify the two ships five thousand feet below. Then it left.

The men watched the mysterious bomber fly off to the southeast. They exhaled a collective sigh of relief. Some looked at the U.S. flag at the top of the mast in the stern, clearly visible. They stood up, gathering their gear to go ashore, causing the ship to rock gently. An officer in short pants went to the crank in the stern to lower the launch for the first landing party.

Then, at 8:05, out of the south, the bomber returned.

Aghast, the men looked up and saw that its bomb-bay doors were open. Fahnestock leapt up and ran to the machine gun in the prow. Barney stood by the wheelhouse door and again pulled out his notebook. The plane was coming in low, its nose pointed at the *King John*. The men on board were still unable to read its markings. Fahnestock swung the machine gun toward the sky. The noise shook the boat. The first bomb, a five-hundred-pounder, was dropped. Most of the men flattened themselves on the deck before it exploded on the water, sending up a cascade of spray. Barney scribbled in his notebook: "bombed by 2 eng. plane—500 yd. miss." The boats zigzagged frantically, the *King John* heading toward shallow water, the *Timoshenko* out to sea. Barney grabbed the doorjamb of the wheelhouse. He stood there looking out, guiding the captain away from the path of the bombs.

The plane rose, veered around in a long loop, and banked. It came in for a second run, lower this time, its machine gun strafing and diving directly at the *King John*. Fahnestock fired back and some of the men raised their M1s and shot blindly into the air. Another bomb came plummeting down, sending a waterspout one hundred feet into the air. The plane rose, left again toward the southeast, and curved back. Now it was strafing the deck of the ship and taking machine-gun fire. A third bomb smashed near the port side of the bow. Fragments screamed past or thudded into the thick wood of the sideboards. Fahnestock, hit in the back, slumped over the gun. Barney wrote quickly: "Fahn shot 50 cal." The plane dropped its fourth and last missile near the stern. An antipersonnel bomb, it exploded on the water's surface and a fragment flew off and came thundering toward the boat. The men close to Barney huddled on the deck and looked up, to see him lurch. The heavy splinter caught him in the back of the neck. He fell inside the door, onto the floor of the wheelhouse.

The plane disappeared into the blue sky and suddenly it was quiet, as if nothing had happened. The birds stopped shrieking. Dazed, the soldiers began to stand up, touching themselves, checking their gear. Natives on the beach launched outrigger canoes to come to help them. The officers took stock. None of the bombs had scored a direct hit. The *King John* was damaged and barely serviceable. Eighteen men were wounded, and two were dying. Fahnestock, hit in the spine, was taken to the beach and expired in the arms of a friend. Barney, wrapped in a GI blanket and bleeding profusely, was placed in a canoe paddled by a native. By the time it reached the shore and soldiers lifted him off, he, too, was dead.

The two bodies were laid out on the sand, where villagers gathered, talking softly and shooing the young ones away. A third man, badly wounded in the legs, was set down, too. The ammunition and supplies were carried to land. The Papuans helped care for the wounded, holding their hands and comforting them. Later, rations were handed out, but some of the soldiers were too upset to eat. The sand fleas began biting, and they moved farther inland. Then the bodies of Lieutenant Fahnestock and Barney Darnton were carried back out to the ships and the *King John* and the *Timoshenko* returned slowly to Wanigela. From there the bodies were flown to a new American hospital at an old Catholic mission outside Port Moresby.

The funeral was held two days later, at 9:00 a.m., in the small military cemetery called Bomana, twelve miles to the north. The towering Owen Stanleys were shrouded in clouds and bombers were coming and going on a nearby airfield. The hillside was covered in mud and in places with the flaming red blossoms of a croton tree. Barney's simple redwood coffin, draped in an American flag, was transported on an open truck. Six correspondents dressed in khaki were the pallbearers and hoisted it off the truck and carried it up a slope and placed it next to Fahnestock's. In a long line of khaki, five generals stood with hats off, including General Harding, who had given Barney permission to accompany the troops. An Episcopal minister delivered the eulogy. Taps were played, fighter planes skimmed the treetops, and a rifle squad from the 126th Infantry

Regiment of the 32nd Division fired two salutes of three volleys over the white crosses. Nearby were the graves of American fliers who had died on missions.

The following day, my mother got a phone call from *The New York Times*. The publisher, Arthur Hays Sulzberger, and his wife, Iphigene, drove out to Westport to meet with her. General MacArthur sent a telegram, then released a statement saying that my father had served "with gallantry and devotion at the front and fulfilled the important duties of war correspondent with distinction to himself and to *The New York Times* and with value to his country." President Roosevelt sent my mother a letter of condolence. Later that week, as she recounted years afterward, she heard a booming noise that seemed to shake the house to its foundation. She rushed outside in time to see five planes, flying low in V formation, dipping their wings at our rooftop.

She never remarried. She had had her allotment of love, she said. Barney's older brother Robert sent her the letter our father had written before shipping out, the one that explained his decision to go off to war. She kept it in the center drawer of her vanity table right up until the end of her life. From time to time she would pull the letter out and read it, less frequently as the years went by. And each time she read it, she would weep. As far as I could tell, the part that provoked her tears, the sentence that broke her composure, was always the same: his expression of confidence in her. "Bob and Johnnie can safely be left to her. She isn't the stuff that cracks under a bit of difficulty." Afterward she would replace the letter in its worn envelope and put it back in the drawer. Sometimes she would say to me, "The two of you would have gotten on so well—you are so much alike." On those occasions when I was standing near her, even when I was older, unable to console her and unable to put things right, I was flooded with a welter of emotions. I felt self-conscious, as if someone were watching us—me standing there awkwardly, her crying. Far from helping her overcome her grief, I couldn't even share it. I felt helpless and ashamed of my helplessness and, strangely, disconnected from what was happening—even a little embarrassed by it.

The plane trip took forty-eight minutes. The aircraft flew over the jutting ridges of the mountains, obscured from time to time by heavy mist, and then dropped low over the green canopy of the tropical rain forest and the coastal mangrove swamp. It put down on a grassy strip in the middle of a damp field. Barney climbed out. So did the soldiers, moving awkwardly in full battle gear. A group of seven native women, bare to the waist and carrying bunches of bananas and pawpaws, chattered and stared at the DC-3, then turned their backs and disappeared into the jungle. When the piercing sound of the engines cut out, the men heard silence for a moment. Then abruptly the solid green walls around them echoed with the cries of raucous birds and the droning of insects. Suddenly they were in a different world, one that made the dusty roads and tents and squat huts of Port Moresby seem like bustling civilization. The place was Wanigela, a mission station rapidly turning into an American supply depot on Collingswood Bay, sixty-five miles south of Buna.

The men were ordered to form up on the edge of the field, then walked along paths cut through towering eucalyptus until they reached a small bay. There, at anchor, waited the two ships. Fluttering from their masts in a languid breeze were flags not seen in these contested waters since Pearl Harbor, ten and a half months earlier: the Stars and Stripes. The soldiers massed on the beach under clouds of mosquitoes. Above the ebb and flow of the surf could be heard the sounds of men slapping their necks and foreheads. They rowed out to the trawlers.

Barney thought the *King John* looked like a pirate ship and jotted that down in his notebook. He boarded it, along with Fahnestock and fifty-six men. The soldiers sat down, squeezing in among oil drums lashed to the sideboards and crates of ammo. The first arrivals picked the choicest spots along the sides and under the launch suspended upside down in the stern. Another forty-six men climbed aboard the *Timoshenko*.

Shortly after noon, the two ships lifted anchor and set off, following the coastline several miles out. The shore was lined with leaning palm trees and deceptively placid-looking beaches. It was mostly overcast and, when the sun broke through, unbearably hot. The going was slow. The diesel engine chugged away, sending a which dominated the skies during daylight hours from their feeder base at Rabaul, New Britain.

The next morning, October 17, Barney got up at dawn and took a jeep to Laloki airfield, outside of Port Moresby. At 8:00 a.m., he boarded a DC-3 along with a contingent of troops from the 128th Infantry Regiment of the 32nd Division. "I still don't see how these things can fly," said the congenial private next to him. "This beats walking," said another. Barney reached into the front breast pocket of his uniform and pulled out a notebook and a thick, dark-lead army-issue pencil. He jotted the remarks down. He believed you could never collect too many quotes, and you never knew which ones would come in handy later on. The soldiers were National Guardsmen, young men mostly from farms and small towns in Wisconsin and Michigan. They had been rushed up by air transport from Australia and they were scared. The places where they had trained, at Camp Livingston, Louisiana, and then Camp Cable, near Brisbane, with its semiarid terrain, looked nothing like the steaming haze they could see from the plane's portals. Everything about New Guinea was foreign and forbidding. The jagged mountains were impassable and the jungle impenetrable. The island was filled with exotic animals—one species of kangaroo actually lived in trees—and most of them were dangerous. The troops heard stories of man-eating crocodiles and huge bats and wild boars and poisonous snakes, not to mention cannibals and headhunters. At night a man's imagination could turn a shrieking cockatoo into a charging Japanese soldier, a branch crashing down from a rotting tree into a grenade. Already they had been ravaged by mosquitoes bigger than any insects had the right to be, along with wasps, scorpions, cockroaches, leeches, flies, and biting ants. Some men were already laid low by malaria or dengue or blackwater fevers. They were sweltering in the heat and soaked by the tropical downpours. Their uniforms, still wet from hastily applied green dye, a last-minute stab at camouflage, made everything worse: The dye closed off the breathing spaces in the cloth, so that wearing it was like being wrapped in canvas. In private reports, the top commander had rated the Americans "barely satisfactory" in combat efficiency.

CHAPTER 2

For years my brother and I associated our father with a ship—not the creaking trawler he was on when he was killed, but a gigantic Liberty ship named after him: the SS *Byron Darnton*. The wartime merchant vessel loomed large in our family's iconography. Our mother raised us on stories about her. She told us how the *Byron Darnton* had valiantly plied the treacherous Murmansk Run, carrying war supplies from Scotland and Iceland into the stormy Arctic, defying German submarines, to keep the vital Russian front going. I used to imagine the ship cutting through a sea of ice to reach the frigid port, a deep-throated whistle announcing her arrival, stevedores with frosted beards raising their hands in gratitude before leaping into action as cranes swung across the hold to lift out tanks and crates of ammunition.

Then we heard of her sad ending in March 1946, as she made her final voyage home. She ran aground in a gale somewhere in Scotland. Everyone on board was rescued only minutes before she broke apart. A tattered flag, one of the few items saved, was presented to my family. It hung on a wall over my brother's bed throughout our childhood, not far from a watercolor of the ship that was done by a member of the crew and sent to our home in Westport.

The *Byron Darnton* was built in the Baltimore shipyards and launched in December 1943, an event seminal in the life of our tight-knit family. *The New York Times* sent a photographer and Meyer Berger, one of its top reporters, to cover the christening. Our mother is captured in a photo, wearing a handsome coat with a fur collar and a round fur hat, swinging the champagne bottle in a wire casing covered with red, white, and blue streamers as a port official nervously backs away. Berger sets the scene. He describes the launching platform from which we children look out, "wide-eyed, on the busy yard, on plumed smoke white in the frosty air." Somewhere a whistle screams. Loudspeakers pour out music: the "Marines' Hymn" with its opening line, "From the Halls of Montezuma," and "Song of the Victory Fleet." For a moment, workers on other ships stop their labors. "A welder bent over deck plates not far away, raised a mask and disclosed a frail, fair-haired girl." Another whistle sounds to signal the torch men to burn the cribbing plates. The gigantic 10,500-ton merchant ship begins to budge. My mother gamely swings the bottle—"her aim was hard and true"—and it bursts in an explosion of spray as the ship gently slides down the ways, "as if feeling the water, gliding easily into the river."

Later, my mother described that day in a book she published. Entitled *The Children Grew*, it is her account of how a woman raised two small boys alone, a largely anecdotal guide based on her experience and aimed at other families that had suffered losses of husbands and fathers in the war. She wrote about herself in the third person. One chapter is devoted to the ship, beginning with the christening, told with characteristic verve and bravado. ("The occasion had had its amusing moments—the obvious fear that she'd miss when she swung the bottle. As if she could. She'd batted too many baseballs in her childhood to feel any doubt of her ability to connect with that big hulk.") She found it amusing to refer to Barney's ship as "she." At one point, she wondered how her sons, "with just that mouse's view of a great hull," could feel a personal connection with such a towering mass of steel.

As rectification, she later arranged a visit to the ship in New York harbor. In vivid detail, perhaps rendered even more vivid by the romantic haze of her recollection, she recounted a glorious day. A sleek launch speeds us from the Upper East River to the Hoboken docks. Two red fire tugs with whistles screaming come out to escort us. On board ten men stand at attention in an honor guard and Bob responds appropriately. ("He drew himself straight, raised his right hand in correct salute, held it a moment, then calmly proceeded to walk in great dignity between the guard.") The captain greets her with a corsage of gardenias. We're given a tour of the ship, from the engine room to the bridge, and allowed to pull the cord of the air horn, which bellows across the harbor. Finally, in the officers' mess, the two chefs lay on an imperial meal, with a desert that is half apple pie and half cake, because each one wants to present his specialty. The feast is consumed under a large painted portrait of Barney, which dominates the room. She wrote, with her gift for hyperbole, "She and Bob, particularly, looked at it long, she still with a bit of sharp pain with her love. But, as she looked at Bob's adoring gaze, she saw the uplifted face alight with an uncomplicated love and with belief, as some men look at the stars. 'It's almost as though the ship were Daddy, isn't it, Mommie?' he whispered."

Throughout the war years, we kept in touch with the ship. We gave the crew a music library. They sent us presents, including an ashtray fashioned in the ship's shop from the cylinder of a downed Nazi warplane. One gnarled old mate, she wrote, sent her something made out of the ship's twine—a pillowcase, perhaps; she was never quite sure. And a young man who worked in the engine room, an aspiring writer, sent her a novel he had written for her appraisal. Of the *Byron Darnton*'s demise, my mother was philosophical: "The ship had served her purpose and nobly. It was almost better to lose her in a valiant two-day fight against forces stronger than she, than to think of her degenerating into a sluggish banana boat." She ended the chapter this way: "What interesting compensations Nature and men try to make. The loss of a father is a dreadful loss. But how many boys have a ship all their own? How many boys have a whole ship's crew of men trying to take some part of his place?"

Today, neither my brother nor I have any recollection of the ship herself or of any of its crew members, who, in fact, meant very little to us. We were too young—Bob four and a half and me two—to

remember either the christening or the visit. It's impossible to reconstruct what we—the two mice—were thinking and feeling as we
looked up at that towering hull. But I suspect that our mother had
no idea of how important an icon that ship would become or how it
is psychologically possible for children to turn an inanimate object,
even a 10,500-ton hunk of metal, into a totem for a missing father.
Now, when I read the *Times* article, itself yellowed and crumbling,
I notice details that escaped me before, touches that Meyer Berger
put into his story. He wrote how "awed" we were by our surroundings. He conveyed an impression of how small and vulnerable we
appeared, tiny figures wrapped in winter snowsuits, dwarfed by the
cranes and scaffolds, overcome by the din of sirens and whistles,
gaping up at the ship that rose far above us like a mountain. Held
in the arms of a nurse, I threw my head back, trying to see the top
where the letters B-Y-R-O-N D-A-R-N-T-O-N stood out large and
white across the upper bow. My brother had hoped to be the one
to christen the ship. For more than a week, he had rehearsed the
ceremony, repeating "I christen thee SS *Byron Darnton*. I christen
thee SS *Byron Darnton*" in the hotel lobby all morning. But when
the time came, when he stood on a nail keg and tried to lift the
bottle encased in wire with the steamers flying, it was too heavy
for him. Tears welled in his eyes and he gave up. Looking at the
huge white letters far above him spelling out his father's name, he
whispered something to our mother. She turned and asked a question of the port official, who nodded yes. My brother pulled out a
blue crayon and carefully scrawled his name—a "BoB" in a shaky
hand, the way he had seen it on the last page of his father's letters.
He wrote it upon the ship's immense keel, inches above the water-
line. Meyer Berger spotted this and a photographer captured it on
camera. Moments later, as the *Byron Darnton* slid down the ways,
the letters were lost to view even before the ship touched the water
on that cold afternoon in Baltimore.

Over the years, memories that you don't fully possess fade away.
The flag has long since been packed away in a carton and stored in
an attic. So have most of the photographs and the yellowing newspaper article. Only one copy of *The Children Grew*, inscribed to a
friend of my mother who left it behind, survives on my bookshelf.
Our mother died many years ago, in May 1968. By that time I had

already begun working for the newspaper for which my father gave his life. Only later did I wonder: Was I acting out of my own free will or was I playing out a destiny laid down for me years before?

I was three months old when my father left home and eleven months old when he was killed, and so I have no memory of him. The slate is blank. My brother, two and a half years older, doesn't remember him either, though a legion of small, grainy photos attests that they spent those early years together. One shows Barney awkwardly holding Bob as a newborn; his back looks tight, his muscles tensed, as if he were cradling a Fabergé egg or a miniature bomb. A series of snapshots captures them sledding: Barney sits on the sled, a tiny snow-suited boy on his lap. He pushes off, wrapping his legs around him as they descend a tiny slope, open-mouthed in excitement, and finally they end up sprawled in a snowbank—the figures hard to make out because the image is hopelessly blurred. I imagine my mother dropping the camera and rushing over to make sure they're all right.

All that. And neither of us retains any memory of him. Yet in that place where memory might reside, there's not a vacuum. Not having a father present didn't mean not having a father. There wasn't just an absence in my life. There was the *presence* of an absence, and that presence, along with snippets of information and my mother's recollections and bits of writing that came my way, filled my imagination. They led me, eventually, to romanticize his life and to mythologize him. I was dealing with a mythic entity, something that possessed no physical substance but was capable of exerting influence and power. It was like a ghost in a child's nightmare, a shadow at high noon that is almost invisible. Was the specter benign or malevolent? The question didn't even arise. It was simply there, as large and overwhelming as a ship.

I know it may sound peculiar, but over the years I became superstitious about my father. The truth is that when I was very young, I lived in a world apart. It was a world of magic, where boundaries between the real and the supernatural were porous and where things seemed to cross back and forth as effortlessly as clouds scurrying their shadows across farms and cities. Who was to say which was which? I tried to piece things together on my own and to make sense of events and scraps of information without recourse to outside wisdom. I rarely sought explanation or guidance from adults, whom I held in suspicion. As a result I was prone to misunderstandings. I evolved some odd constructs to explain what was going on around me. Many of my misconceptions centered on my father. Much of the time I didn't think of him at all, at least not consciously, for the simple reason that he wasn't part of my everyday life. But some of the time, in odd moments, I would wonder about him and what had happened to him. I was apt to question whether he had, in fact, stopped existing altogether or whether he, or parts of him, somehow carried on. When courting, my parents chose Orion as their constellation—and later it became magical because she could see it from our backyard in Connecticut and he could see it from the South Pacific—so at night I would search for the three stars of Orion's belt and stare at them. At times they made me feel an almost mystical connection with him. I was like a shepherd from a past age on a hillside under the night sky, awestruck in the presence of the gods.

Lying in bed in the evenings, unable to sleep, I evolved an elaborate ritual, which lengthened over time. First I recited the Lord's Prayer, followed by a series of psalms. I added more memorized passages from the Bible and then a prayer of my own. My compulsion was such that if I found myself saying so much as a single line by rote, I had to start over from the beginning. Otherwise, some unnamed but spectacular horror would befall me or my family. As a result, I often ended up repeating many times over: "Our Father who art in heaven, Hallowed be thy Name . . ." And at some point the words "*Our* Father" conflated with "*My* father" and I found myself imagining my father seated on some kind of heavenly throne. On occasions when I was bad—which I was convinced I was much of the time—I imagined him peering down at me and I tried to surmise his reaction: Disapproval? Disappointment? Anger? Whatever it was, it was remote and judgmental, in keeping with the spirit of the Old Testament, not compassionate or familial. The construct gave rise to a host of theological questions. How strong were his powers? Could he see through rooftops and ceilings? Did his dominion extend over the whole world or just over me? Within a few years, of course, when I became more rational, I discarded the idea of him as a deity, though on some level the essence of the construct lived on in the recesses of my mind like a half-remembered dream. For a long time, even though I didn't fully believe it, I found I couldn't quite reject it.

One of the stories that I heard from my mother—so early on that I couldn't possibly say when I first heard it—was that she perceived her husband's death the moment it happened. There he was on the other side of the earth, fourteen thousand miles away, and the second the bomb splinter entered his brain and extinguished his life, my mother knew it. She was in her home in Westport on a chilly autumnal day. A couple had just been married by a preacher in front of the fireplace in our living room, a quiet wedding attended by a handful of close friends and family. My mother was alone in the kitchen, washing a few dishes, when abruptly she was struck by an overwhelming sensation that Barney was in trouble, that he was trying to send her a message. It was a powerful feeling, one that made her need to be alone. She put a plate down in the sink and stepped outdoors. She walked across the lawn until she came to a tree and sank down beneath it. "The feeling was so strong," she used to say, "that I felt I had to speak out loud. I said, 'What's wrong, darling? I know something is deeply wrong.' And then I knew what it was." For the remainder of the day, she felt odd, and on the following day came the call from the *Times*. The timing matched up. As a youngster, I did not find that episode at all incomprehensible or even unnatural. Quite the opposite: It was the linchpin connecting my magical world to the afterlife, and as such I welcomed it into my private religion.

That religion was replete with various ceremonies. Every so often I would rummage through the bottom of our mother's closet to find a wooden box containing his posthumously awarded war medals—the Purple Heart and two others—and I would spread them on the bed to admire and fondle them like a medieval Christian handling a saint's bones. On a table in our living room we had a patriotic globe dotted with stars to mark the scenes of major American battles. There was one star for Buna. In my naïveté I believed the manufacturer had placed it there to commemorate the spot where my father fell. I used to spin the globe with my eyes closed to see if my finger would land on it, like a Tibetan monk spinning his prayer wheel.

As I grew older, many of these feelings and recollections gradually dissipated. Months would go by in which I would scarcely think of my father at all. But then something would happen to jog me out of my everyday concerns and bring him back center stage. This was especially true after I graduated from college, married, and began at the *Times*. In the mid-1960s, a number of editors and reporters who had been around since the war still worked there. They would say they remembered him vividly, but, to my exasperation, their recollections were invariably vague. They would say only that he was "witty" or "debonair" or "handsome." Once, a long-retired city editor invited my brother and me to his apartment to see some footage of Barney in a home movie. The two of us sat on his couch, a stiff drink in hand, as he cranked up an old projector. Black-and-white images flickered upon a luminous screen. "There he is!" he yelled as the back of a man's head crossed from one side to the other for all of three seconds.

As my time at the paper grew, the number of reporters and editors who had known Barney dropped away, but every so often reminders of him surfaced. In the early 1970s, I covered City Hall out of the pressroom there, and two years after I left, I received a package in the mail from a woman who had been Mayor Beame's deputy press secretary. Inside was a book entitled *The Dictionary of Misinformation* and a note directing me to look at page ten. There I read that the famous quotation "Anybody who hates children and dogs can't be all bad" was not, as generally believed, uttered by W. C. Fields, but spoken by none other than Byron Darnton. He made the wisecrack in an elevator, descending from a party in a penthouse apartment, where the host had punished a misbehaving dog. The remark was picked up by a reporter friend, Cedric Worth, and published in the November 1937 issue of *Harper's*. Later it was used to introduce Fields at a banquet and so became associated with him and eventually attributed to him.

Over the years, I encountered a number of these mementos and reminders. Some came in the form of letters out of the blue, written by his fellow war correspondents or servicemen. One, from a retired colonel in Texas, Mark T. Muller, called him "a dedicated true professional" and included a Kodachrome color snapshot of him grinning as he poked his head into the top turret of a B-25.

The authors of the letters sometimes said they had been meaning to write for years and had finally decided to now that they had been "rummaging through old papers in the attic" or "putting my affairs in order." I took the explanations as code, meaning they were tying up loose ends because they were feeling that their days were numbered. Other reminders of Barney came in the form of articles he had written decades ago, popping up on the Internet as the data bank reached further back in time.

By far the most dramatic memento of all turned up in December 1975, only weeks before I was to leave for Africa on my first foreign assignment. I was in the midst of preparing for my departure, running around trying to secure visas, complete my inoculations, and read up on wars and insurrections from Rhodesia to Angola. One afternoon, as I passed by the bank of mailboxes on the edge of the city room, I saw a package wrapped in brown paper stuffed into my box. Something about it struck me instantly as momentous. I took it to my desk and opened it. A note under the letterhead of the *Chicago Tribune* appeared. It was written by one Harold E. Hutchings, an archivist at the newspaper. He said he had been cleaning house and come across an item at the bottom of an old filing cabinet. He was sending it on to Abe Rosenthal, the *Times'* managing editor. "We have acquired this sad memento of the war in the Pacific," he wrote, "which the *Times* may wish to keep, or pass on to the appropriate recipient." A secretary in Abe's office had passed it on to me, unaware of its significance.

My hands began to tremble as I carefully unwrapped the parcel. Inside was a notebook with a thick cover, on which was written "N.G. 1942, Buna." Above that, my father's name was neatly printed. There was a date: "Oct. 17, 1942." It was his last notebook, the one he carried with him on his final day. Slowly, I turned the pages. There was his handwriting, broad strokes in pencil. I scarcely breathed as I read it. He wrote about the trip aboard the DC-3 from Port Moresby and the soldier next to him saying, "I still don't see how these things can fly." He wrote about the plane flying over "very thick jungle—many white birds," then landing in Wanigela on a strip that was "just grass cut down" and about the women carrying bunches of bananas and pawpaws. He saw the *King John* and wrote that it looked like a pirate ship. Then, the next morning, collecting color for his story, he jotted down impressions of the trip along the coast. He noted at 6:00 a.m. that it was "just turning light." He saw that "the high indigo mountains have emerged" from the night. He wrote that the men caught fish for stew and that grenades were distributed to the troops. Then, at 8:00, he made that fateful entry: "Plane across course. Jap or our?" The plane returned and his writing was hastily scrawled now and came in fragments: "bombed by 2 eng. plane—500 yd. miss." And the final note: "Fahn shot 50 cal." The next page was torn out. I realized that must have happened at the moment the shrapnel struck, or perhaps as the notebook slipped from his grasp as he fell to the deck inside the wheelhouse.

For a long time, sitting there in the city room, I couldn't speak. I don't remember much of what I did do, but I recall the numbing sensation that comes with a flood of contradictory emotions. I felt chilled and warmed at the same time, both scared and comforted. Why had the notebook turned up now, after thirty-three years? Why had it come just as I was about to embark on my own journey, off to cover conflicts in a vast continent? Was it so far-fetched to imagine that it was some kind of message? If so, what message? A warning? A laying on of hands?

I took the notebook in to Abe, who was seated behind his desk in the center of his managing editor's office. In his excitement at the discovery, he ordered up a news story about it. It turned out that the notebook had been taken from my father's body by E. R. Noderer, the *Chicago Tribune*'s correspondent in the Pacific. He'd brought it home, intending to give it to my mother, but instead left it in the cabinet. He had retired and moved to Florida two years before. "A reporter's notebook," the *Times* story said, "is perhaps his most professional possession, for in it are his observations and his perceptions, the brick and mortar of his job." A week after the story appeared, another letter came to me. This one was from Sheridan Fahnestock, the son of the man who was killed along with my father, who had read it. He had become a reporter, too, working on the *Bulletin* published in Bend, Oregon. "I don't know about you," he wrote, "but in our family the Darnton name was always special because our fathers died together." Immediately I wrote him back;

the same was certainly true in our family. We corresponded for a while, until distance and time separated us again.

Over the years, as my wife, Nina, and I raised a family of our own—two daughters, Kyra and Liza, and a son, Jamie—I mused about these tokens and mementos and recollections. I came to think of them as visitations from my father. They were like notes washing ashore in bottles, messages from Shakespeare's "undiscover'd country from whose bourn no traveler returns." I suppose that this kind of irrational thinking was a continuation, in lesser form, of the superstitions that had ruled so much of my childhood. But sometimes I almost wonder, Is it even remotely conceivable that perished souls live on in some kind of parallel world and decide from time to time to reach in and tweak our own?

If this is true, then what happened in June 2005 is proof that my father's ghost has an extravagant sense of humor. In that month my brother and I heard that there exists on a remote Scottish island called Sanda a tavern called the Byron Darnton. At first, I was disbelieving. But I went to a Web site, and there was Sanda, a mere stub of a place thirteen miles off the southern tip of the Kintyre Peninsula in the North Channel—that is to say, in the middle of nowhere. It was home to thousands of sheep and a smattering of stone buildings and—here was the odd part—a year-round population of exactly one person, an enterprising fellow who single-handedly had constructed a pub, proclaiming it to be the most remote in the entire United Kingdom. And he had named it the Byron Darnton! This was too much. What was a tavern named after my father doing on some godforsaken island in Scotland?

The mystery was quickly solved. The Web site said the tavern had gotten its name from an old shipwreck, some kind of vessel that had smashed against the island's rocky western shore long ago. Of course! The SS *Byron Darnton*! In a single phone call, my brother and I came to a quick decision. We'd travel to Scotland and go to Sanda. Our wives would go with us. Then we'd raise a glass—or several, or perhaps many—to the memory of our father. If Barney has indeed been trying to get my attention, I thought, he has certainly succeeded.

Some weeks later, Nina and I took the overnight flight from JFK, changed at Heathrow for a plane to Glasgow, then rented a car for the long drive in the Highlands, which would take us past Loch Lomond and the pine forests of the west coast. We spent the night in an elegant castle overlooking Loch Fyne, sleeping in a canopied bed in a vast chamber, the walls coated all in white, guarded by suits of armor and broadswords mounted over the stone fireplace. The next day we ended up in Campbeltown, an old-world sea town with thick wooden piers, salt spray in the air, and seagulls resting on rooftops.

There we were met by the driver of a RIB, or rigid inflatable boat, built around a solid hull with inflatable tubes at the gunwales. We were handed rain slickers and we climbed down a ladder to board and sat side by side on motorcycle saddle seats with raised handgrips. Minutes later, we were out of the harbor in the Mull of Kintyre, bouncing off the waves and doused by spray. When we hit the churlish waters where the Irish Sea converges with the Firth of Clyde, the waves practically washed over us. We tightened our hold on the handgrips as the boat bucked and bounced. After some forty minutes, the driver pointed to the horizon and yelled in a thick burr, "Thar she is." In the distance, rising starkly out of the dark water, was an imposing island, shaped like a gigantic upside-down spoon. As we drew nearer, I could make out rolling green hills and, closer still, the white dots of sheep and dark lines of stone walls. We entered a quiet bay. A row of gray stone buildings was set behind a fifteen-foot seawall. They looked as if they had been there for centuries.

We pulled up to a jetty. A man rushed over, fastened the boat, and thrust out a calloused hand in welcome. Dick Gannon was a slight man in his mid-fifties with a white beard, thick-lens glasses, and the unkempt look of a person living alone. He had been preparing for our arrival—we had explained the purpose of our visit in an e-mail—and he was eager to show us around. He grabbed our bags and walked ahead, but I stopped dead. A sign perched on a wooden stand at the end of the jetty read BYRON DARNTON TAVERN. It was strange to see that name suspended in midair in a place that was at the ends of the earth.

We dropped the bags off inside a stone cottage and headed for the pub. In front a dozen people sat at picnic tables and in lawn chairs, sipping drinks and gazing over a half-moon bay of stones washed by gentle waves. The scene was a study in holiday serenity. The tavern presented itself as an eighty-foot-long, sleek stone building under a slate roof. It bore a large hand-painted sign that depicted the island set between raging white surf and billowing white clouds. Once again there was that improbable name: B-Y-R-O-N D-A-R-N-T-O-N. We crossed an open-air courtyard and entered. Inside, the room was vast and cheery. The walls were stone with pine cladding, and wooden tables were spread around. The obligatory dartboard hung in a corner. Suspended from the walls were T-shirts and white life preservers with BYRON DARNTON painted in bold red letters. At the far end was a handsome three-penny bar made of sandstone and topped with thick mahogany. I grabbed a stool next to a large jar of home-pickled eggs and contemplated the selection: five ales and beers on tap and upward of thirty whiskies. My father would have approved.

I chose a lager and settled in while Dick sketched the history of Sanda and told us about his tribulations in getting the pub built and up and running. When it came time to name it, he thought of the most dramatic event of recent times—the night the *Byron Darnton* struck the rocks just below a lighthouse on the treacherous western coast. For fourteen hours, the ship foundered. Lifeboat crews from Campbeltown tried to reach her and convince the captain to abandon ship. Finally, only minutes after all fifty-four passengers and crew and a husky dog were taken off, the ship broke in two. Over the years, divers stripped her of everything worth taking. "We had no idea where the name of the ship came from," Dick said. "Or that there was any history behind it, or a living family. We simply liked the sound of it—struck us as poetic."

Nina and I spent part of the afternoon with a group of men outside. Most of them had come over on yachts from Red Bay in Northern Ireland. I bought a round of drinks, which seemed to open the door to a lifelong friendship. Six of the men, our own age, were particularly friendly, and when we told them the object of our visit, one exclaimed, "I read about you on the pub's Web site! You're famous!" He bought us a round. Curiously, for all their boozy camaraderie—they invited us to sail back to Northern Ireland with them—they turned evasive whenever we asked questions about them. We found out why three hours after they had gone. Dick remarked, "Do you happen to know who you were drinking with all afternoon?" He anticipated our surprise with a smile. "Pink Floyd."

The next morning, Bob, his wife, Susan, and their daughter, Margaret, arrived in a motorboat. They dropped their bags off at their cottage and we all went to the tavern. Bob and I posed next to the sign. Moments later, we were inside, and I watched Bob take it all in with the same incredulity that I had felt twenty-four hours earlier. Dick disappeared behind the bar and we heard the pop of a champagne cork. Flutes were filled and passed around. I looked at my brother and he looked at me. He proposed a toast. "Here's to the memory of Byron Darnton," he said, sounding oddly formal. He raised his glass and I raised mine. "Here's to the old man," I countered. We refilled the glasses several times.

Afterward, Bob and I walked across the waist of the island to visit the remnants of the wreck. Black-faced ewes scattered at our approach along a path though the bracken and wildflowers. The path dipped through a valley and reached the windswept western coast, where seals sunned themselves on the rocks and colonies of razorbills and puffins nested. It ended at the foot of a tall white lighthouse, built in three stages on the top of a towering crag. A giant outcropping, nicknamed Elephant Rock, was connected to it by a thin eroded strand, much like an elephant's trunk. We had timed our walk to arrive at low tide and we had been told where to look.

And then we saw it, on the rocks, about thirty yards offshore, a heap of metal rising up about eight feet into the air. It was covered in yellow lichen and green moss. With effort, we could just about make out what was—or had been—the bottom of the hull. Resting next to it was something that looked like a propeller and, twenty feet away, another mound of dark metal. They looked strange and out of place in the mudflats, like pieces of sculpture.

We tried to approach it. I stepped down onto the moss-covered rocks at the water's edge. I wanted to see if I could climb over and touch the battered hull. I even wondered if this might be the section on which Bob had written his name. He circled around the other side and stared at the hunk of metal. I yelled something to him, but he appeared not to hear me. The rocks were too slippery, so I could not get close. I didn't feel like trying to wade through the cold brine. I gave up.

After a few minutes standing there and looking around, we decided to return to the other side of the island. As I walked beside Bob, I told him, joking, that I hadn't been able to see his name. By way of reply, he smiled weakly. We were mostly silent. Something about the sight, that vast hull that once had seemed to rise up like a mountain, reduced to this, a pile of metal covered with moss and barnacles, was saddening.

What was I feeling? It was hard to tell. On one level, I was glad that we had seen the *Byron Darnton,* or what was left of her, after all these years. I imagined how excited our mother would have been and how dramatic she would have made our little encounter in telling it to her friends. But I also felt something else, a disappointment, almost a disillusionment. The experience wasn't what I had thought it would be. It wasn't satisfying or revelatory. I wondered, Who was Barney really? What was he like? Why did he go off to war, leaving behind a wife and two small children? Questions that had lain dormant for over sixty years, or that I had never dared to ask, began to surface, seemingly out of nowhere, and demand answers.

Why, if he was such a dominant figure in my mental universe, had I resisted learning about him as a living human being—all this time? I didn't know. Something had stood in my way. I remembered a story I had heard about a Native American tribe in northeastern California (called the Ajumawi, I later learned). They venerate a mountain (called Simloki) and especially the mountain's shadow. At sunset the shadow glides over the bowl of a wide valley and takes an hour and a half to reach a mountain range some twelve miles away. On the evenings of solstices and equinoxes, Ajumawi men race to get there first—a feat that is physically daunting and just barely possible. They know the shadow is sacred and to be revered. A running man may measure his progress and the shadow's movement by looking at the trees, but he must not look back at Simloki until he reaches the end. If he does, he will be struck down.

Standing there on the shore of Sanda, having reached the age of sixty-five and having just retired after working nearly forty years at my father's paper, with a long, happy marriage to sustain me and three fine children now in adulthood, I was finally ready to look back.

CHAPTER 3

Not long after I returned from Sanda, Jamie gave me an extraordinary present for Father's Day. I had guessed that it was something special from various hints and the fact that he had shut himself in his room for hours on end, working to the blast of hard rock with a supply of scissors, glue, and other paraphernalia. He finally emerged, carting a large black scrapbook, which he placed before me.

Using a new data-retrieval program in his college's computer system, he had assembled the complete run of my father's stories in the *Times*. They were not printouts, but exact reproductions, complete with grainy photos and the jagged lines of print produced by the long-gone Linotype machines. He had arranged them chronologically, with chapter headings, such as: "Barney Arrives in the Pacific." I was moved by his gift and especially by that touch—by his using a nickname for his grandfather, who to him was only a shadow of a shadow, as remote as the doughboys of World War I or the soup kitchens of the Great Depression. He had no doubt picked it up from me, but when had I ever used it?

I flipped through the stories. There were fewer of them than I had thought. I was struck by the realization that my father's time at the paper had been one-fifth of my own. My bylined clippings, recently mailed to me in creamy white folders from the morgue that was being dismantled, would tower over his, even accounting for the fact that in his day bylines were much harder to come by. That was not the way I had imagined things. I had somehow thought my work was at best a footnote to his.

I began to read. Some of the stories were familiar to me—I had read them long ago. This time I took a hard look at his style. It was unadorned and elegant and without artifice. It reminded me of Hemingway and Steinbeck, the way he used strong Anglo-Saxon nouns and active verbs and held back on flowery adjectives. If he used a word like *village* or *brook* or *tree* and the sentence called for it to be used again, he didn't search around for synonyms; he used the word again. This set up a pleasing, at times almost poetic cadence. His leads were straightforward—he just leapt right into the subject. He didn't tie himself in knots to concoct an opening paragraph with clever subordinate clauses and all sort of bells and whistles to make it sound like the Second Coming. His writing was the real thing.

At times he referred to American soldiers as "our boys." This was no doubt a prerogative of his middle age, but it also reflected the mood of the country. In World War II, we were engaged, all of us, in a fight to the finish. The enemy was evil incarnate and dedicated to destroying our whole way of life. There was no middle ground; no one stood on the sidelines, and that included the American war correspondents. As if to emphasize the point, the reporters and photographers were actually in the U.S. Army—they wore uniforms, were subject to military command and discipline, and held a noncombatant status equivalent to that of captain.

In his coverage, Barney was passionate about the American airmen. He was amazed at their prowess and their footloose bravery. In letters home to our mother, he was continually struck by how young they were. "You would be enthralled by what goes on in the sky now and again, and by the kids who do it," he wrote. "A high school loose in whining motors." Port Moresby and Townsville, in Queensland, Australia, where the airmen were based, were small places, and Barney personally knew many of the pilots and crews from interviews when they returned from missions, exhausted but grateful to be alive. In the same way that Ernie Pyle became known as the GIs' reporter, he became known as the aviators' reporter.

Barney's fascination with the airmen was in part a reflection of his thwarted ambition. As an infantryman in France twenty-four years before, he had toyed with the idea of becoming a pilot, a not uncommon aspiration among the young men raising their eyes from the muddy, rat-infested trenches to the primitive flying machines soaring above. But his passion for the pilots and crew also came from the exigencies of the reporting situation in the Pacific. At this stage the war was being fought in the skies. Airpower was key, and everything rode on whether the American airmen could turn back the Japanese dominance gained from their capture of strategic air-fields.

Early on Barney ran up against the U.S. Army censors and bridled under their thick blue pencils. He was among the first to abandon the daily press conferences and hopscotch around north-ern Australia, catching military and civilian flights to reach Ameri-can air bases. While dozens of his colleagues cooled their heels in Melbourne, he interviewed pilots and bombardiers to get firsthand accounts of their missions, telling readers what it was like to zoom down on bombing runs on Japanese destroyers and engage in dog-fights with Japanese Zeros.

His copy, cleared by the censors under the dateline "AT A UNITED NATIONS AIR BASE, Southwestern Pacific," was filled with color and human beings speaking in real language. He wrote about a lieutenant who managed a perfect crash landing even though he had shrapnel wounds in his throttle arm, no landing gear, and a Japanese Zero firing on his tail. And about a downed pilot who made it back to base after two days in the jungle; swimming a river, he was attacked by a crocodile, which bit him twice, until he finally plunged his eight-inch-long jungle knife into its throat. A nineteen-year-old Brooklyn boy, a turret gunner on his first mission, candidly admitted his fear up until the point that he shot down a couple of Zeros; asked how he felt about his first kill, he suddenly stopped, turned serious, and said, "Kind of funny." Another pilot told of being trailed by a Zero, which moved so close that it almost joined his formation. Strangely, it did not fire. He looked over and realized the Japanese pilot flying parallel to him was dead.

One of my favorites is about Jerry Crosson, a thirty-year-old former policeman from Staten Island who had just returned from his first bombing run. Seated before an unappetizing lump of meat in the mess hall, Crosson waxed nostalgic about New York, describing a fantasy night out on the town. First he'd go to a Broadway musical. Then he'd "very much enjoy a dinner at the Rainbow Room in Radio City." He'd choose a table overlooking midtown Manhattan and he'd order trout cooked in wine sauce, a mixed salad, a good dry white wine, and plain vanilla ice cream. Seated across from him, and dancing with him between courses, would be his girlfriend, Miss Valina P. Hurst, also of Staten Island. He had planned to marry her but didn't get around to it before "the Japs busted my marriage up." He was planning to rectify that once he got home. The story ended: "Jerry would like Miss Hurst and his parents to know that he is feeling fine and he would like the rest of the United States to know that he and his colleagues are fully confident that they can dispose of the Japanese if supplies and planes keep coming this way." The *Times* went all out on the story. Editors sent a reporter to Crosson's father's house and another to Miss Hurst's house, where she was found dressed in a new Easter ensemble of powder blue. At first she thought the reporter on her doorstep was a neighbor's joke, but then she realized it was for real. She said she was sure her fiancé would "come back and we'll have our evening." The Rainbow Room was contacted and said it would be delighted to serve the couple, gratis, and the chef, Frederic Beaumont, said he personally would attend to the trout. The editors put the story on page one and splashed photos inside.

I turned to the end of the scrapbook. There was Barney's obit and the accompanying photo, one I had seen scores of times. He stood tall in his uniform, staring into the camera with a jaunty smile, his hands clasped behind his back, his cap at a roguish angle. On the following page came his last story, printed posthumously. He described the lives of the correspondents in the Pacific and compared the conditions they endured with those of the correspondents in the Great War—an assignment, I surmised, that had been dreamt up by the *Times Magazine* editor back home.

I envisioned him at the correspondents' hut in Port Moresby, gamely deciding to write the damn thing. Maybe it was a certain "let's get it over with" attitude, or maybe it was the topic—a personal recollection demanding the use of the pronoun *I*—but his writing seemed to open up and soar as he looked to a future when the peace would have been won and the soldiers would return home.

Typically when he wrote a story or a letter home, as I came to learn from letters from his colleagues, he took his typewriter out on the veranda or under a tree. That was probably what he had done this time. The flies were buzzing around in the hot sun and so he decided to put them in his story. He typed: "SOMEWHERE IN NEW GUINEA," then:

> *If the flies will please get off my arms and out of my mouth and eyes, I will write a little article comparing the job of war correspondent in this war and in the last one. In the last war I was not a correspondent, but I saw some in France. It was pretty near the front, too. They were accompanying an eminent visitor. . . .*
>
> *It was near the Ourcq River where there had just been some trouble. Company B was lying in the shelter of a low ridge. Members were somewhat battle-shocked, very hungry and very dirty. And they knew they were soon to go over that ridge where more trouble awaited them. These war correspondents came along, looking very clean and well fed and asking a lot of questions. You took one look at them and knew there wasn't a cootie among them. You disliked them.*
>
> *One difference between war correspondents in the last war and this war is that this time I don't dislike correspondents. I hope the soldiers don't.*

He described the mundane details of everyday life. The correspondents had it better than the soldiers, he said, because they had a shower—an open-air pole attached to a bacon tin with holes punched in the bottom and connected to a hose. He talked about hitching rides in planes, the difficulties in transmitting copy, and the godsend of a fifteen-hour time difference in meeting deadlines. He also dealt with army press relations and the censors, for whom he uncharacteristically expressed sympathy.

> *A man who has spent his life in newspaper work is apt to believe that in the long run the best thing to do is to tell the truth. If the truth hurts enough, the necessary corrective will be automatically generated. Military training is likely to produce a different point of view—the attitude that the best possible face must be put on things. . . . All of which makes operations difficult for those who have to carry out the general principles laid down by their chief.*

Finally, he spoke of a new sense of optimism in New Guinea—a great change from when he had first arrived—and of the resolve of the airmen. He said that there were more American planes and fewer enemy attacks. Calling upon his own experience, he said the mood felt like the midsummer of 1918, when the Americans had pushed the Germans out of the Marne. But there was a big difference—in the attitude of those doing the fighting.

> *The correspondent in this war, unlike his predecessor of twenty-five years ago, can find manifold evidence that the victory will be well used. Young men who are doing our fighting are, to a surprising extent, thinking about the war's end not only in terms of getting back home to their wives and sweethearts and getting away from danger and discomfort. They are thinking also in terms of what kind of world we shall have after peace comes. They are thinking realistically. Above all, they want the United States to be kept strong on land and sea.*
>
> *The politician who preaches "normalcy" at the end of this war will find some hard-headed opposition. He will find these men assured and matured beyond their years. . . . He will find that they want, not national escape to irresponsibility, but peacetime compulsory military service for youths now growing up. . . . He will find a greater love of peace than ever and*

with a realization that peace is not automatic but must be secured.

These I believe are the views of the fighting men. I do not think a correspondent in 1917–19 could have found this realistic thinking about the future among our men in France. I know there was none of it in B Company. We wanted only to get it over with, to get home and forget there ever had been a war. It is stirring to see this change in attitude. It makes the dust all right, the flies all right, the heat all right.

A man can climb the high hill near the airdrome just up the road and watch the bombers and fighters go forth. He can see the yellow bombs being loaded in their racks. He can see maintenance men keeping the strips in shape and chow trucks bearing food to pea-shooter pilots on the alert. He can see ambulances rush up to home-coming planes.

From the high hill near the airdrome a man can see his countrymen building with blood, sweat and toil the firm resolution that their sons shall not die under bombs, but shall have peace, because they will know how to preserve the peace.

I had grown up reading and rereading this particular story and listening to the tales my mother told me about my father. They helped form my early ideas about war and peace and about journalism and the indispensable service it provides to a democracy.

In trying to re-create Barney's life in Australia and New Guinea, I had a number of letters written by correspondents to my mother and later to my brother and me. First among them was a fifteen-page, single-spaced letter written four months after his death by Carleton "Bill" Kent of the *Chicago Daily Times*. A lanky midwesterner with an easygoing manner and a finely hewn sense of humor, Kent was among the fifteen reporters, photographers, and cameramen who shipped out on the SS *Monterey*, a cruise ship converted to a troop carrier, on February 18, 1942. They were informed only that they were bound for somewhere in the Pacific. There was little to do for eighteen days, and the boredom was killing. Like correspondents on downtime everywhere, they turned to alcohol and high jinks. Kent recounts "the great election for boat drill warden." Told they needed a leader to organize an evacuation that might follow an enemy torpedo, they asked Barney to take the position, but he declined. A draft-Darnton movement exploded: Votes were purchased with whiskey, coalitions formed, and posters cropped up everywhere, exhorting ballots for Daruton, Darnton, Darnley, Dalton, Darnkampf (his name had been misspelled in the ship's paper). DARNTON FOR DOG CATCHER, one said. Another: DARNLEY THE RAIL SPLITTER. HIS BOOTS ARE BIG ENOUGH. Moments before the polls were to open, the organizers of the draft-Darnton faction retired to a stateroom in a celebratory mood, sure that Darnton couldn't come up with enough votes for anyone else to forestall his election.

"We were pretty smug," Kent recalled, "waiting for the electorate's voice to begin bellowing for Darnkampf. But Darnton was game. In on our smugness swirled a sinister figure, cloaked in an army raincoat and wearing a handkerchief mask to cover his up-sweeping mustache. He handed over a letter, urging us to whisper to each of ten friends the information enclosed, and crept out, chuckling hideously. The letter urged all right-minded men to vote against Darnton." Among other things, he was rumored to be "Roman Catholic and unpalatable to the farm vote." The ugly whisper campaign failed: Barney was elected by a landslide. And when the drills were held, things turned serious. He insisted that the correspondents, who stood last in the order to reach the boat deck, move quickly and in an orderly fashion. "We developed precision, probably for the first time in our lives," recalled Kent. "We weren't allowed to dawdle over our aperitifs."

After a violent gale, the *Monterey* put in at Brisbane, and the correspondents had their first encounter with military obstructionism. The base commander informed them they were prohibited from writing about the convoy, visiting military installations, or filing stories of any kind. This was a blow to all of them, but especially to Barney, since he had found a B-17 pilot willing to take him and several others to Darwin to write about the damage there from a Japanese bombing raid. The trip was vetoed. They were ordered to Melbourne, but red tape delayed their departure. "We made febrile, slightly alcoholic tours of the city," wrote Kent. "Mostly we stayed in our almost elegant apartments, vying with each other in sports like seeing who could lift the heaviest highball. The drinking on the way over had been a little crude. . . . Darnton wanted to get back on a firm foundation. But although his ingredients were pretty decent and his proportions perfect, the martinis were never very good. They tasted as if someone had soaked lead pencils in them. He was bitterly disappointed. Later I found out why they never appealed to him. I think that a few shakes of nostalgia had been added as a denaturing agent."

Eventually, they made their way to Melbourne, headquarters of the Australian armed forces and the small contingent of American troops. They ran into bewildering rules for multiple credentials and blanket restrictions on filing just about anything. But on March 17, a big story broke: General MacArthur had slipped through enemy lines in the Philippines, arrived in a Flying Fortress near Darwin, and was making his way south. The news was embargoed, but it was too big to contain and slipped out. Three days later, the general arrived in Adelaide, stepping out onto the station platform to deliver his now-famous statement: "I came through and I shall return." Only a single foreign reporter, from United Press, was there to hear it. The others, including Barney, 480 miles away in Melbourne, were forced to lift the text from the afternoon *Melbourne Herald* because the army neglected to give it out.

MacArthur's arrival inspired hopes in the press corps that their filing headaches might end, but they got worse. The general's top public-relations man, Lt. Col. LeGrande A. Diller, instituted draconian censorship. A daily communiqué contained little military information and a lot of puffery. In early April Barney pulled Kent aside and proposed a partnership to hitch rides to the American air bases up north and see how the war was going from there. Kent accepted the deal with alacrity. "I came to life," he wrote. "Here was a sturdy oak for my ivy-like tendrils." They grabbed a commercial flight to Townsville, on Queensland's northeastern coast, which was serving as a base for bombers striking Rabaul and other Japanese strongholds. En route, the plane had to overnight in Brisbane. At dawn they were informed at the airport that there was a seat for only one; silently, they dug in their pockets for a couple of shillings and flipped them. Barney won.

Kent described what happened next:

But as I started to drag myself out of the office and back to the hotel, Barney went into action. I heard him screaming to the youth behind the desk that it was absolutely imperative that both Mr. Kent and himself get to Townsville that same day. We had obtained our tickets in Melbourne on the highest type of military priority—a priority so high and mighty that he couldn't reveal the source of it to a civilian—and there would be hell to pay over this in government circles. Finally the bewildered boy said he thought he could cram both of us on the plane, but would have to take off our luggage and send it up the next day. Barney agreed to that readily, in the office. But when we got out to the airdrome, he began storming, his face dark with rage and flecked with foam. The agent in charge yielded, and Darnton and Kent and their luggage, excessively heavy, were flown to Townsville. From that day on, I felt about Darnton like the B-17 radio gunner who told us how his Fortress fought off 15 Zeros in a 45-minute melee over the New Guinea mountains. He pointed at the pilot, Maury Horgan, and said, "When the war's over I'm going to do two things—buy all the Boeing stock I can get, and follow Captain Horgan around like a dog." Only I didn't want to buy Times stock.

In Townsville, they stayed at a grim hotel, summoned to dreadful meals by the cook, who would stand on the back stoop, smashing a hammer against a steel pan. But they were the only two American correspondents, and the pickings were good. They talked a lot about their wives. One night they both decided to write home, dragging their typewriters downstairs and setting them up on opposite sides of a table. They started in. "That is, Barney did," Kent wrote. "I sat there for 45 minutes, making false start after false start. I got frantic. I tore up every sheet of paper after getting a driveling paragraph onto it. And Barney sat there, swiftly and surely beating out page after page to you, knowing what he wanted to say and how to say it. I despised the man."

In the cool evenings, they'd sit around talking endlessly about what they'd eat and drink when they returned to civilization. "Barney talked a lot about martinis. He used to tell me about his middle-of-the-week days off in Westport—how he would get up late, eat a big breakfast, and loll around the house until the gloaming. 'Then Tootie would go out in the kitchen and stir up a batch of martinis. The pleasantest sound I can imagine right now would be to hear the ice hitting the sides of the mixing glass out in that kitchen.' Long pause. 'They were always just right. I know that, generally, women aren't any good at mixing drinks. But let me tell you, Mister, Tootie can make the best martini in the world.' "

Being away from general headquarters meant more freedom in reporting, but it had its perils. Following a tip, Barney and Kent hitched a ride on an observation plane to Charters Towers, an old gold-mining town, where they came up with an important exclusive—interviewing B-25 pilots who had just returned from the first bombing raid on the Philippines. The raid was led by Maj. Gen. Ralph Royce. They filled their notebooks and wrote lengthy dispatches, but by this time it was late. They woke up the town postmaster, bribed him to arouse the telegraphers, bribed them to open their wires, and sent the stories through. They retired for the night, feeling the satisfaction of a job well done. Days later, they discovered that General Royce had flown from the Philippines straight to Melbourne, where the news was released to the forty or fifty correspondents. Their own dispatches had been intentionally held up and limped into their home offices some seventeen hours later. "We realized that MacArthur's headquarters always was going to beat us on major spot news breaks," Kent wrote. "Even if we got it first, our stories would be held up in favor of a mass release at GHQ, where the good general could be assured of a large and good press."

There was a solution and they took it: get closer to the war by going to New Guinea. In late April, they caught a B-17 to Port Moresby. They landed on a strip in a valley that was, as Barney noted, as deep as a part in a gigolo's haircut. It started to rain and despite the muggy downpour a swarm of mosquitoes descended upon them. What was alarming was that the Royal Australian Air Force officer who signed in the pilot, naked to the waist, didn't seem to notice them. A truck slithered along a muddy road past a row of gum trees and deposited them at a muddy gully leading to a large sagging tent and lean-to, the camp's kitchen and mess hall. There they joined the line for round steak, peas, and carrots, ladled by a fat, toothless, and cheerful mess sergeant from a crude wood-burning stove. Seated on long wooden benches, they saw that the ceiling of the tent was so black with flies, the canvas didn't show through. They listened in to the talk of the American fliers, young men, they noted, who a year ago had probably not ventured out of their states.

"Was you in Suva?"

"Yeah. The whole town stinks of coconut oil. The natives smear it on theirselves."

A bomber pilot asked his sergeant bombardier, "Did you get any beer tonight?"

"No. But I got to watch an Aussie drink a bottle. I drooled for half an hour."

A major stood up and addressed the fliers. "You men got mosquito bars with you?" Dead silence. "Well, you better have."

A blond fighter pilot in flying overalls spoke up: "The mosquitoes were so thick on the inside of my mosquito bar last night that they had to fly a traffic pattern."

They interviewed pilots from Chicago and New York until the billeting officer came for them. They slept on canvas cots in a shed with other men, tossing and turning because they hadn't tucked in their bars right and the mosquitoes were mauling them. An unknown voice whispered from across the room, "No use to fight 'em. First the little ones dive bomb your bar and open holes for the big ones." The next morning they were up at 4:40 a.m., back in the mess hall, interviewing pilots and crewmen, who were waiting for life-restoring coffee after a sleepless night of their own, soon to go off to fight the Japanese.

It was clear that Port Moresby was practically defenseless and that the Japanese could take it if they could just manage to get there. But very little of this pessimism found its way into Barney's dispatches. He accentuated the upbeat and when he talked about hardships he did it with humor. He described the ferocity of the mosquitoes by quoting a gasoline truck attendant at an airdrome: "I put forty gallons of gas in one the other day before I realized it was a mosquito, not an Airacrobra." Mostly he emphasized the spirit of his beloved aviators. YOUNG, STRONG, FEARLESS read the boldfaced headline of a two-thousand-word magazine piece. It began with the bomber pilots and navigators receiving mission instructions. It described their mood, what their downtime was like, where they got their news, and how they had found a swimming hole and took dips in the buff. It ended with a poker game in which a slow-talking southern boy, the winner of a Distinguished Flying Cross, kept up a chatter while examining and reexamining his hand and finally raised the bet. "He scared out everybody. Which should have won him the Distinguished Poker Cross—for he held two fours."

In early May Barney returned to Australia, to find the relationship between correspondents and MacArthur's press officers had deteriorated even further as the war was heating up. He wrote about the Battle of the Coral Sea. Between news developments, he wrote features. He told about soldiers playing baseball on the Fourth of July, and how a shipment of Benny Goodman and Glenn Miller records, played by a soldier in a music store, caused a traffic jam in the street outside. In a story about American nurses, he noted that Australian women overcame a shortage of nylons by painting imitation stockings on their legs. He interviewed pilots in hospital beds. One had been bitten by a snake that had somehow found its way into his cockpit. Another had single-handedly taken on forty-five Japanese Zeros and lived to tell about it. A third had devised a scheme to lure Zeros into high-speed chases that burned up their gas.

In early June, Barney was back in Port Moresby. He wasn't allowed to say that in his letters home because that would run afoul of the censors, so he simply called it "this place." His letters were upbeat: Living in "this place" was tough, but there were compensations: turquoise seas, outrigger canoes, and odd characters like the stiff-upper-lip British plantation owner who treated them to a meal. The birds, however, were another matter. "You would not like them. I'm sure of that. . . . They perch in a tree above you and emit such things as 'That's lousy; throw it away.' Or 'Wasting cable tolls, wasting cable tolls.' The other day we threw stones at them. No hits." He sent home a piece of metal from a downed Zero.

In mid-July, he returned to Australia, basing himself in Brisbane. He moved with a group of other reporters into a large two-story house surrounded by a veranda. For the first time, he lived in luxury. Oil portraits of royals lined the hallways. There was a library, a billiard table, a badminton court, a flowering garden, and three servants to tidy up. A sign out front—WAR CORRESPONDENTS' CONVALESCENT HOME—mystified the locals. A sympathetic Australian neighbor sent over an offer of calf's-foot jelly and then became puzzled when he noticed that the so-called disabled reporters were chasing one another around a badminton court, whooping it up. In July, MacArthur and his entire entourage moved to Brisbane, too. The general arrived in a maroon railroad car, guarded at both ends by American MPs toting tommy guns and wearing white belts and white gloves. The apparition gave the high command the nickname "the circus."

In August, Barney wrote about the battle over the Solomon Islands (the beginning of the Marines' assault on Guadalcanal) and the abortive Japanese attempt to seize Milne Bay, on the eastern tip of New Guinea. His news stories were taking on a new, more ominous tone. The buildup of American forces was insufficient to meet the Japanese threat in New Guinea and the enemy had seized the initiative. They had begun a land drive from the northern coast over the Owen Stanley Mountains, following the treacherous Kokoda Trail, aimed at taking Port Moresby. MacArthur downplayed the Japanese move, claiming the mountains, which rose to thirteen thousand feet, were an insurmountable barrier. By September, the Japanese succeeded in crossing the mountains, reaching a plateau only thirty-two miles from Moresby—a fact that the American censors deleted.

Barney decided it was time to return there. He arrived in Port Moresby in mid-September, to find the situation looking better close-up than it had at a distance. The Japanese were giving up their drive over the mountains. And finally, with new planes coming in, the Americans were winning the air war. The number of Zeros in the sky was dropping. His reports carried a tone of optimism. "Now we're cooking with gas," he quoted one army air forces officer as saying. "We have got sixty two Jap planes in the last four weeks to four that they got of ours."

Privately the Aussies seethed because MacArthur's communiqués referred to the troops up against the Japanese as "our" troops or "Allied" troops, which gave the misimpression that the Yanks were the ones turning the tide. But Barney's dispatches, written closer to the action, were careful to give credit where it was due. He always called the soldiers Australian, and the U.S. censors allowed it through. Barney became popular with the Aussie journalists and sometimes bunked down with them in their quarters seventeen miles out of town.

In Port Moresby, Barney moved into the correspondents' hut. With four rooms for cots draped in mosquito netting and an open veranda, the flimsy plasterboard cottage could accommodate a dozen or so newsmen. Food was an unending diet of corned beef, beans, crackers, and tea. On October 2 came a surprise. MacArthur and the "circus" breezed in for a whirlwind visit. He landed just before dusk in a B-17 bomber at the Seven Mile Drome, as the reporters stood on the bank of a revetment to watch. When the hand shaking and saluting was done, a soldier bellowed, "Time for chow." Some of the newcomers misheard it as a warning of an air raid and quickly scattered.

The next morning, MacArthur rode in a staff car toward the Kokoda Trail in a jeep with chains on all four wheels. He sat in the front, splattered with red mud and grasping the windshield so tightly, he couldn't wave at the soldiers coming down. The men going up opened ranks to let him pass, unsmiling and sweating under their loads. At the end of the road, where the trail began by plunging into a gorge several hundred feet deep, he got out, made some observations, signed autographs, and took a cup of coffee from a cook called "Gestapo Gus." Then he turned to leave. He was twenty-two miles from the Japanese line, the closest he would come. The reporters had shadowed him as best they could. Barney wrote 2,500 words—enough for about two and a half columns. Diller carried his and others' copy back and warned that they wouldn't be released for some time. When a British reporter arrived from Brisbane almost two weeks later, he said the dispatches had been badly cut and changed, because the censors deleted references to the general going as far as he could in the jeep.

But by then, Barney had other concerns. For he had gotten the okay to go on the trip with the 32nd Division and was preparing to fly to Wanigela for his trip to Pongani. He wrote his story comparing the role of correspondents in the two wars and soaked his feet in water to break in his new boots and wrote his final letter to our mother.

At this point Barney was no longer working in tandem with Carleton Kent. Kent later heard about what happened at Pongani, about what went wrong, and then did some reporting to verify it. He recounted it this way:

> *Someone fired Barney with enthusiasm over the story possi-*
> *bilities of such a trip, and he easily wangled a spot aboard the*
> *ship. Possibly it was the enthusiasm of Lt. Bruce Fahnestock,*
> *who had cruised those waters for years on schooners in vari-*
> *ous scientific expeditions, which sold him the idea.*
>
> *That same night a signal was wirelessed back to Air Corps*
> *headquarters, warning that an American ship would be in the*
> *waters below Buna, and for God's sake don't bomb it. Bar-*
> *ney, Bruce, the ship's small crew, and a contingent of 32nd*
> *Division men and officers took off on the dangerous, but not*
> *foolhardy, mission.*
>
> *Something had happened, however, to communications*
> *between Wanigela and Air Corps headquarters. The warning*
> *signal wasn't received in time to advise pilots assigned to early*
> *bombing missions in the Buna area. Soon after sunrise, some*
> *of our B-25's came over the ship.*

Kent's reporting was accurate.

Those words my father hastily scribbled in his notebook—"Plane across course. Jap or our?"—were prophetic. For the plane that bombed the *King John* was an American B-25. It had taken off from Port Moresby early that morning on an armed reconnaissance mission and was returning to base when it spotted the two ships.

As Meyer Berger was to write years later: "It turned out, bitterly enough, that one of Barney's beloved 'high school kids' had made a grievous error; he had mistaken the *King John* for a Japanese craft because it was so far forward of any previous American position."

I don't know precisely when my mother heard that my father had been killed by friendly fire, but the news was not totally surprising. General MacArthur's initial statement had called his death "accidental." There followed a period of confusion and censorship as MacArthur's press officers scrambled to find out what had happened and released information to the *Times* in dribs and drabs.

My mother saved all the messages. The first one came on October 20 in compressed, urgent cablese:

DARNTON KILLED FRONTLINE NEWGUINEA STOP PUBLICATION
FORBIDDEN PENDING ANNOUNCEMENT EXHEADQUARTERS

Two days later came a curt message, apparently in response to a query from the *Times:*

CIRCUMSTANCES UNAVAILABLE YET

And five days after that, Colonel Diller sent another:

SHRAPNEL WOUND LEFT SIDE OF HEAD KILLED DARNTON
INSTANTLY STOP DETAILS NOT YET KNOWN

And five days after that, still another:

WHILE ON SMALL BOAT RECONNOITERING OFF NORTH COAST
NEWGUINEA DARNTON KILLED BY AIRBOMB STOP SINCE WOULD
GIVE VALUABLE INFORMATION DETAILS PRESENCE BOAT OFF COAST
SHOULDN'T REVEALED STOP

No one seemed eager to press hard to find out the cause of the miscommunication. In his letter, Kent wrote:

I know you feel as I do, and as do all his friends—that there's no use trying to find out who is to blame. The young pilot, lacking the warning, simply did his duty. None of Barney's friends tried to find out why the all-important signal was delayed. I hope the army did, to avoid a second such tragedy. I want you to feel certain of this: that Barney would have never gone on the trip if he had thought the chances were against him. . . . He always played it safe. He always meant to come back to you and the kids, and said so. He was very brave, but he never was a fool about it. Posing against the skyline of a war didn't appeal to him. He took his bombing and strafing raids in a slit trench, because he knew that was the only way.

His death occurred in spite of all his sensible precautions. It was surely an act of God. So I'm not interested in why that signal was delayed. My quarrel is with God.

Two days after the death, General Harding wrote a letter to Gen. Richard Sutherland, MacArthur's chief of staff, saying that "everyone hereabouts is distressed over the death of Darnton and Fahnestock." He added:

I knew Darnton quite well (he stayed a couple of weeks with us when the Division was at Adelaide), and consider him one damn good correspondent and a swell guy. He was hot to be on the spot for the first contact between American Army ground troops with the Japs. I told him that this would probably be it and gave him permission to go.

There's no disposition hereabouts to try to hang the blame for the accidental bombing on any one person or group. The pilot might have done more to make sure that he wasn't dropping his bombs on his own people, but I don't believe that he had been advised of the possibility of friendly craft being in that vicinity. The Air Corps staff might have warned their pilots of that possibility since they knew that we contemplated the move by water. And certainly we should have informed the Air Corps to be on the lookout for two ships the morning they were to arrive. I guess we will just have to chalk it up to one of those things that happen in a war, and remember the lesson we learned at a price.

CHAPTER 4

Mom didn't talk much about the period right after Barney died, but years later she acknowledged how painful it was. Being busy helped at first. There were the obligations and trappings of widowhood—arrangements to be made, letters to write. Condolences poured in from Barney's extensive family in Michigan and from newspaper colleagues and others. Friends clipped obits from papers around the country and sent them to her. Death necessitated a surprising amount of paperwork. She received a dunning letter from a member of the *Times* accounting department, asking if she could account for a five-thousand-dollar advance provided for his assignment. Her reply was straightforward—unfortunately, she had no receipts on hand, she explained—in a tone so neutral, it's hard to tell if she was being sarcastic; she sent a copy of both letters to the managing editor, Edwin L. James, and the problem disappeared overnight.

She corresponded with the New York *Daily News* correspondent in the Pacific, Jack Turcott, whom the army appointed as Barney's executor. He collected some of Barney's belongings and sent them back—his passport, correspondent's insignia, army uniform, and some photographs—but following what Turcott called "a horrible Australian custom," Barney's typewriter and many other items had been auctioned off among the Australian reporters. "The men who bought the things refused to part with them, despite my urgent pleas and offers to refund the money." He added that he had burned her letters, which Barney had kept carefully tucked away, to spare her the sorrow of seeing them again. In doing this, he said he was following the counsel of another correspondent, who was a woman and therefore presumably knew about such things. "She said you'd be sure to read them over and over again, which was just the thing you shouldn't do." I doubt my mother appreciated the preemptive solicitousness.

Once these arrangements were out of the way, she encountered a sudden void. After the flurry of obligations and commiserations, for which she steeled herself, not much happened. Communications from New Guinea tapered off. The letters of condolence came less frequently, then stopped altogether. The war went on. Buna, after a bloody campaign that lasted months instead of the one week that had been anticipated, was eventually taken. The American counteroffensive moved on, island by island. At some point Barney's body would be transferred back to the States, but there was no word when. The reality of his death hit home.

After several months, she packed up and moved us to Washington, D.C. She got a job there as an "information specialist" in the publications section of the Office of War Information, the agency set up in June 1942 to handle war news at home and propaganda abroad. Under the former CBS newsman Elmer Davis, the OWI was a sprawling bureaucracy that cleared everything that was for public consumption. It vetted posters warning of spies and saboteurs and critiqued newsreels of the fighting and approved radio series such as "This Is Our Enemy," which portrayed Hitler's perfidy and Mussolini's buffoonery. Exactly how she obtained this position, I never learned, though I know she felt strongly about participating in the war effort. Her background was in the professional world of New York City—before giving up her career for motherhood, she had been an advertising copywriter and magazine editor—so she was well qualified. Perhaps an old friend of Barney's, Milton MacKaye, a magazine writer who also joined the OWI, recommended her. In any case, as someone who could string words into a decent sentence and was a war widow, she was a natural choice.

I, of course, do not have any personal memory of those days, since I was experiencing them from a crib and a stroller. My brother doesn't remember them either. There are so many blank spaces that I can't reconstruct them with certainty. I believe that our mother faced the challenges bravely—she had been raised to regard stoicism as one of the higher virtues—but I believe it more from a sense of who she was than from any objective facts. Like most children, I never sat her down and plied her with methodical questions about the past. As a result, I'm dependent upon stories and comments that she let drop at random—*my* memories of *her* memories, meaning they are twice filtered and doubly unreliable.

But I do have her book, *The Children Grew*. It purports to tell our family story and it presents us as a tight-knit threesome standing up against the world. With wisdom and instinct, she solved the problems of raising two sons without a father. She opened the story with a powerful image. She described Barney's departure from our home in Westport. He was wearing his uniform. He leaned down and told Bob that he would be gone a long, long time but that he would be coming back. "Never forget that," he said. Then the door closed and the boy "pressed his face against the glass of the French door for a long, last look, his arms spread-eagled across the frame as if in embrace. . . . Did the child remember those parting words? How would it affect him, who had never known a broken promise, to find this promise broken, perhaps the largest of all?"

Later she recounted how easy it was to tell Bob that his father wasn't coming back. There was no particular moment in which she had to tell him that he had been killed. (I was too young to require telling.) She simply stopped running eagerly to the mailbox and gradually began referring to "Daddy" in the past tense, until one day, Bob, puzzling over some flowers that had withered, intuitively grasped the concept of death and said, "Daddy died, didn't he?" As I reread that passage, and try to imagine the scene, I am struck by the implausibility of it, of Bob's precocious deduction and his passive acceptance of a shattering truth. Or, on the slim chance that it might have happened, I'm struck by the realization that our family dynamic centered on repression—all those important words left unsaid and all those primal emotions pressed down out of sight. More true to our inner life, I think, is the assertion that she said we were to raise in subsequent years: "If Daddy had loved us, he wouldn't have gone away and left us." I don't remember saying such a thing, which would have struck close to the psychic bone. Nor do I remember her answer, as she wrote it: "It was *because* Daddy loved you so much that he had to go away. He didn't want hurt or harm to come here to you or to this country where you will grow up. He went away to try to stop it before it would come here." Hers was one of those abstract answers that adults think will lay a child's fear to rest by appealing to some sort of higher logic, thus trumping it, but which children instinctually deem unsatisfactory.

Recently I discovered the carbon copy of a letter that our mother wrote during that first year, describing just how much Bob missed his father. I don't know to whom she wrote, but because it was a contemporary account and because it was intended as a private communication, I trust it more than the version she presented in the book, in which Bob blithely accepted his father's death as part of the natural order of things. In the letter she said that Barney had spent his mornings at home and that consequently Bob had seen him more than most children saw their fathers. She said Bob used to follow him around with his own small lawn mower, small rake, and small shovel, imitating him doing yard work. The father-son bond was especially strong. She then noted, "Bob missed his father tremendously the first six months after he went away. He reassured himself by quoting his father's parting words: 'I'll be gone a long time but I'll be back.' When the time came to seem too long Bob had a tough time for a while. He would wake at night crying. I tried to give him all of me he seemed to need and I think he finally adjusted very well to his father's absence."

It occurs to me now that our mother believed that we adjusted easily because she *needed* to believe it. She needed to think we would all carry on almost as before, that she had been able to shield us from the hard reality that his death was a profound wound that would transform everything. Families that undergo tragedy evolve myths to make sense of the loss and define their place in the world. Our narrative was simple and heroic: We had endured a loss, but it was a sacrifice for a purpose—to rid the world of totalitarian evil—and to give that sacrifice meaning, we had to endure and prosper. We would support one another in the face of adversity, and everything would turn out all right. In fact, everything would continue pretty much as had been planned before. The only way for it to continue was for our mother to become both mother and father, to carry out both roles, of the nurturer and the provider. "Could she do it?" she asked herself in *The Children Grew*. "She would have to." She would become superhuman. There is, of course, a problem with a myth, any myth. While it may embody a noble aspiration and provide a source of courage and moral sustenance, it is, by its nature, founded on a kernel of fiction. And so living a myth is a dangerous business, because fiction is not a solid foundation on which to build a family's life. Our mother was not superhuman—on the contrary, she was all too human.

In Washington, we settled into a comfortable house on Ordway Street in the Northwest section. Back then, it was still very much a provincial southern city, though the war had shaken it out of its longtime lethargy. Despite gasoline rationing (three gallons a week), cars jammed the streets. Briefcase-toting government workers crowded the sidewalks—new ones were pouring into the city at the rate of fourteen hundred a week—and military men hurried by in a blur of uniforms, white, blue, green, and khaki. The Pentagon, the world's largest office building, had just been completed. Temporary offices, long rectangular structures that evoked a sense of purpose, sprang up along the Mall and around the Washington Monument. The White House was newly fenced and guards were posted in boxed shelters. "You're in the Army Now" was a hit on radio, *This Is the Army* packed them in at the National Theater, and celebrities like Hedy Lamarr, Bing Crosby, and Abbott and Costello came to town for war-bond rallies. Restaurants were crowded by day, homes blacked out at night. Everyone smoked. It was de rigueur to exude an air of calm, but, as is obvious from the memoirs of people who worked for FDR, war is nothing if not exciting.

Every weekday morning Mom went off to work at the War Department, housed in a mausoleumlike building on Independence Avenue. It must have been satisfying for her to play an informational role on the home front. For someone close to the news media, what better way than to help disseminate war news to an anxious public? She shared my father's views on the essential symbiosis between the press and democracy, and his death had deepened her conviction that everyone must take part in the worldwide struggle to keep freedom alive. Otherwise—and I doubt she ever allowed herself to think so openly, because it would have been too painful—he would have died for nothing.

But practical considerations intruded. What to do with two young boys? She wrote of her problems finding dependable help. A black maid who had worked for us in Connecticut, Inell Jones, whom we were already deeply attached to, moved with us to Washington, but soon the city's racism chased her back north. A succession of maids followed, coming and going so fast, as our mother told it, that they seemed to walk in the front door and out the back. She wrote that one drank heavily. I paint a vision in my imagination: Mom phones at midday, to no answer, then rushes home, to find the woman sprawled in a stupor on the couch, with me bawling in my crib and Bob lying wide-eyed in bed. Other maids were almost as bad. They'd accept the job and show up only periodically. She posted a phone number for a registered nurse to fill in as a backstop—an expensive proposition—and she was forced to avail herself of it often.

She indicated that money was not a problem—*The New York Times* and an insurance company made a generous financial settlement after Barney's death—but rationing was. She had to scrape together enough coupons to keep herself in coffee and cigarettes, not to mention buying new shoes every six months or so for our growing feet. She gave up on my toilet training and decided to send Bob off to nursery school at the age of three, which in those days was regarded as far too young. But, she told herself, Churchill went off to school at a tender age—a precedent that probably struck her as fitting. She had to pull strings to get him in, and reading between the lines in her book, I get the impression that her reaction to the admissions process was typical. She resented the interview with the school psychiatrist, who had the effrontery to ask if he was "a wanted child." ("Was he? Was ever a child more lovingly welcome!") Then Bob failed at a test of stringing beads—he who "had spent many happy hours stringing beads and spools and buttons, long ago." That night she asked him about it. He said that it was silly, that "I'm too big for that." The whole experience was disheartening, she wrote. It made her feel that she was inadequate, that the job of raising two boys was "too complicated to do well under the most normal circumstances." But she rallied and insisted that she was doing all right on her own. She simply had to trust her instincts; she couldn't rely on help from so-called professionals or even expect understanding from them. "You had to find your own way," she concluded. Counselors were outsiders and people with titles were full of thin theory, knowing nothing about the fire of practice. It would be the three of us against the world.

One day the ubiquitous Meyer Berger, the *Times* reporter, came to Washington to spend time with Bob. He took him around the city, visiting famous landmarks and jotting down the jumble of words that flowed in an unending stream from his young mouth. The result was a *Times Magazine* article titled "Robert, Age 4, in Wonderland." The idea was that, as with the truthful child in "The Emperor's New Clothes," only the eye of an innocent could unmask truths about power and fear in the wartime capital. But now reading the article, which is crumpling and yellow with age, I see that it revealed something deeper—something about the boy, not the city. To a child who had just lost his father, the statues of men on horseback and the monuments to heroes and the wounded in Walter Reed General Hospital and the dead in Arlington Cemetery all stoked his febrile imagination. He was steeped in dread of spilled blood and panic-stricken about planes carrying bombs and obsessed with "the Bad Men," who could drop out of the sky at any moment to kill everyone in sight. The article leaves him standing before the Tomb of the Unknown Soldier in his tweed jacket, short pants, and matching tweed cap, looking around wide-eyed at the marble sarcophagus and amphitheater. He whimpers: "I want to go home now. I want to sleep but not where the soldiers sleep because where they sleep is cold."

In April 1943, Mom joined a protest of fifteen writers at the OWI. They charged that the publications division had turned its back on being an honest purveyor of war news. After much Sturm und Drang, they all resigned. The dispute was covered by the

Times. "We are leaving because of our conviction that it is impossible for us, under those who now control our output, to tell the full truth," read a statement from the group. It charged that the section was "now dominated by high-pressure promoters who prefer slick salesmanship to honest information." The other dissidents included Henry F. Pringle, the Pulitzer Prize–winning biographer; Philip P. Hamburger, *The New Yorker* writer; Arthur M. Schlesinger, Jr., the historian; and Mr. MacKaye (my mother's friend). My mother wouldn't have missed a chance to stand fast on a matter of principle. But there was, sadly, that not so small matter of putting bread on the table, and she took what must have been for her a difficult step. She wrote to the publisher of the *Times,* Arthur Hays Sulzberger, asking for a job, and he graciously offered her a position as a reporter in the paper's Washington bureau. In early June, she wrote him again: "I want to tell you how much I appreciate the opportunity you have given me. I start to work on Monday. My one concern is to measure up to the job you've given me a chance to do. I shall certainly try."

The decision to take the job was nerve-racking, she confessed to me decades later, because she had never worked as a reporter. She hoped that she would be able to pick up the skill of gathering and writing news as she went along, that Barney's talent and techniques had somehow rubbed off on her. I realized that her greatest fears were the same that I had had twenty-five years later, the same for every beginning reporter: that she would not be able to dig out all the facts or write quickly enough on deadline or spot the guts of the story and encapsulate it in her lead. For months, she said, she tried to conceal her fears and inexperience from her coworkers. Returning from covering a story, her notebook stuffed in her large leather purse, she would walk past the entrance to the *Times'* office in the Albee Building and circle around the block two, three, or even more times, trying to settle her thoughts and compose the story's lead in her mind.

The job turned out to be more difficult than she'd expected. And how to juggle both it and the demands of family? There didn't seem to be enough time in the day to pack it all in, leaving for work early in the morning and returning at home in the evening, to find the two of us starved for her attention. Gone were the leisure hours, sleeping late on Sunday mornings. And gone, too—or at least so she feared—was family time given to just being together, not consecrated to planned expeditions like visits to the zoo or Rock Creek Park. It's when you're just hanging out together, she wrote, that kids are most apt to let slip the things troubling them.

She described the first Christmas as a trial, an unsettling blending of seasonal joy and personal sorrow. Presents poured in from family friends, especially for the two of us boys, but on the morning we opened them, when we sat on the floor surrounded by ripped wrappings like piles of leaves, there was no adult for her to share it with—or to give her a gift.

All in all, that first year was one of tribulation. And so, she wrote in her book, halfway through it she did something that only another grief-stricken person might understand. She sat down and picked up a fountain pen and wrote a letter to her dead husband. She described it this way: It was "a long letter, confiding in him the many ways she was failing and how she wasn't sure that she could succeed. And how sorry she was. She had just spilled it out. It had done her good." And afterward, she wrote, she burned the letter, explaining: "In this household, things inevitably got misplaced and one of the boys might have come across it one day. They must not be burdened with knowledge of what a struggle it was for her nor know her occasional depths of despair and fear of defeat."

Truth, however, intervenes. She did not, as she had written, burn the letter so that we would never find it. I discovered it in 2005, stuffed inside a manila envelope, along with scraps of notes and faded newspaper clippings, tucked away in a carton that had rested undisturbed in an attic for many years. It was dated March 27, 1943, six months after he died. She began it this way:

Dearest,

This may seem a little screwy but I'm so much in the habit of writing to you, of having you to communicate with, that I think it might help. There are substitutes for lots of things, but there's no substitute for that intimate communication.

I think we're going to be alright. But it's certainly an odd world without you. I haven't yet found home base in myself, a complete home base, without you. You would be pleased that

*few people, if any, know that. You would be happy at the face
I give the world. You would be happy that I'm managing so
well and understand that I'm not managing better.*

She told him that we children were all right so far and that we
seemed to have adjusted to change. But she worried about spending
so little time with us and about the energy her job consumed. She
had proven that she was able to earn a living and she was proud
that she was contributing something to the war effort. She vowed
she'd rather be a ribbon clerk at Lord & Taylor than fall for a big
salary doing something phony. "I know you'd feel that way." Still:
"I wish I had some of your confidence in me. . . . I'm greedy, I guess,
to give the kids the values we would have given them together." She
ended the letter:

> *I wish you could breathe your talent and experience into
> me—as you have given me so much else of yourself. Darling,
> do you really suppose I'll get used to being without you? That
> first brilliant understanding of what your death meant, the
> rightness of it in terms of large issues, or at least acceptance
> instead of resentment. Then the numbness, stabbed with pain.
> And now this alert carrying on, with the unrelieved private
> desolation. Writing to you hasn't helped as much as I thought
> it might. I guess kidding yourself, even this much, my darling,
> is no way to do. We'll see. I may be able to resolve me by talk-
> ing at you, instead of to you, yet. Darling, I love you. You're
> my guy. And this is still the same world. It must be, even with-
> out you.*

It's clear that her account in the book was untrue in one other
significant respect. In *The Children Grew*, she said that writing him
had "done her good." But in reality, in the letter itself, she noted
that it "hasn't helped as much as I thought," that she was "kid-
ding" herself to think otherwise.

The book is not a reliable account of our childhood. It's such
a perfect reflection of our mother, and her capacity for optimism
and romantic delusion, achieved by gutting out the hard core of
dark truths, that more often than not it points in the wrong direc-

tion. For years I was bothered by the disparity between what had happened and what she wrote had happened. My brother and I joked—with an undercurrent of bitterness, he more than I—that we didn't know if it belonged on our shelves under the category of fiction or nonfiction.

CHAPTER 5

My brother and I were always eager to hear the story of how our parents met. I suspect that's true of most of us as children—probably because on a psychological level the story is really about us. It's our own creation myth, a fairy tale whose ending, equivalent to "and they lived happily ever after," is: "and then, *you* were born."

Except in our case, the story remained tantalizingly vague. Our mother seemed to be telling an expurgated shorthand version. There was no precise moment when she first met Barney, no thunderstruck beginning. They didn't spot each other across a crowded room or happen to sit opposite each other in the dining car of the 20th Century Limited—or if they did, we weren't told about it. It took years for me to learn the reason for this opaqueness, and when I finally did, everything fell into place. It was simple: When they met and fell in love, each was married to someone else. The subsequent disentanglement, necessitating two divorces, was ugly. And so, the beginning of our own particular fairy tale was X-rated.

Of course we didn't see it that way. Privately, as we came to learn the through line of the story in small doses and adorned it with our own imaginative touches, we elevated it to the status of a heroic epic. It made their love seem passionate and even in a way pure. What is love without an obstacle to surmount? Long before I saw a staging of *Romeo and Juliet,* I knew something about star-crossed lovers, and long before I heard of Abélard and Héloïse, I felt an instinctive connection to the romantic proposition that great love will not be denied.

When they met in the mid-1930s, my parents belonged to a subculture of New York literati. Their crowd was made up of magazine writers, newspaper reporters, novelists, and professionals from tangentially connected professions, such as advertising. Early on I got the impression that they were given to fast living and heavy drinking. To some extent they were spiritual heirs to the earlier Algonquin Round Table, though less vicious and backbiting. The ethos was epitomized by *The New Yorker,* which offered a knowing take on life in the anonymous big city, with its manifest excitements and small, hidden pleasures. The magazine, grounded on the unstated assumption that New York was the center of the universe, mirrored them and their aspirations, since so many of them were refugees from other parts of the country. My parents were part of that migration.

I came to know my mother's family much better than my father's. As a young child I visited my grandparents in West Philadelphia. My grandmother was lively and irreverent, always ready to play tic-tac-toe or tell a child a tale. She had a soft spot for people in trouble—her father had been a down-and-out drunk—and I can close my eyes and see a parade of palsied men given room and board in exchange for sweeping the basement. My grandfather, who had been an orphan in the slums of London, seemed never to have recovered from his Dickensian childhood—he was quiet and removed from family life. I found their Victorian house, with its thick-curtained rooms and china bed pans under the beds, airless and claustrophobic. The photos of my mother and her three brothers hanging on the wooden stairwell were unsmiling. My mother didn't reminisce much about her years at home, and the stories that she enjoyed telling, with gusto, were of school yard and outdoor tomboy adventures. She acquired her lifelong nickname, Tootie, on a grade-school baseball diamond the day after she appeared as

Little Boy Blue in a class play; she socked a home run and, cheering her, her classmates shaped their hands into horns and shouted, "Toot! Toot!"

Whatever it was that was wrong in that house caused my mother to rebel. She became a 1920s flapper, complete with a pageboy haircut, short dresses, and long beads. In summers, she followed her passion—acting—at the Hedgerow Theatre, housed in a picturesque 1840 gristmill. She left home by dropping out of the University of Pennsylvania in her senior year and eloping. The man she married was named Clarkson Hill. Because in later years Mom regarded him with such contempt, we never found out much about him, other than that she compared him, like Thomas Dewey, to "that little man on the wedding cake." I did learn that he worked in Philadelphia as a banker and that Mom got a job there as a copywriter for an advertising agency, N. W. Ayer & Son. In 1933 they moved to New York City, where she worked for another ad agency, J. M. Mathes, Inc. Together they apparently led a high life, despite the Depression, just as Prohibition was ending. In an image that probably belongs more to the movies than reality, I envision them like William Powell and Myrna Loy, in a duplex with a winding staircase. She became the editor of a high-quality glossy women's fashion magazine called *YOU* and wrote a racy tongue-in-cheek book called *Ain't Love Gland?* Subtitled *A Psychological Guide to Mating,* it was based on the pseudoscientific principle that various glands dictated personality types and it dispensed worldly wisdom for "streamlining your love life." She wrote it under a pen name, Kate Townsend.

Following Mom's funeral forty years later, two hours after her body was laid in the grave, her moralistic older brother, Ernie, who had labored away with dogged rectitude as a high school principal in Philadelphia, reminisced bitterly about his sister during that time. He told of how she had called to borrow money from him, and his surprise when he went to deliver it. A Japanese houseboy opened the door and ushered him into a marble lobby decorated with potted palms. He told us that as a bitter complaint, and I knew I was supposed to be troubled by it. But I couldn't suppress a smile. For years afterward, that image—my mother living in splendor while the responsible world came to call in the person of Uncle

Scrooge—was emblematic of something I loved best about her: her irrepressible spirit and her Auntie Mame conviction that life was to be lived to the fullest.

By contrast, I had little to do with Barney's family. I did visit them in Michigan when I was thirteen and encountered a bewildering array of cousins old enough to be my father. That's because Barney was by far the youngest of his six siblings. His father, Robert (a name passed down through the generations) was a prominent town elder, eventually becoming the postmaster. In high school, Barney visited New York under the tutelage of an uncle, Charles Darnton, the drama critic for Pulitzer's *New York Evening World*. He got his first taste of the glamour of the big city and his first look at the innards of a newspaper, and he was smitten by both. According to his obit, he laughingly told friends as a middle-aged reporter that it was while watching his uncle pound out reviews on a typewriter that he caught the newspaper bug.

Growing up, I heard various stories about Barney's experiences in World War I. He enlisted out of high school in the Michigan National Guard, which became part of the 32nd Division, nicknamed "Les Terribles" by the French for their courageous tenacity in taking on "the Boche." They were the first doughboys to fight their way onto German territory. When I was twelve, an animal died in the hollow of our living room wall, resulting in a putrid smell throughout the downstairs. My mother remarked that a similar thing had happened to the two of them years before, only Barney hadn't noticed it. She said that he had spent so much time in the trenches, surrounded by bodies, that he had lost "the ability to smell death." I pondered that idea for weeks, wondering what it had been like to have gone through such hell on earth—and whether I would have been able to withstand it.

His obit in the Adrian paper was accompanied by the recollection of a fireman who had served in the same outfit. It was headlined BAPTISM OF FIRE. The man noted that shortly after arriving in Europe, Barney fell ill, was hospitalized, and then had to catch up to his unit.

After the usual greetings and back slapping he wanted to see just what the front line looked like. I walked up to an advanced position with him through a connecting trench. A Frenchman was standing by. We visited a few minutes and Darnton remarked that it sure was quiet. "Don't they ever do any shooting?" he asked. The Frenchman just smiled. He pulled a rifle grenade out of his pocket, attached it to his gun and sent it looping over to the German trenches a few yards away. Darnton watched him quietly. That grenade hadn't any more than landed when German machine guns began to cut loose. Bullets whizzed overhead and one of them clipped off a barbed wire fence post right over us. Darnton ducked. "Gosh," he exclaimed, "they really do shoot over here, don't they?"

He attended the University of Michigan, but, as my mother told the story, after his time in France college life struck him as puerile. He dropped out after two years, toured the old battlefields of the Oise-Aisne and the Meuse-Argonne, and then took up a job as a reporter on the *Port Huron Times Herald*. After a year, he moved to Baltimore to work for H. L. Mencken on the *Evening Sun,* the afternoon paper, which was more prankish than the morning *Sun.* He began writing short stories and got some of them published in Mencken's magazine, *The Smart Set,* and in *Scribner's Magazine.* Mencken tried to convince him to take up fiction as a career. He flirted briefly with the idea but decided against it. I went back and located some of his stories. They were well written but struck me as a bit heavy-handed. I think he was wise to stick with newspapers.

He went on to Philadelphia, where he worked on the *Philadelphia Bulletin* and then the *Philadelphia Evening Ledger.* There he met Ann Hark, another reporter, and they got married. The marriage lasted only a year or so. In 1925, he reached the top of the newspaper heap—New York City. He joined the *New York Evening Post,* in those days a respected paper, first on the copy desk, then as a reporter; he covered both 1928 conventions. Two years later he moved over to the Associated Press, as a day cable editor—equivalent to the foreign desk—and then as city editor of the New York bureau. In April 1932, he married a woman named Eleanor Pollock. Two years later, on April 30, 1934, he transferred to the news staff of the *Times* and began rising in the ranks from reporter to editor. Somewhere along the line, he met my mother. The two Eleanors, Eleanor Hill and Eleanor Pollock, inhabited the same universe of advertising copywriters and magazine editors. So it was natural that the two women would become friends and, together with their husbands, all get to know one another.

Over time my mother dropped tidbits about her illicit courtship with my father, but she never told the full story. When I was in my twenties, we might be eating in a restaurant—say the Oyster Bar at Grand Central or Cobb's Mill Inn in Weston, Connecticut—and she'd remark that the place held a special meaning for her, because years ago she and Barney used to meet there. She'd look around, taking in the changes and subtracting them, and I could tell that she was traveling back a quarter of a century to be there with him, perhaps sitting at our very table. Once, passing a hotel—it was the Biltmore, with its gilded clock, a famous meeting place—she told of how several times, filled with remorse, they decided to end their affair. But each time the separation proved insupportable; one or the other would give in and place an urgent call and they'd resume seeing each other. On one occasion, Barney could no longer stand being apart. He telephoned and she admitted that she, too, had been about to phone. They fixed a rendezvous on the spot—a hotel lobby—but in the excitement, signals got crossed. Barney dashed off to the Roosevelt and she to the Biltmore. For over an hour each waited, pacing frantically and then despairing, thinking the other had had a change of heart. Not until the next day was the mix-up sorted out. As she told the story, she laughed fondly and shook her head, as if looking back at herself as a thirty-year-old and wondering how she had been able to endure such wild swings of emotion.

One summer—it must have been 1936, but I can't swear to that—Barney and his wife rented a cottage near the beach south of Westport, not far from where my mother and Clarkson Hill had rented theirs. This was the turning point in the relationship between Barney and Tootie, the time they became lovers. How did it come about exactly? Here the blank spaces intrude once again. They multiply and spread out to attach to one another, so that, try as I might, I come up with very little. That's not surprising. In personal histories the key moments often drop away, while the mundane ones survive in bureaucratic papers or the recollections of others. In trying to piece together my parents' courtship, I feel as if I'm tracking their footsteps on the beach just as the tide moves in to erase them.

There was, apparently, a literal beach. That much my mother told us. There was a critical day—perhaps a Monday, when Barney didn't go in to work (as a Sunday editor, he had Mondays off). She drove her husband to the train station for his commute to the city. Perhaps for some reason Barney was in the car with them, or perhaps he was back in the cottage. In any case, the two ended up together, walking on the beach, talking easily. A seagull glided in over the water for a landing on the shore. As she watched it, Mom realized that she was deeply, irrevocably in love. Everything that followed came from that moment.

It is natural to want to fill in the blank spaces. I imagine the two couples cavorting together, a run of evenings and weekends of cocktails and dinners in restaurants, four-way conversations in which everyone is talking but two seem to be speaking mostly to each other. They laugh at each other's quips, share looks, and trade observations—a natural affinity. The attraction is masked, which makes it more exciting, the boundaries continually pushing out. With his calm air, his natural authority, his newspaper storytelling, Barney overshadows the feeble bank clerk. I remember Mom telling me how she treasured small, insignificant items that Barney had used—a box of matches, say—husbanding them in his absence, keepsakes to invoke him. I see excursions—drives in the country or clamming or crabbing—when Barney and Tootie find themselves riding in the front seat of the same car or sitting side by side in the same boat, each intensely aware of the other. I imagine them looking forward to the times when they will be together, even as a foursome, then planning other times as a twosome.

And that summer Monday morning when things came to a head—how much of it was planned? They end up on the beach, walking slowly, talking easily, discovering how much they have in common, how much alike they are. It is so different from the frivolous flirtations of the cocktail parties. Other walks follow on other days, then meetings in out-of-the-way places. At some point they make love. And the talks become even more personal, each telling things never told to anyone else. I imagine them, as the affinity deepens, speculating about where this crazy passion might lead them, eventually envisioning the kind of life they might have together, playing out the fantasy. It will be so different from the life they're leading now. It will be without all that pretense and the self-conscious pursuit of pleasure. It will be rich in everyday joys, in the satisfaction of being with someone who understands instinctively what you are about. It will be refreshingly bourgeois. They will have children, something they're both ready for; they'll abandon the city and move to the back country—why not right here in Fairfield County? Barney will stay on at the *Times*—newspapering is almost a religion to him—and Tootie will give up her career and tend to the home. Will she do this, for him? Is she ready to throw it all in and become a housewife? Isn't she, in fact, beginning to feel a nesting instinct, which surprises and delights her? For children, a home in the country, everyday delights. Some evenings, she'll meet him in the city for dinner or the theater. On days off, they'll loll about the homestead, reading until noon, going for a stroll through the woods, mixing cocktails in the late afternoon. It could be glorious. . . .

My brother's reconstruction is a bit different. As he remembers hearing the story, the two were walking on the beach and when the seagull swept down, our mother watched it and realized, in a single lightning stroke, that she was in love. Right away, they went to the cottage, and to bed. Our versions have a lot in common, but on a critical point—when sex comes into the picture—they are mutually exclusive: Mine is more romantic, his more hard-edged. The truth undoubtedly does not lie somewhere in between.

Nervously, I pick up the bundle of their letters. My mother kept them safe, tied with ribbons. At some point she went back and tried to fix the dates, writing them on the envelopes, but sometimes she attached question marks. I have read the letters before, but that was so many years ago, I barely remember what's in them. Besides, this time I'm not reading them in the same way, as a child content to gather a general impression of their love. This time I'm like a detective, looking for clues about their relationship—when it began, what made it happen, and how it developed. I hurry over the letters from later years, those written during Barney's trips to the West Coast after Bob was born and those from the war years, and I come to the early ones. I hope, feeling a flush of puritanism that surprises me, that they don't talk about sex. To my relief, they do not. They trace the outlines of a deepening love. There was apparently a trip to Albany that somehow proved pivotal. Did Barney go there to write a story about Governor Franklin D. Roosevelt and did Tootie accompany him? The word *Albany* becomes shorthand in subsequent letters. It seems to stand for a time when they realized they belonged together and were right for each other. A lovers' code springs up, a series of hidden references. One is to the constellation of Orion, another to a Broadway play of that time. Above all is a sign of two *x*'s inside a circle, meaning that the two of them exist inside "the charmed circle," cut off from the rest of the world.

By Valentine's Day, 1937, Barney had left his wife and moved into the Hotel Murray, at 66 Park Avenue. I know this because my mother sent him a Western Union Valentine greeting there. It reads:

SWEET FLOWS A NAME ON THE TIP OF MY TONGUE
IT'S BARNEY D, THE SUNOFAGUN.
I WOULD CALL IT BLISS DEVINE,
IF HE'D ONLY BE MY VALENTINE.

It was unsigned. She later sent him another telegram, again joking in false rhyme:

BY THE STARS OF ORION,
I SWEAR YOU ARE MINE.

At some point, later in 1937 or in early 1938, Barney returned home to Michigan for a visit while she remained in New York. His letters are chatty, filled with news about family members coming and going in profusion. He wrote about an ex-banker who absconded with thousands in embezzled funds, about a teenage niece telling him over an ice cream cone of her dream to become an opera star, about discovering a great deal of animosity toward President Roosevelt. He ended one letter talking about the two of them:

New York is very far away. You're in New York. But you are not far away. One thing you are doing very well: you come always into my mind when a conversation pauses, when I walk home from town, when I awaken. It is good to go to you a hundred times a day, for thoughts of you are pleasant thoughts.

Her letters, by contrast, seek reassurance about the two of them. She worried and reached for metaphors and confessed and poured out her feelings, signing her letters "Kate"—her middle name—which Barney preferred to Eleanor or Tootie.

You know once I made a promise to myself about you—one you never knew about and one I've lived by. And that is, that with you and about you I would never fake anything. Never simulate a feeling, never pretend a thought. It's a good promise. I've kept it, always. And I always intend to. . . . I know I will never have to mask any feeling of mine for you. Nor will I ever have to force one into being something greater than it is. This is real, you are real, I am real. The realness has started to weld. And will continue until it is truly one.

There follows something that confuses me. My mother spoke of losing trust. She hinted at something that had happened, something that he had done, perhaps, that she had to come to terms with.

The past has to be gathered up, the dross looked at and thrown away, the good integrated into the new way of life—so that I come to you whole and good and strong. . . . But there is this one important exception. I loved you wildly, exultantly—blindly—once. And now I love you with knowledge. And that's better. But this I think is true. With the coming of the knowing love I lost a little trust. That's hardly a fair way to express it. Because of circumstances, a little of that trust that you could love me died—or rather, I am sure—became only benumbed. I have to get used to believing that you love me again.

He reassured her in a letter that appears to have been written the day he received hers.

Look, my dear. Worry a bit about this and that if you want to—but I'm not going to. Before the Great Jehovah and the Continental Congress, I love you, I'm going to live the rest of my life with you, I'm proud of you, I'm nuts about you, I miss you, I want you. I like New York–to–Albany with you. I wish I could marry you tonight. I wish you were here tonight. I can create that tight little circle with you. I want kids with you. . . . In short, you are what I'm about. Past? There isn't any. Future? Nothing else. . . . Ah, Kate, you arch minx, you have veritably stolen my heart.

The letter goes on to describe his joy in spending an afternoon with a nephew, his wife, Laura, and their six-month-old daughter. He found himself transfixed by the new mother. It's clear, I now understand, that he wanted to settle down, to have children. It was this that Tootie was offering him. He wrote:

When they left I walked with her to the car and with a nice understanding of what had been going on in my mind (for I had been staring at her all afternoon—and thinking of you) she suddenly held out the baby to me. It was such sweet hokum and I was so proud. Laura got in the car and I handed the baby in to her. Jesus, Darling, I felt swell!

His letter melted whatever reserve was bothering her. She answered quickly, beginning: "Darling, darling, darling, darling," and said that had she been there with him, she would have felt the same thing about the baby. She said their private circle was "soft and warm and brewing."

And so the story of their love, with its beginning in public scandal, reached its fairy-tale ending. According to my mother's entry in *Who's Who*, my father and my mother were married not long after that—on April 23, 1938.

CHAPTER 6

In October 1943, one year after our father's death, our mother was promoted to the position of women's editor at the *Times,* and we moved to Washington Square in New York City. The following summer she tried an experiment: She rented a beach cottage on a spit of land in Westport—not far, in fact, from the spot where she and Barney had fallen in love. Why she would want to return to a place with so many emotion-laden memories is hard to fathom, unless, of course, that was the whole point: that it was the memories themselves that drew her there. Only later did I postulate that this was her way of clinging to the life they had envisioned together.

By her account it was a good summer. We went swimming and clamming and sunbathing. These activities were amply recorded by the camera of Meyer ("Mike") Berger, a frequent visitor. I dropped my bathing trunks and went about most of every day naked. Bob continued his preoccupation with war, spending much of the time in a child's khaki uniform, learning how to march like a soldier and collecting army insignia. He took naps in a pup tent erected in the backyard sand. For a while, his predilection to play soldier distressed Mom, but she soon evolved a positive explanation, as she invariably did when we engaged in potentially disturbing behavior. She decided that his war games were a kind of therapy—"an instinctive sloughing off of some buried hurt," as she was to write in her book.

She found that she could handle the hour-plus commute to the city and so decided to move us year-round to Westport. Typically, she regarded the decision as a weighty choice between extremes painted in black and white. The city was confining and dirty and dangerous. The country was the only place for boys to grow up, to flex their muscles and fill their lungs with clean air and become strong and healthy. As children, we bought this proposition wholeheartedly. Westport would become the crucible of our childhood, the place that would form and sustain us. During this time, my conscious life began—that is to say, my memory kicks in—and so I can say with assurance that I loved it, everything about it. The Connecticut woods were my Eden.

Without realizing it, my family was anticipating the great postwar migration to the suburbs, where the American dream would search for itself in split-level houses and country clubs and wood-paneled station wagons. But in the late 1940s and early 1950s Westport was not yet a bedroom community. It was a self-sustaining village with lots of forests and meadows, closer in spirit to New England than to the New York metropolis. There were onion farms in the backcountry, unheated bungalows along the shore, and a few redbrick factories along the Saugatuck River. Shopping centers had not yet sprouted on the Boston Post Road, not even supermarkets. Local grocery stores delivered to customers' houses and their deliverymen tried to get through even when blizzards dropped two feet of snow. People didn't lock their doors, and some left their car keys in the ignition. Many artists and writers lived there. So did theater people, because of the summer productions in the one-hundred-year-old red barn of the Westport Country Playhouse. Main Street and the side streets were replete with shops that fascinated children—an Army-Navy store, Western Auto, Klein's toys, a hardware store with wooden floors, a five-and-dime with open bins, and Bill's Smoke Shop, a tiny cabin that dispensed penny candies like jawbreakers and wax lips. The Fine Arts movie theater showed double features for twenty-five cents.

We were ignorant of the social order in Fairfield County's Gold Coast, but looking back it now appears clear cut. Italians were the underclass, but they were moving up, assuming the ownership of liquor stores and restaurants. There were no African-Americans other than maids and a few day laborers. The suburbs had not yet become a subject for sociologists. Richard Yates and John Cheever were not yet sharpening their pencils on anomie and conformity in the land of manicured lawns. Lucy and Ricky Ricardo—or rather, their fictional TV counterparts—had not yet moved in from the Upper East Side. Nor had the Man in the Gray Flannel Suit or the Stepford Wives. At the time, only scores of commuters, not hundreds—virtually all men—joined my mother weekday mornings at the quaint wooden railroad station with screen doors that slammed in the summer and large radiators that clunked in the winter.

Years later, recalling that time, Mom would say that she felt she stuck out "like a sore thumb." A single mother working in the city and raising two children alone was almost unheard of. Returning in the evenings, she'd find the railroad station parking lot crammed with idling cars, the wives waiting to greet their husbands, standing on the running boards to wave, some with martinis already mixed in a thermos. At PTA meetings parents filed into the gymnasium in a phalanx of twos, for all the world like the animals mounting the gangplank to Noah's ark. Wives sometimes regarded her, an unattached woman, with a hint of suspicion. And sometimes men, assuming she must be sex-starved, tried to force themselves on her. One day we stopped going to our family doctor, a mild-looking man with thick, round spectacles, whom I feared because he gave me injections. Twenty years afterward, my mother explained why: During a physical examination he had tried to rape her.

But Mom didn't complain. You played the hand you were dealt and you didn't make any bones about it. "You makes your bed and you lies in it," she used to remark in a resounding stage voice. That was our family ethos and the ethos of the country emerging from the war. She thought she'd be strong enough to carry the burden. After all, as Barney had written to his older brother, "She isn't the stuff that cracks under a bit of difficulty."

. . .

Our first house, bought with the insurance money, was a large Colonial built in 1785. It was set in a hidden valley only a mile from the center of town. Approaching it was a surprise. One minute you were on a well-traveled road overlooking the Saugatuck River and then, after an abrupt left turn under a canopy of trees that seemed to part like a curtain, you were on a tranquil road called Edge Hill Lane. It dipped down into the valley, and the house, the only one on the road, rose up on the right on a bluff behind a retaining wall. It was three stories high, white, with green shutters. The front door, up a brick stoop and under a peaked portico with benches set on either side, announced it as a grand dwelling. We always used the back entrance. We'd follow the driveway, which curved around the bluff and ended near the kitchen. The backyard seemed to go on forever. It held a chicken coop, an apple orchard, an old red barn, and five or so acres of meadow and fir trees.

Inside, the house was a child's paradise of hidden nooks and mysterious spaces. The front entrance gave onto two large living rooms, each with a fireplace framed by ancient Delft tiles, one blue, the other pink. A soot-blackened arm, once used for hanging cooking pots, swung out over the hearth. The main staircase swept up to the second floor, where our bedrooms were. Mine was small and tucked in the back. An enclosed staircase, like a secret passage, led down to the kitchen. The third floor had sparsely furnished bedrooms, which were rarely used. They seemed to cry out for children who should have been born. I used to think they were intended for the large family my parents would have had if my father had lived.

Of the war years, I have only a smattering of memories. One is of a spoonful of bitter-tasting chocolate pudding—bitter, I was told, because all the sugar had gone to the war, something that puzzled me. Why would grown-ups—not to mention soldiers—want sugar? Another is of a gruesome comic book depicting the Nazis as wolves; they wore swastika armbands and their long snouts dripped with blood. I hated them and feared them in equal measure. A third memory is of a family, a couple with a young daughter, who shared our house for a while because of the housing shortage. I enjoyed playing with the girl, especially with her dollhouse, until my brother told me that this was not fitting for a boy.

I have a memory of something else, but it is hazy and diffuse, of a time in 1946 when my mother was away for a long time. She went on an editing assignment to Paris for five months. Our grandmother came to stay with us, and we also had Inell, the maid who had left us in Washington, to see us through. I don't recall missing Mom badly, though I suppose I must have. But for my brother it was a different story. One day, after she returned, the two of them were standing beside our car, when he picked up a stick and raked it back and forth across the radiator. "I used to come out here when you were away and do this," he said, according to her book. "I pretended it was your voice. . . . Then I'd be less lonely for you." She wrote that she suddenly understood "a boy's hunger and need for his mother," a remarkable revelation coming from someone who thought she understood child psychology. And then, with earnest resolve, she said that after that she "managed never to be away for more than a few weeks at a time, at the most."

My favorite possession was a koala teddy bear that my father had sent to me from Australia (my brother got a kangaroo). I slept with it every night and often carried it around during the day, though rarely risked taking it outside. It had a flat rubber nose, two soulful glass eyes, and soft, musky fur that smelled, I thought, of faraway places. I found a small blue-patterned chair that was a perfect fit. I often put the bear there, seated as comfortably as an old man in an easy chair, to supervise whatever project I was engaged in. I slept with it long after its arm and leg fell off and the fur had mostly rubbed off into bald spots.

Christmases were an extravaganza, an agony of waiting, followed by a frenzy of greedy acquisition. While we were sleeping, the tree would somehow materialize. In the morning, we would race down to a blaze of colored lights and sparkling tinsel and the sweet aroma of pine sap and needles. The gifts were set out in stacks as tall as we were. More than anything, I loved the ritual of hanging the stockings from the mantel the night before and the magic of seeing them so stuffed that they hung like mail sacks, almost reaching the floor. My stocking was special. Wartime shortage meant that I had no red stocking to match those of my mother and brother, so my mother took the unused one, embroidered with DAD, and put my name on the reverse side. Ever after, I treated it as a talisman. Hanging it became almost a mystical rite, confirming me in my unspoken conviction that my father and I shared a unique connection.

Did our mother date in those early years? If so, we didn't know about it. I seem to remember—judging from the double names on cards attached to the presents—that her friends came mostly in couples. Undoubtedly they were carryovers from her years with Barney. On Saturday and Sunday mornings, when guests slept over, I would rise early and slip down to the living room. There, I'd look at the detritus of the night before, when I had heard laughter mounting the staircase and sliding under my door. I'd examine the half-filled cocktail glasses, the shriveled slices of lime, the sour-smelling cigarette butts in overflowing ashtrays, and the bits of hardened cheese and crackers or leftover desserts. The assorted leavings were a small window onto the adult world. It was clear that grown-ups behaved differently when we weren't around, that their pleasures were exotic and unimaginable. Who knew what those pleasures were? Someday, I thought, I might comprehend that world and even join it, a prospect that filled me with awe.

As I grew, my horizons expanded outward from the house. Next to the bulkhead cellar door, hidden under a spreading pine bush, I built a miniature village. Ducking under the branches, which blocked passage for anyone bigger, I entered a world of my own making. I would lay the roads and move the cars and rearrange the houses. I ruled over this village with a benign but despotic hand, while in the real world I was small and dependent. My powerlessness was brought home to me every morning because of the terrifying chore of feeding the chickens. Opening the wire gate, I would be set upon by our vicious red rooster, which pecked me on the legs and arms, hard enough to draw blood. Each morning I dreaded the attack, searching for new stratagems to avoid it, but it always seemed to come. I would slip into the coop noiselessly, and just as I finished pouring the feed into the trough, the rooster would dart around the side of the henhouse and come at me with its beak bobbing and wings flapping. Soon I began having nightmares about it. Yet I have no memory of asking to be relieved of the chore. One morning I found the rooster hanging dead on the wire fence. He had caught the spur of one leg in the wire mesh, ripped it half off in his frenzy to escape, and bled. I stared at his body, hanging head-first, limp and lifeless, over a pool of blood congealed in the dust below, and my heart overflowed with joy.

Soon my universe expanded to include the barn, which became a hideaway and my favorite place to play. I spent hours there. Once I peered down from the loft through a second-floor window and spotted a worker who had been using a scythe to cut the knee-high grass in a nearby field. He walked to the side of the barn, ten feet below me, and urinated against the wall. I was shocked at the size of his penis, and I quickly pulled my head back inside the dark loft. It was the first time I had seen an adult male appendage.

When I turned five, I widened my universe farther still, explor-ing the lane out front. I'd follow the slope of the road to a crest, where there was an old graveyard packed with leaning tombstones and ornate crypts. I spent hours there, contemplating, listening to the birds and the humming of the insects in the quiet sanctuary of the place. I walked along the paths between graves, vigilant to avoid stepping on them, and toured the crypts, wondering which one contained the body of Jesus. I strained to peer through thick stained-glass windows to the dimly-lit marble slabs inside. Clearly His would be the most impressive. But which one was that? There seemed to be so many, each one more grand than the one before. To cover my bets, I prayed before different ones on different days, leaving behind offerings of wild daisies on the stoop or interlaced in the protective window grilles.

Returning home, I usually turned off onto the remnant of an abandoned road. The excavation was dug into the hillside, so that at the end I had to scramble up an embankment. It led to a grove of pines. Pushing the branches aside, I came to the top of a tall bluff covered by a patch of moss. From there I had a spectacular view. I could see clear across the river to the cluster of buildings that constituted the rear of Main Street. On the near bank of the river was a crossroads. Spread out beneath me, so that I could see the rooftops, were a brick fire station, a grocery store, and half a dozen houses. From my vantage point, sitting cross-legged on the bed of moss, I would watch the comings and goings of the town. A traffic light blinked yellow at the intersection. A car turned off the Post Road and gained speed on the road below me, shifting gears noisily. A pedestrian crossed the street and disappeared into a photography studio. There was something exhilarating in being the unseen observer, in contemplating the larger world far beyond the boundaries imposed by my size, and presiding over it, a giant leap from ruling my miniature village beside the cellar door.

My brother was old enough to have friends visit, and we often went straight to the barn loft. They usually let me tag along, though not always with good grace. On one occasion Inell summoned us to lunch. Bob and his two friends shimmied down a rope hanging from the loft opening, leaving me behind. I ran to the rear of the loft and tried to lift the door set in the floor. It was too heavy. I ran back to the opening, beginning to panic, and leaned out. That was the last thing I remember. When I regained consciousness, I was lying in my bed in a cast up to my neck—my arm and collarbone broken. My mother gave me a talking-to, about using my head and the need to remain calm in a tense situation and the importance of good judgment. I took it all in happily; I was basking in all the attention. I felt sure she must have also lectured my brother for abandoning me, and that made me feel good, too. From the first he had been told that he must look out for me and protect me, and in this instance he had clearly abrogated his responsibility.

The two of us were settling down into our respective roles. He was the steady one, helpful and responsible beyond his years, having been told early on that he was "the man of the house." I was difficult and uncommunicative, given to extreme moods and prone to trouble. As far as I was concerned, my brother was simply bigger and better in all things—he could run faster, jump higher, articulate better, and understand things beyond my comprehension. In her book, our mother wrote that Bob sailed through the early years, adaptive and friendly and curious about people. I, on the other hand, did everything my own way and took everything hard. To put a label on it, she wrote: "Bob was an Integrator and Johnnie, Johnnie was a Creator." But beneath the rose-tinted generalizations, darker shadows loomed. Bob was already worried about protecting our mother from bad news. One morning he balked at going to school but relented when she insisted he live up to his obligations.

That night, while bathing him, she felt his forehead; it was hot. He had a rash—measles. Why hadn't he told her that morning? "I thought you had enough on your mind," she recalled his saying. "I didn't want to worry you."

I sometimes acted out. One weekend her friends the MacKayes came to stay with us. The three adults were up late into the night, and the next morning, hungover, my mother strove to be the good hostess. But I ragged her mercilessly, talking back, needling her but failing to get a rise out of her. Finally, I shoved a chair in her path and she cracked her shins on it. She grabbed me and spanked me, hard. My howls raised the roof and Milton MacKaye rushed in, concerned. I turned on him, yelling, "Go 'way. Can't me and Mommie ever be alone?"

Not long after that, one of my father's brothers, whom my brother and I had never met, came for a visit. The two of us were told, or we intuited, that this was to be an important occasion. We were to eat lunch early, to allow the adults to talk in the short time available, but when our guest arrived, I refused, and after my mother insisted, I ran off toward a busy road. Once there, I had no recourse but to give up and walk back, in defeat. My mother was mortified by my behavior and took me indoors by the hand. When she returned, my uncle said, "I'd forgotten how naughty Barney was as a little boy. I'd forgotten how he loped, too, when he ran—as Johnnie does."

Looking back now, I realize that she guided my upbringing with references to my father and often said how much I resembled him. If I lay on my back with my hands folded behind my head, she would remark that he used to lie down in exactly the same posture. If I made a wisecrack, she would observe that the two of us had the very same sense of humor. We made a game of expressing an endearment. One would say, "Have I told you today that I love you?" The other would reply, "No." And the reply to that was, "Well, I do." It was soon shorted to: "Have I told you today?" and a quick nod no and a counter nod yes. It was the same game that she had played countless times with him. If I encountered a problem or a setback or felt unequal to a task—feelings exacerbated by having a brilliant, well-rounded older brother—she made me feel better by reciting one of Barney's sayings: "Don't worry. Some

Darntons mature late." All of this made me feel less bad and that I was accepted for myself, though it also planted a hard seed that would sprout over time: my attempts to be just like my father.

At a certain point I took to the idea of running away. Comic strips of the time featured the hobo, a man in ragged clothes carrying his belongings in a simple red bundle at the end of a stick. I identified with that. At the age of six I packed a bundle, filled with clothes and provisions like raisins, and kept it in a corner near the back door. When my mother asked me what it was for, I explained that it was in case I wanted to run away. She raised an eyebrow, but in time she and my brother accepted it as a harmless indulgence. I found it a comfort. You never knew when you might need to hit the road in a hurry. And then, inevitably, came the day I did.

The dispute had undoubtedly been building for some time. I was in a climbing phase and was scrambling up and down the furniture. Inevitably, ashtrays and glassware were sacrificed. One afternoon I mounted a wing-backed chair to reach the mantel-piece, above which hung a painting that had always puzzled me (a copy, I found out later, of El Greco's *View of Toledo*). Where were the roads exactly? Why did they appear and then disappear behind all those splotches of gray-green? I found a letter opener and tried to trace them, scratching the canvas. I climbed down, examined my work, and promptly forgot about it—until several days later, when my mother summoned me into the room and pointed angrily at the painting. "Why did you deface this?" she demanded. I couldn't answer. In fact, I had not the vaguest idea. We talked. She expounded on the principle of private property and the selfishness in destroying someone else's possessions. I felt miserable. She asked me what punishment I thought I deserved, and again I was at a loss. Finally she gave me a clue. Every Saturday, we observed a ritual: The three of us would drive to a candy store near the railroad station, where my brother and I would get to select two comic books from a rack that covered an entire wall. I took the hint. "No comics or allowance for six years." "That's a bit harsh," she replied gently. "How about two weeks?" That was fine with me. I was grateful the subject was settled.

But the following Saturday my gratitude evaporated when we drove to the store and I had to wait outside until my brother emerged with two brand-new comic books. On the drive back my rage grew, until we arrived home and I declared, "I'm not sticking around this joint any longer." I grabbed some food and my hobo sack and slammed the back door. I walked down the valley beside our house, crossed a field of knee-high grass, and entered a small woody knoll. Then I doubled back and crept behind a large fir tree in the center of the field. I found a hideaway under the low-hanging branches. The pine needles smelled sweet and provided a soft bed. I lay down and waited, and I did not have to wait long. My mother came down the hill toward the field—she must have followed my direction—and I could tell from her stride that she was anxious. I drew farther back in the branches and watched. She walked toward me and passed close enough for me to hear the slap of weeds against her knees and to read the fear on her face.

She made a wide loop and disappeared. She began calling my name. I moved farther inside and leaned my back against the tree trunk. I opened a box of raisins and ate them, then an apple that was crisp and sweetly sour. The sound of her calling grew fainter as she rounded the house on the far side. The longer I waited, the better I felt, so I waited a long time, until finally, after an hour or so had passed, I went home. She was in the kitchen, washing the dishes, pretending to ignore me, but I could see relief coursing through her. Sometime after that we talked about my punishment, but we did not speak of my running away, almost as if nothing had happened. But I knew that something *had* happened, something important. I had learned a lesson. Small as I was, I had gotten a little taste of power. It was like the apple, both sweet and sour, and I savored it.

Like Bob, once I started school and left home every day, I felt an overriding need to protect Mom. In first grade, I was cast, along with a dozen other six-year-olds, as a bumblebee in a skit during class, and I told her I needed a T-shirt with brown stripes to play the part. The night before, she stayed up late, sewing a costume much more elaborate than the occasion required—a whole ensemble, complete with translucent wings and springs attached to a beanie for antennae. It was one of the few times she was able to supply me with something special for school, and she did it up proud. The next day I was mortified to discover that all the other bumblebees had simple T-shirts. I was embarrassed beyond belief and I promptly hid my costume in a supply closet. That evening, when she asked how it had gone, I said her costume had been a big hit.

At night, to put myself to sleep, I often engaged in a fantasy of escape. Underneath my bed was a trapdoor. Opening it, I would come upon a tunnel that went deeper and deeper into the earth. It ended in a large cavern, in the center of which was a gigantic carnival with a single ride—dodge-'em cars. All my friends were there—they had similar tunnels under their beds—and we would play all night, smashing into one another and whipping around the course, then return home just before dawn.

I worried, somewhere deep within my core, that I was irrevocably bad—not just naughty or incorrigible, as those big grown-up words put it—but truly bad, as if compromised by some original sin. I carried this sense of myself through the day-to-day routine. It was the reason, I'm sure, that I found it hard to fall asleep and that, when I did, I was often beset by nightmares. One night, lying in bed, I heard, or felt, another presence in my room. I opened my eyes, and there in the doorway stood a man—or rather, the ghost of a man. The light was shining behind him, so that I could not get a good look. He seemed to shimmer, standing there on the threshold, looking down at me. I was gripped by terror and felt my heart thumping. I closed my eyes and lay there motionless, not daring to cry out, but resigned, waiting to see what would befall me. A second later I opened my eyes—and he was gone. I didn't know what to make of this. Something told me that it was the ghost of my father, but if so . . . why was it so frightening? I pushed the memory down and didn't talk about it. I waited to see if it would happen again. It didn't.

Around this time I succumbed to a high fever and fell into delirium, and I confessed my secret. "I'm bad, I'm bad," I said over and over as my mother sat by my bedside, placing cold compresses on my forehead. To read her version of the incident, she was able to convince me that I was good by repeating those simple words over and over—"No, you're good, you're good"—until finally they took hold. Like a miracle, my fever broke. Never again, she wrote, was

I troubled by the thought that I was bad. When I read those words now, I smile ruefully. Once again her book, and her view of life, crossed over into fiction. She was a big one for happy endings.

In 1950, my mother and brother and I went to see a movie called *Three Came Home*. Starring Claudette Colbert, it was (as I later researched) based on the story of Agnes Newton Keith, an American writer in British North Borneo during the war. Mom sat between the two of us, as usual, and we settled in with popcorn and soft drinks. Along with her husband, a colonial officer, and her young son, the heroine falls into the hands of the invading Japanese. They are interned in a camp behind barbed wire, and the husband and wife learn they are to be relocated and separated. Standing on either side of a ditch, they say farewell; he slips a note into her hand, telling her to be strong. She takes the boy with her. At one point, going outside at night to rescue laundry from a storm, she is assaulted by a Japanese guard. She lodges a protest, is beaten and interrogated, and faces execution for impugning the honor of the guard. At this point, I noticed something upsetting. On my left, my mother was sitting stiffly in her seat and tears were running down her cheeks, glistening in the glow from the screen. I looked around in the dark to see if others had noticed. Thank God, they were engrossed in the movie. Eventually the heroine is saved by a sympathetic Japanese camp director. The war ends and the male prisoners, emaciated and dressed in rags, come walking back to their families. Everywhere men and women are hugging and weeping in joyful reunions, but Agnes can't find her husband. Her face registers complete despair. Then, as the music soars, the camera pans up a road to the crest of the hill, and we see him, first just his head, then all of him. He's on crutches but manages somehow to run. They fall into each other's arms, then onto the ground. The boy pokes his head in between them and all three hug. *The End.*

By now my mother was sobbing uncontrollably. As the lights went up, people darted glances at her. I was confused and mortified. It was not often that I saw my mother cry, certainly not in public. On the way home we talked in general terms about the war, careful to avoid any reference to her tears. Once there, my brother pulled me aside and explained what was going on. She was crying, he said, because the husband in the movie came back and her husband did not. He used the word *husband,* not *Daddy.* We tried to make her feel better. We brought her slippers, a glass of water, and I read to her, playing the comedian, until finally she began to laugh—out of relief or just to please us, I'm not sure. What stays with me is the sense of reversal: Here we were, taking care of her. Even more, I remember the fear—fear in seeing a crack in her emotional façade. I sensed that the crack could lead to other cracks, that our world was not as secure as I had imagined. I had thought she was happy and contented, as she had told us she was. But I was wrong. The world was dark and dangerous. Old sorrows could rise up out of nowhere to shatter your world, and there was nothing you could do about it.

Growing up, I did not consciously miss my father, because I had never known him. There was no discernible hole in my life that made it seem less than complete, nothing gone that was definable, like a rip in a fabric or a missing piece in a jigsaw puzzle. It's impossible to imagine your life different from the way it is. And in any case the thought of Barney was not something that arose in the daily routine. I went to school, played at recess, ate lunch in the cafeteria, and took the bus home—all without the dimmest notion that anything could be different. I have memories of scattershot moments in which other people learned of his absence. A teacher taking an impromptu census of likely attendees at a PTA meeting asked us to hold up one or two fingers and, embarrassed, quickly counted me—yet I was proud and continued to hold my one finger in the air for all to see. A kindly woman, meeting me at the beach, asked, "What does your father do?" and, at my response—that he had been killed in the war—she gasped and reddened. I quickly said, "It's all right," meaning it. I added, "I was young. I never knew him." But what stung me, I think now, and why I remember the incident so vividly six decades later, was *my* embarrassment, because it was clearly not all right. I knew of no other family that had lost someone in the war.* What else could her reaction signify but that I was different somehow, singled out, to be pitied.

In our family we didn't speak of Barney every day or even every

---

*Estimates are that some 183,000 American children lost their fathers.

week. That would have been unnatural. But we incorporated rituals about him into the rhythm of our lives. Every time we drove to or from Compo Beach we passed a roundabout with a statue of a kneeling minuteman holding a rifle, and we would say, "Hi, Butch," because, we were told, that was what Mom and Barney had done. And there were times when my mother would be moved by some unseen sentiment to talk about him, and then we two would soak it up voraciously, the way I imagine blind people might listen to a description of a sunset or a forest. In her book, my mother said she was aware of the danger of building him up too much, of creating an idol whose heroic stature would smother us. For this reason, she was careful to tell us about his crotchets and small slipups—why was it, she would wonder, that whenever she asked him to pick up things in town, he would return empty-handed? Or that when she asked for a bottle of ink, he'd bring a spool of thread? We would chortle, she wrote, and then she knew that everything was all right and we were seeing him as a fallible human being and not some sort of god.

Today I smile when I think of her little stratagems and her conviction that they worked. Forgetting to buy items in a store, confusing thread for a bottle of ink—such minor, insignificant failings, they served only to highlight the perfection of the man. In my heart I knew him for what he was—a leader among men, someone who was courageous and idealistic, unafraid in war, suave and debonair in public, witty and warm in private. There could never be anyone better than he and it would be impossible to live up to him.

We learned at some point that he had been killed by friendly fire, but that made no difference in the larger scheme of things. We couldn't, of course, blame the Americans. We blamed the enemy—in particular, the Nazis. If they hadn't started the war, causing him to feel the compulsion to go away to write about it, then he never would have been killed. For a child, the emotional logic hits home with a vengeance. At some point I heard that the young pilot of the plane that had dropped the bomb came to our house seeking forgiveness, but I have no recollection of such a visit and I now doubt that it took place. In my juvenile brain I conflated the pilot with the one who dropped the bomb from the *Enola Gay* on Hiroshima, and I came to believe that he had had a nervous breakdown and was unable to return to his bomber, like Gregory Peck struggling to climb aboard his B-17 in *Twelve O'Clock High*.

Clearly, our family myth was evolving and growing stronger. The storybook life that our parents had conjured up in Westport years before would continue with us as a threesome. We boys were supposed to flourish in bucolic splendor. We would go to good public schools and have family outings—clambakes on the beach, croquet games on long summer evenings, ice-skating on backwoods ponds in winter. The idyll would continue and it would be unchanged—only without one of the principals.

Six years after his death, my mother received notification from the army that Barney's body would be transported to the United States for reburial. She chose the Darnton family plot in a wooded cemetery in Adrian, Michigan, where his parents were buried. They had once visited the graves together. We drove there from Connecticut. I remember nothing of the trip and almost nothing of what happened when we got there. I'm told that uncles and cousins surrounded us, that men hoisted us two boys up in their arms, that there were friendly dinners around large dining room tables, with everybody talking and lots of ice cream. What I remember is the grave site. A coffin draped in an American flag, some words said, taps playing slowly and sadly, and then the sound of gunfire—the horrible sound of the guns going off in volleys, one after another, three times. They were deafening. I gripped my mother's hand and felt nothing but terror.

CHAPTER 7

When I was growing up, I learned about fathers through my friends, but I don't believe I ever envied them. The reason was simple. I couldn't imagine having a father any better than the one I didn't have.

My closest friend was Johnny Ray, or "Raisin," a nickname I gave him so long ago that neither of us could remember when. I met him on my first day of kindergarten. As I was sitting on the floor, feeling abandoned and trying through my tears to build a tower of blocks, he walked over, sat down, and joined in. For the next seven years, we were inseparable. Because our houses were close to each other, it was easy for us to visit, so on most afternoons when school let out, he could be found at my house or I at his.

Raisin's home life was strange and frightening. A brother and sister, much older, had moved out and rarely visited. His mother, Eloise, was a soft, quiet woman, and her nurturing seemed an effort to compensate for his father, Joe. Joe was a tyrant. He rode a motorcycle, wore a black leather jacket, and went on violent binges. When he was home, he thundered about the house, answering the phone with curse words and barking commands. His spine was fused, so he couldn't swivel his head; to look at you, he'd turn his large body square at you. I avoided him at every turn, feeling like Jack and the Beanstalk in the castle of the giant. Now, when I look back, I can see him as a rebellious eccentric. An innovative architect, he had designed and built his own home, a meandering house of five levels, with an interior entirely of wood, and he sailed his own twenty-five-foot boat, *Hardtack*. But back then, he was my bogeyman and the fount of my nightmares. When he was drinking, he threatened his son. Worse, he was mercurial, so that on some days, he would be unaccountably friendly. He would sit us down in front of sketch pads and dash off a few lines for us to turn into completed drawings, or sail us across the Sound to the north shore of Long Island and back. I succumbed to these overtures fearfully, meekly waiting for him to explode. And sure enough, the next day he would be on a tear, crashing about the place like a madman. We would flee to the woods and stay away until dark, then creep back to look through the windows to see if he was still there. If he was, we'd stay out until he disappeared upstairs—the giant asleep in the castle's tower.

His explosions got worse over time. Once he followed my mother into the train station and yelled at her—insisting that her car had cut off his motorcycle—and, to her mortification, demanding to know if she was drunk. His treatment of Raisin became ever more abusive. It reached the height of cruelty on the day of the party for my seventh birthday, an event I had been planning for weeks, inviting everyone in sight and laying down treasure hunts and other games. Moments before it was to start, Raisin's mother called to say he couldn't come. The reason was vague and she sounded shaken. When I called him back, I learned what had happened but prevailed upon him to come anyway. He showed up with a sailor's cap pulled down low over his ears, his face bright red. His father, furious over some minor infraction, had hauled him to a barber-shop and forced the barber to shave off every hair on his head. At first we tried pretending it was no big deal. We scarcely mentioned it. Then, during a game of hide-and-seek, as the two of us were lying in the crevice of an upended tree trunk, Raisin told me the story of his punishment step by gruesome step and lifted his hat to show me what he looked like. His bald dome was shocking—so perfectly smooth and shining—and for some reason the skull under the babyish pink skin seemed immense and freakish. Once again his face flushed red to the roots. I tried to console him, though he was beyond consolation. That Monday he missed school, and the news of what had happened to him spread through the class. The following day, Eloise having obtained permission for Raisin to wear the sailor cap at all times, he turned up. He was at least saved from the ignominy of having to reveal his baldness—that is, until one afternoon when our class was unruly in the cloakroom. The third-grade teacher, Miss Anderson, who had given permission for him to wear the hat, was livid. She marched into the cloakroom and with one quick motion grabbed the sailor's hat, yanked it off, and held it at her side. A stunned silence fell upon the room. Everyone froze and stared at poor Raisin. He turned flaming red and tried to shrink down through the floor. Slowly, the teacher returned his hat and we all filed out silently. I spent that afternoon at Raisin's house, but we didn't discuss the incident. I could see it was too painful to talk about. From that day on, our hatred of Miss Anderson grew to pathological bounds. We cursed her at every turn, prayed for misfortune to fall upon her, imagined tortures to be inflicted upon her. We dug a six-inch grave and buried a doll in it, scrawling her name on a cross made from Popsicle sticks. Two years later, when we had moved on to higher grades and learned that she had, in fact, died, from cancer, we celebrated by digging the doll up, wrapping her in burlap, and burying her again, laying a bunch of dandelions on her grave. Our prayers had been answered.

When I was seven we moved across town. The year was 1948. Harry Truman was elected president, "I'm Looking Over a Four Leaf Clover" was on the charts, and *Fort Apache* was packing them into the movie theaters. Our new place, a rambling two-story white clapboard house on a hilly street called Roseville Road, was smaller than our old one. The move was exciting. I was mesmerized as I watched our belongings being boxed and wrapped and slotted into a huge van. We raced the van to reach the new home first, and my brother and I bolted through the empty rooms and hallways, laying claim to certain spaces, like the hidden hollow under the staircase.

Seeing our old furniture in unfamiliar surroundings was jarring but strangely hopeful—like the promise of a new start.

What made the new house special was the backyard, set in the bowl of a surrounding hill, and the woods behind, which seemed to go on forever. As I grew older, I spent hours and hours in them, sometimes with a friend, sometimes just with Nicky, the black hound dog I got for my birthday. I picked him out of a litter of mutts next to a barn on a farm. On weekday mornings Nicky walked me to the school-bus stop and at night he slept curled up at the bottom of my bed, always in the same place, so that over time his body pressed out a perfect doughnut in the mattress.

The day after we moved in, I met Dickie, a boy who lived just up the road. He demanded to know if I had met "Boss." I shook my head no, envisioning something of a neighborhood bully, and he promptly led me down a hill to an ancient gray house, where "Boss"—to my surprise—turned out to be a fifty-five-year-old retiree. He lived with his wife and an aged dachshund and he liked kids. Given to wearing red-and-black-checkered wool shirts and a day or two of gray stubble, most of the time he seemed to be caring for his property, raking leaves, pruning trees, and puttering around in his garden. He took time to consider our questions, and something about him, the way he treated us as equals who simply happened to be less schooled in the ways of the world, prompted us to ask him things we wouldn't ask others.

"If Jesus was the son of God, why wasn't God angry at us for killing Him?" "If an atom bomb was dropped on New York, would it reach us way out here?" "What happens to animals when they die—do they go to heaven, too?" Most of his answers, I don't remember. It was the asking of the questions and the discussions that followed that counted.

Boss lent us a chicken coop in his back woods for a clubhouse, taught us lore about the out-of-doors, and, when it was cold, made room for us in front of his fireplace and his TV set. There on the tube I followed the hour-by-hour countdown to the execution of Ethel and Julius Rosenberg. When I asked him who they were and what they had done, he turned his back and said simply, "Nothing." If they had done nothing, then why were they going to the electric chair? "Because some people in this country are very stupid—very scared and very stupid."

One day Boss was pruning trees and cutting limbs in the woods behind his house when he called to us. He pointed to a young tree about twelve feet tall and asked us if we knew what kind of tree it was. We didn't. He stood back a couple of paces to look it over and said, "Well, I think we may just have here the beginnings of a lollipop tree." I had no idea what he was talking about, but he explained that when the season was right and the tree was big enough, it was known, under certain propitious conditions to grow lollipops. I remained skeptical. But sure enough, one week later he glanced up at a blue sky, sniffed a warm spasm of wind, and allowed as to how the lollipop season might well be upon us. He escorted us to the site. There was the tree, fully decked out, its young limbs almost touching the ground, festooned by hundreds of wrapped candies and lollipops. I knew, of course, that he had done it, but I pretended to be taken in, and soon I almost believed him, which made the whole thing that much more enjoyable. Walking home that day, our pockets stuffed with candy, Dickie confessed that he wished that Boss was his father instead of the one he had. I wasn't surprised by this, because I didn't like Dickie's father either. He asked me if I felt the same way, and I said no, but I didn't tell him why. Boss was way too old. My father would have been young and dashing. He wouldn't spend the whole day just raking leaves and branches—he'd be out in the world, reporting and writing stories and making important things happen.

Later that day Dickie told me about sex. I was shocked and disbelieving, so he led me into his parents' bedroom and opened up a bureau drawer. Reaching under a stack of socks, he found a box of condoms and showed them to me. I was aghast. The whole idea, the very thought of it, was filthy. That night in my bed, I cried, and when my mother came in to say good night, she asked me what was wrong. I told her why I was upset, and she sought to calm me by overriding my misconceptions, insisting that sex was beautiful, a way that adults expressed their love for one another. But I cried even louder. She was confirming Dickie's horrible revelation. So it had to be true after all.

I didn't have a solid idea of the life of a normal family, one with two parents, although I faithfully watched *The Adventures of Ozzie and Harriet* and, a few years later, *Father Knows Best*. The closest model at hand came from the parents of Scott and Craig, mischievous redheaded twins who were among my best friends. The mother, Betty, with long straight hair and a quiet chuckle, was young and attractive. The father, Russ, was friendly, but he could put on a gruff exterior if the situation called for it. They both worked as photographers, but she stayed home a lot, or at least she was at home whenever we arrived from school. I had the feeling that they expected kids to be a little wild, and approved of it even, but they also set clear boundaries. If I turned up with a small tear in my shirt, Russ would beckon me over; as I stood before him, he'd slip a forefinger from each hand into the hole and, with a loud whoop, rip the shirt from top to bottom.

The twins had their bedroom in an attic that took up the entire second floor. Sleepovers began with pillow fights and turned into free-for-alls that seemed to shake the whole house. There was an unspoken understanding: The first two times Russ came up the stairs to quiet us, we could regroup and resume, but the third time he meant business and we had to obey. I looked forward immensely to these occasions. Once I arrived from school wearing my pajamas under my clothes, and when it came time for bed and I shed my shirt and pants, the whole family collapsed in laughter.

Typically, after school I would walk the mile home from the bus stop and disappear outside until just before dark. I knew the lay of the land for miles around—where the meadows were, where the deep forest, the banks of moss for lying down, the blueberries for eating, and the vines for swinging. On weekends, friends would come over and we would build lean-tos against the stone walls or climb high in the trees, pulling up planks tied to ropes to construct lookouts. On windy days, we'd crawl to the end of the branches and sway back and forth with the gusts.

Much of the time, we played war. We were American GIs on the front lines. The enemies were Germans or Japanese. To guide us, we had plenty of movies over the years, like *Battleground, Sands of Iwo Jima, Halls of Montezuma,* and *Stalag 17*. We outfitted ourselves from the Army-Navy store with caps, canteens, woven belts, and thick-blade bowie knives. We dug foxholes, lugged around heavy battery-crank army field phones to communicate with our imaginary troops and died heroic deaths assaulting pillboxes or pinned down in no-man's-land. We lived much of the time out-doors. In summer, we'd dip our hands in cool streams for a drink of fresh water and on sultry nights haul our sleeping bags deep into the woods and swat mosquitoes and listen to strange rustlings until we'd fall asleep. In winter, we'd make "Indian" fires, piling small twigs in a tepee to cook slabs of bacon and toast fat-soaked bread, or lug a snow shovel to a frozen pond surrounded by maples and birch and clear it for ice-skating, going home only when our toes turned red and numb.

It was a time of consummate freedom. I was living out my mother's dream of a freewheeling, untrammeled life in the country, though at times my wanderings felt more like escape. For my eighth birthday, I was given a new English racer. I often jumped on it, pounding the pedals with all my might until I was speeding wildly. I continued for miles along the side of the road. At moments like that, with the wheels spinning madly and the wind whipping my face, the speed lifted me out of myself and away from my concerns. Much of the exhilaration came from leaving my world behind me, from flight. But flight from what?

Our mother had a smattering of psychology, which she probably picked up in the course of writing stories about children and family. She also knew psychological jargon, which was big in the 1950s, and so while eavesdropping on her conversation, the terms *father substitute* and *role model* would sometimes flicker across the screen of our consciousness. The attempt to find a suitable father substitute was a running subtheme in our household, though it never materialized. Did we, my brother and I—or did we not—want her to find a man to marry? The answer, as in many such situations, was resoundingly ambiguous. On the positive side, the reasons were obvious. Who wouldn't want an adult male to step in as a protector and teacher?

Then, too, there is the following exchange, reported in *The Children Grew*. It happened after I was teasing her about not really wanting to have more children. She countered that to do that, she would have to be married. I replied that "a smart woman like you" could get married if she wanted to. She noted that most men her age were already married. I observed that if she liked a guy enough, she could get him to divorce his wife. Disturbed, she explained that would not be right, and repeated that most of the available men were too young for her.

> "I knew you'd say that. This guy is forty-two."
> "What guy?"
> "The guy I was talking to today. At the playground. He was showing me how to shoot baskets."
> "He's probably married."
> "I knew you'd say that. I asked him. He said not."
> "Then he probably doesn't want to get married."
> "He said he'd be delighted to marry you."
> "John!"

On the other hand, if our father was the ideal role model, and perfect in every way, and if he was already a semiliving presence in our mythic lives, what right had we to countenance behavior on her part that might upset the delicate equilibrium and dethrone him? Her attempts to draft outsiders into the part were at times ham-fisted and embarrassing. When I was ten, she learned that the local Episcopal church was planning a father-son dinner. Fearful that I would hear about it, she somehow matched me up with a perfect stranger. The man, gray-haired, with glasses and a slight stoop, hardly fit my image of what I wanted a father to be. When we met in the church vestry and descended the stairs to the basement, where folding tables were covered with bright checkered cloths and slabs of meat and cooked vegetables were piled on a buffet, we had absolutely nothing to say to each other. I suppose he would have been a nice-enough fellow under different circumstances, but I couldn't wait for the evening to be over, and I had the impression he felt the same.

Into the vacuum of father substitutes wandered one or two other men. My favorite was an uncle named Ben, one of my mother's two older brothers. Ben, a redhead gone bald, was a natural-born hell-raiser. He had flash and a rapier wit and a penchant for playing practical jokes, which were usually aimed at anyone and anything in authority. He drove a red Buick convertible with a mounted searchlight, which he'd shine into our windows when he showed up for impromptu night visits; the beam flashed across my ceiling like a summons for Batman, though in this case it came from the Joker. We'd leap out of bed and he'd pour presents on us as if it were Christmas—crystal radio sets, antique flintlocks, Arabian swords, baseball gloves. You never knew when he would appear or how long he might stay.

Ben had been a bootlegger during Prohibition, according to his wife. Afterward, among other things, he became a lumber sales-man, and with his gift of gab, he once sold Atlantic City an entire new boardwalk. And so he was in and out of the money, usually depending on how well he had done at the track. He carried in his pocket a wad of bills, thick as my leg, circled by a rubber band. He dressed like a boulevardier, with Panama hats, white linen shirts, and, if memory serves, alligator shoes. Stories about how he kicked over the traces as a youngster were legion in my mother's family. Once, he placed a condom inside the church Bible early on a Sunday; flustered, the minister held it up before the congrega-tion, then matter-of-factly asked Ben Choate to repair to his office after services. Ben played hooky during two complete years of high school; he had swiped a stack of blank report cards from the school's administrative office and filled them out the requisite three times a year, taking care not to give himself suspiciously high marks and sometimes including censorious remarks about his comport-ment. He spent those years in a pool hall and learned to play well enough to become a hustler, though I don't know if he ever made serious money at it. I do know that he was the best I'd ever seen. We once took him to the basement of the Westport YMCA, where the rougher crowd of teenagers hung out playing pool, and after suckering them in, he ran both tables. Leaving there, mounting the back stairwell into the sunshine, I felt like a sidekick to Jesse James. Ben called me "Shrimp Boats," in deference to my size, after Jo Stafford's hit song. I was half pleased, half mortified by that—like many of Ben's doings, it evoked ambivalence. My size was the one thing I was most self-conscious about, though there was a kind of relief in the honesty of being called on it.

As Ben aged, he never grew up. I recall the thrill of riding with him at the wheel of his red convertible, watching the speedometer rise ten, fifteen, twenty-five, thirty miles an hour over the limit. More than once, he let us steer. On one occasion, the police siren that introduced "Gang Busters" on the radio came on; he turned it up full volume, pushed the pedal to the floor, and streaked down the highway as cars pulled over on both sides to let us pass. In Philadelphia, where he lived, he was something of a legend. One exploit was particularly famous: He stole a policeman's horse while the cop was grabbing a drink at a bar on Drury Street, signed the register of a hotel room, took the horse up in the freight elevator, and left it there. On my visits to Philadelphia, I used to accompany him on his rounds of the bars, and it was like walking through the door with Hickey in *The Iceman Cometh*. Most of the bars were seedy. In one, the bartender encouraged me to pick a quarter off the bar. I looked at Ben and he nodded. When I touched it, it wouldn't move. I circled my fingertips around it, and suddenly an electric shock coursed through my fingers and shot up my elbow, jolting my shoulder and rattling my teeth. I saw the bartender move his hand from a buzzer behind the bar. Everyone laughed and I felt humiliated. Even more, I resented that Ben, who should have protected me, had used me as a straight man for another one of his jokes.

At least once, Ben brought one of his dubious acquaintances to our house. I remember the man vividly because he looked like a thug but had a certain charm. Ben introduced him as a professional soccer player and, to prove it, asked the man to raise his pants leg. When he did, we saw scars and gashes and black spots of mangled shinbone. My mother seemed much impressed by this stranger.

In thinking about Ben, I can't imagine that she believed he would ever make an acceptable father substitute. She probably thought his visits injected a dash of mad adventure into our lives—which they certainly did—and that this was all to the good. She might have imagined that he was too outrageous for us to model ourselves after him, ignoring the truth that children sometimes assemble a Frankenstein's monster of what they want to become by picking bits and pieces of the people around them.

Ben married a southern belle with luxuriant hair, high cheek-bones, and a soft accent. Her name was Dixie. He met her at a supper club near an army base in Texas. Years later, long after he died and after she had outlived two subsequent husbands, she remembered fondly how he had kept his cap on during that first meeting to disguise his baldness. She never got over him, despite all the heartache he caused her. "I was crazy 'bout him, darlin'," she said, "though you know he had his mean side."

Ben was a serious, unreconstructed, lifelong alcoholic. In reading my mother's letters to my father shortly before the war, I learned that once she had ordered Ben to leave our house just as he was settling in for a long stay, because he was unable to go on the wagon. Often his delirium tremens were so bad that he saw snakes on the wallpaper and spiders climbing the baseboards to attack him. During these times, he sought refuge in his mother's home in Philly, lying in bed upstairs, screaming, while she nursed him and brought him soup. He lived three blocks from her, and when I visited my grandmother's, I often walked to his apartment. I never knew what I would find when I entered the door. Once, the phone was lying smashed in the center of the living room—he had yanked it from the wall connection in a rage—and another time, he was asleep on the couch, sitting erect, and his cat was curled up on top of his head, also sleeping, like a full fur Russian hat. Ben died in 1954, alone in a hotel room, of a heart attack. What killed him was alcoholism. At his funeral he lay in an open casket, bloated, makeup heavily pancaked on his cheeks, his neck swollen to twice its size. His eyes, which used to dance with mischief, were closed, and his face, once so vivacious, was sagging and as inert as a sack of wet clay. It was my first, horrifying look at a dead person, and I never forgot the sight, the final lesson in his lasting legacy.

There was a period in which my mother had a suitor who lived with us. His name was Hub Cobb. I took to him, as did my brother. One afternoon, as he dropped the three of us at home and was about to drive off, he looked over at my mother and said, "Okay, I'll give you a ring later." I followed my brother up to his room, shut the door, and announced that they were about to get married. Stunned, he asked me how I knew. I explained that I had overheard the proposal. My brother demanded the details, and when I repeated the words I had heard, he laughed and told me I was mistaken—it was an everyday expression that didn't mean what I had thought.

Hub's father was Frank I. Cobb, the fiery editorial writer who succeeded Joseph Pulitzer as editor in chief of the *World* and became Woodrow Wilson's close friend and adviser. In 1912, Frank Cobb had purchased a run-down lumber and wheat mill in Weston, Connecticut, to obtain skating and swimming rights on its lake, and in 1936 it had been converted into the restaurant, Cobb's Mill Inn, the place where my parents conducted their illicit courtship. All this, I found out later. At the time, when I was nine or ten, I just knew Hub as a powerful new presence in our household. He was a handsome, strong man with a head of blond curls, reminding me of Van Johnson (*Battleground* and *The Caine Mutiny*). Unlike Van Johnson, who was exempt from the military because of a car crash that left him with plates in his head, Hub had served in World War II. He held the dangerous and lonely position of tail gunner on B-17s and B-25s in the Pacific. Coincidentally, he was based for a while at Port Moresby, though after Barney was there, and later in the Philippines. During the Connecticut winter he wore a handsome leather flight jacket with creases at the elbows and collar.

Hub was a full ten years younger than my mother, though I didn't realize this back then. He didn't really have a full-time job. His expertise was home improvement and he wrote various books and freelance articles as a do-it-yourselfer. That could have proved lucrative, tapping into the postwar boom in suburban home-ownership, but he didn't seem to have much cash. He had already written one book, in 1948, *How to Build Your Dream House,* but, as I later learned, he had traded the rights to a mail-order publisher for four thousand dollars; it sold more than a million copies and he received no royalties. During these years, Hub was constructing his dream house, virtually alone. As a site, he chose a meadow in the deep woods across from the inn. To get there, we'd drive our blue DeSoto down a dirt road so narrow that the branches would sweep the windows on both sides. Once in a while, we'd picnic there, breaking out deviled eggs, sandwiches, soda, and beer for the adults, overlooking first the foundation, then the ever-expanding wooden frame. One day we stopped going. My mother informed me in a low voice that the house had burned down. She was worried that if word got out it would hurt Hub's reputation.

Saturdays, Hub drove into the city for a weekly CBS radio program on home remodeling. One time my bother and I were allowed to accompany him. We had to sit quiet as mice in a corner of the studio while Hub and an interviewer faced each other across a small wooden table with microphones. A red light told us when they were on the air. We had been cautioned to keep quiet, so when the light was on, I scarcely dared to breathe. During breaks, when a commercial ran, they wisecracked. Halfway through the program, something shocking happened. The interviewer threw a question at him and then, just as Hub was about to answer, reached under the table and grabbed Hub between the legs. Hub socked his hand away, all the while talking as if nothing was happening. At first, I thought the interviewer had gone crazy. Then I realized that he was trying to make Hub crack up on the air. He was horsing around. I felt outrage. How dare he do such a thing? Especially in the sacred "on the air" space of a studio—thousands, maybe even hundreds of thousands, of people were listening. What would they think if they knew? Afterward, I didn't ask Hub about it, but he seemed to think it was no big deal. When he left the studio, he shook the man's hand and said he'd see him next week.

Having Hub around was good because he fit my image of what a man should be. One spring afternoon we discovered a nest of copperheads under a rock beside a path to the woods. I was horrified—I often took that path, and I was terrified of snakes, above all copperheads, the only poisonous species indigenous to the area. While I watched from a safe distance, Hub moved the rock and killed them with a rake and an ax. When we discovered a nest of baby squirrels, he constructed a large hutch for them. We fed them until they grew up, but after they gave the whole household a serious bout of fleas, we let them go. Another time, he pulled into the driveway and ceremoniously opened the car trunk and lifted out a blanket. As we gathered around, he opened it, revealing a gift for each of us—a

.22 rifle for Bob and a .22 single-shot rifle for me. He taught us to load and shoot, and after that we spent hours in the backwoods, knocking tin cans off logs and shattering glass bottles from twenty paces. Hub could also fix anything, and that was fortunate, because it seemed something always needed repair in our house. I liked to watch him and to hand him a hammer or screwdriver, slapping it into his palm like an attending nurse in an operating theater. He was casual and even-keeled. One time, after we had bombarded him with water bombs from the overhead lattice of our porch and he didn't lose his temper, he bet my brother and me that we couldn't make him angry—a dangerous wager to make with two young boys. We harassed him nonstop. We followed him, bumping into him. We tied his shoelaces, hung on his back, grabbed his legs. When he built a fire, we piled the logs around him, singing "Don't Fence Me In." Finally, he blew his stack, yelling at us. We demanded payment. "I'm not angry," he yelled. He left the room and never did pay up.

As far as we knew, Hub slept in a library room downstairs, where there was a studio bed. He and my mother were not overtly affectionate around us—at least I have no memory of them snuggling or kissing. But they were clearly a couple. Once, the four of us drove to the next town, Fairfield, to catch the dogwood trees in bloom. The trees were spectacular. In my mind's eye, the image of that particular afternoon lives on, enhanced by the aura of time. Pink-and-white blossoms covered our windshield. They filled the air like snowflakes and piled up in drifts beside the road—a world of soft colors that to this day remains my template of natural beauty. On the way there, as Hub was driving, we passed a sign that said SLOW CHILDREN, and my mother remarked, "That doesn't mean you, Hub. You're not a child." I understood the wordplay and thought her crack was the wittiest thing I had ever heard. I enjoyed the sensation of listening to the banter of two adults, of being a small part of a larger whole, a family on a Sunday outing, with blossoms floating through the air.

I don't know how long Hub lived with us, but I imagine it was longer than a year. One day I noticed that he was gone—on a trip, no doubt. I said nothing. Two days later, I began a project in the basement with Raisin's help. Part of the foundation was a crawl

space that could be reached by opening a door, and we began exca-
vating the packed dirt to create a honeycomb of tunnels. On the
third day, the basement light blew. I tried changing the bulb, but
that didn't do the trick. A short time later, I mentioned this to my
mother and observed that it would be good to have Hub come back
soon to fix it. She gave me a fierce look and exclaimed, "He's gone
for good! He's not coming back. And I don't want to hear his name
ever again." I lived up to her command. She didn't hear his name
again. And after that, we never talked about him, as if he had just
dropped off the face of the earth.

Odd—how memory works. Why do we remember some things,
seemingly inconsequential at the time, after a lapse of decades? Why
does our system of retention decide to record such events in a large
file all its own, marked "Important"? Psychologists insist people
retain memories if the memories attach themselves to deep emotions, even if they're not exactly sure what the emotion is. I recall
ten minutes spent one afternoon on Cape Cod more than fifty years
ago as if it were a seminal event. I was about seven or eight, playing
on a beach in Wellfleet, where my brother and I were taken in for
several weeks by a wealthy Westport family who owned a cottage
there.

Fronting the beach were large clay cliffs. Older boys would scale
them, using handholds and footholds dug into the clay. I tried to
climb them, got about thirty feet off the ground, looked down, and
froze. I was petrified. I couldn't go up or down. I cried out for my
brother, who was on the beach below. He stood up, said something
to two girls in the group. They laughed, and I was mortified. Eventually, he rescued me, climbing up and guiding me down by holding
my ankles, but what I remember most is the laughter.

Later that day an older boy, a teenager, joined us. He was friendly
to us younger kids and protective, too, and he said he would be a
"bodyguard" for my brother.

"Me, too," I insisted. "Will you be my bodyguard?"

"Of course," he said. "For you especially. I won't let anyone get
you."

Shortly afterward, we walked up to the road that wound along the cliff above the ocean. Cars were parked there. He sauntered over to one. "Let's borrow it and take it for a spin," he said, looking in at the ignition key. We jumped in and he started it. I sat in the rear seat, between two other older boys, enthralled by it all—the sense of protection, the larger boys around, the illicit thrill of taking the car. He drove up and down the empty road along the sea grass and the sand dunes and then, after half an hour or so, drove back to return the car. We piled out and went back to the beach. That was all. Nothing more happened. I have no memory of the boy's name and no idea what he looked like, and I never saw him again. But it was a half hour that, for some reason, lives on forever in my memory.

CHAPTER 8

Myths die hard. I suppose that's why I persisted in believing that I was living an ideal childhood despite growing evidence to the contrary. The truth was that the cracks were appearing in the façade, that somewhere along the line things were beginning to go wrong. Exactly when or why, I didn't determine back then—nor did I try to. Quite the opposite: I resisted any such knowledge deep in my bones.

Outwardly, much remained unchanged—at least at first. We still undertook the occasional family excursions on Sunday. We'd rent a rowboat at Captain Allen's to go crabbing, meandering through the marshes with our lines baited and hauling up five-inch monsters whose pincers sent a delicious shiver up my spine. Or we'd pack a picnic lunch and head off through the woods to Devil's Den, a swimming hole where the rocky outcroppings next to a waterfall made perilous diving platforms. If it was a hot summer night and the phosphorus was up in Long Island Sound, Mom would take us for a midnight swim at the deserted public beach; the sweep of an arm or leg underwater would unleash a cascade of shimmering diamonds. If the Brooklyn Dodgers were playing in the pennant race or the World Series, she'd spring us from school and take us to Ebbets Field. And later, she'd let us go by ourselves, covering us with a note to the teacher explaining, should anyone object, that rooting for a baseball team in the championship could be more important than a day in a classroom for a well-rounded boy.

She traded in our sedate DeSoto for a black 1939 Ford convertible. We kids rode in the rumble seat in the open air, feeling like royalty. Sometimes there were four of us outriders, two in the rumble seat and two seated above in the well for the collapsible top, facing into the wind like jockeys. I grew familiar with the underside of treetops all over town. Our drives included excursions with spontaneous detours: a stop for a Dairy Queen cone dipped in chocolate, or a round of miniature golf, or fresh corn at a pick-your-own farm. The car looked like a hot rod. More than once, we'd be pulled over by the police, who assumed a teenager was driving. They'd be surprised and embarrassed to find a respectable-looking matron behind the wheel.

Mom also engaged us intellectually, not so much by introducing us to concerts or ballet but by recommending books and using conversation as a pedagogical tool. She loved a lively discussion and leaned into it, sitting on the edge of a winged armchair with her dress festooned between her legs, her eyes sparkling, holding a cigarette with a hooked finger of her right hand. She could be warm and understanding when that was called for, but mostly she expected us to meet high standards. If we fell short by someone else's measure or failed by someone else's lights, not hers, she defended us fiercely.

And yet there were problems. Mom seemed to be working too hard, or at least this appeared the likely reason for the growing number of evenings when she had to stay late in the city. On the nights she was home in time to tuck us in, something strange and unsettling was occurring: When she came into my bedroom to kiss me good night, we had arguments—over little things, seemingly, resentments that had piled up, tensions between us, awkward misunderstandings. I remember being surprised by this, confused as to why it was happening. On one occasion, I rigged up an alarm clock to ring when my door was opened, a simple device that amounted to inserting a piece of cardboard between the ringer and the bell and attaching it to the doorknob. It was a makeshift burglar alarm and was intended as a sort of joke—or so I told myself—but when she tripped the alarm, her feelings were hurt. Soon afterward she began skipping our good nights altogether. At about this time, contending with my usual difficulties in falling asleep, I began thrashing my head up and down on my pillow, a ritual I adopted, I told myself, to tire myself out.

When did things begin to go bad? I can't say for certain, because there was no clear-cut starting point—it must have been when I was eight or nine. That's when I became aware of my mother as an adult carrying a heavy burden of responsibilities. At times, I viewed her almost objectively, from a distance. I believed that Mom, whose spirit craved nothing so much as to be carefree and spontaneous, was being crushed by responsibilities or some other problem that I couldn't fathom. She needed my help and protection, and yet we seemed to be moving further and further apart. At times, she didn't seem like herself. Sunday mornings, when Bob and I used to pile into her bed to talk and snuggle, lost their laughter. Often she appeared cranky and loath to wake up. Once, talking about Stalin's Russia, she observed that the dictator hated journalists and remarked that if the Russians took over the United States, she would surely be executed. Because I had a child's sense of the world and, having heard so much about the Russians, assumed they were about to invade, I was upset—visibly so. I extrapolated from all the war movies I had seen and envisioned myself as an orphan, hungry and freezing in the snow. I began to cry. Yet she made no effort to reassure me, to tell me that such a thing would never happen.

Sometimes Mom would tell me that she would pick me up and then fail to show. She left me waiting for long periods of time at friends' houses or at the movie theater or somewhere else downtown. Once she was to fetch me from the beach for lunch. I waited so long by the food shack that I got hungry. Eventually, I rummaged in a garbage pail for bits of food—half-eaten hot dogs, soggy french fries, and half-filled containers of soft drink. When she finally turned up, four hours late, I told her what I had done, proud of my ingenuity, and was taken back by her reaction. She seemed inordinately upset.

And yet at other times, she would be her old self, capable and seemingly confident, proposing some new venture, like teaching us to play craps or a quick game of charades. This revolving door of personalities seemed to account for an odd perception I had of my life as it was unfolding—that it was proceeding on contradictory levels. It was moving on parallel tracks that led in opposite directions. One was happy and normal, shot through with freedom and Tom Sawyer adventures and all the normal ups and downs of a cohesive family. The other was a dark underside, in which we were anything but normal and refused to own up to it. Something seemed to be dragging us down, something dangerous, and it was impossible to determine exactly what it was because it was nameless and unidentifiable, like the monsters I used to dread in my bedroom at night.

As Mom worked late and began to fade as an everyday presence in our lives, the void was filled by Inell, our live-in housekeeper. Inell was the same age as Mom. Her skin was wrinkled and the color of ebony. She was from Mississippi, and we children didn't know much about her past. Her last name changed several times—from Jones to Atkinson to something else, reflecting changes in husbands. Sometimes the men would show up at our house, balancing us kids on their knees and bringing a rough whiff of New York City street life. Inell also had a daughter who, I was shocked to learn, was herself a mother at the age of fourteen. Mom told me not to ask questions about her. Inell lived in a back room with an attached bathroom. We were not supposed to go in there—it was her private area—but on those occasions when we were invited in, we readily accepted. The heat was turned on high, the radio was playing a soap opera or an episode of *The Fat Man,* and it felt warm and safe.

Inell was the rock in our lives. It was she who was at home when we returned from school in the early years, and who got us in and out of our snowsuits and cooked dinner for us—hamburgers or fried chicken or pork chops and, on special nights, lemon meringue pie. I loved her cooking, but I was not much of an eater. At the small table where Bob and I ate most nights, I discovered a drawer below my place setting. Each night I ate as much, or little, as I wanted, opened it, and shoveled the remainder inside—a solution that worked fine for about a year, until someone opened the drawer and found a festering pile of mold.

Inell called me "Boss Tweed." She answered my barrage of questions—why school was important, why people acted the way they did, why dogs sometimes bit—with homespun directness. On the day in third grade when I was accosted at school with the unexpected question "Are you a Yankee fan or a Dodger fan?" and I took a stab in the dark and replied, "Dodger," she approved of my selection. I felt I had passed some kind of test. Sometimes her wisdom could be a little too homespun. She planted ideas in my young brain that were not altogether true and that blossomed a long time afterward, like errant seeds. I learned, for example, that pepper could make you sneeze, and as I was inhaling a handful to test the proposition, she told me of a young boy about my age who sneezed so much that he couldn't stop, until he just sneezed himself to death. For years, I tried to stifle a sneeze whenever I felt one coming on. Nor was she perfect in every way. One morning, I was horror-stricken at the bus stop to discover that I had forgotten the paper bag that contained my lunch. She promised to deliver it to school. As the morning drew on, I watched the clock with mounting anxiety; when lunchtime came, and she still had not shown up, I flew out the back door and ran all the way home, tears streaking down my face. I burst in at the front door, to find her calmly chatting on the phone. She was apologetic but not, by my lights, sufficiently so. Inell was so much a part of our lives that we didn't think she would ever leave. She was there, had always been there, and would continue to be there—that was our assumption.

I disliked school. I disliked the regimen and being forced to sit still at my wooden desk, watching the minute hand of the wall clock drag along at a slug's pace. As far as I was concerned, teachers, charter members of the adult world, were suspect. On rare days they would read us a story, which I enjoyed, but mostly they enforced drills and memorizations. Whenever adults asked that patronizing question—"And what do you like best about school?"—I replied with honest enthusiasm, "Recess." I retain a vivid memory of one particular moment: Ascending the school staircase, I paused to peer through a window at a distant patch of blue sky; I calculated the number of years I had been in school and the number of years still to go and I wondered how I could possibly endure them.

In the fifth grade, our school was inexplicably swept by Civil War mania—some merchandiser must have had boxcars of Yankee blue and Rebel gray caps to unload—and recess turned overnight into a make-believe battlefield. That improved things immensely. I chose to be a Johnny Reb. We enjoyed hamming up our deaths and especially lying wounded and groaning while the nurses—girls who up until then had seemed pointless in the scheme of things—bandaged us and whispered sweet nothings so that we might recover. One day the craze passed as abruptly as it had begun.

I was the smallest kid in my class. That meant that I had to develop alternative survival skills. I chose wit and guile. I was forever hatching plots, inventing games, and getting in trouble, and as a result, I had a wide circle of friends. We were comrades of the heart, supporting one another no matter what. We accepted one another's weaknesses and failings, we listened to one another's problems, and we confessed things we would never have told our parents. We knew when to extend sympathy and when to remain supportively silent. We traded bits of information about the larger world and tips on how to contend with it. Our bikes—chrome-heavy Schwinns with balloon tires—lay sprawled on one another's lawns and moved about in packs to other lawns throughout an afternoon. Often we went to one another's houses directly after school and walked home at dusk. Typically, I walked for miles along twisting back roads. During one particular frightening stretch of road, a valley where the trees arched to form a darkening canopy and where strange sounds emanated from a swamp, I used to sing "The Battle Hymn of the Republic" as loudly as I could to keep the evil spirits at bay.

Raisin and I formed a group called "Bosom Buddies." Others were allowed in from time to time, but that was a social concession; we were the two charter members and it revolved around us. Naturally, we got in trouble. At times, though, our reputation for transgressions outstripped our misdeeds. In the fourth grade, on a day that Raisin stayed home ill, I was hauled out of class and taken to the office of the principal, one Mrs. Netta Spangenberg. I had no idea what was going on, but I was ordered to confess. "Confess to what?" I asked, infuriating her further. She grabbed me by both arms and shook me roughly. She shoved me into a chair and told to remain there until I was willing to admit my misconduct. I had no idea what I was thought to have done. This went on all morning—chastisements mixed in with physical abuse and periods left alone to "think about it," until finally, mysteriously, Mrs. Spangenberg reappeared to say that I was free to go. "What happened?" I asked. She said someone else had confessed to the offense, which, I was soon to learn, involved an obscene call to a teacher over the weekend. I lingered for a moment on the threshold of the office—even at that age, I had some sense that a fundamental right had been violated—until she looked up and said, "You can understand, of course, why we all thought it was you. You may leave now."

Raisin was something of a social misfit. He was afflicted with epilepsy. I grew accustomed to his seizures and fainting spells, and when they occurred, I learned to cover him with something—a blanket if we were indoors, a jacket if we were outside—to keep him warm. I'd stay by him and calm him when he awoke, a look of confusion and sometimes panic in his eyes. I wonder now if the disease or some combination of the disease and his emotionally tangled home life didn't stunt his maturity. He was one of those rare children who seem to get stuck in childhood. Things that we did as youngsters, which could be put down to a spirited nature, like tossing cherry bombs into the river or balancing on the peak of a rooftop, were less acceptable as we grew a bit older. I sensed that it was time to move on and that he was dragging us back to an earlier age. On excursions he sometimes carried around his old teddy bear, smelly and mangled, with one eye missing and patches of fur pulled out. To an adult, that must have appeared as if he was pathetically attached to a childish toy. But I knew things were more complicated than that. The bear was subjected to an endless round of tortures and tribulations: If we went swimming, it was dunked underwater; if we climbed a tree, it was dropped, crashing, through the branches; once, on a sailboat, it was tied to the front mast, braving the ocean spray like Odysseus. It was a totem, standing in for Raisin himself. It, not he, was assimilating all these blows to body and spirit.

Some years later, in the sixth and seventh grades, when we boys developed an interest in girls and began meeting up with them at the movies, Raisin did not. A distance grew between us, and not long after that, I moved away from Westport and lost touch with him altogether. About ten years afterward, running into an old friend from those days, I heard that he had gotten into trouble for breaking into a construction shed and stealing a cache of dynamite. Some ten years after that, when I was working as a novice reporter for *The New York Times,* Eloise Ray called me to ask if I could manage to get an obituary of her husband in the paper. He had died of a heart attack. I asked about Raisin and her voice broke. Hadn't I heard? she asked. Heard what? He had died, she said, years before, in a canoeing accident, alone on a Canadian river. When I hung up, I had to sit down to catch my breath. The one person who knew me best during those painful, joyful years of growing up—and the one person I had known better than anyone else, and had loved in a way I had loved no one else—was gone. All those years, in addition to being my one and only "bosom buddy," he was living proof that having a father can be worse than not having one.

My brother and I were very close. Separately, we treasured the emblem of Father Flanagan's Boys Town orphanage: the image of one boy carrying another one piggyback and saying, "He ain't heavy, he's my brother." We made it our own, for it seemed to sum up, if not our situation, our relationship. There was no doubt in either of our minds about which boy was doing the carrying and which was getting the ride. Our bond was strengthened by this gathering sense that things were going off the rails, although we didn't talk about that. I was developing into a mental escape artist; I turned aside hints that all was not as it should be. Bob had taken on an additional role as my protector, which meant that he couldn't share his fears. But I could tell that he was under a great deal of stress. He rarely laughed or joked and seemed weighed down by a burden of responsibilities.

Bob was supposed to become a reporter. That our father's mantle was his to inherit was made clear to him at an early age, following the unsubtle means by which such expectations are communicated from parent to child. I remember any number of discussions about the American press and its sacred duties and many anecdotes about irascible editors and dashing reporters. I, on the other hand, was free to choose my profession, though our mother predicted that I would become an engineer—based largely on the fact that I liked playing with Erector sets and model trains and that whenever we visited New York City, I insisted on stopping at construction sites to peer through the wooden barricades. When grown-ups asked that ridiculous question—"And what do you want to do when you grow up?"—I replied with a single word: "Demolition." If they failed to understand, I became explicit: I explained that I wanted to swing that giant wrecker ball that smashed down brick walls.

From the first, Mom treated Bob as more mature than his age. At times she almost seemed to be grooming him for greatness according to some agenda. A wealthy family, who chose Bob as a playmate for their son in hopes he would be a constructive influence, helped guide her in selecting various activities. When he was still in elementary school, she found him a French tutor, a gray-haired Ezio Pinza look-alike; we dropped Bob off for lessons every Saturday morning. On Sundays he would take horseback-riding lessons at a local stable; I would play with a litter of puppies that lived under a barn while he trotted around a white-fenced ring to the exhortations of an exacting riding instructor. Mom and he would talk about books and art and other such things while I listened in from the sidelines. At the time, I thought he had been chosen for these lessons because he was superior and deserving—only later did I conclude that I had missed out on them because by the time I came of age, our home life had deteriorated.

Over time, Bob seemed increasingly to surpass me. He became ever more serious and ever more responsible. He had a paper route and sometimes used the money to buy his own clothes. On one occasion, he asked me to fill in for him. I followed him to learn the ropes—how he folded the papers, tucking them into themselves, stuffed them into a voluminous canvas bag around his shoulder, and tossed them onto driveways and porches from his bicycle seat. The following day it was my turn. Everything went wrong. The papers seemed too thick to fold and tuck. The bag was too heavy; it pulled my bike over. I tried sticking the papers in wads under the seat, around the wheels, into my pants. Nothing worked. And a deadline was looming, the start of my Little League game. In a panic, I ended up ditching the papers behind a bush on the Post Road and then forgot about it until well after the game, when Bob asked me how it had gone. We rushed out, found the hidden bundle, and delivered the papers in the dark.

Bob's accomplishments accelerated in junior high school. He was a straight-A student and a favorite of his teachers, especially in English. He wrote a column about the goings-on at the school for the town weekly. He was on the varsity baseball and basketball teams and in his senior year ran for class president. I helped manage his campaign, employing a cadre of seventh graders to scrawl posters and hand out buttons. I expected he would win, and when he did, I received the news with a tangled feeling of pride and a sense of my inferiority. When the school's janitor died, a friendly man known as "Pop," Bob addressed a throng of students assembled on the playground for a memorial service and delivered a eulogy whose lofty language was the most beautiful and stirring I had ever heard. He was the school's featured orator. He gave the commencement address in words worthy of Pericles, speaking of "a golden sun that streams down upon this wondrous land" but also warning of "shadows marring the golden light"—by which he meant the vague forces of "insecurity, aggression, distrust, and fear."

At the time, Bob was contending with shadows of his own. He wrote a two-page story for English class that was more than a little autobiographical. It described a boy lying in bed, listening to rats in a house he hates, wondering what life would be like if his father had not died. He contemplates running away to Florida but realizes he must stay to help his mother. He excoriates himself for being selfish and self-pitying and wishes he could be carefree like his friends. At the end he falls asleep, whimpering softly, "I hate death. I hate life." The story, which turned up in an old carton recently, received an A+ from his teacher, who wrote a warm note at the bottom, saying, "I am proud of you!"

. . .

Eventually, it struck me that Mom's working hard under a burden of responsibilities wasn't a sufficient explanation for the changes in her behavior. I tried not to think too deeply about it, but she seemed different, and our family life seemed different. Our weekend excursions fell away and we didn't seem to do much of anything. I would wander through the woods with my hound dog. She slept late in the mornings and still seemed sleepy by the afternoon. We had a special name for this condition. We called it "groggy." The house began to fall apart; a bog of neglect descended. Milk in the fridge was often rancid. Foodstuffs ran out. Things needed repairing and cleaning—a cracked window, a spot on the rug, a fallen tree in the backyard, a lightbulb that had burned out in the living room. But no one did anything about them.

One Sunday morning, after I had been up for three or four hours, Bob called me upstairs, looking worried. He took me into Mom's room, where she was still sound asleep, and pointed to her bed. The blankets had fallen off on one side and there, halfway down the mattress, was a hole six inches wide. It cut deep into the material, like a crater. The edges were black and brown, burned. Mom's cigarettes were there on a night table. I realized with a shock what had happened. She had fallen asleep while smoking in bed. "She's lucky she didn't burn up," Bob said. "The whole house could have caught fire. We could have all been killed." I was horrified. We woke her, but she had no recollection of the fire and didn't seem to place much importance on it.

One particular Christmas stands out from all the rest because it was such a disaster. I had a devotion to Christmas, regarding it with nostalgia as a time of merriment and excess. And as our situation worsened, I looked more and more to the holidays for an infusion of joy, as an indication that things were still normal and functioning. But this Christmas was so miserable it couldn't be whitewashed. I was nine years old. For several years now, I had not believed in Santa Claus, and Mom had given up the pretense that he was responsible for the tree and the trimmings. Hanging the lights and the balls and the tinsel had always been a family affair, and in previous years we had made a production of it, joking and singing. A booby prize went to the person who broke the first ball. But this year, everything seemed off track. We couldn't get it together to buy the mistletoe, find enough wrapping paper, or replace the electric bulbs that had burned out. We couldn't find all the ornaments or the hooks to hang them with. We couldn't even get the tree to stand upright, and when we finally did, it was crooked. But we plowed ahead, an old record of Christmas carols spinning on the turntable. Mom seemed unsteady as her hand wavered over the box of Christmas balls. She picked one, approached the tree, and lunged—and the tree fell over, a jumble of cracking branches and splintering ornaments. Bob helped her up and we got the tree upright again. We resumed, but this time I didn't join in—I retreated to the top of a sofa, lying on the edge, trying to comprehend what I had witnessed, the disparity between what I had dreamed of and what had happened. Then Mom lost her footing and fell face-first into the tree. I opened my throat and did something I hadn't done for years—burst out crying.

But I still had no inkling of what was going on. I had come to rely upon repression as the first line of defense. It's astounding how repression can blot out pain and confusion and be effective even when flying in the face of contradictory facts that are undeniable. It's a willful blindness. The wind can be blowing the trees sideways, the rain pelting down like bullets, the timbers of the house shaking, and yet you're unable or unwilling to admit that you're being battered by a hurricane. My own private hurricane revolved around my mother. But at the time, I was incapable of recognizing that.

Not long after that Christmas, Raisin and I were walking through the woods on one of our typical excursions. We stopped under a tree and sat down to have a snack. We munched on sandwiches and Fig Newtons. We were silent for a while and then began to talk. Our conversation was curiously intimate. I had the feeling that Raisin wanted to tell me something. I looked over at him. Wiping his mouth, he turned to me and said in a voice that sounded different from his usual voice—different enough for me to sit up and pay attention—that he had overheard his mother talking with a neighbor of ours. "They were talking about your mother," he said. "What about?" I asked with a sense of foreboding. He nodded his head in the general direction of the house occupied by the neighbor, a genial white-haired widow. "She said, 'You know what the trouble with Tootie Darnton is?' And before my mother could answer, she said, 'She's a drunk.' And my mother said she knew it, too." I was too shocked to reply for a moment. I was mortified. A *drunk*! Who does she think she is, saying a thing like that? But then I resolved, with a certainty that surpassed any certainty I had ever known, that she was mistaken—deeply mistaken.

"It's a lie," I said. "A dirty lie." And I told him never to repeat it. And that ended the matter.

CHAPTER 9

Another memory boils up, this one from a later time. I was perhaps eleven. It was late in the afternoon on a fine summer day, the sky a cloudless blue. I was lying on a blanket at Compo Beach and my mother was lying on a blanket not two feet away, when abruptly she sat up and out of nowhere delivered a warning. "Watch out for *The New York Times*. They use you like a sponge. They squeeze you dry and then they toss you away."

The remark, uncharacteristically bitter, was a total non sequitur. We hadn't been talking about the *Times;* we hadn't been talking about anything, in fact. She didn't explain herself and I didn't ask her to. Her observation just seemed to drop unbidden out of a blue sky on a summer afternoon—which is probably why it stayed with me through the years.

I disregarded her warning. I ended up working for the *Times* for almost four decades, beginning as a copyboy and moving through various departments and assignments. Others in my family went to work for the *Times,* too—my brother for a year, before I did, and later my wife, Nina, who began writing articles when we were abroad and then worked in New York as a freelance Arts & Leisure reporter, movie critic, and movie columnist. A decade ago, when the paper began whittling down its morgue, the voluminous file of clippings sorted by subject, writer, and other categories, I was sent the collection of Darnton family bylines: my father's, my mother's, my brother's, my wife's, and my own. It arrived at my home in a carton that measured three feet by four feet, so heavy that the postman struggled to carry it. I used to joke that when it came to the *Times*, we were like a coal-mining family in West Virginia, unable to break away from the company store. In short, our lives have been interwoven with the paper from that day in April 1934 when my father first pushed through the revolving door of what was then called the Times Annex at 229 West Forty-third Street down to the present.

During my forty years there, I thought back from time to time to my mother's warning and wondered what had prompted it. Among newspaper folk the *Times* has never been known as a happy shop—there are too many ambitious and clever people crammed into a single city room—but I never had cause for complaint. True, I saw any number of instances of corporate injustice: deserving people cast aside while incompetents were promoted, reputations trashed by rivals, credit given to the wrong people, and editors who nurtured a bullying streak. But to me, these negative aspects were outweighed by gestures of thoughtfulness and generosity and acts of courage and integrity, especially on the part of collegially minded reporters. I'm grateful because the place provided me with a solid paycheck and an adventurous life.

So why was my mother bitter that summer afternoon? Was it because she was aware of slights meted out to others? (Shortly before, a friend of hers, a foreign correspondent named Tania Long, married to the brilliant wartime London bureau chief, Raymond Daniell, had been exiled to a backwater assignment in Canada.) That seemed unlikely. Was it because of all the sexual intrigue, expressed by the well-known dictum "Drink is the bane of the *Herald Trib* and sex is the bane of the *Times*"? (On one occasion, she had told me, Mike Berger's wife, upset over an infidelity, had barged into the bank of telephone operators, threatening to cut out her tongue to dramatize a vow that she would suffer in silence.) No, that didn't seem likely, either.

It wasn't until I began doing research for this book in 2006, trying to figure out what my mother's working life was like when I was a child, that I came upon the likely answer. I was burrowing deep into the *Times*' archives in the hulking old building that had housed the block-long third-floor newsroom since 1913. This was at the time that the paper was preparing to move three blocks away to a modern skyscraper on Eighth Avenue. The archives, a vast compendium of correspondence and personnel records going back more than a hundred years, were temporarily stashed in a makeshift room in the basement, where the presses had been. The floor was fissured with metal tracks that used to carry the plates to the presses, and the smell of ink was embedded in the cavernous walls. As a young reporter, I used to go there to watch the rumbling presses, which sent vibrations through the whole fifteen-story building. They fed off an endless webbed stream of newsprint roaring up from the sub-basement, tended by pressmen dressed in dirty overalls and wearing giant earmuffs to protect their hearing. Now, the place was cold and quiet and eerily deserted.

An assistant in the morgue told me how to find records, which were cataloged by the dates of the reigns of publishers, as if they were monarchs. Then he disappeared. After a while, I managed to locate my mother's file, a single thin manila envelope. I took it over to a small wooden table, sat down, and slowly read through it. Clearly, many documents were missing. Mostly those spawned by the demands of bureaucracy, when she changed departments or jobs, were there, along with snatches of correspondence saved at the whim of various editors. There were memos and transfer slips, which gave a skeletal outline of her brief trajectory at the paper—her time as a Washington reporter, the summons to New York to be women's editor, and her departure. There were also half a dozen letters written by her. The correspondence did not tell the whole story of her time there. Nor was it balanced. On her side there were letters in which she laid down her views about women's news and fleshed out her arguments for coverage and tried to persuade editors to go along. On the other side there were the editors' responses—succinct notes to the publisher, dashed off quickly because they were pressed for time, or remarks slotted into the margins of her letters, seemingly written to preserve a record in case problems developed down the line.

Sitting there, reading these exchanges, I envisioned her as a thirty-seven-year-old woman with two children, undergoing the grind of a daily commute, stepping on the morning train as a mother and stepping off as a working woman doing battle in a man's world. I could see her trying to contend with powerful figures at the paper, men with demanding jobs who didn't believe in coddling employees and who, for that matter, didn't have all that much empathy to begin with. They hadn't gotten to where they were by being soft or sentimental, and if they felt an obligation to my mother because of her dead husband, they quickly managed to suppress it.

Piecing together a coherent narrative from these scattered bits of paper was impossible. But they at least provided a sense of what she'd been up against. At first she wrote warm notes, expressing gratitude for being hired. She didn't lose her equilibrium when the Times' bureaucracy fouled up, as it so often did, assigning her on the very first day to a new job without informing the person she was to replace and later failing to come through with a promised raise. She was so grateful to be there that she didn't raise a fuss. But over time, her letters showed more and more frustration as they recounted her struggles and confrontations with the top editors, and they grew lengthier as the grievances piled up.

The memos offer only a tiny window onto the Times' newsroom of sixty years ago, when women reporters were many times scarcer than the notorious mice that skittered under the desks. Adolph S. Ochs, who took over the paper in 1896 and transformed it into the reliable "Old Gray Lady," didn't like the idea of women on staff. Nor did he believe women should have the right to vote. As Nan Robertson recounts in her book The Girls in the Balcony, during the forty years that he ruled the place, only four women worked as reporters in the city room. While other, less buttoned-up papers were touting their female stars, sometimes to excess, the Times remained a bastion of male privilege. The attitude carried on long after Ochs's death in 1935, even into the early 1970s, when the women organized to press a discrimination suit and won a settlement. When I joined, in 1966, the mice still outnumbered the women many times over.

In my mother's day, almost all the women reporters worked for her in women's news, a small department on the eighth floor. She sat in a glassed-off cubicle, with a deputy, Harriett Crowley, at a desk outside. They faced about a dozen or so writers sitting at desks grouped by subject, the largest cluster for fashion reporting, next to wall charts keeping track of how often items like Saks shoes or Bonwit Teller furs appeared in the paper, information useful in dealing with the ad-sales people. There were smaller clusters for beauty, child care, and home décor. One white-haired reporter covered women's clubs for the Sunday society section. The work of the others was for the most part ghettoized on the daily "home page," which specialized in "the four *F*'s"—food, fashions, furnishings, and family. As Doris Faber, then a young reporter, recalled, "It was pretty much like a cartoon of a mini city room with rows of desks—a beauty columnist at her desk intently reapplying nail polish, opposite a regal old fashion editor frowning at a batch of sandal samples being unpacked by one of her several assistants." Some of the assignments, she told me, made her cringe: "For instance, on the day before Valentine's Day I did a phone survey among well-known bachelors about their plans for avoiding matrimonial entrapment." But occasionally news would break out to be offered to the more important desks in the city room. "I got a front-page story when a transit official speaking at a women's city club talked frankly about raising the five-cent fare."

Five floors below, the *Times'* city room, with its all-male management, was a raging pit of contending egos. First among the titans was managing editor Edwin L. James, a flashy dresser who played the horses and exulted in his reputation as a tough boss. He was the sort of man who flew into rage at a slow-moving elevator, smashing the doors with his cane to let the operator know who was being kept waiting. Another tyrant was Lester Markel, lord of the ever-growing Sunday department, a brilliant newspaperman but a man who was ruthless, scheming, and widely despised. Since Markel had worked closely with Barney, who at one point had been an editor in his department, one might have expected that he would treat Barney's widow with a modicum of respect. He did not. Nor, apparently, did James. He began one memo to the publisher, Arthur Hays Sulzberger, this way: "Mrs. Darnton has sent me a copy of her letter to you. It is true, as she says, that I helped her get started in a technical way, largely because I was a friend of her husband and, after all, I hired him on the *Times,* which probably resulted, indirectly or not, in his being killed." The memo went on to deride her conception of women's news.

Her clashes with the other editors centered on this question of what constituted women's news—how to define it and where to place it in the paper. As women's editor, she had a broad view of women's interests and believed strongly that stories aimed at them should reach far beyond "the four F's." The world was changing, she insisted. During the war, women had held down jobs in factories and other workplaces, and they would never be the same; they might return to the home, but they had an abiding interest in the cost of food, family budgets, labor laws, children, and social issues. This was a far cry from the fare that usually appeared on the home page.

In addition to running this page, my mother was expected to generate stories for other sections of the paper, mostly the national and local news pages. At the *Times,* such a jerry-built arrangement has traditionally been a recipe for failure: The editor of a small outlying department ends up having to beg or cajole the national or city editors into running his or her stories in space consigned to their own stories, something they naturally resist. And in this case, the stories she was trying to place were these larger, thematic pieces of interest to women. Underlying the confusion over how to deal with women's news was the sour rivalry between James and Markel. Caught in the cross fire, my mother was attacked by both, for different reasons. The Sunday editor complained that he was not getting his fair share of the spoils out of women's news, and the managing editor resisted her initiating stories with what he derided as "sociological looking into the future."

Finally, in April 1945, she had had enough. She sent a five-page single-spaced memo to the publisher, Arthur Hays Sulzberger, recapitulating her ideas. She asserted that the paper had "a particular blind spot" when it came to stories of concern to women. "The news value of these stories is not obvious to men or to desks which for years have ignored the interests of women," she wrote. "I refer, to give a few examples, to stories on the development of shortages, among low-priced textile goods for instance; on the needs of children and young people in relation to their health, education, work and well-being and what plans and legislation were in process; on women's new place in industry, which involves such things as equal pay legislation, how they function in the organized labor picture and what will happen to these 20 million, many of whom are heads of families, during reconversion. In my opinion, it is the printing of such stories that will bring new women readers to the paper."

These types of stories, she wrote, should not be confined to the home page, but should be carried throughout the paper. She asserted that she had made strides in the right direction, so much so that that three other newspaper publishers had sent editors to see how it was done.

It is my belief that The New York Times, *through necessity since the paper was so behind the times on women, has been on the verge of developing a significant new convention in newspapering. Just as sports, business news, financial, drama and the arts are special departments, the women's news department has blazed a trail in coverage of news of interest to women, at a time when women are more conscious of their responsibilities in the world than ever before. . . . Also, on pain of being misunderstood, I think I should warn you that we have already built up a fan public of some extent so that if the news they have come to look for is obviously once more ignored, they are apt to resent it and accuse the* Times *of returning to an outmoded policy of "clothes and cosmetics," insulting to women readers.*

And then, in a surprising couple of paragraphs at the end, she said she wanted to "step out"—resign. The bad blood—especially between herself and Markel—had reached the point that "no matter how I worked, or attempted to work, he would soon again become dissatisfied, so that again I would be under personal attack that would make it difficult to do a job and be troublesome all around for the people who work on the paper." She saved the original letter in her files. A copy turned up in James's file, which I held in my hands sixty years later. On it, he had scribbled at the top, "no reason for all this," and, in the margin of a paragraph in which she'd outlined the problem, he wrote, "exactly wrong." She was prevailed upon to give it another try, and she did, but she lasted only another three months before leaving the *Times*.

She then took the job abroad—the one that caused my brother to miss her so terribly—and went to postwar Paris. There, from August to December of 1945, she edited a magazine called *Overseas Women*, which was aimed at women in the armed forces. When she returned, she was struck by a forceful idea: Since there was such an apparent hunger for women's news of a serious bent, not just in New York but everywhere, why not come up with a vehicle to satisfy it? Together with her former deputy, Ms. Crowley, she founded just such an organization. It was called Women's National News Service, a syndicate with its own reporters and editors to specialize in news by and about women. They would offer their service to every newspaper in the country. They would treat women as intelligent adults, bypassing the usual fare of beauty hints, recipes, and advice to the lovelorn and instead concentrating on serious news developments and revealing feature stories.

WNNS began in 1946. It was partly financed by our mother, who put in the insurance money from Barney's death and an additional settlement payment from the *Times*. Exactly how much this amounted to, I have never been able to determine, but looking through a deteriorating file of bits and scraps of paper, I see that savings bonds were issued to her for $24,225, a princely sum in those days. These were cashed in. Initially, the venture looked promising. She beat the bushes and in the first year signed up some twenty-two papers to receive the service, including the *Boston Globe,* the *Philadelphia Bulletin,* the *Baltimore Evening Sun,* the *St. Louis Globe-Democrat,* and the *Cincinnati Enquirer.* They paid as much as $150 a week and in return received a package of twenty news stories and ten features. The stories were assembled by half a dozen editors and writers who often rewrote files sent in by freelancers and seventy-two stringers, of whom ten were in Tokyo, London, Paris, and other cities abroad. Sometimes the New York writers lifted stories from the wires, placing calls to flesh them out. Fashion and beauty columns were held to once a week and struck a practical, no-frills tone. One column on spring clothes for children, for example, said, "nicest . . . we've seen for many a spring [but] unfortunately price tags pose a pretty problem for non-millionaires."

In the first year, the service carried stories about housewives exerting pressure to bring prices down, debates in the Senate on school aid, and the arrest of three women who were testing draconian antistrike laws in New Jersey. There were also pieces about the attitude of Japanese women toward a plan to substitute UN rule for U.S. rule (they were against it) and the attitude of Soviet women toward American broadcasts (they liked them). The staff was well chosen and professional, almost all of them women, and it was varied. Among them was a twenty-one-year-old Hunter College graduate, a West Indian–American named Marjorie Marsie-Hazen, still amazed, sixty-two years later, that "these two ladies employed a 'colored' neophyte."

Initially, WNNS was located on West Forty-fourth Street, but it later moved into the seventh floor of the *Times* building. Occasionally, Bob and I would visit there, pausing in the lobby to look at a large plaque to our father and Robert Post, a *Times* correspondent lost in an air battle over Germany. I recall the exciting bustle of the office, the head-clearing smell of mimeograph machines, and the piles of rough yellow copy paper perfect for drawing on. I knew, in the stealthy way that children acquire such knowledge, that my mother was the co-proprietor and that I was expected to behave in order to do her proud. I disliked planting kisses on Mrs. Crowley's cold cheek, a ritual greeting I was forced to observe, but I enjoyed visits to the telephone switchboard upstairs, where the operators made a fuss over me and gave me wooden pencils with rotating balls on the top for easy dialing. Just around the corner was Times Square, with the Camel billboard smoker blowing giant smoke rings, where we saw the first-run performances of *South Pacific* and *The King and I.*

At the beginning, Mom traveled around the country for speaking engagements at women's clubs, using these occasions to talk about the status of women and their humanistic take on important issues. Women had different, perhaps even deeper, concerns, she told the Woman's Club in Dayton, Ohio. "Men are interested in fires and epidemics. Women are concerned with the serum that may prevent the epidemic." Only the Russians seemed to understand the importance of wooing women with promises of a better future, she told a federated women's club group at a tea in Birmingham, Alabama.

She also engaged in the sort of broad-humored high jinks that press clubs of that time indulged in. She traveled down to Washington to appear in a "Bittersweet" Valentine skit at the Statler in 1952. The conceit was to match up famous lovers. As Mom strolled out in a general's uniform, with dark glasses, a corncob pipe, and a hat with a visor thick with the golden oak leaves called "scrambled eggs"—a ringer for General MacArthur—out from the opposite wing strolled an exact double.

But WNNS began to lose money. For a long time our mother tried to interest her former bosses at the *Times* in subscribing to it. Signing up the premier paper in the country would open the floodgates to new clients, she believed. But her erstwhile superiors would have none of it. In January 1947, she pitched the idea directly to Mr. Sulzberger. She began by saying that she hadn't wanted to capitalize on her prior association with the *Times*. "We wanted very much to stand on our own feet, to prove ourselves. . . . Well, now we would seem to have made good." She said WNNS had a network of seventy-four string correspondents, both in the United States and abroad, and that they often turned up stories before the *Times* did. As a result, her client newspapers, she asserted, "are beating you throughout the country." There was no need to settle the issue of what constituted women's news: that had been obscured by "a lot of theoretical hogwash—so why not just think of it as a catch-all category for news about family, children, health, education and welfare?" Pointedly, she summed up: "It would mean a great deal to us to have you as a client and, frankly, we think you need us, too." She suggested sending over a week's worth of stories for evaluation. Her letter prompted internal memos from both James and Markel, who said they had no need of such a service but agreed, reluctantly, to take a look at it over the course of a week. James, galled by the assertion that her little outfit was more nimble than his mighty enterprise, ended his memo on a sarcastic note. "I am just as bearish on it as when I told Mrs. Darnton we would not want it." Not surprisingly, after a week's worth of stories, WNNS failed the test.

From that point on, the fate of WNNS was sealed. It might have failed anyway. Using the mail to deliver the stories was an anachronism even then, when most other news was dispatched by Teletype. The system was simply too slow. Every evening, a young man traipsed over to the post office on West Forty-second Street with story packets. Hours were lost in sorting them and routing them, two or three days in sending them, a couple more hours on the other end in the newspapers' mailrooms. That meant that the stories couldn't contain breaking news, and even when they were trend stories about significant issues, they ended up sounding like features. Meanwhile, papers everywhere had started hiring women's editors, generating their own coverage. All these factors tended to make the service seem like a frill, valuable enough when times were flush but the first thing to be dropped when they were tight.

Nonetheless, the subjects of interest that WNNS dealt with—the readjustment to life at home, the successful raising of children, juvenile delinquency, family problems, the growing divorce rate—all went to the heart of the pressing social concerns in 1950s America. So the idea at the core of the news service made sense, even if the business model couldn't support it. For my family's sake, it would have been better if WNNS had gone belly-up right away. But as it was, it limped along until 1954, and my mother kept pumping money in, trying to keep it afloat. "It was always a struggle," recalled Henry Stern (later New York City's parks commissioner), who worked there as a City University undergraduate in 1952. "I remember Orvil Dryfoos, who was publisher in training, coming down to ask for the rent whenever it was past due—one hundred and twenty-five dollars a month. He looked sheepish. Sometimes your mother and Ms. Crowley would hide if they knew he was coming."

A balance sheet from that year, 1952, tells the story. Assets: $4,138.34. Liabilities: $107,581.23. Total cumulative deficit: $168,182.93. An accompanying folder in a pile of material kept in an attic these many years tells the same sad tale. It is bulging with scribbled notes, letters from my mother pleading for money and bankbooks documenting a gradual accretion of savings and a precipitate withdrawal of the entire sum.

All of this made me realize in a visceral way, like a punch to the stomach, that she must have been suffering on all those nights when she didn't come home in time and all those Sunday mornings when we jumped into her bed and demanded her full attention. In her attempts to fulfill the dual roles—the provider and the nurturer—she was failing at the one and not doing so very well at the other. The knowledge of this, had she been able to admit it head-on, would have been insupportable. In later years, she used to joke about a cavalier attitude toward financial security, saying, "Money is something you throw off the back of a speeding train." But I knew the attitude was a pose, a defense. On a deep level, she was oppressed by the weight of her failure as a businesswoman.

Nothing that happened to her while she was at the paper hurt her as much as what occurred on November 28, 1954. On that day, the *Times* ran a Sunday book review of *The Children Grew*. She had been counting on the book, in her unrealistic, Micawber-like, something-will-turn-up fashion, to bail us out of penury. She must have envisioned a strong, sympathetic review, which would set off waves of rave reviews elsewhere and turn her failure at WNNS into a moral and aesthetic triumph. It did not work out that way. The *Book Review* editor assigned the review to Shirley Jackson, the author of, among other works, "The Lottery," the misanthropic short story about a town whose citizens achieve civic serenity by holding a lottery each year to choose one of their own to stone to death. The editor undoubtedly thought of Ms. Jackson because she had written a book about bringing up her children—its acerbic tone captured by its title, *Life Among the Savages*. In any case, the matchup turned out cruel. Ms. Jackson panned Mom's book. It was a heartless piece of writing. "Mrs. Darnton brings to her children—and to her book as well—a good deal of soap-opera courage, a fair amount of sentimental mysticism and only the smallest edge of humor." One observation was certainly accurate, if not terribly perspicacious: "Mrs. Darnton's boys live with the image of their hero-father constantly before their eyes." But what followed cut my mother to the quick because it turned the thing she was proudest of—her fortitude—inside out by suggesting she was wallowing in self-pity. "One has the uncomfortable feeling that although it is impossible to quarrel with Mrs. Darnton for her devotion to her husband, her book would be easier to read with just a little less of the last-letter-to-my-sons kind of thing. What may well be courageous, self-sacrificing and noble in the doing can readily become self-indulgent and tear-jerking in the telling."

After that review, Mom, sinking ever deeper into alcoholism, rarely spoke about her book.

In some ways, I suppose, my mother was a visionary. In 1974, six years after she died, my wife and I were invited to spend a Sunday at Hillandale, the Sulzberger estate in Stamford, Connecticut. It was a place of rolling hills and ample forests, cut through by paths that had benches placed at intervals, complete with wooden boxes into which servants had placed copies of that day's *Times*. There we met Iphigene Sulzberger, the grand old lady of the family dynasty. As she was then—the daughter, wife, mother-in-law, and mother of the four successive publishers—she was the not-so-secret power behind the scenes and the keeper of family lore. We got to know her well over the following years, but I remember most vividly that first meeting. She received us in the splendor of the mansion. Nervously, we managed to intercept our three-year-old daughter, Kyra, as she tried to pull priceless vases off the antique tables and pour juice on the carpets. Happily, we all withdrew outside to lounge beside the swimming pool. There Mrs. Sulzberger knelt down as we talked, surrounded by a blanket of grass. She began sifting through it with her aged fingers, picking out crabgrass and putting it in a little pile, as if she were expelling uninvited riffraff. "Amazing how difficult it is to get rid of it," she said. "Why is it that the weeds are always stronger than the flowers?"

Then the conversation turned personal and she began reminiscing about my mother. She said she was "a remarkable woman." And she added, "I followed the goings-on at the paper from a distance. In terms of women's rights and what women wanted to read, she was way ahead of her time. I wish she could have lived today to see herself vindicated."

I thought for a moment of telling her how hard it had been for my mother and how badly she thought the paper had treated her. But I didn't. Mrs. Sulzberger's remark seemed to come out of nowhere, a non sequitur, like my mother's warning about the *Times* delivered on that beach so many years before, and it was difficult to know how to respond to it.

In the summer of 1953, Bob and I were sent to stay with our uncle and aunt and their four children in Media, Pennsylvania. At the time I had no idea why we were being sent there, but I didn't question it. Our three male cousins were close to us in age, and so it seemed natural enough that we should go for a visit. Only years later did I figure out that we were on a forced sabbatical to give Mom a chance to dry out.

The summer passed in suspended animation. David Choate, my mother's youngest brother, and his family lived in one of the early houses in a Levittown-type development in Delaware County, twelve miles west of Philadelphia. It was a small, squat brick house of low ceilings and thin walls, three rooms downstairs, three rooms upstairs. Outside were a newly seeded lawn, a curving black tarmac road set off by high curbs, and one or two baby trees tethered to rubber leashes, as if they wanted to run away. It was a vast flatland still under construction. On either side, as far as the eye could see, were similar brick houses; two blocks away the wooden frames of other houses were going up, and two blocks beyond that, the foundations were being dug, and beyond that, more tarmac was being laid down by road crews. It was the kind of place depicted in scores of cartoons: identical men leaving identical houses carrying identical briefcases down identical walkways.

What I remember most about that summer was the consistency and regularity, a soporific boredom. Every day at noon, our aunt served us children lunch: chicken noodle or tomato soup and bologna or peanut butter and jelly sandwiches on white bread. At six o'clock, dinner at the same oval table with the faux walnut veneer—chicken or hamburgers—except now Uncle Dave was there, a quiet man with a long, melancholy face. Beyond mealtimes, there was little to do. We rarely went anywhere. We hung around in the backyard, waiting for the afternoon start of *Bob Horn's Bandstand* on Channel 6 (the forerunner of Dick Clark), a new dance show out of Philly that made me nostalgic for the girls of Westport, since we had just started boy-girl parties and what passed for dating at the movies. The high point came when my cousin and I figured out how to make some pocket money by carting around a wagon of Kool-Aid and selling it to the construction workers. Bob picked up some cash working as a caddie at a nearby golf course.

The days were hot; the hours ticked by in slow motion. I felt as if I were on a moonscape, a bland, moribund place on the periphery of everything I cared about. And yet I got along with my cousins, and my aunt and uncle were friendly. Eventually, I came to realize that in the midst of all that boredom was something positive. The day-to-day rhythm of the humdrum was medicinal. There was something to be said for consistency and regularity—they made life seem secure. Toward the end of our stay, Uncle Dave took Bob for a stroll to have a talk. He told him that he realized things were tough at home but that there was not much he could do to help us over the long run. At one point he said that the two of us might have to go to foster homes. We should prepare ourselves. Bob didn't tell me this until many years later.

We returned home at the summer's end, to find that our house had come alive. The lawn was cut, fresh lemonade was in the refrigerator, and Mom seemed revivified. She was happy, full of plans and promises, and, most of all, her eyes were large, as if they had popped open. They seemed to crackle with her old animation. I asked her if she had been "groggy" lately and she said, no, not to worry—those days were over; she was feeling much better. And she had discovered the cause of her grogginess. It was the house's well water, which had never been properly tested. It contained some unhealthy minerals. To prove the case, she showed off a watercooler she had bought and installed in the dining room, giant bottles of pure mineral water. We would all drink it from now on. I was overjoyed to learn that our bad days were behind us.

The sad news was that Inell had gone. We didn't learn the details, just that her departure had to do with the "rough patch" we had gone through, the difficulty of pulling together enough money to pay her on time every week. Mom appeared to feel that, after being with us all those years, Inell had been less than loyal in not sticking around. But with characteristic optimism she pointed out that we were big boys now and didn't need her. We'd manage fine, just the three of us. In fact, to ease the transition, she had arranged for us to be invited to dinner at the house of Inell's new employer, the Katzes. Perhaps Inell would even cook our favorite dessert, lemon meringue pie. When the dinner took place the following week, it turned out to be a fiasco. Bob and I wanted only to visit with Inell in the kitchen, while she was scurrying about nervously trying to put on a feast that would please her new boss. She made it clear that we were "underfoot." The dinner conversation was awkward. As Inell served us, I kept looking to her for some sign that she missed us as much as we missed her. Making small talk, Mom noted that I was a fan of "pop music." Mr. Katz brightened at this and promptly showed me his collection of jazz and show tunes, not a single one of which I was familiar with. The kind of music I liked were these new songs with a heavy beat, like Bill Haley's "Crazy Man, Crazy," which were pushing out traditional songs like "Stranger in Paradise" and "I Love Paris" on Lucky Strike's *Your Hit Parade*. "That's not music; that's nothing but noise," sputtered Mr. Katz. Even the lemon meringue pie seemed to have lost its savor.

Without Inell, there was no one at home when I returned from school each day. I reveled in my new emancipation. When friends came over, I'd raid the refrigerator. I'd fix us a snack while pulling out a couple of raw eggs and I'd toss them over my shoulder while they, shocked, tried to catch them before they splattered on the floor. I was signaling: Anything goes in this anarchic household.

We had the run of the place. On a hill in the woods behind our house was a decaying shack, which became a clubhouse for all my buddies. They gathered there after school. One afternoon I engineered an elaborate plot to entice the class bully over. We punished him, strapping him to a bedspring and slapping his belly until it turned red, and then proffered a document pledging that he would straighten out and give up his bellicose ways. He signed it. The rest of the afternoon we all played football.

I still liked creating miniature villages tucked away in hidden places outdoors. But now, the thrill of destruction entered the picture. I designed the bridges and houses to come crashing down in landslides and earthquakes, and on the Fourth of July, I placed firecrackers and cherry bombs in strategic spots—beneath the cars, under the town hall—to wreak mayhem. I'd try to light the fuses all at the same time, which I could never quite manage. I also had a more permanent microworld—an American Flyer toy railroad set that Mom helped me with. We placed it on a twelve-foot-by-six-foot piece of plywood, using plaster of Paris to create tunnels and sculpted hills and, over time, adding a station, a farm, a rural crossroads, and a couple of houses complete with chopped twigs for stacks of wood by the back door. One day, acting on a sudden impulse, I gave it all away and told my astounded mother that I needed the plywood for a tree house. That was only partly true. I suddenly felt I no longer wanted to be the lord and master of such a perfect pretend little community.

I was also developing a fascination with criminals. To some extent, this mirrored society's interest of the time, a remnant of the public preoccupation with gangsters during the great crime epoch of the 1930s and 1940s. Each week, I listened fervently to "Gang Busters" on the radio, my heart racing at the end when the announcer issued a real live "wanted" bulletin for an escaped killer known to be "armed and dangerous." I was sure the killer was in our neighborhood, probably in the bushes outside our house, which kept me tossing and turning in bed. I cadged copies of *The Saturday Evening Post,* which printed stories of bank robbers and killers. The magazine rarely disappointed, illustrating the articles with grainy black-and-white photos, usually mug shots, of ruthless-looking criminals. I especially prized its annual "Ten Most Wanted." Of all the criminals, I most admired Willie Sutton because he was shrewd and acted alone, although it was hard not to make room for the charismatic John Dillinger, who was said to have escaped from jail with a phony gun carved from soap and blackened with shoe polish.

With the help of three friends, I composed a book called *Crime Incopurated* (an unintentional misspelling of *incorporated*), which documented the exploits of our antiheroes. We added essays and short stories, antisocial in nature, and even a section providing tips for criminals, a perverse mirror version of Dick Tracy's "Crime Stoppers Textbook." I took the book to school one day and it created such a sensation during a music class in the auditorium that the teacher spied it and confiscated it. Four hours later, I crept into his office, spotted it on his desk, and grabbed it. As a purloined object, it took on added value.

Not long after we returned from our uncle's house in Media, Mom began working long hours again and then appeared fatigued and began turning groggy again. Sometimes she was so tired, she didn't manage to get up in time to go to work. On Sundays, once or twice, she placed calls to the home of the owner of Calise's liquor store; we would drive there and park around the back and he would open the door to let her in while I waited in the car. She would come back carrying a paper bag. As inconceivable as it now appears, I still had no idea what was going on.

I soon noticed that her driving was erratic, especially at night. When we had to pick Bob up somewhere—say at basketball practice at the junior high school—the trip turned into a nightmare. On winding country roads, our car would weave all over the place, sometimes crossing into the wrong lane and riding up on the opposite shoulder. Sitting in the front seat, I would close my eyes. The headlights would swerve, pointing first at some tree trunks, then a clump of bushes and a driveway. I'd reach over to grab the wheel and straighten the car. Sometimes I simply gave up and put myself in the hands of fate. I'd duck on the floor and cower there with my eyes closed, waiting for the crash. The moment we arrived at our destination and the car stopped, I would heave a sigh of relief. For then Bob would take over the driving. I felt my body relax. I'd climb into my customary place, lying flat in the rear well for the collapsible top while my mother scooted over into the passenger seat and Bob slid behind the wheel. He would frown as he concentrated, shifting gears in an H-pattern as he had been taught by Uncle Ben, sometimes grinding them, straining to sit taller to be able to see better. He was only fourteen. When we'd get home, we'd help Mom to bed, swinging her feet up on the mattress and tucking her in. As a rule we didn't need to undress her, because while she was driving, or attempting to, she was already clothed in her nightgown, which was covered with a robe, and wearing slippers.

Throughout this time, Bob was becoming more and more a lifesaver to me. He had taken over the role of the protector, becoming less of a brother and more of a father. I knew that I could lead a child's life because of him alone, that he was a shield covering me from the dangers that would otherwise crush me. At times, I almost luxuriated in my sense of irresponsibility. With a kind of obsession, I insisted upon my ignorance, upon my right to a childhood of innocence and, even at times, joy. With desperation, I concentrated on unimportant details and short-term pleasures. The knowledge that I had, say, a sleepover date on the coming weekend was enough to sustain me. I remained detached from adults and never told anyone about the problems at home. Even while denying their existence, I recognized that they were at the core of things, a secret wrapped within secrets. Yet I could never get at the core secret, because I did not want to. I saw that the world, tenuous and full of fears, could never be complete or comprehensible to me. I became superstitious and compulsive. If I saw a Lucky Strike pack on the sidewalk, I had to step on it. I never stepped on graves, walked under ladders, or broke mirrors. Any superstition I encountered, I immediately adopted, a fall guy for snake-oil salesmen and religious cranks. If I spun the radio dial and came across a sermon, I had to stop and listen to it or at the least turn the radio off, move the dial, and turn it back on. I carried a rabbit's paw to baseball games and rubbed it while playing right field, praying that a ball would not come to me or that, if it did, I would catch it. I seemed to derive pleasure from superficial, meaningless things and rituals—a collection of jelly glasses with cartoon figures on them, the daily habit of watching *Captain Video* on television, the number of times I could jump on a pogo stick without falling. I became fanatical in my fandom of the Dodgers. Their winning assumed an importance beyond anything else in the universe. I admired Jackie Robinson and Carl Furillo and Gil Hodges, but I loved Roy Campanella; when "Campy" was behind home plate, everything seemed in place. During the World Series, against the unbeatable Yankee machine, I lived and died on every pitch, falling on the couch with my fingers crossed as Joe Black went into his windup. When the series ended in disaster, as it invariably did, I swooned in misery.

I also turned into a religious fanatic for a short period. Convinced that I was destined to spend eternity in hell, I vowed to forsake all manner of petty thievery and other behavior that had put me on the path to fire and brimstone. This was strange, because the denomination in which I had been raised was the Congregational Church, which did not place a great deal of emphasis on the perils of the afterlife. The church I attended was a picture postcard of a New England church, a simple but majestic white clapboard structure with a soaring steeple surrounded by a sea of green grass. Yet somewhere along the line, I came across the darker strains of theology, and I embraced them, imagining a Lucifer personally eyeing me and preparing a future of fiendish cruelty. The transgressions that I and my friends engaged in were minor—shoplifting plastic toys at the five-and-ten and the like—but I knew they were sufficient to send me to everlasting damnation. At one point a group of us began sneaking into the movie theater on Saturday afternoons. We'd wait until the manager unlocked the doors, then slip into the empty theater and hide under the seats when he swept through with a flashlight on an inspection. Clearly, this alone was going to consign me to hell. One Saturday, as we assembled in front of the theater, I announced self-righteously that I was going to pay for my ticket. The other boys were surprised at my turnabout until I began to describe vividly the horrors that awaited me—and them—unless we changed our ways. We all paid. Some days later, one of the boys announced that his parents had told him that hell did not really exist in a physical state; it was a sort of spiritual symbol, standing in for something else, like Santa Claus. I questioned him closely. He articulated the position convincingly and immediately I felt a weight drop away. Shortly afterward, I gave up my fanatical religious phase.

I resumed having arguments with Mom when she came in to say good night. The grogginess was getting worse. She was now sleeping a good deal of the time. When I awoke for school, I saw that her bedroom door was sometimes closed, and when I left to catch the school bus, I would go upstairs on some pretext and see that it still had not opened. She stayed home most days, dressed all day in a nightgown.

At about this time, when I was in the sixth grade, we lost our house. Bob and I weren't told what had happened, but we knew from bits and pieces of information that Mom's business wasn't doing well. In retrospect, it's clear that she had sunk the mortgage into the Women's National News Service. For the time being, until things picked up, we were informed, we'd just have to rent. The place we found was an apartment in a rambling, run-down old house in the poor section of town. The house was a monstrosity, painted battleship gray, falling apart. It loomed up like a Charles Addams cartoon at the end of Saxon Lane, a dead-end street marked off by two crumbling pillars. It was situated just a stone's throw from the river and next to the railroad tracks.

Overnight, we went from a place of about five thousand square feet to one that had five hundred. The apartment had two rooms—a living room, now heaped with our sofas, desks, and other large pieces of furniture, and a bleak bedroom. Sandwiched in between the two rooms was a four-foot-wide galley for a kitchen and a narrow bathroom. Mom and I slept in the bedroom, our beds separated by a bureau and a Japanese screen. Bob slept in a partially enclosed back porch. In winter, he huddled under a mountain of blankets.

The house shook when trains went rattling past. At first, we were kept awake by the noise, but eventually we adjusted to it and were able to sleep. My friends liked hanging out on the riverbank and playing on the tracks. We'd put pennies on the steel rails, step back to watch the train thunder past, then retrieve the smashed bits of hot copper. We experimented with other coins and small items but drew the line at things that couldn't fit into our pockets, for fear they might derail the speeding locomotive. No friend remarked that we seemed to have fallen on hard times, though I imagined them all thinking that. Children are more aware of the climbs and slides on the socioeconomic ladder than is generally recognized. I remember Mom trying to put a good face on things, cheerfully cooking oatmeal for breakfast because it "clings to the ribs" and telling us that the important thing was that the three of us were together. My hound dog, Nicky, came with us, of course, but after a week or so, he went missing. A phone call came from Boss; Nicky had turned up there, just the way he had in the old days after I boarded the school bus. We fetched him home, but after a week or so he disappeared again. From then on, Nicky commuted from our apartment to Boss's house and back, a trip of some fifteen miles, which took him across the busy Post Road, spending two or three weeks in each place. I felt hurt every time he left and grateful when he returned. During one of his sojourns with us, he woke us at two in the morning with ferocious barking. It came from the building's central hallway, then from the front stairs, and finally from outside. A neighbor from across the hall told us that he had chased away a burglar. Eventually, Nicky moved in with Boss and stopped coming to our place altogether.

We weren't used to living in the same house with others and we didn't go out of our way to become friends with our neighbors, as if remaining aloof could keep alive the fiction that we had the house to ourselves. There was one other boy living there; he had an odd tic, a way of screwing his eyeballs to the upper corners of his sockets and when I spent time with him, I acquired it, too. At other times, I would contemplate mortality. I would place my hand over my heart and feel the beats and wonder how many beats I had left in my allotted lifetime.

Mom would have periods in which she appeared to be her old self. I could almost feel her willing these periods on, trying to rally in the face of some unnamed force weighing her down. There were still times in which she could cook up adventures that made life scintillating. I had long wanted a skunk as a pet, ever since seeing the movie *Bambi,* and so for my twelfth birthday, she bought me one. I had been told they made affectionate pets, once they were deodorized. I named it "Airwick" and imagined carrying it with me, looped lovingly around my neck. But sadly, the skunk had been caught full-grown and was not tame. Let loose in our apartment, it hid under my bed, and when I went to pet it, touching the frizzed white strip on its back, it sunk its capped teeth deep into my hand. From there it ran and hid under our claw-footed bathtub, a sanctuary where it remained during the day, emerging only at night or on those occasions when we took hot baths. The skunk was a disaster, and we soon got rid of it.

I was fascinated by the river. To reach it, I had only to follow a short path through a grove of pine trees, emerging on the bank near the base of a giant stone tower that supported a railroad bridge. The river rose and fell with the tides. When the tide was out, a blanket of slippery green slime covered the rocks, and a slightly nauseating smell of pollution and sewage hung in the air. I wanted to set a raft on the river and let it carry me, the way Huck Finn did. A friend and I built a large one by lashing together the heavy creosote railroad ties. It took two weeks to construct it, and just as we were hauling it to the water's edge to launch it, a railroad man peered over the edge of the bridge and spotted us. He ordered us to stop and then, more calmly, explained that the New York, New Haven and Hartford line would be legally responsible if we drowned, which, he said, was a distinct possibility. Several weeks later, my mother bought me a small skiff. It had a large hole in the bottom, which I patched over. A friend and I took it out on the river and made it to the center of town, paddling furiously and bailing out the water that seeped in relentlessly. Once we made it past the town bridge, and then made it back, we never went again. The expedition had lost its romance.

One afternoon my brother, several friends, and I were hanging out on the riverbank, idly tossing rocks at a small white buoy about forty feet out in the water. Only rarely did one of us manage to hit it, and whenever that happened, we'd all cheer. Suddenly, a wild-looking man came screaming down the path, running so fast he skidded on the earth, as if he were sliding into third base. Moments before landing on the ground, he let fly a rock the size of a fist. It struck me in the right thigh. I didn't cry out and no one noticed. The man leapt up and continued charging at us. When he reached us, he was literally hopping mad, yelling something about "private property"—it turned out it was his buoy that we were using for target practice. Eventually, he calmed down somewhat. At that point, Bob saw tears in my eye. Realizing that I had been struck, he turned on the man, straightening up and yelling back, "You hit my brother!" Our friends moved toward him. The man blanched, mumbled an apology, and quickly slunk away. That moment remains a jewel in my memory—I can hold it to the light and examine it from any angle, all of them pleasing: the turning of tables on an adult, my martyrdom, the thrill of gang power, and, most of all, my brother as an avenging angel.

Bob rarely got into trouble, but once he did. He and three friends played hooky at the local swimming hole, Lee's Dam, and were found by the police officer charged with investigating juvenile crime. They were taken to school in disgrace. That evening, Mom and Bob had a talk. She asked him why he'd done it. Hanging his head, he said he didn't know. There was a long silence. She broke it, saying she thought she knew: He had been too good for too long. He must have felt the need to kick over the traces—everyone did sooner or later. His face brightened. "That's it, Mom," he said. "That's exactly it." She hugged him. I heard this conversation from a short distance, standing in the shadows. I, too, had been playing hooky that day—Dickie and I had spent it in the woods, smoking. I told her this—leaving out the smoking part—and she sighed. "What do you think—should I give myself up?" I asked. She finally just laughed and shook her head no.

Not long afterward, the same police officer, a lean man with acne scars on his face, came to our place, looking for me. Raisin had called, his voice cracking nervously, to let me know the cop was on his way. He was coming to retrieve some items that Raisin had stolen from a neighbor's shed—maritime maps, flares, a flashlight, binoculars, and other things. Raisin had asked me to stash them for him, and I had buried them in a grove near the road. I dug them up and had them waiting when the cop arrived. He warned me that there might be serious repercussions, that theft was a felony and so was holding stolen goods. I worried about the threat for weeks and then, when nothing came of it, gradually forgot it.

I began writing gruesome stories for English assignments. I had always liked spinning tales—during sleepovers, we would take turns telling ghost stories, and I was usually nominated to cap the evening with a gothic horror. But now my proclivity for describing eviscerated corpses and the like spilled over into my homework. I would write such passages as: "The cop walked into the bedroom, surprised to find the bed overturned and Mrs. Ferguson's guts splayed upon the wall and her scalp hanging from the chandelier." My English teacher, Miss DeMers, called me in for a talk. Why, she wondered, did I feel a need to write so graphically? Didn't I realize that reading passages like that was upsetting? I pondered the question—I had never thought about it and was curious myself to discover the answer. Perhaps, I said, I wanted to shock people so that they would feel something strongly. Or maybe it was language—I was experimenting with it, trying to find different ways of saying things. Had she noticed, for example, that I had found four different ways to describe Mrs. Ferguson's guts—some of them sort of funny? She frowned and told me not to write like that anymore. From then on I censored myself and was delighted to find that for some reason the stories came out even scarier.

Around this time Mom stopped coming home for dinner. It was hard to predict her comings and goings. She would be groggy for days on end, then abruptly go into the city to work and stay there until long after dark. This was a new development; up to now, especially once Inell had left, she had returned in time to feed us. How would we eat without her? Bob could drive, but he wasn't much of a cook. Still, he tried his hand at making a dinner, invariably thawing out some frozen vegetables and frying hot dogs or hamburgers. That became our routine. A guidance counselor at school somehow caught wind of it, he told me years later, and with feigned casualness asked Bob, "Is it true you cook dinner most days?" Sensing a danger—that we might be separated—he replied, "Certainly not."

On special nights, Mom made arrangements with a small Italian restaurant to feed us on demand. We'd run up a tab eating grinders and she would take care of it later. The restaurant was across from the train station, about a mile's walk, which would have been fine except that the only way to get there was to cross the railroad bridge over the river on a pedestrian walk that seemed more like a catwalk. I was petrified at the prospect. I had seen, from the safety of solid land, what happened to the bridge when a train roared across, how it trembled and even seemed to sway. Once or twice, I had been caught on the catwalk and the wind rush from the engine seemed powerful enough to press me against the wooden railing and possibly hurl me over into the water fifty feet below. Now every evening, twice an evening, I had to negotiate this perilous journey. I timed my trips to avoid trains. I waited on one side of the bridge, peering down the tracks, sometimes putting my ear to them (a trick picked up from the Westerns) until I became convinced that the coast was clear. Then I walked rapidly along the catwalk, ready to break into a sprint at the first sign of a train. The trip back, my belly loaded up with spaghetti and meatballs, was even worse in the dark, though with the advantage that the train's headlight would provide plenty of advance warning, almost enough for me to make it across the catwalk unscathed. It was my very own Bridge of Sighs.

The saving compensation for these problems was my social life. Girls had now become the focal point of my and my friends' existence and we pursued them everywhere, trying hard not to appear as if we were. There were any number of places where we could get together with them; at Miss Comer's dancing class in the gymnasium of the local YMCA, where we wore black suits and white gloves and the popular girls filled out tasseled dance cards in the first five minutes; at Compo Beach, where we migrated to one particular section, spreading out blankets close to one another, the girls rubbing suntan lotion on one another and the boys wrestling in the sand; at the Saturday movies at the Fine Arts, where double-dating, triple-dating, even quadruple-dating meant the possibility of whispered endearments and stolen kisses; at parties, where everyone waited for the moment when the host would produce an empty bottle and place it in the center of a circle; and, of course, at junior high school, where the intrigues were hatched in notes passed around in class and during conspiratorial clusters at recess. Through it all, we boys were led around by the nose. Girls joined us as girlfriends and then broke up with us and switched places in a bewildering parade of matchups that seemed to have been planned without us. We knew nothing about these schemes and suspected that they had been hatched during secret conclaves, but we accepted them passively and willingly. What else could we do? The girls were so much more focused and single-minded than we were. We were clueless.

This frenzy of activity allowed me to persuade myself that things were not so bad after all. I imagined that there were plenty of people worse off than I was—I could see them in class, the boys without girlfriends. Life still had possibilities. And from time to time, Mom would come alive, acting like her old self, to prop up the illusion that our ship was still steaming ahead. Several times I allowed myself to wonder what things would be like if our father had not been killed. It was the year of Eddie Fisher's hit song "Oh My Pa-Pa," which I added to my growing pile of 45s. I sometimes played it on my Victrola when I was alone, trying to look soulfully off into the distance as he crooned about how his dear father would bounce him on his knee, but I was aware that I was striking a pose. I was trying to express something, a deprivation of some sort, even if it was only a caricature of it. I was playacting to determine if the loss of my father was real, while covering up the loss of my mother, which was genuine. It was emotional camouflage.

But soon life was to change radically. One evening Mom announced that she had given up on the business and accepted a job in Washington. We would be moving there. First, Bob and I would stay behind to finish up the school year in Westport, a matter of some nine months. Then we would join her in the capital. The news came as a blow to me, but, being practiced in short-term thinking and immediate gratification, I postponed imagining just how big a change it would be. We were sent to live with a woman we did not know well, a friend of Mom's whom I will call Betsy Evans. She had just moved to Westport after a spell abroad as a career diplomat, apparently after a scandal (I was later to learn that she had fallen in love with a Czech while stationed in Prague; the man turned out to be a spy and she was drummed out of the diplomatic corps). Betsy rented a run-down house on Riverside Avenue. When I heard the address, I was horrified. The impoverished family that had lived there had lost all their children to polio. For two weeks, the school had taken up collections in the classrooms and we all had contributed our pocket change in a mood of self-congratulatory charity. The house, which I thought must have harbored the disease, loomed large in my nightmares. The banisters, the windowsills, the toilet seats—any or all of them could be diseased. We moved in and over time I forgot about the stricken family and the threat.

Bob's room and mine were next to each other on the third floor. The furnishings were basic: a steel-frame bed with a thin mattress and a single chest of drawers—nothing else. The floors were covered with peeling linoleum and the walls were painted a dull green. Downstairs, the house was a little nicer, though small, decorated with European artifacts. Betsy had two Airedales. I learned to say "Come," "Go," "No," and "Good Dog" in Czech so that I could walk them.

The time passed quickly, too much so. I wished it would slow down so that I could stay in Westport forever. We fell into a routine. Before school in the mornings, gathered around the breakfast table, we watched the *Today* show with the congenial Dave Garroway and his cohost, the chimp J. Fred Muggs. The producers sometimes interrupted the show to bring live coverage of atomic-bomb blasts in Nevada, and I soon became fixated on the bomb. I had been primed for years to consider its horrors. We'd seen instructional films in school: scenes of air-raid sirens going off, crowds scurrying off the city streets, families taking refuge in basements. In one film, the father, nailing a curtain over a cellar window, got a whiff of radiation; it struck him like a puff of invisible smoke. But seeing the bomb explode live on TV, watching the tower that held it crumble, the billowing dust, the gigantic mushroom cloud rising up from the desert like an avenging monster—now *that* got my attention. It far surpassed any sci-fi movie. I wrote numerous letters to the Atomic Energy Commission and other such bodies, receiving back a flood of pamphlets and brochures extolling the benefits of atomic energy. But of course it wasn't the peaceful uses I was interested in. It was the monstrous prospect, and mystery, of so much instant annihilation that I found irresistible.

Two days after my twelfth birthday, I returned from school, to find a letter addressed to me in the mailbox. It had a New York postmark, which was unusual. Inside was a short handwritten letter, saying that the writer had been told about my birthday and so was dropping me a note. What a coincidence, he continued, his birthday was the same month. The letter was unsigned. I shrugged and tossed it into the wastebasket. Several weeks later my mother, during a phone call, asked if I had received any mail lately. I told her about the mysterious letter. She said nothing. About a week later, I found another letter in the mailbox in the same handwriting. The author said he was so sorry he had forgotten to sign the letter—he must have been too excited, because just as he finished it, he got a phone call informing him he had been selected as the Most Valuable Player that year. He added, "So I'll sign this one twice." And he did: "Roy Campanella. Roy Campanella." Even from as far away as Washington, my mother could reach out and with her inventiveness make something fine happen.

One day, I broke two beautiful, expensive vases. I was playing ball in the living room, bouncing it against the wall, when the vibration caused a large mirror over the mantel to dislodge and pitch forward. I grabbed the mirror, halting its fall, then watched helplessly as the vases, one on each end, tumbled onto the floor. I replaced the mirror, then picked up the pieces and reassembled them as best I could. Time passed—weeks, months even. I forgot all about it. One Saturday, lying in bed, I heard Betsy cry out three floors below. I ran downstairs and she was holding the pieces of a vase in her hand. I realized she had not yet seen the other one. Slowly, guiltily, I recounted what had happened. When I told her about the second vase, and led her to it, I saw her eyes glisten with tears. She had to sit down. I blushed in shame.

It mitigated some of my wild behavior that I was getting good marks at school. I was moved up to a more advanced math class and the teacher there took an interest in me. He was also the coach of varsity basketball, and Bob, now in ninth grade, the last year of junior high, was on the starting team. The teacher, Gordon Hall, appointed me as official scorer, presumably to give me a position to buck up my self-esteem. I enjoyed traveling around with the team, sitting at a wooden table courtside, along with a scorer from the rival team, assiduously marking down every basket and every foul. But I was conscious of the striking difference between playing the game, dribbling down the court with all eyes upon you, and sitting there anonymously writing down what happened.

Before long, the school year ended. I did not want to leave and found it painful to say good-bye to my friends. I was sure they would soon forget me and that I would pine away for all of them. On the next-to-last day, the math teacher offered me a ride home. As we arrived at the house where I was staying, he pulled the car to the shoulder and peered at it. He frowned and seemed disturbed by the look of it. He reached over and patted me on the back, then grasped my hand to shake it and held on to it for what seemed like a long while. Then, his voice breaking, he wished me good luck.

Two days later, I left Westport.

CHAPTER 11

I drove to Washington with the family of friends, the twins Scott and Craig, who were headed on a sightseeing trip there. I hoped that being with them would make my departure a little easier—as if postponing it by an extra day or so. Bob was not going with us; he had made arrangements to spend the summer helping to build a school on an Indian reservation in New Mexico. Furthermore, he had won a scholarship to Phillips Academy Andover in Massachusetts, so he wouldn't be home during the coming school year. It began to dawn on me that I was now going to live alone with my mother in a strange city.

My sorrow over leaving Westport was lightened somewhat by my excitement over seeing Mom. We had not been in close touch in recent months—as always, I was an abysmal letter writer, and long-distance phone calls were reserved for emergencies—but she had led me to believe that her new job was going well. She was the press officer for the Children's Bureau of the Department of Health, Education and Welfare. Having a full-time paying job, bringing in a regular weekly salary, would be a relief after the financial tailspin of the past few years. The Women's National News Service had finally collapsed in bankruptcy that year, 1954.

My anticipation mounted as we drove down the turnpike, playing games by spotting animals along the way. I began a silent monologue, attempting to persuade myself that things might turn out all right, that Washington was going to be intriguing, maybe even exotic—after all, it was the nation's capital, not even a state. It had no representation in Congress; you could almost claim it wasn't even part of the United States. Plus, I'd get a chance to see the government in operation. Problem was, I didn't believe these rationalizations for a second. I began to long for my hometown an hour after we hit the road.

We arrived in Washington in the early afternoon. I had in my hand a slip of paper with the address of our new place on Newark Street, in the Northwest section. We drove up broad boulevards of embassies and restaurants and drugstores with the curious name of Peoples, across a bridge above the treetops of Rock Creek Park, and up and down various side streets. Houses of brick and stucco faced tiny front yards—a landscape that struck me as puny and confining. We got lost. Eventually we found my new place, a squat, sturdy-looking Victorian structure. Mr. Kuhner parked in front and suggested that I go in first, since I hadn't seen my mother in some time. I knocked at the front door. It was answered by a stooped man with a nimbus of white hair. He kindly explained that he was the owner and my mother was a renter, and he directed me to an adjacent door. It opened onto a staircase leading to the second floor. I bounded up the stairs. No one was home—or at least no one answered my knock. I turned the knob and stepped inside a small room, sparsely furnished. There were two doors. One, I could see, led to a bathroom. I opened the other. The bedroom was dimly lighted and it took a moment for my eyes to adjust. I saw a bed, mussed but empty. Next to it was an easy chair and there, dressed in a nightgown, heavily asleep, her head draped to one side and her mouth open, was my mother. I tried to wake her, but to no avail. She was, I saw at once, too groggy.

I went back outside. I told the Kuhners that Mom needed to rest a bit more—the two adults exchanged quick glances—and they invited me to have lunch with them. We spent the afternoon in a blitz of sightseeing. I became frenetic. I felt a sudden need to burn off energy. I proposed to the Kuhner twins that we climb the Washington Monument as many times as we could. After running up and down four times, we sprawled, exhausted, on the vast lawn of the Mall. Then they took me back to my new home. I said there was no need for them to climb the stairs, grabbed my one suitcase, thanked them, and leapt out of the car. Mom was still asleep when I arrived. I managed to get her into bed, made two peanut butter sandwiches, and, some hours later, found that the couch in the living room converted to a bed. I lay awake for hours, listening to my own breathing.

At some point during the night, my mother came to, slowly and not altogether coherent. She seemed surprised to see me there and asked what I had been doing. My voice dripping with sarcasm, I replied that I had been counting raindrops, looking at shadows, twiddling my thumbs. I saw her expression collapse into hurt and I regretted it instantly. I felt racked with guilt. Who was I to think only of myself and to add to her miseries at a time like this? The next few days passed in a blur.

That summer I was sent to stay with relatives in Michigan. They were on my father's side of the family and so I had not known any of them. They were welcoming. They kept appearing, dozens of them, it seemed, pouring out of cars, coming from different towns. And—to my astonishment—they all had the same last name as I: Darnton. I hadn't known anyone with that name outside our little circle of three.

The start of my visit was rocky. I wasn't sure this new Darnton family would like me, so I had prepared a rough list of jokes and favorite lines, a sort of crib sheet of what I took to be winning witticisms. As I went to my room in the evening, I was shocked to see that the woman of the house—my cousin, though she was more than twice my age—had unpacked my suitcase. The crib sheet had been placed in a drawer. I felt my face redden. She must have read it. I had been unmasked. At the very least, I couldn't use any of my prepared routines. I was on my own, with nothing to fall back on. How would I ever win their admiration and affection? That evening, around the dinner table, I dropped a cutting remark about Senator Joe McCarthy, who was then at the height of his crusade to root out Communists, and the same woman looked me square in the eye and said, "You shouldn't speak ill of Senator Joe McCarthy. He's an American hero." I was taken aback. I didn't know how to respond. I had never met a McCarthy supporter and had been raised to view him simply as the devil incarnate, with no specifics to back up that opinion. I probably wouldn't have offered them even if I'd had any.

Despite the start, the summer turned out okay. I went from relative to relative in a guest-passing relay that crisscrossed the state and eventually landed me in summer bungalows on the upper reaches of Lake Michigan. I slept out on the beach during the warm nights with my first cousins once removed, tried to water-ski, and spent three weeks on a farm. I also learned manners: A cousin who handed me an ice-cream cone was shocked when I didn't respond "Thank you." "What do you say?" she asked, and I could only give her blank looks. She took on my boorishness as a project and put me through a drill—to wait for others to start eating, not to look into the milk pitcher before pouring from it, to hold the door open for adults. By the summer's end, I could pass for polite—barely.

When I returned to Washington, Mom appeared to have improved somewhat. She had been going to work every day. Bob returned, too, and stayed a short while before heading up to Massachusetts. He was the subject of a segment on local TV. At the time the airwaves were filled with the phenomenon of juvenile delinquency and somehow my mother had pitched the idea of doing a countervailing piece on "a good boy." He was it. As cameramen and soundmen and a woman interviewer with a bouffant hairdo traipsed through his room, asking him about his experience in New Mexico, directing him to hold up to the camera the Hopi doll he had acquired there, I watched in admiration. My own brother on TV! It didn't strike me as odd that he was becoming famous—after all, he deserved it—but I could tell that all the attention made him self-conscious and miserable. He was submitting to it with clenched teeth. I wouldn't have traded places with him for the world—though I also knew that there was no chance that would ever happen.

A few weeks later I began Alice Deal Junior High School. After the Westport school, it seemed large and impersonal. During my first period, I got myself pegged as a wiseacre. The homeroom teacher told us to introduce ourselves by citing positive things about ourselves; she called on us one by one, and when she reached me, I glanced up at the clock, noted there were a mere forty-five minutes remaining and said I needed more time. She glared as the class broke up in laughter, then took a deep breath and told me to try again. I said that I had come from a town in Connecticut, and on the spur of the moment I decided to lie: I said I had been president of my class. It was important to me that my new classmates realize how popular I had been and how much I had given up by moving to their school.

As the days passed I felt myself a loner and became shy. I made friends but wasn't particularly fond of any of them, comparing them to the lifelong buddies I had had in Westport. I developed a crush on a girl in my class but never acted on it. There didn't seem to be any boy-girl parties down there. Were they all emotionally stunted? I concluded that my days of intimate friendships and flirtations had come to an end. I missed my New England woods—there was no place to go where you could be alone and lose yourself among the trees and streams. Restless, I explored Washington. I attended several sessions of the Army-McCarthy hearings, went paddle-boating in the Tidal Basin, took repeated tours of the FBI (looking for traces of Dillinger), and haunted the gruesome anatomical exhibits at the National Museum of Health and Medicine. As time went on, I amassed a thick collection of visitor's passes to the public gallery of the House of Representatives, signed by the congressmen and -women (or their secretaries), by passing myself off as a tourist from their home states. I took up trumpet lessons for a while, inspired by the Montgomery Clift character in *From Here to Eternity*. Each evening, I climbed out onto our roof and played taps to the setting sun, until a neighbor yelled at me to shut the hell up and threatened to call the cops.

I pined so much for Westport that Mom sent me there for a couple of days. I stayed with friends and accompanied them to school. My presence in a classroom was so disruptive—girls were passing me notes; boys were throwing things around—that the teacher, whom I didn't know, expelled me. She told me to report back after school. I did. As I entered the empty classroom, I could tell that she had forgotten about me. She had me clean the blackboard and perform a couple of other chores, and then we started talking. I liked her. She asked me if I liked Washington and I said no, that I hated it. She asked me why and I said, "Because I like it here." She said she understood. She had just moved to Westport, she added, and she missed her old hometown. The next day I returned to Washington. My sojourn in Westport only seemed to make things harder to bear.

With Bob gone, a hole was torn in our family. There was no one to look to for guidance, no one to drive the car home safely, no one to take charge in an emergency. Even if we hadn't talked about Mom's drinking—though in later years, Bob would insist he told me about it in the days before he left, something I have no memory of—I'd felt we somehow were confronting it together. Now I was suddenly vulnerable, as if the roof of our house had been ripped away by a tornado and I was huddling, helpless, in a corner.

Mom, meanwhile, bounced from job to job. The list of agencies for which she did public-relations work grew ever longer. She worked for outfits representing American Indians, aircraft owners and pilots, sufferers from arthritis and rheumatism, people with mental illness, criminals on parole and probation, and on and on. Each time, the story was the same: She would start out fine, fired up with enthusiasm, then encounter some bumps along the road, begin to skip workdays, succumb to "grogginess," and then lose the job. The periods of work grew shorter and shorter. We moved into a semiattached house farther up the street. Her mother died and she made it to the funeral in Philadelphia.

Bob came home on Christmas vacation, then Easter. With him in the house, I breathed easier. He seemed alarmed at what he found, though we didn't discuss it in detail. He noticed that we had been selling off our furniture. Once, I took a snapshot of him and inadvertently captured Mom in the background, slumped over in a chair. Weeks afterward, when she saw it, she flew into a rage. Was I trying to humiliate her? I had no idea what she was talking about. I stared at the photo—everything in it struck me as ordinary.

One Sunday, Mom announced that Carleton "Bill" Kent, the man who had been the correspondent for the *Chicago Daily Times* in the Pacific, was coming by for a visit. He and his wife, Janet, and their son lived in Arlington. Mom spoke of him with such respect and affection that it was clear his friendship with Barney gave him a special place in our pantheon. I had never before met a man who had been so close to my father in the war. And yet, during that visit, I acted younger than my age, hamming it up and playing the clown. As the adults sat on the porch having drinks, I took their son, a few years younger, into our backyard. At my instigation, we imitated them. "Let's be boozehounds," I said, and we staggered around, pretending to be drunk, holding imaginary drinks in our hands, chugging them, falling down, and giggling. When the time came for the Kents to leave, I wouldn't let go of the joke. We hiccupped and staggered, and I kept going on about "booze" and "boozehounds" even as my mother's face turned hard. She was clearly embarrassed, but I kept at it. Instead of shaking Kent's hand, I missed it by a foot. Finally, as their car pulled away, I pitched over and fell down in the street. "What is wrong with you?" she cried, turning away in anger. I had no idea, so as I picked myself up, I didn't answer.

The next summer I took a Greyhound bus to Texas and worked on a small ranch owned by Aunt Dixie's brother-in-law. It was a maturing experience. On the way I read my first serious work of literature (*Of Mice and Men*). We passed through the South, and I was shocked and angry at the separate drinking fountains and bathrooms and lunch counters in the bus stations. I thought of Inell: The idea that she would be consigned to separate facilities was infuriating. The ranch was four hours outside of Dallas. I rose every day at 5:30 to help feed the cattle. I learned to ride a horse, toss bales of hay out the back of a pickup, and help a cow give birth by pulling out the calf. I returned home taller and more confident. Mom was sick again, but this time she announced she had discovered the cause. Her liver was diseased, something called sclerosis. She would undergo an operation to have a portion of her liver removed and then she would be fine. "Does this mean you won't be groggy anymore?" I asked yet again. "That's exactly what it means," she replied. She had the operation, recovered at home, and was better for a while. But three weeks later, the grogginess struck again. Perhaps they hadn't removed enough of the liver, I speculated.

I became fearful and obsessive. I was convinced that thieves would break into the house we were renting or that the windows had been left unlocked or the gas left on. I stayed up late into the night listening for the sound of a door opening, a muffled whisper, a tread on the stairs. My room was the first at the top of the staircase, so I felt exposed. If robbers or killers came, I would be the first one they would get. I would creep out of bed, turning on the lights, and carefully make my way downstairs. I'd check the gas taps on the stove and the window locks. Then I'd retrace my steps. Lying in bed, I'd begin to wonder if I had checked everything thoroughly enough. Once planted, the seed of doubt would sprout and grow larger and larger, until I felt compelled to get up and check again. Sometimes I performed this ritual two or three times a night. In between, I was terrified. Every creak made me sit bolt upright in bed. I became so exhausted, I asked to sleep in my mother's bed, and she let me for several nights running. Then she worried that it would become a habit. I knew that she probably had some half-baked sexual theory in mind—but how could I tell her that it was a physical attack that frightened me so? What was at stake was my very survival. At her insistence, I dragged myself back to my own room and there, night after night, I stayed awake until well past midnight or awakened suddenly, my heart throbbing, at two or three in the morning. What was that sound? How many robbers were there? What weapons did they carry? What would they do to me? In the mornings, I would arise slowly, dark rings under my reddened eyes.

One day, on a school holiday, I went with Mom to her office not far from the Capitol. From there I crossed the Mall and went to the Smithsonian. I had been there about an hour and was looking at a wooden display case when a man sidled up next to me, uncomfortably close. As I was gazing at the exhibit, he was looking at me. I glanced at him—his eyes were opened wide and had a crazed look. I moved away around a corner and he followed. I quickened my step and walked through a door into the next room and he came, too, still looking at me with that lascivious leer. I sped into another room, turned a corner, entered yet another room, and stopped before a glass case. I looked up—he was there! Now I ran. I ran through three rooms, found a door to a back staircase, ran down the stairs, opened a door to the outside, and ran up the sidewalk and across the Mall. I didn't stop for six blocks, until I reached my mother's office building. Breathlessly, I told her what had happened. She was concerned, but chided me: Instead of running away, if I'd been convinced the man was out to harm me, I should have reported him to a guard. Later that afternoon, returning home with her on a streetcar, I was convinced I saw the man sitting ahead of us, but when we got off, he didn't follow us. Then I saw him strolling along on the sidewalk. At dinner in a restaurant a few hours after that, I saw him sitting alone at another table. I couldn't be sure—I hadn't gotten that good a look at him—but I told Mom. She said that it was impossible, speaking sharply in a "Pull yourself together" tone. I did. And soon I stopped seeing him.

Mom began staying home even more. She would send me on errands to the drugstore, a few blocks away on Wisconsin Avenue, mostly for Camel cigarettes. She supplied me with a note so that the clerk would sell them to me. She was usually too far gone to check on the change, so after a while I began pocketing a dollar or so. Then I began to keep all of it. She would be too drowsy to remember to ask for it. I amassed a cache of savings. Once or twice she would ask if I had returned the change, and, waxing indignant, I would insist that I had. During those walks to the drugstore, I was trying, consciously, to cope with the bleakness that had descended upon me. I began looking at myself from afar, objectively, as if I were in a movie, a movie about a young boy coming from a house of sickness. He was on an errand; he would soon buy a pack of cigarettes and pilfer the change. Somehow, for some reason, the fantasy made things easier to take.

A boy I knew in school lived on a cul-de-sac near Richard Nixon. He, like me, had been taught to despise the vice president, though we weren't altogether sure why. One afternoon, we armed ourselves with four eggs, went to Nixon's house, approached the front stoop warily, and threw them, hearing delightful smashes as they splattered on the façade. Then we ran as fast as we could. We knew that Nixon wasn't living there at the time—he was occupying the vice president's official residence—but the act of petty vandalism still felt gratifying.

Our basement had a Ping-Pong table, but now Mom was no longer capable of playing with me. I built a makeshift darkroom there and tried my hand at photography. I began hanging out with a boy who lived up the street; he was small for his age and pale and clearly headed for trouble. Together we turned the basement into a shooting gallery. We propped up sheets of plywood and fired the .22 rifles at them from a distance of twenty feet. Sometimes the bullets would ricochet from the rocks in the walls and go dancing around our heads. The danger was part of the thrill.

After a year Mom and I moved again to a small brick house on Forty-sixth Street, a tree-lined road close to Chevy Chase, Maryland. One morning I woke up and found a man downstairs. He was partially dressed in a crumpled suit, his breath smelled sour, and he was moving slowly. I could see that he was drunk. He explained that he and my mother had had a few nightcaps and he had stayed over. From somewhere, he produced a football—it was mine; I must have left it around—and he began holding it in different grips, showing me how to spin a spiral. He put his arm around my shoulders. I imagined that somewhere in their drunken revelry, Mom had said how sad it was that no man was around to show me manly things and that he had decided, in his stupor, to fit in a quick lesson. I despised him. He soon left, wobbling down the front stairs.

For a few months afterward Mom seemed to be functioning, but then she hit rock bottom. She stopped going to work altogether and stopped getting dressed, instead wearing her nightgown and moving between her bed and the couch downstairs. I functioned on my own, making my breakfast before school, running a paper route after school, and helping to prepare dinner. I had no idea where money was coming from or how much of it was left.

I began simply disregarding her. When a friend came over after school and seemed surprised to find her lying asleep on the couch, I told him to pay her no mind. I fell into a routine, and it became important to maintain it. I became addicted to classical music—the louder, the better. I loved Mussorgsky's *Pictures at an Exhibition,* Strauss's *Till Eulenspiegel's Merry Pranks,* Tchaikovsky's *1812 Overture,* and, most of all, Beethoven's symphonies. After school, I would retreat to my room, close the door, pile the records up to play automatically, and turn the volume up as high as it would go. Lying on my bed, I lost myself in the thundering chords blasting around. It was like being in an echo chamber. The music—transformed into brute noise—obliterated all thought.

At some point in all this, Mom took a spill down the staircase.

She broke the second toe of her right foot, and the toe turned yellow and blue and became misshapen. It was twisted halfway up, like a bent twig. Somehow, I got her to the doctor, she hobbling in and out of a taxi. She came home with a cast that covered her right foot and went all the way up her leg; it was open at the toes, where her second toe had a pin running through it, held in place by a metal brace protruding from the cast like a large staple. The steel entering the fleshy side of the toe was hard to look at. As might be expected, she did not take care of it—nor did I, for that matter—and one day I noticed that the toe had turned almost black. We went back to the doctor. It had become infected. A closed cast was put on and remained there through a long convalescence.

At school we were given an English assignment—to write a short story. I worked on it all weekend. It depicted the end of the world in an atomic holocaust. In a forest a few survivors were holed up, but they were facing an invasion by an enemy who had started the con-flagration with a missile strike. The men were hiding behind pine trees with their rifles at the ready—a lift from Hemingway—and discussing the perfidy of the invaders as shadows began moving up the hill toward them. The payoff of the story came at the very end: The reader naturally assumed the guilty ones were Russian, but in the last paragraph they learned the invaders were American. The teacher asked me to read my story to the class, and I readily did so. Afterward, there was a stunned silence. He asked for comments. The first person to raise his hand said he doubted that I had writ-ten it. Others backed him up. The teacher cut short the debate—he said he was sure I was the author. I was thrilled at the reaction; it couldn't have been better.

By now we had been living in Washington a year and a half and another Christmas was coming around. To me, that meant one thing: My brother would be coming home. I was aware that our situation had deteriorated seriously since his last visit, but I had no idea what could be done to arrest the slide. I didn't believe he'd be able to make things better—that seemed beyond possibility—but I looked forward to feeling once again that rush of relief, the relin-quishing of responsibility once he was in the house. I anticipated his homecoming by preparing the most impressive gift I could think of—a collection of paperback books about famous artists. The books discussed the artists' distinctive qualities and were illustrated with their most famous works. I spent my purloined savings on them, purchasing them one at a time from a store on Western Avenue in Chevy Chase. I accumulated them over months, until finally I had twenty of them, a stack ten inches high. I put them in a shoe box and wrapped them carefully.

When Bob came home, he was distressed by what he found. I knew this not because we talked about it but because he seemed so preoccupied. He was uncommunicative. He rarely smiled, and he parried my questions about his life at Andover with half answers. I could hardly wait to give him the present, and on Christmas morning, when he barely acknowledged it, I was crushed. To this day, I don't know exactly what I was trying to do—I don't know whether the gift was intended to brighten his homecoming or whether it was an expression of love, since I missed him so much, or whether it was a bribe of sorts, intended to make him sit up and pay attention and figure a way out of the mess we were in. Once the holidays were over, he returned to Andover.

It was a late Sunday afternoon on a mid-January day in 1956. The sky had been a strange opal color all day and now it had begun to sleet. Slivers of ice slanted down from the leaden cloud like spears. The ice coated the streets and sidewalks and roofs with a glaze and crystallized around tree branches, bending them to the ground. I was upstairs in my room, perhaps doing homework—luckily, not listening to the drums and trumpets of the classical music that I loved to play at full volume.

I heard a scream from downstairs—an unearthly sound, unlike anything I had ever heard. It began as a low rumble, almost a moan, then ascended higher and higher, until it became a piercing cry. It was loud and wordless, the sound of a human throat opening up and giving vent to every bit of noise it was capable of.

I leapt up, tore around the banister, and ran to the stairs. Halfway down, I saw my mother sprawled in the center of the living room floor. She was thrashing about, her limbs flailing in all directions, her eyes wild. Her feet and hands pounded against the floor. She lay on her back, flopping up and down like a fish. There was another sound, a playful growling. I saw that our dog had grabbed the fringe of her nightgown. He was leaning back, his paws planted firmly on the floor, tugging at it. He let go, danced around, and then grabbed another piece. Had he attacked her? No, I knew he hadn't. She was having some sort of convulsions. I ran to her and kicked the dog hard in the ribs. The dog yelped and retreated to another room. My mother was still thrashing about, her hair covering her eyes, saliva flecked around her mouth. I tried to hold her down, but she was too strong for me. Her jerky movements rocked us both into the air.

I jumped up and ran to the front door and fled outside. I almost toppled down the front steps, which were covered in ice, and lost traction on the sidewalk, slipping and sliding, my arms windmilling like a cartoon character's. I made it to a neighbor's house and pounded on the door. A man I did not know came to the door. I could see a woman behind him, sitting in an easy chair, her mouth open in surprise.

"Come. Please come. Come quick," I pleaded. "My mother."

That was all I said. The man took his time fetching his coat, which bothered me. He walked carefully along the slippery sidewalk, leaning first against a banister, then a tree trunk, then holding his arms to his sides, with his palms down, to brace against a fall. We came to our front stairs. I saw I had left the door open. I went first. When we got inside, Mom's convulsions had stopped. She was still lying in the center of the floor. Her eyes were wide open, staring up at the ceiling. I knelt beside her and said over and over, "Mom. Mom. Mom." She looked up at me, frowning in confusion. She opened her mouth as if to speak but said nothing. She kept looking at me, then away, then back at me. She was dazed.

"Where . . . where am I?" she asked. She looked at me again. "Who . . . who . . ." I could see she did not know who I was. I told her not to worry, that she had had some sort of fit but that she would feel better soon.

The neighbor and I lifted her onto the couch. Now she was surprisingly light to carry, and docile. I got a blanket and covered her with it. The man didn't seem to know what to do.

"I don't know what it is," he said, "but she seems better." He didn't seem to think it strange—or if he did, he didn't say so—that my mother didn't recognize me. He said there was nothing more to do and he walked out the door and headed back to his house. I could see him out the window, carefully negotiating the icy sidewalk, in a hurry to get home.

Mom was still frowning and looking totally confused. She was regarding everything—the chairs, the drapes, the doors—as if she were trying to figure out where she was. That she didn't know me, her own son, was deeply upsetting. I ran to the phone and looked up the number of her doctor and called her. The ring tones seemed slow. The doctor answered the phone herself.

"You must come, you must come," I said, my voice breaking. "My mother is . . . She's lost control of her muscles. She fell on the floor and her arms and legs were moving all over the place. And now she's stopped, but she doesn't know anything. She doesn't know who I am. You have to come. You have to send an ambulance."

I heard the doctor's voice, her tone sharp.

"Have you looked outside?" she asked.

I did, through a window that was just above the phone. I could see the ice still coming down in sheets.

"Nothing can get through," she said. "Not even an ambulance. You'll have to handle this on your own."

I knew that her cold tone was intended to brace me up, but I hated her for it. She gave me instructions. If the seizure—for that's what she called it—was to reoccur, I was to get a spoon and hold it in my mother's mouth, pressing down her tongue so that she wouldn't swallow it. That was very important. She mustn't be allowed to swallow her tongue, for she could choke on it. Did I understand? I said I did. She said some more things, but I don't remember them precisely. I was thinking of the spoon and how to manage it.

After the phone call, my mother seemed to come around. She knew who I was, but there was a remnant of confusion. She had no idea what had happened, and I decided not to tell her. I just said that she had been sick but now was okay. After that, I made her some soup, but once she had taken a few sips she didn't feel like eating it. I made her a cup of tea. I fed the dog and felt his ribs—I was worried that I had broken one when I kicked him so hard—and he seemed okay.

I stayed close by Mom. Two hours later, we were sitting side by side on an upright couch, a love seat, in the small room between the living room and the kitchen. I had put on the television as a distraction. We were watching *The Ed Sullivan Show.* An act came on—jugglers, or maybe seals in an inflated rubber pool, bouncing balls on their noses—when I heard the sound again. It came from about one foot away and made me jump, that same low groaning. Then it rose up and up, an opening of the vocal cords, all playing at once. I heard the audience applauding on the television. The dog danced back and forth in a half circle around us, barking. I ran to the kitchen, found a large spoon, and ran back. Now Mom had slid down the couch, her body half on and half off. Her legs began to tremble on the floor, and so did her arms, which were on the couch. She arched her back. I threw myself on her arms, and when her mouth flew open, I thrust the spoon into it. I tried holding her tongue down, but her head was thrashing from side to side. I got behind her and put her head between my knees and held the spoon in place. Its handle was vibrating and I could feel her teeth clamping down. I held on like that. After some time—three minutes, five?— she stopped moving and then fell limp. I removed the spoon. She had frothed at the mouth and out of it ran rivulets of blood. Maybe I had pressed down too hard. But she was still breathing. I got her back on the couch. Now she looked up at me, again dazed and lost, with an almost childlike pleading. Again, she asked where she was, what had happened.

Later, when she recovered, she leaned against me and I got her upstairs and into her bed. She fell asleep. I stayed there, sitting by her bed for a few hours, the spoon on a bedside table. Then I took the spoon into my room, just across the hall. I lay down in bed with my clothes on and put the spoon on my dresser. I didn't want to sleep. I had to stay awake in case she had another attack. I listened for that sound again, the unearthly scream. After another hour or two, it came. I ran into her room and shoved the spoon back into her mouth. We rode this one out more easily, it seemed. Then I gave her some water to drink and went back to my room. There was one other attack, around midnight. She then fell into a deep sleep, and I must have also.

I don't remember much about the next morning. I looked in on her and found her still asleep, then made my breakfast and went off to school. The weather was warm, so despite the ice storm of the previous day, the school was open. When I got home that afternoon, Mom was missing. I hadn't been there more than ten minutes when the doorbell rang. Two women were there. I let them in. One went to sit down in an easy chair, but I stopped her just in time—the chair was broken, its back legs propped into place. The other woman went to sit in another chair, but I stopped her also—that chair was broken, too, in the same way. They were like booby traps. The women sat together on the couch and exchanged glances. I noticed the floor was filthy, with piles of dust in the corners. I suddenly saw the room from their perspective—how odd and dysfunctional it must have appeared. I blushed and was angry at them. The women said that my mother had been taken in an ambulance to recover in a hospital. They explained that they were from Alcoholics Anonymous, a group that helped people with drinking problems. It was then and there, sitting in that room on that long-ago afternoon, that I finally understood everything. I knew, as if the proverbial lightbulb had been switched on in my head, what the problem was, what had made Mom "groggy" all those years. She was a drunk.

The doctor telephoned and said I'd be staying with her for a few days. She picked me up in her car. I disliked her intensely, and her whole family. She had a son slightly older than I was, and I was pleased to see that he was afflicted with a bad stutter; it was nearly impossible to understand what he was trying to say. At least, I thought, I can talk properly. A week later, I went back to our house in time to prepare for Mom's homecoming. When she arrived, a transformation had taken place. Her eyes were wide open—I hadn't seen them that wide for years, it seemed—and they were once again animated. She told me where her bottles were and together we unearthed them—dozens of empty gin bottles stashed high up in cupboards and in the rear of closets. I carried them to a garbage can in the back alley. She didn't ask me many questions about her convulsions. Two days before they occurred, she said, she had abruptly stopped drinking altogether—a forced withdrawal because she had run completely out of money. It was the sudden cutoff of alcohol to her system, she had been told, that had brought them on. She had been lucky: In some instances, convulsions like that proved fatal. In any case, she said, she was never going to take another drink as long as she lived.

And she was true to her word.

CHAPTER 12

After Mom came home from her week in the hospital, filled with dramatic tales about the bizarre mental patients she had encountered during her stay in the psychiatric ward (which is where they placed alcoholics in those days), she joined AA. She had tried the twelve-step program several times before, I was to learn, but the hook hadn't caught. This time, it did, and the reason was clear: She had hit rock bottom. The realization had finally struck home that her life, and our future, hung by a narrow thread. That was the crucial first step on the road to recovery.

I didn't tell Bob right away about her recovery—why, I'm not sure. We rarely talked on the phone, I never wrote letters, and I had stopped communicating with just about everyone. I hadn't told anyone, other than her doctor during that one phone call, about the convulsions. I went to school, as if nothing had happened. Some two weeks later, Bob called from Andover. His voice was strained as he asked me how Mom was doing. He fired questions at me. I cut him off to tell him what had happened, saying that she had had these seizures but was better and that she had been magically transformed. It was a miracle! Our family would be restored; our lives would become sane again. I repeated these assurances over and over. Eventually, he sounded somewhat relieved, but I don't think he believed me—his tone was still skeptical.

Fifty years later the two of us were sitting at a dining room table in my apartment in New York City when we began to discuss our childhood. We didn't do this often, preferring instead to make one or two passing references to how deluded we'd been and let it go at that. But this time we talked about what had occurred on that icy evening in Washington. Several times over the years I had told him about the episode, but never in detail. Now I described it from start to finish. When I looked up, I saw he had tears in his eyes. He was silent for a while and then told me that his visit home had been a traumatic turning point for him. Shocked at how low Mom and I had sunk, at how the household had stopped functioning and was sliding into poverty, he realized that he alone could save us. So he came to a difficult resolution: He would quit school and stay home and make some money and get us back on our feet. He wrote Andover, informing the school of his decision; the dean wrote back, telling him he was making a big mistake and strongly urging him to return to complete his studies. After much soul-searching, he followed the dean's advice. It was, he confessed, his eyes brimming with tears, a wrenching moment, perhaps the worst in his life. In his overheated adolescent mind, the decision not to quit high school constituted an abandonment of us to save himself. He was going to cut the cord. Figuratively speaking, he had packed his suitcase and was going to walk out the door into his own future, drawn inexorably toward self-preservation, like a protagonist in a coming-of-age novel or like Tom Wingfield, the young man in *The Glass Menagerie,* running off to sea to escape the suffocating home with the nagging mother and the lame sister, fleeing a life that would crush his dreams, only to be crushed by the burden of guilt. The discussion confirmed what I had often thought: that though Bob had managed to leave, he hadn't gotten away unscathed.

Neither had I. For years after that night in Washington, I had a recurrent nightmare. I was in the house on Roseville Road in Westport. The ground-floor rooms formed a long passage to the front door. Upstairs, the bedroom corridor ran parallel to the one downstairs, and the two floors met at an enclosed staircase next to the door. My mother, downstairs, had lost her mind. I was upstairs. Frantically, I called the doctor, and as I was pouring out my fear that my life was in danger, I heard something on the line—a click: My mother had picked up the extension. She told the doctor that she was fine, never better. But then her voice started to rise and got louder, until it hit an echo chamber and became deafening. I dropped the receiver and ran toward the staircase for the front door. It was a long way. She did the same—we were running *toward* each other. I knew I must beat her to reach the door and escape unharmed, because she was carrying an ax. As I bolted down the staircase and reached the bottom, I turned to look in her direction—that's when I would wake up, sweating, my heart pounding.

Gradually, once Mom recovered, our lives began to improve. She obtained a job in New York City, doing PR work for a criminal justice organization. This meant that she would have to relocate there immediately, but I would stay in Washington to finish up my last year at Alice Deal Junior High School. Arrangements were made for me to move in with a family—the third time in four years that I had been farmed out. I didn't object; at this point, I think, I suspended all volition and just drifted along, following the current. I didn't know the people I was to stay with, the Reynolds (which is not their real name; I'd rather not identify them). They were new acquaintances Mom had made through AA. Mrs. Reynold was a hard-driving lawyer, red-haired, with pale skin, outgoing and assertive. Mr. Reynold was a mild-mannered accountant. He drove a Henry J, was thin as a shadow, spoke in almost a whisper, and was self-effacing. He was the one who was the recovering alcoholic. The two were so different, it was hard to imagine what had brought them together in the first place, not to mention what kept the marriage alive. They had a one-year-old girl, whom I was encouraged to think of as a baby sister.

It was odd being a surrogate child, dropped into someone else's family, a full-grown adolescent delivered overnight, the way cartoons of the time depicted a stork landing on the roof with a babe in diapers. I tried hard to fall into step with rules and rituals that circumscribed what had been an existence without boundaries. I would sleep in the guest bedroom unless guests were there, in which case I'd be given a cot in the study. I was to wake up every morning at 6:30, dress, and then cook myself a single egg in a metal poacher that formed it into a perfect circle. I was to receive a weekly allowance of five silver dollars for lunch money. After school, I was to do my homework, concentrating on math in order to raise my grade. Dinner was at 6:00 p.m. I was to show my math homework to Mr. Reynold, who would check it over, and then at 9:00 p.m., I was to file into their bedroom to kiss each of them good night. I found them, night after night, reading in their crisp pajamas, sitting up in beds on opposite walls, as far from each other as possible. The experience, I imagined, was like being drafted into the army, but it turned out that the routine, once I got used to it, wasn't all that bad. I sensed that it helped keep dissolution at bay, for I knew that all was not well in this house. The place was eerily silent, lifeless, without affect. Even the baby seemed abnormally quiet. At dinners I tried to keep up a cheerful monologue; otherwise, a silence would descend, punctuated by the rhythmic clicking of Mr. Reynold's false teeth. When he spoke, his wife often contradicted him or simply spoke over him. He and I formed an unspoken alliance, expressed through sympathetic glances. After he corrected my math homework, he took to patting me on the shoulder. I decided that in the divorce, I'd go with him.

During these four or five months, I cut myself off from the few friends I had. I rarely invited anyone over after school, taking the trolley alone with my pile of schoolbooks. In the afternoons, I would take long walks with my dog or watch, with a gnawing sense of shame because it was below my age level, Disney's Mouseketeers singing and dancing and offering phony companionship. I cannot say that I was unhappy. I was feeling almost nothing at all, which was a relief of sorts.

A year before, I had applied to Andover and been turned down. I scored badly on a qualifying test, and at my interview with a school alumnus, I had barely talked. Now I applied again, and this time—miracle!—I was accepted. I was told that I was being given a scholarship, though I would have to repeat the ninth grade, since the test revealed that I was behind in vocabulary and other areas. Mom conveyed the news of my admission with great excitement. Another member of my school class was selected to go to Exeter, Andover's rival. He was tall and handsome, a football player and a good student, just the type of standout applicant who deserved to go to prep school. I felt that I—a mediocrity in terms of skills and grades and an athletic prowess hovering safely in the middle ground—did not. I believed I got in on my brother's coattails.

That spring, for Easter vacation, I joined Bob and Mom in New York. I have a vivid memory of our first night, the three of us walking down the sidewalk holding hands. Mom hugged us, wearing her familiar perfume, I cracked jokes, and Bob laughed, and we all felt good—a family reunited and whole. We stayed in a tiny studio apartment in the Roger Williams Hotel. Sleeping on a roll-away bed next to an open window, I couldn't fall asleep for a long time. I listened to the sounds of the city, that inchoate cacophony—taxi horns, subway rumblings, sirens, laughter—all filtered up and down the canyons into a steady low roar. I felt I was listening to the distillation of something powerful, like a distant waterfall. The first morning I was so excited, I got up early, while my mother and brother were still asleep. I stepped outside onto the sidewalk and stood at the corner of the building, gaping. A friendly doorman came over for a chat. He spotted me as a greenhorn and, leaning against the building with his hands in his pants, he clued me in about life in the big city. It was a place to be careful. It was dangerous: Everyone had some kind of scheme; you always had to be on the lookout. It was a rough place, he said, looking at the passersby as if he could spot their games. I knew instantly this was where I was born to be.

And two months later, I was. I said good-bye to my surrogate family and waited for a taxi. I was leaving my dog behind. Our car, the beloved Ford convertible with the rumble seat, would not accompany us, either. Mom had left it for repair at a local garage and it stayed there so long, the owner charged rent and impounded it. Mrs. Reynold, wiping tears from her eyes, stood on the threshold, holding the baby. Mr. Reynold walked me to the taxi and hugged me more tightly than I thought him capable. I gripped their good-bye present—a large, handsome suitcase—and the taxi took off for Union Station. I felt a rush of joy. I was glad to be leaving it all behind—them; Washington; Alice Deal; the steaming Mall; the stupid avenues named after states; the Mint; the FBI, with its underground pistol range; the medical museum, with its damaged fetuses in bottles; the grandiose Capitol dome. Only my dog would I miss, but him I regarded as a necessary sacrifice. As the taxi carried me down Connecticut Avenue, I looked out the window at a world suddenly come alive with novelty and possibilities. Not too long afterward, I heard that the Reynolds had separated, then divorced. I was happy for him.

In New York, we moved into a small apartment overlooking Madison Avenue and Sixty-third Street, a rent-controlled fifth-floor walk-up. "It sharpens the memory," my mother cracked as she showed it to me. "You don't forget anything when you go shopping." On the ground floor, just outside the front door, was a hole-in-the-wall laundry presided over by a stooped old man whose arm bore a concentration camp tattoo. On the second floor, a two-foot sign announced THE FIXIT MASTER. No neighbor I passed going up or down the creaky wooden stairs ever said hello; most didn't even nod. The apartment was two good-size rooms, a living room and a bedroom. There was no kitchen—only an open closet with a half refrigerator, on top of which was a two-burner hot plate. Next to the closet was a tiny bathroom with a floor speckled with old octagonal penny tiles and a porcelain sink that doubled as the water supply for cooking and washing dishes. Somehow, reaching up to crowded shelves for supplies, balancing pots and pans in elaborate configurations, allowing some to stay warm with just an edge resting on the scorching hot plate, stirring in sauces, and parking frying pans on the sink, Mom was able to whip up three-course dinners.

Our lives centered on AA. The meetings were held in a church in the Murray Hill section, and Mom insisted on taking us to some of them (this was before there were separate sessions for AA family members). I found them excruciating. I was embarrassed by everything—by being there, by her being an alcoholic, by mingling with other self-described alcoholics. People fussed over me, which only made me feel more conspicuous and out of place. At the first meeting, Mom told me later, a man looked me over and cracked, "He's either a midget or an arrested alcoholic." When she was called upon to recount her problems with drink, Mom's spiel was eloquent. She skewered the rationalizations and self-deceptions of the down-and-out alcoholic. One bit, delivered with theatrical timing, brought down the house. She would hold up her right hand, curling her fingers around an imaginary tumbler, and say, "One day I finally realized that what was poisoning my life was right inside this glass. And so I changed from well water to bottled water."

Most of her friends, at least the new ones we saw most frequently, were from AA. They were a varied lot. One, a first mate in the merchant marine, visited us every time he was in port; he promised to get me a union card and a berth on a freighter—my dream from an early age—and only after my mother's death did he confess that she had buttonholed him and told him in no uncertain terms not even to think of it. Another, a big-boned, sexy, redheaded actress who kept slipping off the wagon, became almost like a daughter to her. Once, a small army of six—myself included—was assembled to rescue a distressed drinker from an abusive husband on Staten Island; we plotted our strategy on the ferry on the way out: We would set up a protective circle around her while she packed her bags—like defensive linemen for the Giants, I thought. Luckily, her husband was not at home, so the extraction was easy. Whenever a "pigeon"—a newcomer to the program—called, Mom would stay on the phone for what seemed like hours, talking slowly and gently, as if she were persuading a suicide to come in from a ledge, helping the person regain some glimmer of hope, an inkling of control over a life spiraling downward.

That first year, when Bob came home on vacations, it felt good to have our family together again. And it was a relief to acknowledge the invisible, or not so invisible, hand that had been dragging us down. But typically, we didn't talk about the hard times we had been through or the reasons for them—carrying on, in theory, the illusion that they had been little more than temporary setbacks. We fell into our respective roles: Mom as mentor, Bob as prodigy, and me as wise guy. But something had changed, something that made our old triad impossible to sustain. Bob had grown beyond us, so that even when he was there, part of him seemed to be elsewhere. Around the dinner table he and Mom still carried on their wide-ranging discussions—about F. Scott Fitzgerald, El Greco, obscure points in Christian theology—but the passion seemed to have evaporated. He didn't appear to expect much from the exchange; he was simply going through the motions to humor her. His sights were trained on a distant horizon. Psychologically, he had already left home for good.

Recently I came across a letter that Mom wrote during those hard years in Washington. It was to a Darnton relative in Michigan, and typically, she spent a certain amount of ink bragging about us. "Bob is at Phillips Andover and doing amazingly well. They've put him ahead two years in English, one in French, one in math. So he'll have at least one year of college under his belt before he gets there. He's getting honors, too, which means a scholarship along with his athletics, school paper and class officer activities." She went on for quite a while in this vein and then turned to me: "Our lovable Johnnie, I'm afraid, will bloom too late to have such returns as he goes along. We tried for a scholarship for him—at Bob's insistence—but he didn't make it. I am just as well pleased because I think he needs home a bit more. Barney used to say he was one of the Darntons who matured late. And John is indeed very much like his father in many ways. If he matures into anything close to the person his father was, my cup will run over."

Bob and I had fallen into a division of labor that had been marked down for years. His role was to excel and to replace Barney. Mine was to rebel and to *become* Barney.

In reading the letter now, I realized that one of Mom's major achievements was to provide me with an essential love and acceptance. No matter what happened, or what I did, I never doubted that I was loved. In instilling this, she lessened my feelings of being overshadowed by my brother's accomplishments—as Bob was my shield from her and her alcoholism, she was my shield from him and his success.

At the time, I did not understand this dynamic, and my feelings toward her were changing. I loved her, of course, but the bonds that had bound me to her had broken. The hard truth was that she had failed conspicuously in her heroic attempt to provide us with a mythic ideal childhood. I accepted the fact that she was an alcoholic and felt stupid for denying such an obvious truth for so long. Now, looking back, I could see clearly the mileposts I had missed all those years. Seeing them made me feel idiotic and deceived. I didn't think of alcoholism as a sickness—the idea of its being a disease was not yet current—but as a weakness, even as moral depravity. I had seen her helpless, flailing about on the floor, and the image was burned into my brain. As a result, I had cut myself off. I could no longer accept her as a parent or as an authority. I was, at the age of fourteen, a free agent, responsible only to myself. No one could tell me what to do. It was frightening, but even more, it was invigorating—exhilarating. I was on my own and would forge my own way.

Soon I was to experience the sensation—callow, selfish, and unspeakably delicious—of a young man who at long last was leaving home.

CHAPTER 13

W hen Bob and I left for Phillips Academy Andover in September 1956, we had no money, and so we had to hitchhike to Massachusetts from New York. We got hold of a map, marked the route in pencil, and set out, each of us carrying a suitcase. I had packed a couple of neckties and wore an old herringbone jacket that I had picked up somewhere—jackets and ties were mandatory at Andover—along with a new pair of chinos. I was excited. I had never hitchhiked before. And here was I, my thumb out on a busy highway, on the threshold of a bold adventure.

We left early in the morning and made good time. By midafternoon we had reached Boston and found ourselves entangled in the web of highways encircling the city. A timid man with a small mustache picked us up and took us to his house for lunch. My suspicions were on alert. Growing up in the 1950s, we didn't discuss homosexuality, but somewhere along the line boys learned about "queers" and we warned one another to avoid them. I was mistaken. Our host, a professor at MIT, gave us homemade soup and sandwiches on thick slabs of bread and engaged us in lively, avuncular talk. Learning that we were students at Andover, he impressed upon us the importance of science and the rewards of choosing it as a career. How he envied us, he said, posed as we were on the brink of adult life. Decisions we made now would have a cascading effect throughout the years to come. Then he escorted us to the entrance ramp of the route north of Boston and left us there. As the cars whizzed by, I stood on the roadside, well fed and excited about the future. I was in thrall to the infinite possibilities ahead. It was dizzying to contemplate them, the twists and turns to come, each one leading to new twists and turns. I felt impervious to harm, filled with blind confidence.

When we arrived at Andover, I got my first view of the campus. Both sides the road gave way to great green seas of pristine grass and perfect stone walls. In the distance were ivy-covered brick buildings and windows with creamy white trim. As if on cue, a bell tower clanged majestically. Other students were arriving in cars driven by their parents. They parked in front of dormitories, unloading trunks and stereos and soft armchairs.

I wasn't nervous about starting school. I had Bob with me. He was to be a senior and I a freshman. As I already knew but soon was to see for myself, he was a star on campus—the head of a student civic organization, on the honor roll, a deacon in church, a member of the debating team. As always, his accolades were oppressive to me, since I had little hope of matching them, but at the same time a source of pride. I didn't mind being "Darnton's younger brother." Standing in his reflected glory would bolster my own status. Now that I had been transported to a new place, I had been given the gift of a fresh start—the opportunity to put Washington behind me and carve out a new identity. I felt as if I were walking out of a dank cave into a sun-splashed meadow.

I found my dormitory, an old white house on the edge of campus. Half a dozen other boys lived there. One of them, a lad from Texas named John Daniel, became an instant friend and roommate. We shared an interest in reading—he introduced Dylan Thomas to me, and I Sean O'Casey to him—and we talked long after lights-out from our beds, which were on opposite sides of the room. Our friendship was strengthened by a rare bond—the fact that his father, too, had died.

During this time of my life, I stopped thinking about my father altogether. I had more immediate concerns—making new friends, fitting in to a new place, going to classes, and studying. I was working on my new identity, becoming more extroverted. I didn't think of myself in relation to my family or my past, but was immersed in the present. I fell in step with Andover and took to its traditions and challenges. New arrivals were subjected to hazing by seniors, who had only to utter two words—"Hey, prep"—to get them to haul their furniture upstairs. Rivalry with Phillips Exeter Academy was intense; their school colors were red (ours were blue), and every morning we filed out of daily chapel chanting, "Whadda we eat? Whadda we eat? Red meat! Red meat!"

Life was regimented. The regimen was enforced by the ringing of chapel bells from a wooden steeple, which dominated the campus. In the mornings, we had to dress quickly to make it to breakfast in the Commons, the building that housed the four dining halls. There was a fifteen-minute window, between 7:05 and 7:20, to check in and so escape a demerit (five demerits and you were placed on probation). The bells started ringing about once a minute and then sped up progressively, so that by the end, as you were running full out, sweating even in winter, your lungs burning, they came at you like a machine gun. After breakfast, there was the same clanging choreography to reach the mandatory chapel service. Then classes started with bells and buzzers of their own. And so it went throughout the day.

The odd part was that I liked almost everything about it. I liked studying in the library, sitting at a long wooden table with green lamp shades. Around me, bookshelves mounted to the ceiling and high overhead windows let in slanting rays of sunlight. Sometimes, deep in a book, I'd hear a familiar cough and know my brother was in the same room. I liked the cavernous gymnasium, the clanging locker room and steaming showers, and the long afternoon break for sports, galloping down a soccer field, trying to learn tennis and get the hang of pole vaulting. I liked the late-afternoon classes—English in Bulfinch Hall, a jewel box of a building, designed in the style of the great architect. We sat in wooden chairs set in a circle, listening to teachers in tweed jackets expound on the crafts of reading and writing and inculcate respect for literature. ("You don't judge great books—great books judge you." "Never say: 'The author is *trying* to say . . .' The author *is* saying—you're *trying* to figure it out.")

On Saturday nights we attended first-run movies in the assembly hall. On Wednesdays guest speakers were imported to inspire us; most were worldly businessmen who confided the secrets of their success. They were introduced by the dean of students, G. Grenville Benedict. Benedict, balding, face flushed, given to wearing pinstripe suits, was the most charismatic figure on campus. Loving the limelight, and in love with himself, he paced up and down the stage when he talked, jangling the change in his pockets and speaking in rotund sentences that resisted colloquial grammar. I liked listening to him; he could make a routine announcement of a change in schedule sound like a summons to battle.

I was bursting with school spirit. The night before the single greatest event—the football game with Exeter—we congregated on a hilltop, standing around a huge bonfire. As embers flew up into the night sky, the football team would arrive on a flatbed truck, like Greek warriors, and we underlings would let loose in bloodthirsty chants and screams. Our faces, glistening in the reflected flames, were frenzied. We lost ourselves in the mob, a primal submersion to tribe that, with only a small tweak of the dial, could lead young men to sign up for war.

Over time my enthusiasm for Andover was mitigated by some hard-edged realities. There existed, I was soon to learn, a strict social hierarchy. Boys who were deemed cool were at the top of the heap, especially if they were athletic. The guiding principle was to achieve an ineffable quality of worldliness, a pose of having seen everything and being surprised by nothing. It was epitomized by a singular bodily stance, slouched against a wall, hands in pants pockets in such a way that the jacket tails hung over them in front, like a bloodhound's ears. The dress was conforming: wrinkled jacket, tie askew, chinos, and dirty white bucks. The best compliment was to be called a "cynic." The most devastating insult was to be called a "weenie." In the atmosphere of social categorizing and ostracizing found only at an all-boys school, we deified the strong and handsome and we vilified the weak and homely. We assiduously avoided all risk. Intellectual prowess didn't enter into the equation—except at grade times. Three times a year, classmates were rank-ordered on a bulletin board, the highest at the top, the lowest at the bottom, occasions that constituted revenge for the weenies.

Halfway through my freshman year, I noticed something else. A speaker came to our Wednesday assembly from a union hall in New York City. He delivered a rabble-rousing stem-winder about workers' rights, and in response students in the hall rose up out of their seats, shouting him down, waving dollar bills in the air, attempting to heap ridicule upon him. I was flabbergasted. What was this? People I knew, friends, had suddenly gone berserk. Their faces were red and they were screaming. They were displaying their colors, defending their class. A realization struck me like a lightning bolt: I was different. I was a scholarship kid and I was in the minority. Class divisions that I had never been aware of, that I had certainly not encountered in the public schools of Washington, D.C., materialized, as suddenly vivid as wrist stamps under the ultraviolet that determined who could enter a country club dance. I had unknowingly crossed a no-man's-land and had infiltrated the camp of money and privilege. The scales fell from my eyes. How could I have been so blind to the way society was ordered? This cocoon was for rich white people. There was one black boy in my class and one in my brother's class, too. We had a number of Jews, but not too many.

Once clued in, I cultivated my newfound knowledge and began to notice things—how some of my friends had dresser drawers full of fine starched shirts, how others skipped meals and paid for cheeseburgers at a diner on campus, how on Saturdays they walked into town to casually buy new blazers or madras jackets at the Andover Shop. I began to see how the world was organized to fill their needs and prerogatives. Toward the end of senior year, recruiters from Harvard and Yale and other Ivy League schools arrived on campus to make their pitches. They came to us—we didn't have to go to them.

On vacations I returned to our rent-controlled apartment in New York. During the winter break, I undertook a bizarre venture with some friends from Westport. We got hold of tuxedos and wore them to crash society balls in the city. We'd learned the fire staircases and hidden corridors of the Plaza and the Pierre and other fancy hotels and simply walked in through the back door. We'd take to the dance floor and flirt with the girls, usually after smuggling in a bottle. There was, of course, the attraction of the opposite sex, but the thrill of it, the exaltation, came from penetrating the closed world of the upper class. I reveled in being a barbarian at the gates. And sooner or later in the course of the evening, I'd pick a sympathetic young girl and try to impress her by admitting I didn't belong there. Almost always, the girls went along with the game, and some were even intrigued by it. But once, my ploy landed on a less than sympathetic ear and my name was taken and I was summarily ejected from the ball. The following day my mother received a phone call from a woman with a cultivated accent who was on the organizing committee. Was it true that I was a student at Andover? Yes, my mother replied. Well, in that case would I be interested in attending the next dance legitimately? I wasn't. I told my mother to hang up. And from that time on, I never crashed another ball.

During the Easter break, I spent some time with the family of an Andover friend named Nate, who lived in Wilton, Connecticut. His father was a journalist, a writer for *Life* magazine, and his mother was a poet, and he had a younger brother and sister. Sitting at their dinner table, before a feast of baked ham and steaming vegetables served on fine china and drinking water from crystal glasses, I felt I had stepped inside a Norman Rockwell painting. The father, a handsome man with a wayward shock of hair, stood up when he carved at the head of the table. He questioned his children with a store of paternal wisdom. The mother gently chided him when he seemed to be exerting too much control. I was witness to the power and wholesomeness of the American dream. This, I told myself, was the way my life would have been had my father lived.

In my second year at Andover, after Bob had graduated and moved on to Harvard, I was pleased to note that I could survive very well on my own. Somewhat to my surprise, I found that my grades were strong, especially in science and English, that I had many friends, and that I was moving ahead in the sort of extracurricular activities that were useful for getting into a top-notch college. I liked writing stories and I entered an essay contest. I needed to write about something personal, something moving, so I chose to write about attending an AA meeting. I pulled out all the stops. I poured on the rhetoric and scooped out the metaphors and applied a heavy helping of the pathetic fallacy. I described the thunder and lightning before the meeting, how it rent the skies and a downpour drenched the streets. Then I wrote about how the congregants, slipping quietly through the side door of a church, convened to tell their stories and bare their souls in a redemptive communion. I described how open they were, how appealing, how they accepted me into the group and how uplifting it all was. Afterward, when we emerged, the city's streets were washed clean and the cigarette butts had disappeared down the storm drains and the sun came out and the air was fresh—and so on. Barely a single syllable was honest—what I described was the antithesis of what I had actually felt. I won the contest.

During summer vacation of my sophomore year, I drove with two of Bob's friends from Harvard to Boulder, Colorado, and from there took a Greyhound bus to Yakima, Washington, where I had arranged to take a job in an apple orchard. I was given a room in a tiny makeshift cabin on a hillside overlooking the trees. The work was brutal. I arose at 6:30 in the morning, fixed breakfast, put a sandwich in a paper bag, and joined a work crew. Ten hours later, after backbreaking labor on the top of a ladder, thinning apples from heavy boughs by squeezing them off at the stem, with only two five-minute breaks and half an hour off for lunch, I would return to my cabin, so exhausted that I could barely stand. But then, after frying a hot dog for dinner and washing it down with lemonade, my limbs began to ache pleasantly. I would sit outside as the sun went down over the brown lava hills in the distance, watching the long arcs of the sprinklers over the treetops below and listening to the buzz of the cicadas. On those evenings, alone, with my thoughts vitiated by fatigue, I felt entirely at peace.

The work crew was made up of the descendants of "Okies" and "Arkies" who had migrated west during the dust storms of the 1930s. They lived in squalid quarters in the single-road town of Wiley City in the valley below. They were a hard lot, straight out of The Grapes of Wrath—wrinkled before their time and tanned a permanent brown, with crooked and missing teeth, and outfitted in bib overalls. They turned their weekly paychecks over to a local store that provided groceries and, on Saturday nights, enough hard liquor to send them into oblivion. The children had no formal education—nor had the adults, for that matter. During breaks, the conversation would range widely over issues that aroused their curiosity. I was astounded at the level of ignorance. Debates would break out, sometimes running for days on end: Was Chicago nearer to California than New York? Which was closer to the Earth, the Sun or the Moon? I was allowed to toss in my view, but it carried no more weight that anyone else's. They were astounded to learn, after questioning me in a group conversation that turned awkwardly personal, that I was still a virgin at the age of fifteen. "Hell," said one. "I lost my cherry in a haystack at eight."

I went on a weeklong church retreat up in the mountains. We camped and lived on fish plucked from a cold lake. The twenty or so young people divided themselves into two groups, the good kids and the less good. I straddled the two, but by the week's end I had gravitated toward the misfits. I was an object of fascination to their leader, a young man with slicked-back hair, tight black pants, and motorcycle boots, who went by the nickname of Paladin, after the character in the TV series *Have Gun—Will Travel*. Paladin, like others in his circle, was of Swedish extraction, and I was surprised to discover that other locals looked down on them, considering them shiftless and dirty, especially those who still occupied "Swede Hill." After the retreat ended and I returned to work, my quiet evenings at the cabin came to an end. My new friends would drop by, a scruffy gang in rusty cars and broken-down pickups, and take me for a night out. They had little to do. The prime activity was hanging out on a strip of odd lots and hot rods in downtown Yakima. Once Paladin invited me to his home on Swede Hill. It turned out to be a tumbledown shack. Banging around inside, his father raged in a drunken stupor. We beat a hasty retreat, and leaving I saw Paladin's face had turned scarlet. We didn't talk about the incident and never returned to his home.

By the summer's end, I had accumulated enough cash from my paychecks, fifty dollars a week, to buy a small secondhand Harley-Davidson. Learning to ride it, I ended up in ditches a number of times, but eventually I got the hang of it. I resolved to ride it across the country, heading home to New York. I set out in late August with a bedroll and bag of clothes strapped to the back.

I barely clocked twenty miles before it broke down. I wheeled it to the nearest motorcycle shop, and had it freighted and shipped to Boston, which gobbled up all of my remaining money. I was forced to hitchhike, but I found the going easy. I went south to San Francisco and then east across the mountains, following Route 30 straight through the fields of Nebraska to Chicago and then on to the turnpikes and New York City. It took me five days. Waiting for rides, with no one in sight, I sang songs on the roadside. I bought postcards in every state and sent them to my mother ("Welcome to Iowa"). I memorized every ride I got and the gist of every conversation with every driver. I had discovered a glorious way to travel. I could go anywhere in the country—for free. I thought of myself as a rambling man, stepping in and out of lives, listening to the dreams and confessions of strangers while speeding along the roads on long afternoons and lonely nights, the original rolling stone.

In my junior year at Andover things began to turn sour. My affection for the place had worn off and I began to strain at the many restrictions. I kept a dog-eared copy of Kerouac's *On the Road* on my bedside table. I took to wearing a black turtleneck sweater—faculty members would occasionally pluck the neck down with a forefinger to see if I was wearing the mandatory tie underneath—and also to smoking, which was allowed twice a day, during fifteen-minute breaks after breakfast and dinner. In the second semester I became embroiled in a controversy involving the student literary magazine, *The Mirror*, of which I was the deputy editor. I wrote a short story about a junior faculty member trying to win the affection of unruly students in a dormitory; his efforts at enforcing discipline were ham-fisted, and the students rebelled. I recounted the story from the students' point of view and at the end I abruptly shifted the perspective to that of the teacher, seen alone in his room, weeping. My thought was that this sudden shift would jolt the reader and force him to see everything that had gone before in a new light. I doubt that it worked. But in any case, the story bought me a great deal of grief. I based it loosely on an apprentice teacher who had been there a year before and was now gone. The editor of the magazine, a senior, inserted the teacher's initials into the story's title, thereby undermining his anonymity. The magazine was printed and then suppressed by a faculty adviser before it was distributed, and the student newspaper broke the story. I was called in and reprimanded, and I didn't defend myself. I didn't mention the fact that it was not I who had come up with the title—to do that, I thought, would be to implicate the editor. The issue was raised at a faculty meeting, where I was loudly condemned, and the decision was made to take away my scholarship.

At the start of summer vacation, a teacher spotted me on the side of the road—hitchhiking to New York—and reported me to the dean. I was informed by mail that this was a serious offense. I wrote back indignantly, declaring that I had had no alternative because I had had no money for the fare home and that, given the same situation again, I would be forced to do the same thing. My ploy—the indignant pose of an impoverished but proud student—worked. I was told that I would start my senior year on a somewhat lenient form of disciplinary probation. By the time the letter reached me, I was well into a summer of wild adventure and unbridled freedom. I was going off the deep end.

That critical summer began, not by accident, on the road—more specifically, at a gas station cutoff on the Jersey side of the George Washington Bridge, a good spot for getting rides west. I had managed to indoctrinate three Andover friends into the glories of hitch-hiking, and we decided to set out for San Francisco. We would travel in pairs and meet up in Chicago in three days, precisely at 6:00 p.m., on the steps of the Art Institute. From there, we would make our way to the freight yards and hop a train west. I was in the second pair, delayed by twenty-four hours as I awaited the arrival of my partner. We had poor luck in getting rides (I hadn't calculated how much longer it would take for two people) and we finally made it to the rendezvous with only twenty minutes to spare. The reunion was joyous—the four of us danced on the sidewalk of Michigan Avenue. Our friends had assessed the situation and had purchased a carton of food for our time in the boxcar. We took a bus to the vicinity of the freight yards.

Then things began to go wrong. We stopped off in a bar to buy bottles of water. Next door was a junkyard of demolished cars, and as we were crossing it, two police cars drove up. We split up, hid, and waited until they left. We reassembled out on the street, but one of us was missing. From inside the yard we heard shouting. A companion and I returned and saw a large black man stomping on top of a car and waving a gun. Gently, taking care not to surprise him, we calmed him down—he turned out to be the night watchman—and we rescued the fourth member of our group, who was still shaking with fear. By now it was getting dark. We circled the junkyard, following a chain-link fence that trailed off above a ravine. We plunged down it, into swamp water up to our waists. By the time we found the yards, we were exhausted, soaked, and filthy. But at least we were there!

Now the problem, in the bewildering jungle of tracks and signals and switching engines, was to find the right train. We had been told that railroad detectives searched the cars before they left, so to elude them, you had to catch the train as it was leaving and gathering speed. We talked to a signalman in a tower; he said a train was due to leave for Los Angeles at five in the morning and he would alert us. We spent the next few hours practicing our technique on trains still being assembled. The first person was the spotter. He would choose the car, toss in the food, and hoist himself up, then ten yards away the second would join him, and those two would help the third, and they'd pick up the fourth as the train accelerated down the line. We got to be pretty good at it. Finally, the moment arrived. Our signalman yelled down: The next train was it! We took our positions and waited anxiously. The engine came on strong, then the boxcars. They flew by, rattling loudly. The doors were closed. Our spotter was on the wrong side of a curve in the tracks, so he couldn't get a good look at the cars to come. Before we knew it, the entire train had thundered past. We were downcast, ashamed in front of one another and the signalman. We stayed there, hoping for another chance. At dawn two railroad detectives spotted us. After a brief interrogation, they drove us to a highway heading west and told us to get out of town.

We split up again. My partner and I, after five days scrambling for rides, were in Tucson when we found ourselves next to a freight train idling at a crossing. We asked the engineer where it was bound and he said it was going to Los Angeles. We jumped on board and lay down on a flatbed car right behind the engine. Four feet above us was the belly of a truck riding piggyback. We were ecstatic—here we were at last, riding the rails. We imagined how jealous our two hitchhiking partners would be. The train took off slowly, with the cars banging against one another. It plodded through the desert all night, pulling off frequently to stop at sidings for hours on end. Each time, the cars smashed against one another, like giant dominoes, jolting us awake. By morning we were hungry and caked in dirt, but still enjoying the adventure—until an encounter that took away the romance. As I looked back along the train, I saw two men way behind us, jumping from car to car, approaching us. We could see them only when the train rounded a bend. Their going was slow and they were invisible much of the time, but each time a bend came, they had moved closer than we'd expected. After about half an hour, they reached us, two wiry men poorly dressed. One of them had lips chapped so badly they were cracked open and the sores inside were bright red. He mumbled something and the other man told him to speak up. He did, suddenly almost shouting. He asked us if we had ChapStick. When we said no, he looked disbelieving. He climbed up into the cab of the backward-facing engine to look, he said, for a first-aid kit. While he was gone, the other man, thin as a rail, with matted hair, complained about him. Ever since they had left prison together some months back, he said, the guy had been following him around like a whipped dog. The first man returned, his mission unaccomplished. He looked at our two small suitcases and then at us and then at the other man. He touched a bulge in his pocket. The other man looked away, as if in thought, then turned back and looked at us and then at the first man. Slowly, he shook his head. A couple of minutes passed in silence. Then they got up and left as they had come, jumping from car to car, away from us. I breathed deeply. They could easily have robbed us and rolled our bodies off the train.

The train pulled into Los Angeles in the evening. We got off and called an Andover buddy, who said he'd be happy to offer us a place to stay. The problem was, he couldn't pick us up right away. I read the nearest street sign to him. He had never heard of it. We were in some kind of manufacturing area. He said he would come shortly after midnight. We killed time. Nearby, we found a pie factory, and so we spent the last of our money to buy a lemon meringue pie for his mother. Then we sat down to wait—hitchhiking does nothing if not teach patience. We waited—and waited. He didn't show. At 3:00 a.m., we ate the pie. We found a fleabag rooming house and slept on the floor of the second-floor corridor. At 6:30, I awoke. My friend was yelling—a man who had opened his door and found him curled up there was kicking him in the stomach. We bolted away and left quickly, then hitchhiked north to San Francisco. There, another Andover friend took us in.

In San Francisco, my friend Steve, from our quartet of hitch-hikers, introduced me to friends, who he said were wild. The first night, one of them, a football player at UCLA, took us out for a ride. He leapt out of Steve's car, ran over to a garage, lifted the door, and emerged at the wheel of a shiny black car. It belonged, he said, to a police detective. Anyone else want to take a ride? I hopped into the passenger seat. On the dash was a police radio and on my side a searchlight. We drove into the Presidio. I tried to yank down the rearview mirror, but it wouldn't budge. When he gave the word, we both jumped out, sending the car careening down a hill, where it smashed into a tree.

The summer continued in that vein. I bummed around, picking fruit in Northern California and getting odd jobs at shape-ups on the grittier sides of towns. I ended up working on a construction crew that was building a school in Santa Barbara, where I joined up again with my buddy Steve. We got to know some locals who liked making trouble. A handsome young man named Keith knew how to hot-wire cars and seemed to steal them as a matter of convenience to get around town. Once or twice we joined him, until one evening we crashed a car into a concrete gateway pillar. Neighbors rushed out, worried looks on their faces. We ran off. Separated, we made our way back to town, hiding in the bushes as every car passed. I resolved to give up car theft. At one point, Keith invited us to move into a house whose owner was away; he had been hired to look after it. He broke a windowpane to simulate forced entry; that way, he could explain the damage. We stayed only a couple of days. I learned that the owner was in rehab, and I didn't like messing up his house.

In August, we hitchhiked to San Diego and crossed the border into Tijuana. The town was filthy and disgusting. Every two steps, it seemed, we were accosted by pimps and dealers. There, going up a back staircase to the second floor of a whorehouse, in a room with toilet paper tossed in a corner, bullied by a pimp into buying a rubber for five dollars, I lost my virginity.

At the end of the month, I hitchhiked home. I had spent the night before my departure at a fancy party with a girlfriend named Denise; I had borrowed a tuxedo from her friend and gotten so drunk that I'd vomited all over it. The next morning, Steve drove me to my starting point, the beginning of the Golden Gate Bridge. We shook hands and he left. As I stood there, hungover, the taste of vomit still in my throat, depressed at the prospect of all the miles ahead and filled with self-loathing, I wondered what in God's name I was doing.

Somewhere along the line, I had evolved the philosophical notion that experience was all. The importance of adventures was in the living of them. Added up, they would build character and endow understanding. Each bizarre encounter, each brush with danger, each passage through yet another crazy set of circumstances was another tale to tell, a notch in my belt. In lost moments, waiting by a deserted roadside, with my gut rumbling from hunger, I'd remember all the rides I'd had up to that point, as if they made a significant pattern. I'd reconfigure my life on the road, summarizing it like the biographical bullets I used to read on the back cover of paperbacks: The author went to sea as a merchant marine, worked as a short-order cook in Hong Kong, taught English in Peru. Somewhere in this jumbled journey through the underbelly of America, I thought, would come wisdom and meaning.

After such a summer it was difficult to turn back into an upstanding prep school boy. I managed to make it through most of my senior year. I was breaking rules about smoking and drinking but avoided getting caught. At one point I was called in by Dean Benedict and chastised for having a "negative attitude." I protested—the soul of innocence—but he had me dead to rights. I spent a good deal of time in the infirmary with fake illnesses, made convincing by high fevers, induced by holding thermometers up to lightbulbs. My grades were suffering badly—I was in advanced courses, like calculus, and skipping so many classes that I was hopelessly behind. By now, I detested Andover—everything about it. Looking at the boys seated around me in chapel or in the dining hall, boys who were my friends, I saw hypocrites and conformists. It was the school that had done that to them, I told myself, the school—with its dictum: "Our goal is not to build boys but to mold men." Andover had methodically misshaped them into soulless achievers ready to assume positions of privilege they had not earned.

Despite my attitude, my prospects for college were looking good. In the last semester, I was given an "A rating" by Harvard, meaning that I was a shoo-in as a candidate for admission, provided I remained a student in good standing. I did not. With only months left to graduation, one Saturday night I left campus in a car after signing into my dormitory; I went to a bar in the nearby town of Lowell and had half a glass of beer. My absence was discovered when my mother tried to phone me and the housemaster couldn't locate me. The horrible part was who was driving the car: my brother. He had come up from Harvard to visit me, along with his girlfriend, and she and I had convinced him on the steps of my dormitory to keep the evening alive. "Let's go somewhere," I said. He was reluctant to get me in trouble, but neither did he want to look like a spineless killjoy. In the bar, we had a grand time. There was an open mike, and he and I sang a hillbilly song, "As Fer as I'm Concerned," until we were practically booed off the stage by the barflies.

In my dorm my housemaster waited in ambush. He had been alerted to my absence when my mother had phoned. He interrogated me, and I tried to lie my way out of it. I said I had been in the infirmary. He knew I had not been; he had called there. He said he smelled alcohol on my breath. I did a quick calculation. Could I save the situation by making a clean breast of it? Of course. I admitted what I had done and apologized for placing him in the position of having to make such a difficult decision: He could report me, and end my time at Andover, or he could ignore this unfortunate incident, knowing that I had learned my lesson and that I would never do such a thing again. I stopped, my heart racing, waiting for his response. He looked me in the eye. "I'm not in a difficult position," he said quickly. "I have no choice. I must report you." Within two hours, Dean Benedict and another faculty member convened a meeting of two and expelled me. When Benedict told me, he seemed to display the superior air of a man whose verdict had been vindicated. The next morning, I was to be on a train to New York City.

I didn't feel shook up by leaving. I felt quite the opposite—almost a kind of exhilaration. I took a moment from packing to slip outside my dormitory and carve my name deep into a wooden bench along a pathway. I was leaving my mark. My housemaster called me in for a last-minute talk. He wondered what had gone wrong, why my trajectory at Andover had been so promising and then had gone into a tailspin. I was touched by his curiosity, if not his concern, and I tried to gather my thoughts. I didn't tell him about my growing disillusionment—my distress at losing my scholarship, my anger at the social conformity, my jealousy of my classmates' money and privilege. None of this was clear to me at the time. Nor was I able to dig into a deeper truth: that Andover had become a symbol to me. The school often spoke of acting in loco parentis, and I had come to accept this literally. For me, Andover had become an authority figure. It had taken the place of my mother and the entire adult world. I wanted to fight against it and overthrow it. How much better to turn my back on the treadmill competition for top grades and credentials and instead assume the role of the one who refuses to go along, who works to bring down the whole system. I would go out with a bang. My expulsion would complete my résumé—I was now typecast in the role I coveted: the rebel, the troublemaker, the outsider. I didn't tell my housemaster this because I didn't know it. I just felt this strange new sense of exhilaration. I looked him in the eye and croaked, "Something's wrong with this place. You ought to let in girls."

One agony of my expulsion was my brother's involvement in it. He had been reluctant to take me off campus, knowing that I, not he, would be running the risk, and he knew how big the consequences were. The iron dictate of our family was that he, in his role as father substitute, would protect me. Now he had thrown that obligation to the winds. Moments before I was to leave Andover, the phone rang. He was on the line and he began by saying that he hadn't been able to sleep that night, that he wanted reassurance that I had returned to my dorm without getting caught. I took a deep breath and told him I had been expelled. He responded with a long, low moan, a groan of pain.

He met my train in Boston. We would ride down on the train to New York and confront Mom together. On the way, our conversation uncharacteristically turned to our childhood. For the first time, we began exchanging confidences about it, about what we remembered and how hard it had been. He said he wanted to tell me something that he had vowed he never would. It was something that he had seen as a young boy. What was it? I asked. He paused, as if he were reconsidering. Then he began. Did I remember that time Uncle Ben came to visit years ago? The time he brought along with him a buddy, the soccer player, the man who had lifted up his pants leg to show us all the scars on his shin? I remembered perfectly. The next morning, Bob said, he had gone into our mother's bedroom. She was asleep, and sleeping next to her was the man. The sheets were in disarray and he was naked and lying on his side; his penis was hanging down. "I sometimes wondered," Bob said, "years afterward, if she had asked Ben to bring someone along, you know, a kind of stud to sleep with her." I was shocked at his revelation, but even in the midst of it, I wondered how he had been able to stash it away inside himself all these years, like a small bullet imbedded in the flesh.

It's odd how the past is never really past, how it can rise up to club you when you least expect it. I didn't feel upset by his revelation, not as much as I later thought I should have been. Something had insulated me from it, maybe all the years that had passed in ignorance. I wondered how the episode had affected my brother, husbanding through childhood that shocking primal image of a stranger in bed with our mother. And why had he chosen this particular moment to reveal it? Was it a means of reducing our mother in our eyes, so that we could face up to her? Or was it proof, at a time when he was open to the accusation that he had abrogated his most important responsibility, that he really was capable of protecting me, that he had been doing it all that time by keeping that bullet wound secret?

When we made it to New York and saw Mom, there was no recrimination. She saved all of her umbrage for Andover, insisting it was too puritanical for boys of creativity and spirit. Typically, she was on our side, no questions asked.

Over the years, I've told the story of my expulsion from Andover with a kind of perverse pride. In the telling, I sometimes try to minimize the role my brother played, shading the narrative a bit, emphasizing how his girlfriend and I had to persuade him to act against his better judgment, protecting him as he should have protected me. But there's no getting around the repercussions the expulsion had. There I was—one minute on the threshold of getting into Harvard, the next scrambling to find a high school to graduate from.

Recently, reading letters between Andover and my mother—letters in which the school demanded payment of back tuition amounting to $675.63 and refused to release my transcript until it was made, and in which my mother attacked the school for expelling me—I came across a stark assessment of Bob's role in the affair. The letter was from Benedict, explaining that the disciplinary committee sought "extenuation in the fact that John's absence from bounds was in the company of his brother." Sadly, he said, the committee could not. He went on: "I am myself in doubt as to just what happened between the two boys. John insists that the initiative was his, that he worked hard to persuade Bob to take him along and finally succeeded. Be that as it may, I should expect that the business would be one which would lie heavily on Bob's conscience." His letter struck a truth deeper than he knew.

But as I dug into the correspondence more, I realized that for years I had been omitting some important details in telling the tale. I was astounded to rediscover what I had once known: that I had been properly chastised for a "negative attitude," that I was failing two courses—chemistry and calculus—and that, in fact, I had already lost my "A rating" to get into Harvard. Who knows? Perhaps I wouldn't have been admitted there in any case. I abruptly recalled that I had already been breaking serious rules at Andover, taking swigs from a bottle of rum hidden in a bench and smoking cigarettes in prohibited areas. I was itching for trouble, in full-fledged rebellion.

These were facts that had dropped by the wayside in my narrative, as I'd honed it over the years, confident that no matter how

I tried to downplay Bob's guilt, it would shine through, a kind of irredeemable sin, and that my attempts to minimize it were likely to come across as rather noble and even touchingly loyal, as befitting a brother.

Every good story demands a coda. Twenty-five years after my expulsion, a new dean invited me to a reunion. He said there had been a "grassroots" movement to have me return and added that if I did, Andover would give me a diploma. My first response was to fire back a refusal, saying, "Sadly, your capacity for forgiveness outstrips my own." But then I relented. My old Andover friend Nate, who turned out to constitute the entire grassroots movement, persuaded me by insisting: "If you fall off a fence, you must go back and touch it."

The twenty-fifth reunion was a bust. It was held in a cabin in the woods, a place I had rarely visited as a student, and not many classmates showed up. The dean put in an appearance and made a speech. At one point, turning to me, he allowed as how an "injustice" had been done to a member of the class but added that the record was vague as to what offense I had actually committed. "They don't even know," I thought to myself. He ended by saying he could not confer a diploma—that would require approval from the board of trustees—but had been empowered to offer instead "a certificate of attendance." He gave it to me, already framed.

I stepped onto a tabletop and made a short speech. Looking my former classmates in the eyes, I said I had come back not to honor Andover but to see them, since what counted in the long run was not loyalty to an impersonal institution but the friendships formed there. I explained I had gone off campus and consumed half a beer, and, holding a glass with half a beer remaining, I offered a toast—to them, not the school—and downed it.

When I sat down, a man I recognized as something of a campus cut-up all those years before sidled over for a chat. His name was Tom. He said that he, too, had been expelled.

"Really?" I remarked. "What did you do?"

He said that his roommate, Ned Evans, known to come from a wealthy family, had found a condom in a drawer. Ned blew it up.

They played with it, batting it back and forth like a balloon and brought it outside. When the housemaster's toddler came by, they gave it to her, and the child ran off with it, skipping around a corner. Within minutes, they heard her mother scream.

"That must have been horrible," I said. "So you had to leave right away?"

He smiled.

"Not at all," he said. "I stayed."

I was mystified and asked him to explain. "My roommate's father called the headmaster of the school and asked him, 'What building do you most need?' The answer was a new science hall. He said, 'The day my son graduates, you'll get it.' "

I was aghast.

"You don't believe me?" Tom said. He reached into his pocket, pulled out a map, and pointed to a darkened silhouette of a building that was labeled EVANS HALL.

I did not keep my certificate of attendance.

CHAPTER 14

I went to the University of Wisconsin in Madison by a roundabout path. After I was expelled from Andover, no private school of any repute would take me on to finish out the year. I enrolled in a place called the Searing School, a small tutoring outfit of tiny cubicles in a walk-up off Lexington Avenue. I needed only four credits to graduate. My teacher was a soft-spoken young man from Mississippi, who sported a fine mustache in the style of William Faulkner, his hero, whose works he assigned, along with Hawthorne and Henry James. He had moved to New York in hopes of making it as a writer and lived with his wife in a tiny apartment on Horatio Street in the Village. They invited me there to talk about writers and writing. We drank cheap Chianti. The relationship felt like something I must have read about once, life in the Village in gentler times. I celebrated my "graduation" with a night of drinking at the Subway Inn, a smoky dive on Lexington and Sixtieth Street. My diploma was supposed to come by mail, but I don't remember ever seeing it.

That summer I finally got my fill of hitchhiking. I thumbed my way to Lake Tahoe, California, to meet up with my friend Steve. When I arrived and he wasn't there, I turned around in a huff and hitchhiked back to New York. I had run out of money, rides were scarce, and truck drivers, worried about insurance, had stopped taking on passengers. Some of my encounters were dicey. A car driven by two African-Americans, who were drunk, plowed into another car on the Pennsylvania Turnpike. Before the police arrived, I tossed away a bottle from the backseat and, my head aching, walked to a service area to thumb another ride.

Back home, I worked for a while as a soda jerk at a Walgreens. Then I went to Cape Cod and got a job at a summer camp in exchange for steamship fare to Europe. I had enrolled by mail at Lycée Henri-IV in Paris; my intent was to spend a year there, learn French, and reapply to Harvard, which had advised me to spend the year in "a constructive way." My time abroad didn't work out as I had planned. I lasted only one week at the lycée. I found the boys there immature—they threw spitballs when the teachers' backs were turned—and the rote learning dull. But I soon immersed myself in the language and culture. I obtained a certificate from the Alliance Française and haunted the cafés and parks and museums. I walked the Left Bank streets at all hours, smoked pot, read the classics, fell in bed with a Parisian named Jacqueline and multiple others, tried passing myself off as French, and wrote a couple of bad poems. Most of all, I matured. It was a time for introspection, and I wallowed in it. I had been lucky that stealing cars hadn't landed me in trouble. It was time to look to the future. In short, I felt myself beginning to grow up.

I reapplied to Harvard, filling my application with a laundry list of books I had read in French and an essay arguing that French culture was superior to American. Only a French poet, I insisted, could write a poem about eating a seagull. Harvard turned me down. A friend recommended Wisconsin, which had rolling admissions, and I applied there and was accepted. That summer I got a job in New York, working as a medical attendant for paralyzed patients at the Rusk Institute of Rehabilitation Medicine on Thirty-fourth Street. While I was there, my childhood hero, Roy Campanella, the man who had commemorated my birthday, was admitted; he had been in a car crash and was paralyzed from the shoulders down. His room was in a private area on the third floor, and we were all told not to bother him—he was said to be depressed. I had visions of talking to him, encouraging him, inspiring in him the will to carry on. Several times I slipped up to the third floor, but each time his door was closed. Then, one afternoon, I found it open just a crack. I pushed against it and peered inside. Campy was lying on his back, surrounded by machines, his eyes closed. He was inert, his large bulk covered by a blanket. I looked at him for a moment, listening to the machines. I was on the threshold of a great moment, but I didn't know what to do. I decided not to wake him. He was beyond my help. I backed out quietly, drawing the door closed, and never saw him again.

I entered Wisconsin in the fall of 1961. I hitchhiked to school, again with a single suitcase. At the first lecture, I spotted a beautiful young woman with dark hair, worn long and straight in the bohemian style. She entered the lecture hall late, mounting a side aisle and trying to appear inconspicuous. I looked at my watch and shook my head; she smiled. I gave her my seat. She sat on my raincoat, and when I picked it up after the lecture, it was flattened and wrinkled. She was flustered when she handed it back to me. We didn't speak. But by chance we found ourselves in the same English section two days later. We went out to lunch. And so I met Nina Lieberman from Brooklyn.

I played it cool and didn't ask her out for weeks, though we often seemed to fall in together after classes. We walked in step, I remarked. Our first date was memorable. I convinced her one evening that it was permissible to borrow one of the rowboats that were stacked upside down at the boathouse—not all of them were padlocked—for an outing on Lake Mendota. She packed a picnic basket. She was sitting in the boat, waiting patiently as I clamored over a pile of lumber to look for something to use as a paddle, when a police cruiser came around the bend. The officers threatened arrest and put us in the cruiser. On the way, I was showing off, wisecracking, until one of them turned around and blurted, "What's a matter? Don't you want to be treated like a white man?" "No," I countered, "just a man." At the station house we were given a lecture about the inviolability of private property and then released. The police drove us back to campus and, suddenly friendly, put the siren on at my request. It was still sounding as we drew up to her dormitory, and the housemother, who happened to be standing in front, dropped her mouth in surprise and glared at us. All in all, I thought, it was an auspicious beginning.

On our second date, we went to an Italian eatery. Still flush in my road warrior, "I'm from New York City" stage, I remarked over a cup of coffee that I wouldn't mind dating a young Wisconsin girl: "You know, somebody who works in an ice-cream parlor . . . somebody who's never heard of Kerouac."

Nina smiled and joked, "Who's Kerouac?"

When I walked her to her dormitory that evening, she went to fetch a blanket for me—it was already getting cold at night—and when she handed it over, I covered us, and standing underneath it, I kissed her. We began going out and soon spent most of every day with each other. I was, I realized, for the first time in my life, in love. But it took a long, long while for me to be able to say that out loud.

In one of our first classes, an introduction to anthropology, the professor assigned us to write our autobiographies. Taking a leaf from my mother's book, I wrote a sunny version of my childhood, skirting over the rough spots and emphasizing the times of spontaneous fun. When the paper was returned, I wouldn't show it to Nina. She entreated me; I refused. She grabbed for it; I held it out of her reach. We proceeded like this down the sidewalk until, coming to a mailbox, I dropped it in. That settled the matter. For years afterward, years in which she helped me deal more honestly with my past, she asked me why I had done that. I came to realize that, on a level not quite conscious, I hadn't wanted to present her with a pack of lies.

We were cultural opposites. Nina grew up in an attached house in Sheepshead Bay, Brooklyn, the daughter of a furrier who emigrated from Russia, by way of Cuba, as a boy of thirteen. She went to the High School of Performing Arts, hoping to become an actress. She had never tasted an artichoke or stepped inside a church. I had gone to a fancy prep school, had a home address that sounded rich until you saw it, and had never tasted a bagel or seen the inside of a synagogue. She came to my house for Christmas and I went to hers for Passover.

I was schooled in repression and had never, to my knowledge, known anyone who had been to a shrink. Nina was a believer in ferreting out secrets and the truth, and over time she relentlessly pried me out of my shell. In courting Nina, I realized years later—she, of course, was the one who pointed it out—I was incorporating the rituals of my parents. Orion was our constellation. I took to asking her, "Have I told you today?" On our first vacation together in New York, we went to the Oyster Bar, where my mother and father used to meet. And we talked of how we had been destined for each other. I was convinced that the relationship between my mother and father had been perfect and that any relationship I had would be perfect also. Later, the attempt to replicate the ideal made for problems. When Nina and I had arguments—often because I would turn up hours late or disappear somewhere without calling—they caused me to question the strength of our bond. I was sure my parents had never fought; after all, I had never witnessed such a thing. It took years for me to learn how people who love each other actually behave.

My major was experimental psychology. I spent untold hours in the laboratory running experiments on rats, gradually ascending the evolutionary scale as high as monkeys. Eventually, I would become more interested in Elizabethan literature than in a Skinner box. I hung out in the Rathskeller, the basement of the student union, which was frequented by New York radicals. I lived off campus, had little money, and didn't eat regularly. For two years I subsisted on meager food and meals Nina bought me. When we ate out, we instituted an elaborate charade: I would claim not to be hungry and she would be famished, so famished that she would order for two. When the food came, she would quietly push one plate in front of me.

I lived by my wits. I shoplifted at the Kroger supermarket, slipping packages of hot dogs into my pants. I scammed the two bookstores on State Street, stealing textbooks from one and selling them back to the other, and vice versa the following day. Finally, I got a part-time job in the psych lab and earned honest cash. During summer vacations, I worked in New York: as a souvenir salesman at the top of the Empire State Building, a Sky Ride attendant at Coney Island, a mail sorter in the bowels of the General Post Office on Eighth Avenue. But invariably I had to hand over my earnings to pay Mom's households expenses and rent. In my third year, I couldn't scrape up $362.52 for out-of-state tuition. The parents of a classmate from Long Island lent me the money and Bob helped pay them back.

Wisconsin was politically active in the years I was there, from 1961 to 1966. (I stayed an extra year to mop up my incompletes.) I was arrested as a freedom rider by Spiro Agnew in Baltimore County, went to the March on Washington, and took part in innumerable demonstrations against the Vietnam War, including the levitation of the Pentagon.

For most of these years, Bob was away at Oxford, a Rhodes scholar. He obtained a doctor of philosophy degree in eighteenth-century European history from St. John's College, and while there he married his Harvard sweetheart, Susan Glover—the same girlfriend whom I had met on that fateful Andover weekend. Mom borrowed the money to attend their wedding in an Oxford church, but I stayed home, looking for work. Before I found it—at a post office on the Upper East Side—I was desperate for money. Several times I sold my blood for ten dollars at a dingy walk-up blood bank on Forty-second Street.

Bob and Susan returned to New York and, with a heavy heart, as it turned out, he went to work at the *Times,* assuming the mantle that had always been his.

On a break from the university, I went to visit Bob down at the police reporters' "shack" on Centre Market Place. He had just begun work as a reporter at the *Times* and was undergoing the initiation rite for beginners back in those days, the early 1960s—covering the murders, suicides, and other crimes coughed up by the city. On the police beat, he was in the belly of the beast, a scholar rubbing elbows with cops who couldn't care less about the Enlightenment and wizened police reporters who couldn't construct a sentence, calling their stories in to rewrite instead. He read a tome on the Italian Renaissance by hiding it inside *Playboy.* When I first heard him speaking on the phone with "the desk"—an editor on the city desk—it was clear to me that he didn't belong there. He nasalized his vowels and hardened his consonants to sound like a street guy. It wasn't really him—or, as he might put it, being grammatically correct, it wasn't really he.

Its nickname, the shack, was not a misnomer. The place was a gritty three-story tenement across from the old police headquarters, sandwiched between bail bondsmen and storefronts that sold firearms, ammunition, and bulletproof vests. Inside were offices for the various newspapers and wire services, dingy rooms with little more than banged-up desks, linoleum floors, ratty window shades, and, of course, the essential telephones. Outside, the distinguishing feature was the dozen or so lightbulbs protruding from the façade like illuminated bumpers on a pinball machine. Each one was a different color (blue for the *Post,* red for the *Times,* and so on). When one lighted up, that was a signal to the reporter—who might be down on the sidewalk, escaping from the heat or playing poker—that someone was calling him. That way, he could dash inside to take the call.

When I entered the shack and climbed up the stairs to the *Times* office on the second floor, I found Bob seated behind a desk, his suit jacket hanging from a hook on the door. A police radio was blasting static into the room. From the hallway sounded the thuds of a large bell in an annoying irregular staccato—code, he explained, to indicate the location and severity of a fire. Only the old-timers could decipher it. I was blown away by it all. Ghosts of Edgar Allan Poe and O. Henry haunted the place. I had entered a Stygian underground, a locale where the pulse of New York City could be heard beating, in toxic fitfulness, twenty-four hours a day.

There were no women, other than the naked photos on faded calendars. I was introduced to some of the veterans, including Patrick Doyle of the *Daily News,* nicknamed "Inspector" for his ability to extract information from cops at crime scenes by suggesting that he was their superior, calling "from headquarters." Some of them, I was told, employed multiple names for suicides, depending on such nuances as whether the "leaper" jumped off a bridge or a building. In my father's years, when there were all those daily newspapers around, between twenty and thirty reporters were assigned to the "cop shop," but now the ranks had thinned to less than a dozen at any one time. Mixed in among them were young reporters earning their chops.

One of them, Nicholas Pileggi, then working for the Associated Press, suggested it was time for an early-evening banquet. In remarkably short order a sweep of the building produced a happy band of ten, including hangers-on, which moved down Mulberry Street toward a renowned Italian eatery. They left one reporter behind to cover for them and answer their phones. I tagged along, impressed by the cohesive spirit and the "us against them" mentality—in which the "them," I quickly learned, was not the police but their respective newspaper bosses. We commandeered a long table that was soon heaped with bottles of wine, calamari, spaghetti, veal piccata, and other Italian delicacies. We ate for two hours. From time to time a phone attached to a nearby wooden pillar would ring and someone in our party would answer it, cupping his palm over the mouthpiece so he could hear. The caller was the reporter left in the trenches. "Hold on," our guy would say, turning to the group. "Two-alarm fire, Mott Haven, no injuries." All agreed: not worth filing. Ten minutes later, another call: "Body in a trunk in Bed-Stuy. No ID." Same response. And so I learned a second lesson that day: The city's pulse could be monitored at a distance—with a little help from friends. And that could be fun. Reporters were underpaid, but they were a scrappy lot and they extracted compensations. After a year at the *Times*, Bob quit, returning to his first love, history, beginning a long and distinguished career.

When I graduated from Wisconsin, Nina and I got married and I needed a job. I passed a test to become a copy editor at McGraw-Hill, an entry into publishing, but I wasn't looking forward to it. Days before I was to report for work, my mother happened to mention that when our father died she had been given a letter from the *Times* publisher, promising us boys a job if either of us wanted one. The letter had been lost long ago, but perhaps something could be arranged. Did I want a job there? I thought so. She placed a call to an assistant managing editor at the *Times,* someone she had known from the old days, and I was taken on as a copyboy. I was excited at the idea of working there, recollecting that evening I had spent with my brother down at the police shack.

In the same way that my father dated his obsession with newspaper work to the days and nights he spent in New York with his uncle Charles Darnton, the drama critic, I would later look back to that meal on Mulberry Street and regard it as the time I got hooked on the same profession.

CHAPTER 15

For twelve years, not a drop of alcohol passed my mother's lips. At times it seemed she was teasing us: If a stranger offered her a glass of wine, she would raise it to her nose and sniff it with the ceremonial frown of an expert, appraising. On these occasions Bob could barely restrain himself from grabbing the glass out of her hand. Finally, with a judgment—"The bouquet is superb"—she would quietly put it aside. It was an odd dance. To this day, I don't know if she was testing herself, proving that alcohol wasn't something to be frightened of, or testing our forbearance, or sending a message to the stranger that she wasn't a killjoy. Or perhaps, given that wine and spirits were so meaningful to her generation, both as a touchstone and a metaphor for the good life, she simply couldn't bear to pass up the nostalgic ritual.

In the job market she did not do as well. Here, the damage was done. She had lost too much ground in taking short-term, low-paying positions, and her résumé was filled with too many unexplainable blank spots. She never again found a job that measured up to her talents or experience, and she had trouble holding on to the jobs she did manage to land. After PR, she worked for a few years as an editor at *Parade* magazine, the Sunday newspaper supplement, and then got piecemeal employment wherever she could. She went long periods without a salary and was hard put to support herself. Scraping together the rent—the less than princely sum of ninety-eight dollars a month—was dicey. More than once, the landlord, who happened to be the golfing reporter at *The New York Times,* threatened eviction. She dreaded, in her mid- and late fifties, going out on job interviews and would often come home feeling humiliated when someone half her age treated her cavalierly. One time, while being grilled about her résumé, she left in a huff, blurting out, "Why don't you just look me up in *Who's Who?*"

We remained poor. The small neighborhood grocery store two blocks up on Madison Avenue allowed us to charge goods, and Mom invariably was way behind in paying the bill. I hated the place. When I was sent to pick up an order she'd placed by phone, I dreaded the look of the man at the checkout counter, his narrowed eyes and set jaw, as I uttered the words "Charge it, please." Mom ran up a stack of IOUs from her friends. They covered some twenty years. A long time afterward, I found them placed in a folder, along with copies of letters she had written describing the desperation of our situation and asking for a little something "to tide me over," along with promises to repay the sum soon. There were also four or five letters from the friends who made the loans, begging for them to be made good. I recognized the names on the letters—people who long ago had been regulars in our lives and who had probably dropped us, I concluded, as deadbeats. I doubt she ever repaid any of them.

Increasingly, without work and a wide circle of friends, Mom led a solitary life. She visited museums and took an occasional meal out, but mostly she stayed home, reading, knitting sweaters, and watching television. From time to time she wrote magazine articles and took up exotic hobbies like mixing potpourri—collections of herbs, dried flowers, and spices, which were given names like "Walpurgis Night" and "Ophelia's Bouquet." She lived for the days when I would come home on vacation. Then she would pour out observations and thoughts bottled up over months and regale me with stories of her encounters with New Yorkers. My friends loved to sleep over, taking the roll-away bed, while I took the couch, so that they could talk late into the night with her. She'd sit on the edge of her winged easy chair, her elbows resting on her knees, smoking and drinking scalding coffee, dispensing worldly wisdom and helping them sort out their lives.

I noticed age tugging at her. Her hair thinned and turned gray, rising in a nimbus around her head. She put on enough pounds to be called plump, her skin began to loosen, and she had bags under her eyes. But those eyes still sparkled with mischief. Her face was so open and welcoming that strangers often talked to her on buses or in coffee shops, and when she told of these meetings—or recounted any story for that matter—she acted them out, moving her hands swiftly, like a conjurer.

By the time I was in college, our relationship evolved into an easygoing, bantering friendship. I called her by the nickname "Darty." We played Scrabble and drank no-cal ginger ale. She taught me a parlor trick she had learned long ago, a way to startle onlookers—how to stick a pin in your thigh without it hurting (the trick is to tighten the muscle). I taught her the "Gypsy lady" card trick, in which the fall guy picked a card at random, called a number I provided, and she guessed it (there was a code in the name he asked for). I sometimes used the trick to astound a barroom full of strangers and win a night's worth of drinks. She'd ham it up, speaking in some kind of half-French, half-Balkan accent and demanding that the card be held close to the receiver so she could "read" it. Once she muffed the code—she pronounced the card to be the queen of diamonds and it was the jack—but she quickly recovered with a witty excuse: "Zee moustache—eet does not come across zee long distanz."

These are the times, and this is the way, that I now like to remember her.

Sometime in the late fall of 1966, Mom began to feel run-down and experienced vaginal bleeding. She went for a checkup and had a Pap smear, something she had neglected to do for many years. It was positive for cervical cancer.

At this point Bob and I, both newly married, were starting out on our careers. He had gone to Harvard as a junior fellow. I had started as a copyboy in August and Nina was working as an editorial assistant at Random House. We had taken over Mom's apartment on East Sixty-third Street after convincing the landlord that we could handle the rent, which went up to $108 a month, ten dollars more than my weekly paycheck.

We had thought long and hard, before the illness struck, about where Mom should live. By now she wanted to luxuriate in a full-fledged retirement, somewhere outside the city, preferably in a small town with character. It also had to be an inexpensive place, so that Bob and I could support her with modest contributions from our piddling incomes. That was a tall order, but we hit upon a solution. She could move in with her eldest brother, Ernest Choate, himself a widower. During the depths of the Depression, Ernie, the most responsible and conscientious of his siblings, who for years had banked his teacher's salary in Philadelphia, had had the foresight to purchase a vacation house in Cape May Point in southern New Jersey. It was a spacious and attractive three-story cottage divided right down the middle into two sections connected by a single door. And best of all, it was only one block from the Atlantic Ocean. We presented the idea to Ernie and his two daughters and they approved it. He was probably lonely, the daughters said, and Tootie would certainly provide lively company. She could even cook him meals. Though they hadn't been close over the years, living together would give them a chance to repair their relationship. And the partitioning of the house was ideal: If they got on each other's nerves, they could go off to their separate domains and sulk in privacy. We would pay something for her upkeep.

We went down to investigate. The cottage seemed perfect. It had a large screened porch, which caught a breeze on long summer evenings. At night a lighthouse a quarter of a mile away cast luminous beams across the bedroom ceilings. Seagulls cruised the sky above, the driveway was lined with seashells, and on windy days the crashing of the surf could be heard from the front doorstep. A stone's throw away was a sandy beach. Mom would love taking walks on it. The deal was done and she moved in. For months, from the reports we got—largely from her—everything seemed to be going just fine. Then, after spotting the bleeding, she saw her doctor in New York and discovered that she was ill.

She underwent surgery at Roosevelt Hospital in New York. The operation seemed to go okay, though the doctors were cautious in predicting a full recovery. Take it one step at a time, they advised. Clearly, the prognosis would have been better if she had had regular screenings and they had caught it earlier, they said, but still they insisted, in that balancing act of dispensing hope alongside truth, that these things sometimes took an unpredictable course. Bob helped her check out of the hospital and was shocked to see that when she signed her name, she wrote "Eleanor Hill"—her name when she was married to her first husband. "Why did you do that?" he asked. She looked down, shocked and flustered by what she had done, and quickly changed it to "Darnton."

Now we faced a new dilemma. She had to undergo a course of radiology and would require care during and after the treatments; we could hardly ask Ernie to take on this chore. We didn't have enough money to hire a full-time nurse. How could we arrange transportation for further checkups or administer medication or just be by her side to bolster her morale? I was tethered to a full-time job at the paper, working nights, so it fell to Bob to relocate from Boston to Cape May. Dutifully, he assumed the lion's share of the burden of taking care of her. When he arrived, he found that brother and sister had fallen to bickering like an old unhappily married couple. "Their relationship was horrible," he recalled many years later. "They were just picking at each other. Ernie's resentment was very visible in all his exchanges with her. He wanted to enlist me on his side in their little squabbles, kept feeding me stories about how badly she treated him. That's when he told me how long before she had asked him to loan her money and when he went to give it, the door was opened by a Japanese houseboy. I resented him—here she was, dying of cancer, and he was running her down."

Bob spent a miserable six weeks there, driving her to the county hospital for radiation sessions several times a week. "The doctor was quite frank with me. He said she was dying. I remember asking him how to cope with Mom, what to say about her illness. He said most people in her condition don't want to know, they don't ask, 'Am I going to die?' And sure enough, she did not. So that issue was never joined. She never talked about dying. And the doctor never told her."

Barney Darnton shipping out in February 1942.
His last notebook turned up thirty-three years
after his death.

Reporters and photographers on the SS *Monterey*. Barney is standing on the far right. *(Wisconsin Historical Society)*

The correspondents' hut in Port Moresby *(Wisconsin Historical Society)*

In Port Moresby, soaking boots to break them in. This is the last photograph of Barney. *(Ed Widdis / Courtesy of Joe Larkin)*

Posing in a slit trench. LEFT TO RIGHT: Robert Sherrod, *Time;* Barney; Tom Yarbrough, Associated Press; Carleton Kent, *Chicago Times;* Major Elbert Helton, U.S. Army.

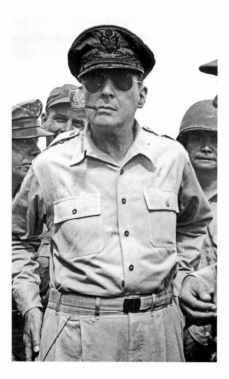

General MacArthur
*(U.S. Army Signal Corps / General Douglas
MacArthur Foundation, Norfolk, Virginia)*

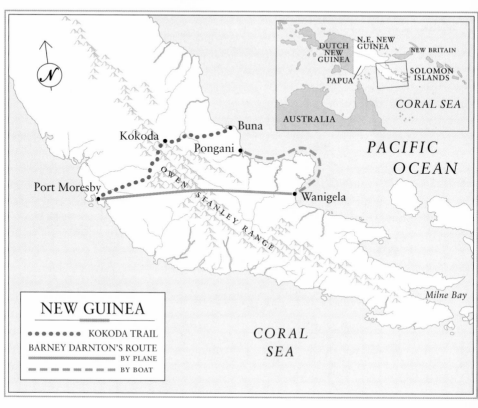

NEW GUINEA

•••••••• KOKODA TRAIL
BARNEY DARNTON'S ROUTE
━━━━━ BY PLANE
━ ━ ━ ━ BY BOAT

Barney examining a B-25 at Amberley Field, Brisbane *(Colonel Mark T. Muller)*

Troops aboard the *Timoshenko* on the way to Pongani shortly before the bombing *(Neil Sandery)*

The *Timoshenko* and *King John* (RIGHT) at Sydney harbor

Wounded carried ashore at Wanigela after the attack at Pongani *(Australian War Memorial)*

Barney's casket, carried by correspondents, at Bomana War Cemetery, Port Moresby
(Wisconsin Historical Society)

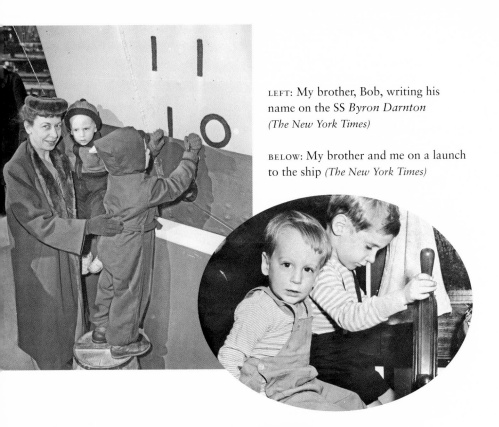

LEFT: My brother, Bob, writing his name on the SS *Byron Darnton* *(The New York Times)*

BELOW: My brother and me on a launch to the ship *(The New York Times)*

Bob and me at play

Mom, Bob, and me at home in Westport

Bob and me with my beloved hound dog, Nicky

My mother early in her career

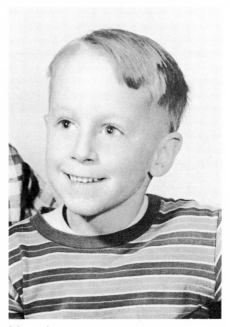

Me at six or seven

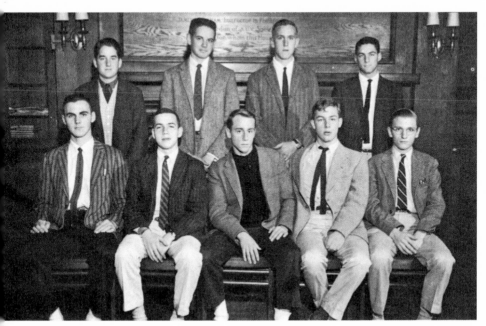

The staff of Andover's literary magazine. I'm in my indispensable black turtleneck.
(Courtesy of Pot Pourri *yearbook)*

ABOVE: Nina's and my wedding photo

LEFT: Mom in 1966

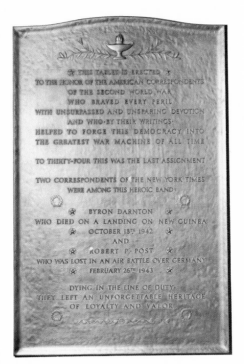

The plaque from the lobby of the old *Times* building *(The New York Times)*

Meeting Charles Garry and Huey Newton during the Black Panther trials *(The New York Times)*

ABOVE: Covering Idi Amin's fall in Uganda *(The New York Times)*

LEFT: Befriended while with the guerrillas in Eritrea *(The New York Times)*

With Lech Wałęsa on a plane awaiting takeff at Gdańsk airport

Speaking to Metro reporters as their new editor, 1986 *(The New York Times)*

Nina at Sanda, Scotland

Bob and me visiting the pub in Sanda

Lieutenant Bruce Fahnestock, yachtsman and explorer, was also killed on board the *King John*.

Robert L. Owens at his ninetieth birthday party. He helped bring Barney's body ashore. *(Sherita Hatch)*

Flight and ground crew of *Baby Blitz* in September 1942. David Conley is standing on the right in the front row. *(Jack Heyn / Courtesy of the Alexander G. Evanoff Collection)*

Pongani villagers during Nina's and my trip

Donald Oiroembo, the chief's son, negotiating

The chief, Cyprian Oiroembo, presenting me with a necklace

Alexander Girewo telling of viewing Barney's body

Mom put on a stoical front. She didn't complain about the treatments, though they exhausted her. She approached them with a kind of forced gaiety. Once, when she lowered her drawers to lie naked on the radiation table, the technicians burst out laughing. She had painted a smiling face on her rear end.

In the evenings Bob would try to mediate across the dinner table. The situation became increasingly untenable. Ernie could not let go of his resentments—both petty ones over what he saw as day-to-day slights and long-buried ones over how she had lived her life; she was, by his lights, reckless, irresponsible, and a spendthrift. After a few scotches, a tight grin would come across his face and he would let fly sardonic comments. Mom acknowledged the sacrifices Bob was making. At one point she remarked, "Someday, in the future, you'll be glad you did this."

That Christmas we all gathered at the seaside compound. Nina and I drove down in the morning, and Bob and Susan were already there. With Ernie at the table, we had an awkward meal—the joviality was distinctly forced—and then we exchanged presents. Ernie handed me a carefully wrapped gift; it was heavy, and when I opened it, I was surprised at his generosity—it was an electric carving knife. He gave Bob and Susan something equally expensive, like a new radio. Then he reached behind and handed Mom her gift—an unwrapped carton of Camel cigarettes. There was an embarrassing silence. He merely grinned.

Our family retreated to Mom's side of the house. Someone suggested a walk on the beach. We were just about to put on our coats when we fell into an impromptu discussion about finances. Nina's father, a generous man who had welcomed me into his family, had been paying our share of Mom's upkeep to supplement our low salaries, and he had raised an intriguing point. For all these years, why hadn't she arranged to receive Barney's Social Security? Surely she could use it now. On the drive down, Nina and I had talked about it—the additional money could be a lifesaver. I asked Mom about it. At first she dismissed the idea, seeming to laugh it off. But when I insisted, she seemed embarrassed and turned defensive. Did I think that was something she hadn't thought of? There were plenty of times she could have used that money, she said. That wasn't the point, I insisted. She could use it now, so why not apply for it? She fell silent, looked down, then looked up, almost defiantly. "Well, there's a reason I can't. I won't get it." She stood there, eyes blazing. "You see, your father and I were never married." For a moment, none of us spoke. My brother turned white. Susan held her breath. I looked at Nina and saw she was struggling to contain her surprise.

We asked her to explain. She turned girlish, laughing, as if it were no big deal. They were married, for all intents and purposes, she said—certainly in each other's eyes, which is what counted. But why hadn't they actually gotten married? What was the reason? She waved one hand. Sentences came tumbling out, but they didn't add up to an explanation. They were already living together, so people assumed they were married. And it had taken a while for Barney's divorce to come through. And a piece of paper couldn't make them feel more married than they already did. Besides, it wasn't so easy in those days for a divorced person to get remarried in New York—a lot of bureaucratic red tape was involved. They would have had to run off to some justice of the peace in Maryland, and since everyone thought they were already married, it would have been embarrassing if that had gotten out. And Barney had been cables editor at the Associated Press. He was widely known. AP reporters were everywhere and any one of them would have instantly recognized his name. Besides, they led their lives as if they *were* married—why, they had even picked a date to celebrate as their anniversary—the one in *Who's Who*. How could they now go back and change it? And so on.

We stopped pressing her and put on our coats for the walk on the beach. It was cold, and the wind whipped up the sand. I was stunned. Bob and I looked at each other. We trudged along the sand and came to a large piece of driftwood. Mom, dressed in a thick sheepskin coat, leaned against it, already winded. We stood around in a circle and talked some more. She said she was surprised that we were taking this so seriously. "Especially you, John," she said, looking over at me. "I always thought you'd be pleased." I looked back. "Well," I said, "I always identified with Edmund the bastard." How to tell her that this one bit of news threw everything into question, that it had the potential to overturn the mythical superstructure she had so carefully assembled over the years? Did this mean they hadn't been the ideal couple after all? Had he not loved her enough to marry her? Why in God's name would he have gone off to war without providing her with the legal protection of a wedding certificate? And if he hadn't loved her, did that mean, by extension, that he hadn't loved Bob and me?

I never got satisfactory answers, though I broached the subject delicately several times in the months to come. Years of learning not to question things or dig too deeply had fortified my ability to live on the edge of ambiguity, even about something as fundamental as this. Over time, I came to more or less understand her position, though research in the bowels of New York City's marriage bureaucracy would later reveal an important piece of the puzzle.

Mom's stay at Cape May came to an end when one of Ernie's daughters called Bob to say her presence was just too upsetting for her father. He had seen his own wife die of cancer, and so going through it a second time, watching the deterioration of his sister, would be just too much for him, she insisted, having little idea of the real situation. To make herself perfectly clear, she ended the conversation with a straightforward demand: "Get your mother out of there."

I found a small apartment for Mom in Westport and we moved her there. She settled in quickly and seemed glad to be back in the town that had meant so much to her. She made a new group of friends through AA; they included one or two women like her, tough, dry-eyed women who had worked at professional careers when that was no easy thing. For some months, her health even seemed to be improving. I began to nurture the hope that she might actually recover. She talked of wanting to buy a car. Much to Bob's annoyance, she bought him an expensive present, a leather attaché case—on money that he was providing. She borrowed several hundred dollars from a friend. Nina and I had been planning a two-week trip to Europe that summer. We decided to go ahead and take it, and when I told Mom of our decision, she responded with an uncharacteristic flash of anger. "Go ahead," she warned. "You'll come back and find me stretched out on a marble slab." In our ignorance, assuming she was improving, we thought she was over-dramatizing and wasn't in any danger. She seemed so much better that her death seemed far off in the future. We stuck to our plan. I couldn't conceive of her death or grasp the process of dying. When we returned from Paris, Rome, and Venice, Mom seemed, to my boundless relief, to be no worse.

But in the fall, she deteriorated again and her doctors ordered another operation. Bob and I accompanied her to Norwalk Hospital. "I remember her being wheeled down the hallway on a gurney," Bob recalled. "I saw the back of her head as she was wheeled off. Then she raised her arm and waved her hand grandly in the air—that seemed so much like her. It brings to mind the expression 'throwing your hat over the windmill,' one of her favorites. There was something so gallant about that gesture."

Mom came out of the operation with a colostomy bag. She seemed much worse, physically and mentally. She was dispirited and moved slowly under heavy medication. Again, we faced the question of who would look after her. Bob approached a cancer society in Norwalk to ask for assistance, explaining that we had virtually no money. An official there listened carefully, then turned to him and said, "You have a Ph.D.; you can take loans and pay them back." Bob left, seething with anger that our society offered no help for someone poor who was so desperately ill. We obtained a list of local people, mostly African-Americans trying to scrape together a few bucks, who would move in with dying people and tend to their needs. There followed a succession of them, some better, others worse—a situation that reminded me of her attempts to find nannies for us when we were small children in Washington.

Then came months of unmitigated hell, a series of mishaps and emergencies that required us to rush to Westport in shifts. Mom would fall or a caregiver would quit. She was on heavy medication. Her discourse was rambling. She'd fill reams of copy paper with notes for a novel set in New York in the forties and fifties; people from her past surfaced as characters, with notations that captured their essence. I gave her a bath. She was so thin, her bones poked to the surface of her legs and back and hips. Her skin was wrinkled and hung loosely from her arms. That horrible brown bag was always there, attached to a brown tube that disappeared into her abdomen.

We moved her into a hospice on the Post Road. She was in a double room, her belongings reduced to essentials that fitted inside a metal cabinet next to her bed. Her coat—cloth-knit, fashionable—hung in a wall locker, looking too gay for a garment never to be worn by her again. She didn't complain, and she had moments of lucidity. Visiting her was disconcerting because she seemed so distant. We would hold her hand—her bones felt like the proverbial twigs in a glove—and not have much to say. When Dr. Martin Luther King, Jr., was assassinated in April, she rallied briefly to discuss politics and the sad state of the country, but soon she turned quiet again. We tried to be friendly and upbeat to the staff, in hopes that they would treat her better. One Sunday, she seemed peaceful and serene. She told me Barney had come to her in a dream. "He said, 'Don't worry, everything will be all right.' He was waiting for me. He even held out his hand toward me. He said I would join him." I thought of the story of his death—how convinced she was that he had come to her at the moment of dying, contacting her from the other side of the world. If a spirit could conquer space, why not time? Now, in the days to come, Mom was increasingly not there. She smiled at us occasionally, didn't talk much, held our hands loosely, already occupying another space.

She died on May 15, 1968, at the age of sixty-one. Neither Bob nor I was with her at the time. Bob, at home in Boston, got the call. He phoned me. He began in a throaty voice and as soon as he got the words out, he broke down and sobbed. I did not know what to say. Soon we hung up. I was alone in the apartment. I went outside to the staircase and sat down on the top step, not knowing what I was doing, too stunned to feel anything I could put into words. I had known that she would die and that she would die soon, but I had not truly grasped the fact. I sensed the world already shifting for me, the axis tilting a bit, and I wondered if it would ever be the same.

Preparing for the funeral meant running a gauntlet of chores. At the nursing home we discovered that someone on the staff had stolen her watch, the one fine piece of jewelry remaining to her. We were too distraught to demand an inquiry. The funeral home director made a hard sell for an expensive casket and service. He didn't understand that we weren't willing to go into debt to give her a grand send-off. "The Italians," he said, "now there's a people who do it right. They really love their mothers." Bob was instructed to go to her apartment and bring back her clothes, the best ones he could find—and told not to forget the stockings. He didn't. When he dropped them off, he walked by a half-opened door; there was a young man—someone he recognized from junior high school—holding the leg of another corpse in the air, trying to slide a stocking down a lifeless limb.

The service was held at the picture-postcard Saugatuck Congregational Church, the very one Bob had been confirmed in. I had never been confirmed, and now we were both atheists. The church was not as filled as I would have liked. But some old friends, including Mr. and Mrs. Kuhner, turned up. The minister had not known Mom, and at Bob's request, he did not deliver a eulogy, instead reading passages from the Bible.

Sitting in the front pew, staring at the coffin a few feet away and imaging my mother's body inside it, I felt peculiar—I was not crying, but I couldn't see properly. Wherever I looked, rays of blinding light poured in, forcing my sight into a narrow tunnel. The rays of light seemed to have weight—they were pressing in on me from the sides. I couldn't take in much of what was happening around me. The sensation disappeared after the service, but it came back at the grave site as we sat on folding chairs on a grassy slope and watched her casket being lowered into the ground.

Afterward, a dozen or so people came to the tiny backyard outside Mom's apartment. Among them was Uncle Ernie. We served lemonade, and family and guests sat around on chairs sinking into the damp grass and reminisced. After an hour or so, most of them left, but Ernie stayed on and began, with a strange grin, tossing up unpleasant memories. He talked about the Japanese houseboy and the money Mom never paid back. Did he want us to compensate him? I looked at his glass. He wasn't drinking scotch and he was turning nasty without it. He cleared his throat to get our attention and then looked meaningfully at us. "You know," he said loudly, "your parents were never married."

I looked at him and, depriving him of the pleasure of disillusioning us, said, "We've known that for years."

When I returned home, I found that a company had sent me a laminated copy of my mother's obit and a bill for it. I took the prepaid return envelope, attached it to a box, filled the box with heavy rocks from Central Park, and dropped it in a mailbox.

CHAPTER 16

Three months after my mother died, I was made "staff" at the *Times*—which is to say, I was promoted to reporter. I was distinctly a novice (no one there used the term *cub reporter*). I've often thought how much pleasure the knowledge of that promotion would have given Mom. For one thing, she would have seen it as a vindication of my talent and of her faith in me, the slow starter. But even more significantly, she would have seen it as a step toward assuming Barney's mantle, which my brother had cast aside.

After several months I began receiving a byline on my stories. As a result, some people who had known my parents learned of me and my whereabouts. One day a letter arrived at the paper. I opened the envelope, to find elegant old-fashioned penmanship on thick cream-colored stationery—perfumed. It began: "How wonderful to see the Darnton byline again!" I skipped to the signature at the bottom: "Mildred Blake." Then I read the letter. She explained that my father had been a close friend, that she and her former husband had been newspaper people, too, and had known him on various papers a long time ago. Would I be interested in meeting her? I replied immediately. And so it was that Nina and

I found ourselves one cold Sunday afternoon in the late fall taking a train to Dobbs Ferry. We climbed a steep hill to an immense stone and cedar-shingled house. It sat on a bluff of denuded foliage high above the Hudson. We stepped onto a stately porch with fluted columns and white railings. As I rang the bell, I looked at the door anxiously. It was flung wide open. Standing in the frame was a plump, matronly-looking woman in her seventies with glasses and thick white hair. The moment she saw me, she stepped back, peered at me from head to toe, and said, "Ah, yes, I see it—you *are* Barney's son." I mumbled something—I don't remember what—feeling both pleased and embarrassed.

Milly ushered us inside to a couch in a book-lined parlor, where a blaze was going in the fireplace. Two other elderly people were there. One was Vincent Riorden, her former husband. She had divorced him in 1935, she told us later that afternoon, and the split-up had been amiable—so much so that even after she remarried (her second husband was deceased), she and Vinnie got together to commemorate it. Laughing, she said she had proposed an article to *Ladies' Home Journal* on how to celebrate the "silver anniversary of your divorce" and had received a polite but very firm rejection. The other person in the room was Mary Francis, a slender woman with shimmering white hair that fell to her shoulders, Vinnie's longtime partner. As we took our places on the cozy couch, Nina and I felt that we had entered a tight circle of people who knew one another so intimately they could communicate with the raising of an eyebrow.

Vincent, who had multiple nicknames, including "Vinnie," "Binny," and "Speed," had the look of a man who had lived hard. His rugged Irish face was flushed with the pink-and-purple spider veins of a heavy drinker. In fact, he already seemed pretty much in his cups on this early afternoon. He didn't say much as Milly talked, recounting how their lives had intersected with my father's when they were all young in Michigan and then wove in and out over the next twenty years.

That afternoon she told an abbreviated story of their friendship. (I've filled it in from many meetings since and from talks my brother had with her later.) As a beginning reporter in Adrian, Michigan, Milly had known of the Darnton family. My paternal grandfather, Robert Darnton, as postmaster and head of the school board, qualified as an eminent town father—important enough to be interviewed every time he arrived at or departed from the train station, which she staked out for the *Adrian Daily Telegram*. She had met Vinnie while on the *Michigan Daily*, the university's student paper. They were married in 1920, became reporters, and met Barney at a boardinghouse in Port Huron. He helped them both get jobs on the *Times Herald*. It was a lively town, where sailors and lumberjacks mixed it up in the bars, to the delight of the city editor, whose mantra, Milly wrote in a delightful sketch, was: "Give us this day our daily crime." When Barney went to Baltimore to join Mencken's irreverent circle, he enticed the two of them to join him, sending back letters describing the joys of what Milly, following Mencken, called the "Maryland Free State" (because it never passed a state law supporting Prohibition). With bootleggers, the Ku Klux Klan on the Eastern Shore, and an iconoclastic editor who thumbed his nose at the "boobocracy," Baltimore was even more wild and wide open than Port Huron.

As Milly talked, I got a stronger sense of my father, or at least one side of him. He was catnip to women, she seemed to suggest, and he loved to drink. This picture seemed to bring together pieces I had already known—those letters home eulogizing cocktails, the hints from acquaintances that he was a bon vivant, Mom's description of him as a self-described "lapsed Catholic." Except that this time around the portrait was more complete: I was getting it directly from people who had lived with him—and *before* he had met my mother. As Milly talked, a question struck me: Had she been in love with him? Had he loved her? She was vivacious, intelligent, scintillating—much like my mother. She would have been Barney's kind of woman. I tried to envision her in her twenties, thin and bright-eyed and eager. I imagined the two of them having martinis in a bar somewhere, Barney getting high, beginning to look at her more as a woman than a friend. I imagined the talk turning more intimate, Barney reaching over to touch her knee. I looked over at Vinnie. Did he seem more reserved because of drink—or were his memories of Barney not quite as congenial as Milly's?

Milly continued the trajectory of their past. She told of Barney's moving on to Philadelphia to work on the *Ledger*. There he met his first wife, Ann Hark. It was hardly a match made in heaven. Ann was six years older, straitlaced, the daughter of a Moravian minister, and she was deeply interested in the Pennsylvania Amish. One weekend, Barney and his new wife came to visit them in Baltimore. As usual, the newspaper crowd was drunk. One inebriated scribbler fantasized staging a burlesque of the Virgin Mary, complete with a chorus of nuns. Ann was shocked. The next morning, she and Barney slipped away early. Their marriage fell apart shortly afterward.

Barney moved on to the big leagues, New York, in 1925. Hard-pressed for money, he shared a ratty apartment with two other reporters. It had only one bed, and since each of the three worked a different shift, each could claim it for eight hours and not a minute longer. One of the three, Milton MacKaye, was, like Barney, a newly arrived reporter on the *Evening Post*. "Mac" was a large man, ruddy-faced, with a stutter, and he was a bon vivant with a wicked sense of humor and the magnetism of a born raconteur. He was drawn to women and women liked him. He and Barney were to become inseparable. The Riordens followed Barney to New York—once again, he gave Vinnie a boost, this time onto the *Post*. Barney moved in with them. They shared a four-room apartment on the second floor of 80 MacDougal Street, a platonic ménage à trois. Living there was pleasant. Their row house had a tranquil backyard that joined the gardens of neighboring brownstones in a common courtyard. Barney stayed with them there for two years, from 1926 to 1928.

They worked hard and played hard, wading deep into the bohemian life of Greenwich Village in the Roaring Twenties. They palled around with fellow newspaper people. At the time, New York had seven morning papers and four evening papers, so there were plenty of like-minded people for friendship. My father's crowd included a number of reporters who harbored aspirations of becoming well-known writers. They felt sophisticated and liberated, having sloughed off midwestern rectitude and Babbittry. They drank a great deal, making the rounds of mid-Manhattan hot spots and Village speakeasies. Getting plowed on Saturday nights was a social obligation and a point of pride.

At this point Milly paused in her recitation and poured me another drink. She had come to where my father met his second wife, Eleanor Pollock. Vinnie nodded knowingly and looked into the fire. Eleanor Pollock—"Pollie," as she was called—was spirited and exuberant, even wild. She was not beautiful in the traditional sense, but she had so much animation that she was irresistible. She cursed—which was unusual for a woman in those days—and drank only brandy. Like Milly, she was a working woman, holding her own in the world of advertising and magazines, accustomed to dealing with men in a flirtatious workplace. At the time Pollie was engaged to be married to Lindesay Parrott, a reporter on the *Post* who, like my father, was soon to migrate to the *Times*. Barney and Lindesay were friends. Parrott was tough and proud of it, specializing in seedy crimes and trials. He covered the Lindbergh kidnapping and many of the other famous criminal trials of the twenties and thirties. During the Snyder-Gray murder trial (Ruth Snyder hired Judd Gray to kill her husband for insurance money), Parrott remarked that he was looking forward to witnessing the first electrocution of a woman. He moved on to the *Morning World*, which died, and then to the International News Service, the agency founded by William Randolph Hearst. Sometime in 1929, INS assigned him to Moscow. Barney and Pollie saw him off at the pier. Parrott took Barney aside to ask a favor. "Take good care of her until I return," he said.

"That," pronounced Milly, "turned out to be a mistake." As she said this, Vinnie took a deep sip of his scotch. She continued the story. When Parrott returned a year later, Barney and Pollie met him dockside, holding hands. They told him that they had fallen in love and were engaged. And sure enough, in April 1932, they were married. Parrott was deeply wounded and carried a lifelong grudge against Barney. Ironically, after he moved over to the *Times,* the paper assigned him to my father's job after Barney was killed in the Pacific.

I was astounded. This was certainly a more detailed—and intriguing—version of my father's second marriage than I had ever imagined. But what about his subsequent marriage to my mother? How did that happen? Here Milly demurred. She didn't know much. During the mid-1930s, Barney drifted away from her and Vinnie. (Other people subsequently filled in the parts she was reluctant to spell out.) Vinnie was still covering the courts and there was the hint that alcohol was hurting his career; meanwhile, Barney was forging ahead and hanging out with a group of big-time reporters and accomplished writers. Mac MacKaye, having covered the Seabury Commission, which exposed widespread judicial and police misconduct, wrote a book about it, *The Tin Box Parade,* and was becoming a successful freelancer. There was a general sorting out between those who were moving up and those who were getting stuck.

In fact, Milly said, "I never met your mother. But I saw her once." It was one Christmas at Bloomingdale's. Looking over the selection of cards, Milly saw a young woman—dark-haired, strong features, sparkling eyes—speaking to a saleswoman. She was asking for cards to be engraved "Byron Darnton." At this point in her story, Milly looked into the fire and her mind seemed to float back to that moment three decades earlier. "I had heard Barney had a new gal, and I thought to myself, So here she is. I looked her over. She was stylish, well dressed, seemed full of life. She looked like his type. I didn't introduce myself."

On the train back to the city, I tried to absorb this new portrait of my father. Alongside the family man and the patriotic idealist, another Barney Darnton was taking shape. This one was more hard-boiled—an ambitious reporter, a heavy drinker, a womanizer who seduced his friend's fiancée—not at all the father I had grown up with. But the more I thought about it, the more real this new version seemed to be. And the odd part was that it hadn't come as a total surprise. Without knowing all the facts, I had on some level already imagined him like this. I must have picked up clues along the way, almost subconsciously. This new, somewhat bohemian portrait was not fully fleshed out; it was still just a silhouette. But the question I now had was how to square it with the old portrait—the more conventional one of the doting father and loving husband. And what did all this suggest about my mother?

I didn't let these questions preoccupy me. As was my habit, I shelved them for years and went on with my life, working as a newspaperman and raising a family of my own. But my brother took up the questions and began talking to people about Barney. In 1986, he gave a talk at the Princeton Club (he was then a professor at Princeton). After he spoke, he was approached by a tall, slender woman with bright blue eyes, the wife of an old Princeton grad, who inquired, "Are you Barney Darnton's son?"

"Yes, I am," Bob stammered. "Did you know him?"

"Very well. We used to go drinking together in Greenwich Village in the twenties."

They sat down together in a corner and talked. The woman, Mildred Gilman Wohlforth, a former crime reporter for the *New York Evening Journal,* eighty-nine years old, was a fount of information. She told him about the places they drank, the books they read, their friends and lovers. Patting his knee, she said, "You know, we had no morals at all." With a smile, she added, "But I never slept with your father." She patted his knee again. "Too bad. Then I really could have told you something." Bob decided on the spot that he had to know more about these people.

With her help, he made a list of thirteen names—our parents' contemporaries. He tracked them down. Some were alive, although barely, passing dismal final days in nursing homes. Their memories, as he put it, were "clouded over." Others retained memories, but fragmented ones; they recalled key turning points in their own lives, not in our parents'. He took notes on what they said and compiled lists of books to read, places to look for journals and other source material. He became taken with the idea of doing a book about our father. We would research and write it together, the historian and the journalist, each with specialized strengths, prying out information from the not-so-dead past. Strictly speaking, the book would not be a biography; it would be a story of the times, a depiction of the world of newspapers in the 1920s, 1930s, and 1940s. I suspected—but I didn't tell him—the project would be therapeutic for him, that perhaps one of the reasons he'd become a historian was to ferret out the secrets of his own beginnings. I knew he would reject such an idea vehemently. He's not one to indulge—which is how he thinks of it—in psychological soul-searching.

In any case, the project died on the vine. At the time I was the *Times'* metropolitan editor, taken up with chasing daily stories about crime, race, and poverty in the city, and, as I've said, I wasn't gripped by the emotional prospect of delving into our parents' history. Then Bob gradually lost interest before he got down to writing anything. And twenty years later, in the mysterious way these things happen, *I* became gripped by the idea of writing about our parents. As my career as a newspaperman was coming to an end, I began to think back over my life, wondering what had influenced the choices I made. Surely it wasn't chance that made me go into the same profession as my father. And to work for the very same newspaper. How many decisions could be traced back to those Sunday mornings when Bob and I tumbled into our mother's bed and listened to the stories of our father? Why did his spirit keep intruding into our lives? But it was only when I went to Sanda Island and stood next to my brother, looking at what had been the hull of the SS *Byron Darnton,* that I began to think back on the questions left unanswered and decided to investigate them.

Bob turned over the notes of the interviews he had conducted long before. That was a good thing, because by this time virtually all the principals were dead. His interviews were invaluable and contained some intriguing surprises. In 2010, he pulled some of his information together for an article in a journal called *Raritan* to be published the following year. It was titled "The Old Girls Network," a reference to the fact that many of the interviewees were women who had kept in touch with one another, offering up a kind of communal testament to what those days were like.

One of the sources Bob got to know was Milly Blake, the woman from Dobbs Ferry, and he pried some more crucial information out of her. In particular, he wrote about an incident that happened at the Minetta Tavern in the early 1930s, an incident that bore an eerie resemblance to the scene I had imagined. She and Barney were sharing drinks and she confessed that life with Vinnie had become impossible, that she was thinking of leaving him. Barney responded by saying, "If you break up, let me know." Was he offering sympathy—or something more? She didn't know. But then several years later, in 1935, when she told Barney that she was getting divorced and was about to marry another man, he took it badly. Obviously hurt, he stood up and left the room. As Bob listened to Milly tell the story and looked over at her, he was struck with an odd thought: that she was almost saying she could have been Barney's wife, that she might, in another life, have almost been his mother.

Years later, when I began interviewing people, I was talking to the offspring of those he had interviewed. Still, they had vivid memories of their parents' lives. And there were plenty of books about Greenwich Village. Putting all this together, I began to get a feel for the libertine men and women of the Jazz Age. They were urbane and polished, with an appreciation of the bon mot, a low tolerance for sentiment, and a thin overlay of cynicism. They consumed books. They exalted Sinclair Lewis's gimlet eye and were greatly influenced by Hemingway's stark style (described by Milly as "cat killed rat"). They took in the plays of Eugene O'Neill at the Provincetown Playhouse as well as movies with the Marx Brothers. They were mostly poor in the 1920s but managed to live pretty comfortably in the 1930s, even during the Depression, because newspaper salaries, though hardly exorbitant, were at least regular and magazines paid a lot. For a night out on the town, the men dressed up in tuxes or white tie and tails and the women wore long, clinging gowns.

Prohibition sharpened their mania for the forbidden fruit. They made bathtub gin at home, adding juniper berries to distilled alcohol, and they haunted speakeasies along the Tenderloin and in the Village. Once Prohibition ended in 1933, the speakeasies converted to bars and the clientele barely had to shift bar stools.

An important feature for the New York literati was the weekend getaway. On Fridays, they would knock off work early and pile into trains to go to Long Island or, as was the case with my parents' crowd, the Connecticut coast. Easing the passage with a drink or two in the bar car, they would pour out at Westport or Fairfield or as far north as Madison, where Mac MacKaye rented a place not far from the water. They would spend two days talking shop, downing drinks, and playing croquet and badminton and games like charades and "murder" (the guest who drew the short straw killed off the others by catching him or her alone somewhere, like in a dark closet—sometimes a prelude to romance). They worked on gigantic jigsaw puzzles and pounded out songs like "I've Been Working on the Railroad" on a baby grand piano, tossing off quips and flirting. It sounded like an uneasy mix of innocence and hedonism.

Sex was the organizing principle. The weekends in the country and long nights drinking in the city made for frequent couplings. Men—even when married and, in some cases, *especially* when married—made passes at the nearest women, married or not.

Women, having long ago cast off the remnants of Victorian prudery, often responded positively. Sometimes they even hung their hats for certain males and went after them.

Children were the great stumbling block. Some didn't want any at all. Others had them but raised them almost as an afterthought. "I had a strange childhood because there was only one other child in my parents' circle," said Bill MacKaye, the only child of Mac and his wife, Dorothy. "No one wanted children." Still, he remembers fondly the excitement of meeting the train on Friday evenings, of adults crowding around the piano for songfests and prodigious amounts of drinking. At one point the MacKayes had an apartment on Jane Street in the Village. They used a basket to lower the cat down to the street. "Everyone talked of going to Europe. They were constantly having people over, and the rule was if you came over to visit, you had to throw all your pennies on the floor. Periodically, my mother would sweep the pennies into the corner and they would be collected—the kitty for a trip to Europe. There were never enough to get there, but people were charmed by the idea of being separated from their pennies."

Bob located Dorothy MacKaye, who was in a nursing home in Washington, D.C. Years before, she had written mysteries under the name Dorothy Cameron Disney. One was titled *The 17th Letter,* published two years after Barney's death, and it incorporated him in the story. He's Max Ferris, news photographer and the best friend of the married protagonists, two reporters named Paul and Mary Strong. He disappears on assignment in Iceland after mailing back sixteen letters; the seventeenth is nothing more than a mysterious theater program, and they set off to find him. I devoured the book the moment I got it. Much to my disappointment, Max isn't a memorable character; he makes only a fleeting appearance at the end. But the book intimates a lot about the bond of friendship between Barney and Mac: "Breaking up a bachelor establishment wasn't always easy for the girl who accomplished it . . . not that Max Ferris was the sort who would openly sulk and gloom because his best friend had found a wife. . . . But there had been no withdrawal, no break in the friendship that meant so much to both men."

When Bob talked to Dorothy, a frail woman propped up in a

wheelchair, her memories slipped in and out of focus. But she was able to come up with a few anecdotes. Some of them captured aspects of Barney's personality, like his flair for the dramatic. When she gave birth to her son, Bill, Barney visited her hospital room not with a bouquet but with a seven-foot-tall dogwood tree. Others concerned Mac's philandering. Although he had never promised to be faithful and she had never asked him to be, his romantic escapades became difficult to ignore. Once, at a party, she opened a kitchen door, to find him passionately kissing the hostess. She closed the door and summoned her energies to blot out the knowledge of what she had just seen. "I did not have to open that door. If it had remained closed, I would not have seen anything. I will not let that door determine the course of my life." But of course she had seen it, and the memory dug in deeper and deeper, until it was one of the lasting few that disturbed her in her life's twilight.

She spoke of Mac and Barney as inseparable as "Castor and Pollux." They had so much in common: both from the Midwest, both from religious backgrounds, even both burdened with given names heavy in literary import—Milton and Byron—which they rejected. Their personalities were different—Barney was calm and soft-spoken; Mac was all energy and movement, the last to give up on a party—but it became clear, the more that Bob talked to these elderly women, that Barney shared Mac's philandering ways. At the *Post,* they were known as the two "skirt-chasers." One time, they found themselves in New Haven on "tap night," when Yale's secret societies induct new members. "They went up and down the crowded sidewalks outside the *Evening Post* office, tapped the prettiest girls on the shoulder, and whispered, 'Go to *my* room,' " Dorothy said. "Nobody called the police. They got a lot of laughs, and so did the girls. Whether they collected any phone numbers, I can't tell you."

The ethos of the time is captured in a book written by Ursula Parrott, who had been married to Lindesay Parrott before he took up with Pollie, the woman my father seduced away from him. The Parrotts were divorced in January 1928 and shortly afterward Ursula produced a novel titled *Ex-Wife,* initially published anonymously. It created a scandal, becoming the *Fear of Flying* of its day, going through nine printings, and ending up as a movie, *The Divor-*

cee, starring Norma Shearer. It depicts the life of a woman who is spurned by her shallow husband and then becomes "a Modern Woman." She succumbs to a meaningless round of highballs and dinners, draining advertising jobs, and empty affairs with newspapermen. The setup is a little ridiculous—the heroine sleeps with her husband's best friend and hides the fact by pretending she has committed a multitude of infidelities—but it ends as a rather moving portrait in loneliness. The trade-off for all this glamorous freedom, it says, is lack of stability and commitment. *Ex-Wife* was followed by a rival book, *Ex-Husband,* covering the same ground from the point of view of the enraged man. It was also of anonymous authorship—some claimed that Lindesay Parrott himself must have written it. I was told that Barney is a character in the books, but if so, he's disguised so well that I couldn't figure out which of the parade of adulterating men he is supposed to be.

Ursula Parrott's life, incidentally, turned out miserably. Lindesay left her, according to members of her family, because she became pregnant and he wanted no children. He would have nothing to do with the baby, a boy named Marc, who was raised by grandparents in Boston and sent off to a boarding school. His mother saw him once a year. She married three more times, wrote thirteen more books and various screenplays, but spiraled downward, dying a penniless alcoholic in 1957. One of the last articles written about her said that she was accused of stealing silverware from a couple who had befriended her.

In May 1986, Bob achieved a breakthrough when he met Barney's second wife. At the time, she was eighty-six years old and living in Arlington, Virginia. The intermediaries were two members of "the old girls network," Edith Evans Asbury, a longtime *Times* reporter, and Mildred Gilman Wohlforth, the woman who had introduced herself to Bob at the Princeton Club. Bob had told them about his project, and they invited us over to a Manhattan apartment on East Sixty-third Street, reminiscing while serving champagne and hors d'oeuvres. After a few drinks, Edith Asbury began pestering her friend: "Call Pollie. Call Pollie." Eventually, Mildred Wohlforth went to the phone, dialed a long-distance number, reached Eleanor

Pollock, and placed the receiver in Bob's hand. He was nonplussed. It was an extraordinary feeling, he said later, to be talking to a woman who had known Barney so intimately, having lived with him for ten years—three times longer that our mother had. It was all he could do to blurt out an invitation to take her to lunch the next time he went to Washington. She accepted, somewhat warily. Above all, she didn't want to meet him at her home.

He took her to the Jockey Club. They were both eager but awkward, eyeing each other across the table. Pollie didn't want to be tape-recorded and Bob decided that taking notes would inhibit her, so he tried to memorize their conversation. She said she had been following both his career and mine. Right away, he saw similarities to Mom—she was expressive, fast-talking, animated. She waved her hands in the air so that the bracelets on her wrist would jangle. Carefully, he began with questions about that era—the books, the places, the people. Unlike those of others he had interviewed, her recollections were sharp and her answers specific. Like them, she talked about the free-flowing alcohol and the speakeasies. Chumley's at Bedford and Barrow, with its unmarked door and escape route at the rear, catered to writers, whose framed book jackets hung on the wall. At Jack Delaney's on Grove Street, the bartender, Joe, sang songs and would warn of an impending raid by shouting out the name of a gangster: "Get out. Johnny Torrio is in town." For elegance, nothing could beat the Washington Square nightclub of Barney Gallant, who shared an apartment with Eugene O'Neill. His philosophy was: "No isms or cults are any good. Every man should be his own Jesus."

Pollie summed it all up, saying, "It was new, we were young, and things were happening. I can't wave a wand and make you see Ruby Keeler tap-dancing 'The Stars and Stripes' at Texas Guinan's and Texas greeting everyone with 'Hello, suckers.'"

For the first time, Bob was getting solid information about his father, and he soaked it up. Barney was a dapper dresser (he once spent $7.50 for a shirt, a lot in those days). He was well read but by no means an intellectual. His politics were not far left—he was basically a "Knickerbocker" Democrat, with a soft spot for Al Smith and Jimmy Walker. Pollie and Barney lived at 43 Fifth Avenue, in a building filled with Tammany people. Their social life was busy.

They played poker with James Thurber, dined with Edna St. Vincent Millay at Squarcialupi's on West Fourth Street, and hung out with writers like Philip Wylie and Sinclair "Red" Lewis. The night Prohibition ended, they and the MacKayes dressed up to the nines and celebrated at the St. Regis. At the same time, Bob was also hearing some disturbing new things about Barney: He was "strange," "an unhappy man," "had a lot of ego," and, above all, was "restless."

And then there was all that sleeping around. Barney "loved women and ran after them," Pollie observed. Shortly before she and Barney married, in 1932, he and Mac went off to the Bahamas on a junket. As the ship approached New York, Dorothy MacKaye suggested they take a harbor craft out to meet it, but Pollie refused. She didn't want to surprise them—there was no telling what they might find. And she was right. On the return voyage, the two had had a competition to see which one could bed down an attractive young woman. Barney won. But Pollie insisted that underneath all the sleeping around and misbehaving, Barney was deeply conventional. "He loved women, was always chasing after them, but he wanted them to stay in their place, at home. You would call him a male chauvinist pig today. But it was a different world then. We were amoral. All that switching of partners hurt, but we wanted to have a good time, as much fun as possible, and to hell with the stuffed shirts."

The philandering of Mac and Barney fell under the rubric of "Don't ask, don't tell." It was not something their wives chose to confront. The men were not romantic hedonists, searching for Blake's palace of wisdom on the road of excess. Rather, the motivation was more superficial—the lure of novelty and the thrill of the chase. They did it because they were allowed to do it. The times condoned it and skidded over the emptiness that lay at its heart, much like the ethos of their favorite novel and secular bible, *The Sun Also Rises*. Their morality possessed a strain of rectitude and conventionality. Pollie stressed over and over how Barney was seized by the idea of having children and living a quiet life in the country, counterbalancing his ever-present sense of restlessness.

When he accepted the assignment to cover the war in the Pacific, Mac phoned Pollie to tell her. "I just laughed," she recalled. "It was so like him. I told Mac, 'He got Tootie. He got the boys. He got a house in the country. Now he's running off to Australia.' Mac hung up on me."

After her meeting with Bob, Pollie sent him a letter, elaborating on things she felt she had perhaps glossed over. She repeated her assessment of Barney. He was personable, witty, charming, intelligent, and a hard worker. He loved the theater (the play *Journey's End,* about soldiers in World War I, made him cry). He liked jazz—in particular Libby Holman singing "Body and Soul" and "Can't We Be Friends?" Then she added as an afterthought, "He was not a drunk. But he could and did get drunk. When he drank, he reached out for the nearest woman. I walked in on him at parties (by mistake) a couple of times, and while it was not in flagrante, it could have been had the opportunities been different. He was, I think, completely amoral but expected everyone else to be of Puritan stock. Harsh judgment on my part? No, I don't think so."

Bob was to meet Pollie one more time and correspond with her over the ensuing couple of years. Throughout, she refused to delve into certain areas. She couldn't shed any light on the mystery of our parents' failure to marry—in fact, she had a hard time believing it, given Barney's basic "bourgeois" nature. She tried to keep in check her strong animus toward Mom, but failed. She said Tootie had been her best friend, had taken Barney from her, and had seemed to want everything else she had. Once, she actually said, "Have you ever considered that your mother was a nymphomaniac?" She then ticked off a list of men she said Mom had slept with, topped by Meyer Berger, the *Times* reporter who had been a frequent visitor when we were children. Bob was so shocked that, in scribbling notes to recall the conversation, he forgot that assertion for a couple of days.

Set against what Pollie told him were memories of things Mom had said long ago on those rare occasions when she had talked about Barney's second marriage. Shifting the blame, Mom insisted that Pollie was the one who effectively broke up the marriage, because *she* was given to sleeping around with all sorts of men. Confronted with a straightforward choice, Bob didn't know which one to believe.

I did. When Bob turned over his notes, including that scurrilous remark about nymphomania, I felt that Pollie had hoodwinked him. I was sure that for all her insistence that she was refraining from speaking ill of the dead, the remark was not an offhand comment. It had been dropped with malice. She was extracting revenge.

Pollie died in November 1991, at the age of ninety-one. She didn't leave any close relatives. I discovered years afterward, in talking with Bill MacKaye, that there may have been another reason she lost Barney: She couldn't have children. The one thing Barney wanted—progeny—she couldn't provide.

Bill, who had been close to Pollie, the friend of his parents, added other bits of information, which further complicated the picture. He said he had overheard "whispered conversations when your mother came on the scene." One was that there had been "a rivalry for your mother's affections between your father and another chap—his name may come to me as we talk." He elaborated: "I mean your father had strayed into Tootie's arms and Pollie was quite certain that Tootie was the instigator of this, that she wanted Barney, had set her cap for him. But your mother was also pursuing this other chap."

He then revealed a second piece of information: "If I'm not mistaken—but you know the timing on this—I think part of Tootie's technique in setting up housekeeping with Barney was that she got pregnant. And I think my father thought that they'd gone off and seen a judge or something, but why they would have given that impression and not done it, I don't know." A few moments later, he said he had heard that Mom "snagged" Barney by getting pregnant. I knew, on this point, that he was reflecting Pollie's take on things.

We talked for a while and then I mentioned a name that reminded Bill of my mother's other suitor. "That's it!" he cried excitedly. "You've got it. That's who it was."

The name was Cedric Worth, my father's friend from the *New York Evening Post*, the man who had passed along the quotation "Anyone who hates dogs and children can't be all bad."

At this point, I was tempted to throw up my hands. Lindesay Parrott. Ursula Parrott. Mac and Dorothy MacKaye. Pollie. Milly. Tootie. Barney. And now Cedric Worth. Everyone, it seemed, was sleeping with everyone else, or trying to. Jumping in and out of bed had certainly made for some lighthearted shenanigans and no small amount of intrigue. But underneath that sophisticated revelry, I thought, it had been a serious and cruel business. It broke up friendships and ruptured marriages. The ethos was captured by a sardonic remark that Barney once tossed off to my mother, which she didn't tell me until I was grown up: "It's not wedding bells, but cheap hotels, that's breaking up that ole gang o' mine."

The story has a footnote. Their lives had not stopped interweaving. I learned that Lindesay Parrott—he who had lost Pollie to Barney in the 1930s—had come back into Pollie's life sixty years later. He moved into her apartment in Arlington, Virginia, and she nursed him there until his death. That was why, when Bob first telephoned her, she had insisted that he meet her in a restaurant, not in her home. Bitter to the end, Lindesay Parrott had said, according to Dorothy MacKaye, "No son of Barney Darnton is coming to my place."

I looked at Bob's notes, scribbled during the train ride back to New York after his interviews with Dorothy and Pollie. He ruminated on the paths their lives had taken, large outcomes that hinged on random happenings and what at the time seemed like small moments—a request to a friend to look after a fiancée, a misunderstood signal over drinks at the Minetta Tavern, a kitchen door opened at the wrong second, revealing a husband kissing someone else. In retrospective old age, these moments loomed large and were seen for what they were—pivotal.

"While history happens at the level of great events," Bob wrote, "these micro-events get washed out. Yet for the individuals, the latter *are* history: the past as looked at across a distance of 50, 60, 70 years. Who's to say that their past, however individual and anecdotal, is any less history than the Big Story line we know in conventional narratives?"

CHAPTER 17

The dashing foreign correspondents of the 1930s were gone when I started at the *Times* in September 1966. I remember my first day vividly. The night before, I had been too nervous to sleep. By morning, I felt worse. Gulping down my coffee, I followed it with a tranquillizer—for the first time in my life I needed a pill to calm down. The reason seemed obvious once I entered the busy lobby of the headquarters on West Forty-third Street. Across from a bust of Adolph Ochs, the publisher who had made the *Times* great, was the bronze tablet to the memory of Byron Darnton and Robert Post, two correspondents "who braved every peril with unsurpassed and unsparing devotion and who by their writings helped to forge this democracy into the greatest war machine of all time." I was entering my father's cathedral.

In the elevator, I remembered visiting my mother in this building; back then the elevators had operators who would tip their hat to her. I got out at the third floor, where the newsroom was. A receptionist at an imposing wooden desk called a copyboy to meet me. I was ushered through a pair of swinging doors and along a passageway behind a frosted-glass partition. I could hear phones ringing and the buzzing of many conversations on the other side. Then I got my first glimpse of the city room—a cavernous space extending the length of an entire block, with windows at either end. To one side were the senior editors, seated at clusters of desks shoved next to one another. Copy editors lined the rim of crescent-shaped desks, some actually wearing green eyeshades. To the other side, reaching all the way to Forty-fourth Street, was the reporters' area, row upon row of metal desks with large typewriters that could be flipped upright or collapsed out of sight. Even in midmorning, there was a certain bubbling activity, the promise of exciting things to come. A dozen or so men were talking on the phone or typing. One stood up and slipped on his jacket, his side pocket bulging with a notebook, presumably to go out on an assignment.

My job, it turned out, wasn't in the newsroom itself, but in a room beyond. I was to work for the *Times* News Service, next to the communications department. As stories and cables piled in from foreign and national bureaus, I was to grab copies and run them off on a mimeograph machine and then distribute them to *Times'* clients on an upper floor. After half an hour, the machine turned my hands purple—they looked as if I had thrust them into a pot of dye. I had been there about a week when an enthusiastic political reporter named Clayton Knowles heard my name and asked if I was related to Barney Darnton. I said yes. He grabbed me by the wrist and took me over to meet the deputy metro editor, Arthur Gelb. Gelb, a tall man, whose arms seemed in perpetual motion, greeted me warmly. He said he had joined the paper some years after my father's death but had certainly heard a great deal about him. "He was a legend," he concluded, looking down at my hands as if I had contracted a disease.

Over the months to come I studied how the newsroom functioned. I learned to read the reporters' status by the placement of their desks—the top ones, Homer Bigart and Peter Kihss, were up front, and the pecking order extended all the way to the rear. I learned who was good and who was not, who was respected and who drank too much. I came to know when a big story was breaking, not so much from people dashing around shouting—that was a Hollywood stereotype—as from an indefinable perception that the well-oiled machine was shifting to a faster gear. The city room was an impersonal place. When an editor on the metro desk wanted a reporter for an assignment, he'd grab a microphone and boom out the name and the reporter would lope up an aisle under the searching eyes of his colleagues, some of whom hoped he would bungle it.

I was at first acutely conscious of my father and wondered if people were comparing me to him. Every now and then I would run into people who had known him. They invariably said something positive and innocuous—how "nice" he was or some such thing—and I felt pleased but also embarrassed. I was curious to know more but reluctant to press them for details. I didn't want to appear anything other than cool and in control, professional—which was the way I imagined he must have been. As a consequence I couldn't shake the feeling that I was in his shadow, even if it wasn't apparent to everyone else. I would sometimes look at the older reporters standing around gossiping or telling jokes, and I'd imagine him there, at the center of the action.

Over time my nervousness wore off, in part because the jobs were so menial that there was little chance to slip up. I worked hard, mostly at nights, and I gradually was promoted from copyboy to news clerk and then news assistant. At first I answered calls on the foreign desk. Then I wrote captions on the picture desk. After that I moved to the metro desk, where I kept track of assignments and copy and handled news tips. And finally I compiled the daily news summary, which ran on the front page of the second section. I was watchful for signs that management was favoring me as some sort of legacy, but this did not appear to be the case. Other copyboys and -girls—girls were just starting to be hired—seemed to be following the same trajectory.

By this time I had decided I wanted badly to be a reporter. I examined the stories written by my role models and tried to imitate their style. I assimilated the values of the paper and learned the institutional lore, much of it passed on from older reporters in anecdotal form. The stories they told encapsulated lessons—about accuracy, objectivity, street smarts. There was the tale of the reporter whose career was shot when he secretly slipped away from Chile the night before the coup against Salvador Allende. There was the reporter fired for inserting the name of a phony award in a routine commencement story. And there was the hero who covered segregation agitators in Mississippi and learned to look inconspicuous by taking notes inside his jacket pocket.

I realized that I had been hearing similar stories all my life from my mother, who remained starry-eyed about the paper despite her travails there—except that her stories, I now learned, stretched credulity. One tale she recounted with relish was meant to illustrate the paper's incorruptibility. Years ago, when the legendary Carr Van Anda began his job as managing editor, he had typed out his resignation and kept it in his desk drawer. As she told it, Adolph Ochs himself came down one day to see him, bearing a wedding announcement of a family member that he wanted to see in the paper. "Certainly," replied Van Anda. "And while you're here, here's something for you," he added, reaching into the drawer and handing over his notice. Ochs read it, then sheepishly took back the announcement. I myself told that story dozens of time, until I knew enough about the *Times* to realize there was no way it could have happened. The wedding of a publisher's relative was newsworthy, and besides, no editor, not even a legendary one, would have been likely to buck his publisher over so trivial a matter.

The chasm between news assistant and reporter was wide, and to make the leap, the beginner was expected to write feature stories on the side. Coming up with a subject august enough for the *Times* was difficult. One day I heard about a man harboring an incredible menagerie of animals in a makeshift pet store on Fulton Street. He was being forced out by the city to clear the way for the new World Trade Center. Pythons, monkeys, Amazonian fish—all of them had to relocate. At last I had found a human-interest story. I interviewed the animal lover, a rotund bearded man named Henry Trefflich, not once, but twice. I arranged for a photographer. I stayed up almost until dawn writing and rewriting the story, trying to make each word perfect. I went to work, handed the story in to an assistant metro editor, who assured me it looked good, and went home that evening exhausted but triumphant. The next morning, I ran out to get the paper. I couldn't locate the story. I flipped through the pages several times and then saw the fruit of my labor—shrunken to a six-line caption under a photo of Trefflich holding a chimp.

In the summer the *Times* allowed news assistants to fill in for reporters on vacation. This meant receiving assignments from the desk—and the likelihood that the stories would be printed. I was assigned to cover a Fifth Avenue parade of veterans. I was nervous, wondering whether I could write fast enough on deadline. What would happen if I choked? Would there be a big blank spot in the paper? I checked the clip files in the morgue to see how past parades had been covered, went to Fifth Avenue, crammed a notebook full of quotes and descriptions, and went back to the office to cobble together a story. Sweating, I typed out my lead, which I cribbed from one I had found in the morgue: "The tramp, tramp, tramp of marching feet resounded along upper Fifth Avenue yesterday as . . ." The next day, I found in my mailbox a dupe of the story, marked with the initials of Abe Rosenthal, then city editor. He had scribbled a note that consisted of a single word followed by an exclamation point: "Cliché!"

Somehow, over time, I learned enough and assembled enough clips and impressed enough people to be promoted, one of a small handful to rise from within the ranks. In August 1968, after a two-week vacation, I entered the building as a reporter. I was assigned to a desk in the very last row and drew journeyman assignments. Soon after that, I found myself at the police shack. Close up, it lost some of its glamour.

That was the fall and winter of the bitter Ocean Hill–Brownsville school strike, which pitted the largely white, largely Jewish teachers' union against African-American parents and activists in a struggle for "community control." I trudged around the streets, interviewing people on the picket lines or in their apartments, trying to figure out what was going on. Mostly I did legwork for the big-name education reporters. In those days, on returning from assignments, we lined up in front of the night city editor, Sheldon Binn, a brilliant, no-nonsense newspaperman. One by one, we would move up, eventually taking the seat next to Binn, who would fire off two or three questions to get the essence of the story, dispense space ("a buck" meant a full column), and assign a "slug"—the one-word name that would track the story on its circuitous journey through production and into print. Each time I approached Binn, half of me wanted to be told that I had fallen on a big story—big enough for page one—while the other half felt paralyzed at the thought.

It took a long time for my capabilities to catch up to my ambition. But I eventually settled into the rhythm of reporting and writing and yelling "copy" the moment I finished each page. I derived a thrill from the knowledge that by the time I was working on the third page, my second page was being copyedited and my first was being set in hot lead by a linotype operator in the composing room upstairs. In midafternoon, trucks delivering newsprint backed into the loading bays on Forty-third Street, sending fourteen-hundred-pound rolls crashing into place. It sent a jolt through the newsroom, like the rumbling of a hungry beast. Phones rang, reporters barked questions, typewriters clacked, and the loudspeaker would boom out directives—"We need copy!" or "Keep it tight!" The frenzy mounted through the early evening. Then magically, at 7:10 p.m., like a baseball game that ends with a walk-off, it all stopped. Reporters leaned back and relaxed. Copy editors finished up the one or two stragglers. People would approach the city desk and ask for a "good night"—permission to leave. And soon the presses in the subbasement would start up, sending a tremble through the building. The beast was digesting.

One of my early assignments was covering Connecticut. In those days the state was the bailiwick of a single reporter. I was provided with a car and a one-room office in downtown New Haven; the office had frosted glass on the door, like a private eye's. I covered everything that happened: summer riots in Hartford, dreary debates in the legislature about the state income tax, student sit-ins, racism in the Waterbury Police Department, the admission of women to Yale. And of course I wrote countless features about life in suburban Fairfield County. Nina and I moved to Westport. It felt odd to be living there after such a long absence and to be viewing it through the eye of a chronicler.

These were the tumultuous times of the late sixties. My political views were left of center—I had carried my antipathy toward Richard Nixon into his presidency—and I felt an affinity for the counterculture. I was friends with some of the provocative agitators, like Jerry Rubin, who tried to persuade me to abandon objective journalism, which he insisted was impossible, and go to work for a more compatible publication, such as *The East Village Other*. I resisted the argument. I had been inculcated with the belief that the highest form of journalism was the honest type practiced by quality newspapers. Objectivity, at least as a goal, was the key. I thought if I laid the facts out fairly, and other reporters did the same, and readers were open-minded, chances were that people would end up reaching the same conclusions I held.

While I was in Connecticut, a big story broke. The Black Panther Bobby Seale was indicted for murder—a young Panther, interrogated as a possible informer at the local chapter, had been killed after a visit by Seale—and so the stage was set for a high-profile trial. On May Day in 1970, thousands of antiwar and antigovernment activists poured into New Haven for a massive demonstration. The police fired ample quantities of tear gas at protesters on the town green, but the event did not ignite a leftist uprising as the FBI had warned. Eventually, Seale's trial ended in a hung jury and the case against him was dropped.

For one particular story, I went to JFK to meet a party of Black Panthers who were coming from the West Coast. Their plane was late, and as I bided my time, I stared up at the giant board of destinations: Istanbul, Addis Ababa, Bangkok, Cairo, Jerusalem, Hong Kong. The names seemed infused with poetry. I felt a restlessness almost as palpable as a bodily ache. I had to see these places and experience them. Was this, I wondered, what my father had felt?

My stories from Connecticut were enough to secure me a promotion as "chief suburban correspondent," a new position. In theory, I was to roam the outer urban areas, uncovering trend stories of sociological import. I was a flop, and after some months of desultory work, I was consigned to night rewrite as a punishment. Night rewrite is to a newspaper what the emergency room is to a hospital—a place of intense boredom, punctuated by periods of unmitigated panic. I disliked it, but eventually I got accustomed to fielding multiple phone calls from legmen, writing "quick and dirty" sidebars, and piecing together big stories quickly. The blank spaces in the paper never appeared. I was cured of my anxieties over writing on deadline.

After two years, I was taken off night rewrite and sent to the pressroom at City Hall. If the police shack was the toxic pulse of the city, Room 9 was its reptilian brain stem. The door was covered with brass plaques of all the city newspapers that had died.

Inside, the walls were covered with dust, ancient press releases were stacked on the windowsills, and the desks were jammed so closely together that even whispers could be heard by rivals. The air was rife with intrigue and, at Christmas, the closets magically filled with cartons of scotch from well-wishers doing business with the city.

I arrived there at the mid-tide watermark of the John Lindsay administration and stayed two years into the Abe Beame administration. These were important and changing years for the city. Federal money was still coming in, the old-time bosses still had some power, a reform movement was under way, crime was up and city services down, and everyone worried about racial riots. The corridors of power were peopled by Damon Runyon characters in government clothing.

During these years our bureau of three or four reporters covered a lot of budgets, a goodly number of scandals and elections, and the ceaseless ebb and flow of government and politics, sometimes with what might be called distinction. But I could never dispel the feeling that the truly important parts of the power structure remained unseen, like a huge machine whose operations were 90 percent underground. I concluded that the real business was conducted in secret, at closed meetings of the Board of Estimate, which passed on all city projects; in off-the-cuff meetings between real estate developers and borough presidents; and at long, leisurely lunches in Brooklyn or Queens steak houses. On those occasions when I wrote an investigative piece, the reaction was instantaneous. It reminded me of Mike Royko's line that "a reporter is to a politician as a barking dog is to a chicken thief," and I felt we should be producing dozens and dozens of such stories every week.

Though I didn't always realize it, my reporting sometimes took me to the same haunts my father had frequented. I have a vivid memory of interviewing an assistant district attorney in the Bronx: We left the templelike courthouse on the Grand Concourse and went to a cozy bar, where after a few drinks he filled my notebook with off-the-record nuggets. Thirty years later, I came across a letter written to my mother by Jack Turcott, Barney's *Daily News* colleague in New Guinea. Turcott reminisced fondly about their reporting days in New York—in particular a press conference in the

Bronx courthouse, called to give out information on Bruno Hauptmann, the kidnapper of Lindbergh's baby. The melee of fifty reporters was so wild, the elbow jabbing so intense, the prosecutor lost his glasses. Turcott and Barney left the shouting horde, repairing to a nearby bar. To their delight, half an hour later the prosecutor's press secretary walked in, told them his boss had not spoken a word, and then provided a full account of what he would have said. "Barney and I had a second drink and then we agreed that the man who doesn't get excited always gets much further than the man who erupts," he wrote.

In March 1975, I received a call at home from Paul O'Brien, the press spokesman for the city comptroller, Harrison Jay Goldin. He sounded shaken and, after giving an ironclad pledge to allow him to talk off the record, I understood why. The city had just held a sale of notes and bonds—a tradition-laden ceremony, during which banking syndicates place their bids in a little green tin box in a chamber in the controller's office—and something unheard of had occurred: The box was empty. No one bid. O'Brien sounded like the voice of doom. "What's this mean?" I asked. He didn't equivocate. "No one is willing to loan us any money." "But how about the city's bills?" "We can't pay them." "But . . . the policemen, the firemen, sanitation workers . . . what's going to happen? Who'll pay them?" "Not us. We're broke."

And so began the long saga of the fiscal crisis, a story with twists and turns that kept New York on edge for months. The *Times* left most of the daily coverage to me and a young colleague, Steve Weisman. Although scores of press conferences were held by city officials who sought to explain and justify their budgetary legerdemain, I remember exactly one. After half an hour of arcane mutterings by James A. Cavanagh, the portly deputy mayor, I raised my hand and asked, "Is it too late to drop this course?"

One result of the fiscal crisis was that the foreign desk began to look kindly on my request for a foreign assignment. For years, I had wanted to go abroad, but I had a problem. The starting point for many foreign correspondents was to go to Vietnam. I was implacably opposed to the war and, given all the stories I had heard about my father in World War II, I couldn't conceive of covering a conflict that I did not wholeheartedly support. That struck me not just as antipatriotic but, on some level, deeply wrong. Years later I realized my stance was absurd, but at the time I steadfastly refused to consider a posting to Saigon. As Asia was cooling off, however, there was another part of the world that was heating up—Africa. When I was offered the job of West African correspondent, to be based in Lagos, Nigeria, I leapt at it. Nina was game. We figured our girls, Kyra, then four years old, and Liza, two, were young enough to adapt to a new country without trouble. For Nina, who had obtained a master's degree in theater arts from Columbia and another one in child development from the New School, it meant embarking on a future without a clear career route, but she was up for adventure.

Down at City Hall, my colleagues congratulated me on my new assignment. But not everyone understood. One day, I ran into Howard Golden, then a Brooklyn councilman. He and I were cordial to each other but hardly close. His face fell as he put his arm around me and led me off to a quiet corner near the grand marble stairway. "John," he said, his voice oozing concern. "I hear they're sending you to Africa. What happened? Did you mess up?" For him, New York City was the universe and City Hall was the solar system, and the idea of giving it up was beyond comprehension. I hastened to assure him that it was my life's ambition. He walked away shaking his head.

For months I prepared for my assignment, reading up on Africa, getting inoculations, and undergoing briefings from officials in Washington, including one at CIA headquarters. My request for a resident visa to live in Nigeria wasn't approved. It wasn't denied, either; it was simply left to languish in limbo. Finally, the foreign editor suggested that I head off alone, find a country in West Africa to base myself in, and then send for my family. I left on a cold day in January 1976. Nina and the girls were there to see me off. I kissed them and then walked up the red carpet of the futuristic passageway of Saarinen's TWA terminal, carrying my portable Olivetti.

Only a short time earlier I had received that mysterious package from Chicago that contained my father's last notebook. At this point I was keenly aware that I was following in his footsteps. All the stories I had heard about him had had their effect. The myth was irresistible. Part of what I was and what I felt had come from him, even his restlessness. Now I was about to test myself on the same ground that had become his last stand.

CHAPTER 18

A s a newly minted foreign correspondent, I found my entry into Africa anything but easy. Six hours after arriving in Abidjan in the Ivory Coast, I ate a hot dog and collapsed with food poisoning. My father, too, my mother had said, had begun his foreign tour with an illness—except that his was caused by a bad batch of vaccine.

After two days in bed, sweating out a recovery, I was able to get up and investigate the capital, looking into communications and airline connections to see if it would be a suitable base for covering the continent. I decided against it—there seemed to be too many white Frenchmen pulling strings in back offices. So I moved on down the coast to Ghana. I liked Accra immediately—the languid, sultry air, the sweetness of the people, whose universal greeting was, "How is life?" Rickety buses painted with philosophical fragments such as DEATH OF MOTHER IS END OF FAMILY and THE BEAUTYFUL ONES ARE NOT YET BORN plied the potholed streets. I registered at the Ambassador Hotel, which had seen better days—my room had only one working lightbulb—and requested a call to New York. "Certainly," said the cheerful desk clerk. He could book the call for Saturday morning. I looked at a calendar: It was Wednesday. I concluded Ghana was a bit too laid-back for a bureau.

During these initial weeks, I felt a need to communicate with the foreign desk, to let the editors know what I was up to, a hangover from my days as a local reporter. But after a couple of calls, during which it was obvious that my editor was barely listening, it dawned on me that no one in the home office was waiting to hear from me. At first, the realization made me feel as if I had fallen off the edge of the map. Here I was, contending with all these logistical difficulties, and they didn't even care. Then the implications sank in and I felt a flood of joy. I was liberated. My schedule, my life even, was my own affair. I alone was responsible for myself and my family. Now all I had to do was to prove that I was worthy of this freedom, that I could be a top-notch correspondent, that I was smart enough and quick enough to be Barney Darnton's son.

In Accra I managed to meet the Nigerian high commissioner, an expansive gentleman who served me tea and enjoyed discussing New York's fiscal crisis (I was just the man for that). He chuckled while mopping his brow and smoothing the wide sleeves of his *agbada,* a spectacular embroidered robe. During our third meeting, he abruptly leapt up and pumped my hand. In a stentorian voice, he announced that he was going to give me a present: permission to enter Nigeria on a onetime visa.

The plane trip from Accra to Lagos normally took forty-five minutes. Mine, due to inexplicable delays, mechanical problems, the nonappearance of the flight crew, and the crush of a crowd at the ticket counter, took eight hours. I arrived at Ikeja airport wilted and worn-out and handed my passport to an immigration official wearing mirrored glasses and an imperturbable expression. He demanded to see my return airplane ticket. But why would I need that, I ventured, since I was coming in? Without it, he said, I couldn't enter. Case closed. He summoned the next person in line. I protested. I begged. I mentioned a certain letter from a certain high official of the *Times,* complete with a stamp and ribbon, informing anyone who cared to read it that I was to be the officially credited correspondent for an important American newspaper. Could I introduce that document into our discussion? The man did not say yes, but he didn't say no, either. The letter, I recalled, was in my suitcase, and at that moment I happened to look through a window and see the luggage truck crashing into an overhang. Bags were falling onto the ground, collapsing like accordions, bursting open. The baggage handlers walked off. Passengers, businessmen with set expressions, fatalistic from years of coping with West Africa, crawled along a conveyor belt to squeeze through the opening of hanging rubber straps, no easy task, since the belt was moving in the opposite direction. They looked like hamsters on a wheel. I joined them. I made it outside and miraculously located my suitcase, when the truck inexplicably took off. It drove around the terminal building to the front, where I and a few other passengers managed to leap off. I looked around, congratulating myself. I was in Nigeria. But then I remembered that my passport was still in the custody of the immigration official. I entered the terminal and saw an Air Ghana counter. I bought a ticket back to Accra, walked through to the arrivals area, and presented the ticket to the official. Without so much as a raised eyebrow, he stamped my passport, handed it back, and gestured me through. Clearly, Nigeria was unlike any other place on earth, a sort of alternate universe in which rationality and the normal laws of cause and effect didn't apply.

I found a taxi, which carried me for miles and miles along a stark highway, the driver stopping only once to renegotiate the price we had already agreed upon. The road was black except for candles flickering on roadside tables bearing pyramids of goods, presided over by big-busted women wrapped in flame-colored kaftans. Dark figures darted between the cars. I was dropped off at a white stucco house on Ikoyi Island. It had been rented long ago by the paper and was now occupied by an amiable Australian. He welcomed me with a stiff drink in one hand and a bottle in the other. I fell asleep with geckos staring down at me from the ceiling.

In the morning, I slept late. I turned on the radio and heard military music. A shaky voice made an announcement: "I bring you good tidings. The government has been overthrown." Ten hours in the country—eight of them asleep—not knowing a damn thing about Nigeria and still less about the government, I had stumbled into a coup. I dressed, ran out the door, and made my way downtown, through streets jammed with fleeing cars and pedestrians. At the Reuters office I was mounting the stairs when a man came running past me. "I'm Darnton, from *The New York Times*," I yelled after him. He paused for a moment. "Colin Fox, Reuters." He reached the bottom of the landing and shouted over his shoulder, "Welcome to Nigeria!"

Luckily, my reporting reflexes kicked in. I located the bullet-riddled limousine of the head of state, Murtala Muhammed, abandoned on a highway, and saw the pool of blood in the backseat, where he had been riding. I teamed up with Fox—we rode around in his open MG, looking like clueless tourists—until the tanks took over the now-empty streets. Soldiers packed into Land Rovers pointed guns at us. "No road!" they shouted angrily, and we quickly retreated. Throughout the day, power seesawed between the military in office and the rebels challenging them, until finally it appeared that despite Muhammed's assassination, the coup attempt had been beaten back. I filed through Reuters and spent the night at their office. As I lay on the wooden floor, the Teletype machines murmuring in the background, my stomach growling with hunger, I relived the events of the day. I felt a warm satisfaction. I had gotten the story out. My baptism had been difficult but successful. I suddenly felt that this crazy profession—with its camaraderie, adrenaline-fueled excitement, and proximity to important events—was right for me, that I had been born for it.

The following day Fox and his family were expelled from the country—he had filed an overblown story on tribal violence in northern Nigeria, a sensitive subject six years after civil war. I left his office moments before it was ransacked and padlocked and saw him taken away in a Black Maria. Later I heard that he, his wife, and young daughter were taken up country, placed in a dugout canoe, and pushed across a river into neighboring Benin. Except for an Agence France-Presse man, I had become the only resident Western correspondent in the country.

I flew to London and escorted Nina and the girls back to Lagos. I knew Nina was not one to break under hardship—in that respect, she reminded me of my father's assessment of my mother. Still, her taste for adventure surprised me. The fetid streets, bordered by open sewers, jammed with cars, bicycles, and people carrying everything from small bundles to furniture on their heads, struck her as exotic. But I could see she was wondering how to set up a life for us here. After the grinding two-hour trip from the airport, she asked, "When do we get to the nice part of town?" We were just about to pull into our driveway.

I set about establishing an office. I bribed a telephone repair man to obtain a line for a working telex. We enrolled Kyra at an international school. It was adjacent to a military barracks, and to get there each morning, we had to be cleared by guards waving automatic weapons. Lagos lived up to its reputation as a difficult place. Phones didn't work, electricity was a sometime thing (NEPA, the electric company, was said to be an acronym for "no electrical power anytime"), and corruption was rife. Everyday transactions like getting gas meant forking over paltry bribes, called "dash." The wet heat was oppressive. The streets were clogged with traffic jams euphemistically called "go-slows." To try to unsnarl them, military police pulled out long whips and used them on feckless drivers.

After fifteen months, it was our turn to be deported. I had written dozens of articles about Nigeria's praiseworthy efforts to grow more food and surmount various other problems, but four or five of them proved displeasing to the military authorities. One was about piracy in Nigerian harbors, another about a military raid on the commune of a charismatic musician and political dissident whom I had come to know, Fela Anikulapo Kuti. The American ambassador, Donald Easum, warned me that he had heard some rumblings of discontent from inside Dodan Barracks, the seat of the military government. I considered lying low for a while and concentrating on covering other countries, but then something happened that cried out for exposure. The two-and-a-half-year-old son of our steward, Martin Anoweh, fell ill one night. We rushed the child to the main children's hospital, a crowded, dirty, and depressing place. After the medical person on duty failed to find a vein for an IV, the boy died of dehydration. The hospital treated the case perfunctorily, and the staff yelled that Martin was to blame for his son's death. From that point on, we were forced to pay bribes at every step—to retrieve the body from the morgue, to cut through needless paperwork, to be allowed to enter the cemetery, and finally to persuade the grave diggers, suddenly "on break," to bury the makeshift coffin. Martin was devastated. His grief was deepened by the cruelty of every official he encountered. A doctor provided me with accurate statistics on infant mortality, proving that the problem was much worse than officially admitted.

The story created a furor. Not long afterward, plainclothes police from the National Security Organization searched my office and my home, confiscated files, and escorted me to a prison compound surrounded by ten-foot walls topped with razor wire. Inside, a warden, a tall man stripped to the waist, with an angry scar encircling his midriff, confiscated my clothes. He placed me in a dungeonlike cell. During the next eight hours, I was interrogated several times by a young man sharply dressed in civilian clothes who asked me to identify my sources. I politely declined. Eventually, he told me that I had to leave Nigeria because my stories had put the country "in a bad light." The next morning, Nina and our girls were placed in a holding cell while I was escorted to buy our plane tickets—on the first flight to anywhere. We were taken in separate vans to the airport, placed in detention there, and put aboard a plane bound for Kenya. Moments before takeoff, a man bolted up the ramp and tossed our passports in my lap. When we arrived in Nairobi, the foreign press corps met us at the airport, whisked us to a hotel, and treated us to dinner and drinks.

We finished out the four-year assignment in East Africa, where life for foreigners was comparatively idyllic. West Africa was crowded and tumultuous. The climate and the tsetse fly had kept away Europeans. It was the center of culture and art, the historic empires of Mali and Songhay, the Gold Coast slave trade, and the sand-swept cities of the Sahara, where Tuareg in robes of indigo blue rode camels. East Africa was still something of a colonial preserve. It was the home of *White Mischief* and Hemingway's green hills, the game parks, Isak Dinesen's farm, and Masai warriors walking down the Nairobi sidewalks swathed in red kangas and carrying spears. Naturally, foreign correspondents based themselves in East Africa.

We were a privileged band, flying off to cover coups and revolutions, helping and competing with one another. One day we'd be trekking to Timbuktu, another ordering from room service at a Paris hotel during a layover to catch a connecting flight between Senegal and Zaire. This was before the great droughts and famine in the Sahel, AIDS, and the genocides in Rwanda and Darfur, and the child warriors and slaughters in Kenya, Liberia, and Sierra Leone. All that changed everything and made Africa a dismal place to live in and write about.

The stories I covered weren't lacking in drama. I watched as Lt. Col. Mengistu Haile Mariam, the Ethiopian dictator who had smashed five vials of red blood to proclaim the revolution's "red terror," littered the streets of Addis Ababa with bodies. I chartered a plane to fly into Uganda as Idi Amin was being toppled; I searched his house, looking in his freezer to see if rumors were true that he kept human hearts there (there weren't any), and I photographed the blood-soaked walls of his prisons. I met illegally with banned poets and writers in Soweto during the protests against South African apartheid. I accompanied guerrilla and rebel movements from the Ogaden to Angola.

One of my most memorable moments came in Eritrea, where I tagged along with a Marxist rebel group. Sleeping under the stars, I was awakened one morning by something tugging at my hair—a monkey. The poor animal, it turned out, had been adopted from the wild by a rebel commander, and now it was adopting me. I was flattered but also a bit nervous—the authoritarian commander, clearly jealous, disliked me heartily and more than once joked about leaving me lifeless in the bush. I told him the monkey would be brokenhearted; he didn't laugh.

These were high times for foreign correspondents, before the advent of satellite phones and other innovations in communications cut down on independence. We could disappear in the vastness of Africa for weeks at a time and go months without speaking to "the desk." Because the quandaries of time and space worked in our favor, we could pretty much decide what was worth writing about. It was truly a wonderful deal: Someone handed you a credit card for travel and telex charges, patted you on the back, and sent you off. In return, you had all kinds of adventures and wrote home about them. In this respect my days of foreign reporting were closer to what my father had lived than they were to the experiences of correspondents who arrived only a few years after I did.

We called ourselves "hacks," a British term intended to deflate the pomposity of those who took the job too seriously. We didn't engage in high-minded discussions about what we were doing. We must have looked ridiculous, with our safari suits and elephant-hair bracelets and even juju charms. In retrospect, some of our exploits were silly—like getting drunk and climbing out of hotel bathroom windows in Marxist Ethiopia to evade the Ministry of Information's "babysitters." Such times remind me of Barney and his crew in Australia and New Guinea—the drunken carousing, the need to blow off steam, and then the serious business of reporting the war.

In the course of these adventures, I didn't feel that I was immune to danger, nor did I seek it out. I didn't stop to think if I was consciously or unconsciously trying to replicate Barney's life. But I recall hearing that one of my colleagues wondered if I had a penchant for risk taking that stemmed from a desire to emulate my father. And I remember sitting down in a hotel room in Khartoum, before a long trip into a contested area of Ethiopia, and writing a note for Nina, thinking she could look to it for comfort in case anything should happen to me. The wording of that note, now that I think back on it, echoed the wording of the letter my father had written to his older brother on the eve of his departure to the Pacific.

But I think it's true to say that, like my father, I tried to avoid unnecessary risks. I'm reminded of an incident in Uganda when Amin was fleeing. Our small band of correspondents encountered a crazy quilt of contending forces: Libyan troops defending Amin, Tanzanians ousting him, and Ugandans fighting on both sides. It was the kind of anarchic situation old African hands found most perilous. At one point, we ventured into a no-man's-land. Behind us were the Tanzanians, who offered protection; ahead of us was chaos. There were snipers but also, presumably, civilians to be interviewed. We stopped every three or four blocks to decide whether or not to go on. Finally we halted in a crumbling alley. A correspondent for *The Washington Post* said we should turn around. A reporter from the BBC said we should go forward. The first said we were courting danger needlessly, the second that we were obligated to find out what was going on up ahead. The deciding vote fell to me. I said, "Let's go back."

In the early summer of 1979, over a shaky phone line in Mozambique, I talked to the *Times'* foreign editor, who asked me where I wanted to go on my next posting. Anywhere but Eastern Europe, I replied, thinking of the gray weather and the gray landscape and the gray lives under communism. Two weeks later I received my assignment: Warsaw.

We took a ferry across the Baltic to a Polish harbor town whose name we couldn't pronounce (Świnoujście). On the drive to the capital, we stopped for coffee and had to mime our order. Along the way, fresh from the red flame trees and purple frangipani of East Africa, we passed unspeakably drab villages. In Warsaw, we drove past tracts of soulless government housing, huge buildings rising up like radiator blocks. We checked into the one international hotel, the Victoria. Its lobby was largely deserted except for money changers and prostitutes. We walked to a nearby department store; there was little for sale. We went to a grocery store; its shelves were stacked with bottles of vinegar. Nina was upset. A voice inside me whispered, I'm not sure we're going to be able to handle this.

But it was in Poland, which I came to appreciate and love, that my journalist's lucky star provided me with a story that made headlines around the world. Within a year Lech Wałęsa, an unemployed electrician with a Pancho Villa mustache, would scale the wall of the Gdańsk shipyard, and the striking workers there would found Solidarity, the free-trade union that pried Poland from the grip of the Soviet Union and breached the monolithic wall of communism.

When I arrived, I was the only American correspondent to cover the six countries of Eastern Europe from Warsaw. I moved the bureau there from Yugoslavia. The Polish authorities seemed of two minds at the prospect of having the *Times* headquartered there. But I'm sure it appealed to their nationalism and their practicality: Attempts to use me could prove useful in the ever-complicated balancing act between Washington and Moscow. Aside from one or two bizarre anonymous calls that we blamed on the secret police, the government was mostly welcoming. Three days after our arrival, we were given a tour of the capital by a rather stiff young man from Interpress, the government propaganda agency. He showed us the Royal Castle and the Old Town, painstakingly reconstructed after the devastation of the Nazi occupation. We then asked to visit the Jewish ghetto, where Nina's father had hidden while fleeing from Russia sixty years before. After that, he took us to the statue of

Chopin in Lazienki Park. We asked to see the Umschlagplatz, where the trains took Jews to the Treblinka death camp. And so it went, seesawing back and forth, the guide's defensiveness growing, until finally he ushered us into a small church. Stealthily looking about to see if we were being observed, he pointed to a wall and told us to examine it. There were lists and lists of names—war dead—and after each the word: Katyn. "The dates, look at the dates," he hissed. They were the same, too: 1940. It took a few minutes for me to understand. The guide was referring to the wartime Katyn massacre, in which some twenty thousand Polish officers and citizens had been executed in an area occupied first by the Russians, then the Germans. The dates signified that, in contradiction to the official line, the atrocity was Stalin's doing, not Hitler's. We took away a deeper lesson: He was introducing us to the dark side of Eastern Europe, to states that were slaughterhouses, a place where Germans killed Jews and Russians killed Poles, where the cobblestones were steeped in blood and thousands, even millions, of innocents could slip into graves hardly noticed and barely mourned.

Poland rounded out my education on governmental repression. Our phone was tapped and our house was bugged (on one occasion, a lightbulb in our entry started flickering and humming; within two hours, unbidden workers arrived to repair it). What the eavesdroppers were interested in, we learned from our friends, was not our thoughts about the Party or our geopolitical views. They couldn't have cared less about that. What they wanted was scuttlebutt: who was sleeping with whom, who had a drinking problem, who wanted to go abroad. *That* was useful information.

When we arrived, the press and TV were tightly controlled by the Polish United Workers' Party. There was an official censor's office downtown—everyone knew where it was. The media had achieved a sort of negative credibility. During my first week, a cabdriver, learning where I was from, enthused in broken English about New York, which he had never visited, observing among other things that he imagined that there was very little crime there. Taken aback, I asked him where he had gotten his information. Polish radio and TV, he said: "All they say is bad crime in New York." The driver, like many Poles, had taken what he'd heard from the official airwaves and turned it upside down. A friend of mine, a Polish playwright, half joked that he preferred to get a negative review because that would ensure a larger turnout. In the absence of good information, rumors abounded and jokes conveyed truths.

When discontent reached the boiling point in the summer of 1980, we were on home leave. On a flight from Phoenix to New York, I was paged by a stewardess, who told me someone would be waiting for me at the airport runway. A messenger was there with an instruction from the *Times:* Proceed to Poland on the next available flight. I did, while my family stayed in New York. A day later, when I approached the Lenin Shipyard in Gdańsk, a worker examined my credentials, opened the front gate, and said, "Welcome to Free Poland." In the cavernous hall where the strikers were assembled, the names of companies going out on strike were read over a public-address system to loud applause. Minutes later, I was surprised to hear "*The New York Times* has joined our strike!" The hall erupted in thunderous cheers.

One of my first interviews was with Anna Walentynowicz, the fifty-year-old crane operator and grandmother who had set off the strike when she had been fired for political activism and refused to leave.* I asked her what were the workers' strongest grievances. She fixed me with a stare that was anything but grandmotherly, saying, "It's not so bad that the government screwed up. I mean, anyone can screw up. What's galling is that they refuse to admit it. The papers tell us over and over that our lives are getting better and better. And we can see that they're getting worse. That's what really gets to you—the lies." One of the first things the workers did was to start their own newspaper, churning out a two-page leaflet on an old mimeograph machine. They named the paper *Solidarność* and gave it the famous red logo under the Polish flag.

As I looked around, the workers with transistor radios glued to their ears, listening to the Polish-language broadcasts of the BBC and the Voice of America, seemed stunned. They actually could do something—say vote on a new list of demands—and hear about it over the air within minutes. The speed was confounding. To them, government broadcasts had always come with a substantial delay

*In April 2010 she was among ninety Poles who perished when a plane en route to a memorial ceremony at Katyn crashed at Smolensk, Russia.

to allow for censoring. Who knew that news could be fast and accurate? This was something totally different and exciting, and it had a radicalizing effect. The outside world was paying attention to what they were doing. As I watched all this, I realized that the hunger for a free flow of honest information is something deep and natural, almost a visceral need to a healthy society, like food and water to the human body.

Covering the strike was difficult because the government had cut off all communications in the north of the country. That meant that I had to fly from Warsaw to Gdańsk, hitchhike five miles into the city (the taxis were on strike), do my reporting, and then return to Warsaw to file. But there was an upside to this. The episodic nature of my visits highlighted changes in the workers' mood and attitudes as the protests spread. At first when I spoke to them, they were shy and awkward, usually refusing to provide their names. But by my third visit, I noticed a sea change. Now the strikers approached *me*. They demanded to be interviewed and insisted that I take down their names and addresses, spelling them out laboriously, and they readily posed for photographs. Decades of fear of reprisals from the authorities had melted away.

The upshot of the strikes, of course, was capitulation by the state and the establishment of Solidarity, the first non-Party workers' organization in any Communist regime. Over a period of sixteen months, it operated aboveground and attracted some ten million members, turning into a revolutionary force for expanding the boundaries of freedom. The process was anything but smooth—there were strikes, police raids, firings of Party leaders, threats from Moscow, and maneuvers by Soviet troops. For me, it was a roller-coaster ride on an endless stream of stories. Where once it had been impossible to obtain any information, now there was a glut—people were consumed with democracy, exciting conversations went deep into the night, and the whole country seemed to have turned into one big university coffee house brimming with ideas and cigarette smoke.

Then came December 13, 1981, when Gen. Wojciech Jaruzelski imposed martial law, shutting everything down in the space of a single snowy night. As an exercise in raw power, it was awe-inspiring. Solidarity leaders, meeting in Gdańsk, were brought from their hotel rooms in handcuffs. Lech Wałęsa was put on a plane and taken to a distant villa, where he was placed under house arrest. Overnight, all communications with the outside world were severed. A country in the middle of Europe, at the end of the twentieth century, simply dropped out of sight, as if it had been sucked into a black hole. It wasn't so much a matter of putting Poland into one big concentration camp, as some commentators said at the time; it was more like putting each and every person into an isolation cell.

Like everyone else, I had no idea martial law was coming. At 10:00 p.m., I wrote a new lead on a story, and when I went to file it shortly after 11:00 p.m., my telex was dead. I picked up my phone. That line was dead, too. Still, I didn't think anything drastic had happened—fluctuations in service weren't all that uncommon. In a heavy snowfall, I drove to Piękna Street, where the foreign wire services had their offices. When I arrived, everything was in an uproar. Phones and telexes weren't working, people were rushing up and down the halls, and rumors were flying. A small band of us trudged through the snow to the local Solidarity office, where we saw police carting files away. A young man huddling in a doorway told me they had arrested half a dozen activists there. I filed through Reuters—the only agency with a computer line—and then made forays around the city for updates as the army took over and set up roadblocks. At 6:00 a.m. General Jaruzelski announced martial law. The Reuters line died. So here I was, at the center of the biggest story in the world, with no surefire way to get it out.

Nina had left for London only hours before to help a Polish friend whose play was opening there. We had a housekeeper who lived in, so Kyra and Liza were not alone. But in the morning I left them at the homes of close friends, diplomats whose children were the same ages as ours. I finally managed to file through the secret communications system of the American embassy, sending my story as classified material through Washington. But the next day when I went to file, I ran into a snag. Other reporters had asked for the same privilege, and so the embassy had decided to allow a single dispatch each day; we could all contribute to it and it would go to all of our papers. This was a good solution for the embassy, since it wouldn't overload its line, and it was good for Poland, since it would get the story out, but it wasn't ideal for the half dozen American reporters, since we were competitors.

We had no choice but to go along. For days and then weeks, we convened in the embassy at 3:00 p.m. to write a communal story we referred to as "the camel" (a horse designed by committee). We had no idea whether the stories were being used or even received, since our papers had no way of contacting us. We later learned that our camel was feeding every media outlet in the United States.

At the outset, the authorities announced that we would have to submit our reports to the censors. The censors were men in military uniform presiding over two telexes in the office of Interpress. I didn't even consider it and took no small delight in evading the authorities to get my copy out. I used "pigeons"—that is, people—as couriers. For the most part, they were Westerners who had been stranded in Poland and were now able to leave. I met them at the airport or in the lobby of the Victoria Hotel and handed over my stories with the phone number of the *Times'* foreign desk at the top of the first page. Because I wasn't sure of the risk to the courier, I camouflaged my first story as a letter to Robert Semple, the foreign editor, meaning that I put a salutation at the beginning, "Dear Bob," and ended it with "Yours truly." It wasn't much of a disguise, I thought as I handed it over to a Swedish businessman who was taking a ferry to Stockholm, but it might slip past a hurried Polish border guard who wasn't fluent in English. The story, I later learned, got through. Confused by the format, Semple reached Nina in London and asked her questions. Would I be expelled if it were published under my byline? She replied sensibly: Since I had written it as a letter, why not print it as a letter? And so the paper did, salutation and all, boxed on the front page. That made it seem even more dramatic, like a message that had been passed through a tiny crack in a wall—which, in a sense, it was.

To ensure that my stories arrived, I made two carbon copies, sending a total of three copies of each one. I named each story after a woman, beginning with the first letter of the alphabet, and wrote the name on the copy, instructing the *Times* to notify me by telegram—the only communication system still standing—when the story arrived. Soon the messages began pouring in: "Abigail says hello." "Betsy sends her regards." "Carol has recovered." I became adept at enlisting pigeons. One was an American secretary taking the Chopin Express train through Czechoslovakia to

Vienna. Another was a businessman who carried the story in a hollowed-out Marlboro box. A third was a West Coast hippie, who nonchalantly stuffed it into the bottom of his boot. A fourth story went out aboard a private plane that was medevacing the British ambassador, who had suffered a heart attack. What amazed me was that I asked dozens of people to act as pigeons and not one, not a single one, declined.

Soon I hit upon a foolproof arrangement. A German photographer for *Time* magazine agreed to help smuggle out my copy. The Polish authorities had insisted that all news photographs be developed inside the country and submitted to the censors. But *Time* had recently switched to color photographs, and, as there were no chemicals on hand to process the film, the authorities permitted this one photographer to ship his film out undeveloped, presumably keeping a close eye on him while he was shooting. Each time he was to make a shipment, he contacted me. I'd trot over to his hotel, spread my story on his bathroom floor (turning on the tap to foil the bug in the room), and he'd photograph it page by page. At the top of the first page was that same old number for *The New York Times*. And presto—off it went to *Time* magazine's photo department, which then sent it on to West Forty-third Street. The scheme came just in time, because the flood of departing Westerners had turned into a trickle.

After a week, Nina managed to talk herself aboard the first LOT flight from London and turned up on our doorstep at midnight, lugging a suitcase filled with meat from Harrods. She said that as the plane was about to touch down, the stewardess thanked the passengers, all Poles returning home, for flying with the airline, saying she hoped they would "fly LOT in the future." Her remark set off peals of bitter laughter. They knew they wouldn't be flying for quite a while.

In Poland, resistance continued, but in muted form. There were sporadic reports of strikes and other protests. Local phone service came back, but each call was preceded by a recorded warning that it was being "monitored." Underground leaflets and laboriously typed bulletins—samizdat—popped up like mushrooms after a rain. My Volvo suddenly began acquiring a lot of flat tires, often just before curfew, so that I'd have to sneak home, dodging patrols on the deserted streets. "Ah," said one tire repairman, holding a sharp screw that had been carefully placed between the treads, "I haven't seen one of these for . . . oh, more than a decade."

Eventually, as far as the outside world was concerned, the Polish story began to fade—down to the bottom of page one, then inside the paper, then to one or two appearances a week. Over time, things settled into an eerie kind of stasis. Men in uniforms read the nightly news. Some six thousand Solidarity activists were held in prison. Newspapers, their staffs vetted for political reliability, resumed publishing and toed the official line. Christmas was dreary. We put a wreath on our front door and a handyman attached a Solidarity button to it. Kyra, then seven, feared the repercussions and removed it. The man upbraided her: "Just because Solidarity is not allowed, you don't like it anymore." She cried.

For those friends of ours still at liberty, Nina and I scheduled a New Year's Eve party to try to raise their spirits. We managed to wrangle some hors d'oeuvres from diplomats who had access to the embassy commissary and we laid in plenty of alcohol and put up some streamers. But by 9:00 p.m., no one had turned up. By ten o'clock, we opened a bottle and resigned ourselves to drinking alone. Perhaps we had been foolish to believe they would run the risk. Then we heard a caravan of cars pull up. Dozens of our friends poured out. We later learned that they had been debating whether or not to come for two hours. The party turned out to be one for the books. Singing and shouting, they fantasized about leaving Poland. At midnight, they toasted one another with cries of "Happy New York!"

In the second week of January, I scored an important exclusive. The highest-ranking Solidarity leader still at large was Zbigniew Bujak, the twenty-seven-year-old head of the Warsaw chapter. Moving from house to house like the Scarlet Pimpernel, he had become a symbol of the resistance. Through contacts, I asked for an interview. On the day it was to materialize, I was given instructions to change cars and taxis, and I finally met up with activists, who blindfolded me and took me to a large house in Praga, on the east bank of the Vistula. But the long-anticipated encounter was called off at the last minute. It was too risky, I was told. Instead, I wrote up a list of ten questions for Bujak and days later was told to appear at 8:00 p.m. on the third-floor landing of a certain apartment complex close to the river. That evening, it snowed heavily. I parked my car blocks away from the rendezvous and doubled back twice, looking at my trail of footprints in the snow to make sure I hadn't been followed. I climbed the stairs and waited on the dim landing. Minutes passed. By 8:20, I began to despair. Then I heard the front door downstairs open and close. Up the staircase came a young woman wrapped in a thick fur coat. She looked at me and smiled, then unbuttoned her coat and reached into her skirt. She pulled out a sheaf of papers, handed them to me, and left without a word. The next day, I filed the story, in which Bujak spoke of his underground activities and called for the peaceful overthrow of the military "dictatorship." It landed on page one. (The story has a footnote: Fifteen years later, back in Poland, I was interviewing a woman who was a top editor at *Gazeta Wyborcza,* the major post-Communist daily. She fixed me with a stare and said, "You don't recognize me, do you?" In that moment, I did. "My God, it's you!" I exclaimed. She gave me a smile, which hadn't changed over the years.)

During this time, the Polish authorities tried a carrot and stick approach. The head of Interpress, a suave man who was persona non grata in the West, dangled the prospect of an exclusive inter-view with General Jaruzelski. Perhaps it would come more easily, he suggested, if my stories would only show some appreciation for those in power. I did the opposite. Acting on a tip from a source in the Catholic Church, I heard that guards had severely beaten Soli-darity activists in a prison up north, and I wrote the story. The gov-ernment denied it and suspended my credentials for a week. Later the primate, Józef Glemp, confirmed the beatings in his address during the annual pilgrimage to the shrine of the Black Madonna at Czestochowa.

I was informed I had won the Pulitzer by Abe Rosenthal, who called me in Warsaw. I was on deadline—the remnants of Solidar-ity had inaugurated an underground radio broadcast and asked people to respond by flashing their apartment lights, which thou-sands did. I spoke to three or four editors—they passed the phone around—and I could hear champagne corks popping in the background. What really pleased me was that the *Times* article about the awards noted that I was the son of Byron Darnton. For the first time, I felt worthy of my patrimony.

By the time I left Poland five months later, demonstrations had broken out once again in Gdańsk. They were put down brutally by the police. I took a plane to Warsaw, my clothes still smelling of tear gas, and from Warsaw I went to join my family in New York. As the plane lifted off, I stared down at the meadows and forests—those subtle pastel shades of brown and green—and I thought of the friends we had made and the Poles we had met and I was convinced the underground resistance would grow.

I didn't think of my father every day or even every week while I was abroad. But in looking back, I believe that his presence—or something like it—was close. Whenever there was a hint of danger or an obstacle to overcome, an answer came to me from somewhere—from stories I had heard or values I had assimilated or a spirit I had unknowingly acquired.

Sometimes my experiences paralleled his so closely that it was downright eerie. For one story, I signed on in Djibouti to accompany an American crew smuggling coffee out of Uganda. On the way back from Entebbe, flying above a missile range in the restricted airspace of Ethiopia, the pilot, who was something of a cowboy, ushered me into his seat and disappeared. He stretched his legs, enjoying my discomfort as I sat there, my hands frozen on the controls. Three decades later, I read in the diary of one Capt. Alexander Evanoff, commanding officer of the 13th Squadron of the 3rd Bomb Group, that on June 17, 1942, his plane carried Barney Darnton from New Guinea to Charters Towers in Australia. Apparently, a bit of a cowboy himself, he handed over the controls. "I enjoy letting Darnton fly," he wrote cheerily, "but I believe that he is leery of trying anything."

When I returned to the *Times* to work as an editor after a decade overseas, the plaque to my father was missing. During a tasteless redecoration, it had been removed, along with the beautiful green-veined marble facing that had lined the lobby. It took months to locate the plaque—it had been stashed in a storeroom somewhere—and years to get it displayed again. Seymour Topping, the managing editor, took up the cause and eventually persuaded the publisher to hang it on a wall next to the foreign desk in the newsroom. In June 2007, the paper moved to a spanking new skyscraper on Eighth Avenue, but the plaque did not make it into the new quarters. Instead, the paper named a conference room on the fifteenth floor after Barney.

CHAPTER 19

In the summer of 2006, shortly after I retired, Nina and I drove
out to Michigan so that I could visit my father's relatives and
learn some things about him. I had gone there at the age of thirteen,
when I left Washington and fell into the embrace of a large midwestern family I had not known before—or since. Over the years
my only contact had been through greeting cards sent by one uncle,
Tom. They arrived like clockwork one week before Christmas and
one week before my birthday. In precise block letters he would write
a short note, usually about the weather, and include a five-dollar
check. I rarely answered him. I sometimes wondered, Why does
this man, whom I wouldn't recognize from Adam, keep up this
one-sided correspondence? Is it love for his long-dead brother? A
sense of obligation to the family left behind? Then I learned something about Tom that put it in perspective. He had been a banker;
during the Great Depression, he had lost a good deal of money
and ended owing thousands upon thousands of dollars. It took him
something like three decades, but he paid back every cent. Simply
put, he was a man who believed in doing the right thing.

Tom had died years ago, along with my four other uncles and my aunt. In fact, even some of my first cousins had passed away. I was not hopeful that I would come away with a stock of stories about my father. But it seemed to me that if I was to write a book about him, this was the kind of journey I should make. As we crossed the Michigan state line, I thought about the people I was soon to meet. I believed that my father had been different, that he'd been the only one with the gumption (a word they would probably use) to leave the roost. I was convinced he had had a special quality, a restless gene, which made him go off to war and bounce around the country looking for better jobs while they stayed close to the homestead. Of course, I was mistaken.

But our first stop seemed to fit my preconception. It was a pleasant but sterile retirement community in Marysville, called Snug Harbor. It was the home of Louis Dunn, the son of my aunt Clare, and his second wife, Marian. Louie, ninety years old that week, was a gentle, soft-spoken man with an oval-shaped face, a large furrowed brow, and a few wisps of white hair. He had worked for forty-two years as a reporter, city editor, executive news editor, and editorial-page editor for the *Port Huron Times Herald*—the same paper where my father had started. Over coffee, he explained it had been no coincidence. He had idolized my father and resolved to follow in his footsteps. Barney had gotten him the job.

Louie disappeared into another room for a moment and returned with a carbon copy of a letter Barney had written the editor, asking him to hire his nephew. I recognized my father's casual style. ("He's dead set for newspapering and I think he'll make the grade.") Louie reminisced a bit. He recalled that in his sophomore year at Notre Dame, he and a friend had gone down to New York to meet Barney and my mother, who took them out to a nightclub and got them roaring drunk. "I was a country hick. What did I know? I got sick in the hotel." The next morning they stopped off to say good-bye and Barney poured him another drink. "He fixed me up—what is it, the tail that bit the dog?" Barney, he said, was his idol. "I mean, it was one of those darn things, I don't know. He was very debonair. He wasn't flamboyant about it. He smoked and drank, had a little mustache, a good-looking guy and kind of big city, big stuff. He had covered the Al Smith campaign. He was kind of your ideal of the really debonair city guy."

Louie's father, president of a mutual savings bank, had wanted him to go into banking. "I kind of broke his heart, I think." He fished out another letter from Barney, this one written to congratulate him for getting assigned to cover the Sandusky bureau. It was filled with avuncular advice. "There is no place like a small town to learn what the newspaper business is about, even though it may not seem that way when you are undergoing the process." Something in the letter caught my eye: Barney began with an apology for not writing sooner, explaining that he'd been busy—"getting married and settled in the country." *Getting married.* So Barney had wanted his family to believe that he and Tootie had wed. I didn't ask Louie if he knew that this was untrue. If Barney had wanted his family to believe it, then who was I to disillusion them?

Nor did I ask Louie why he had turned his back on his dream of working for a big-city newspaper. The answer emerged when he started talking about his first marriage. One day, he said, his wife, Ardiel, came down with what she thought was the flu. It quickly worsened. She had trouble breathing, was rushed to the hospital, and then into an iron lung. She had contracted polio. For the next twenty-four years, until her death, she was an invalid. Louie looked out the window at a distant view of a lake. "In the newspaper business, you know, you have to move around. You don't stay put."

We talked about all kinds of things, our grandfather, who was so distinguished and looked like Woodrow Wilson, the Catholic Church, the war, and how much newspapers had changed. He spoke slowly and chose his words carefully to be precise and to avoid exaggeration. I thought he was someone who exuded common sense and integrity and that he must have been one hell of a fine editorial writer.

That afternoon we drove five hours to Charlevoix, a resort town on the northern shore, where various branches of the Darnton family had summer cottages. Charlevoix is located on an isthmus between Lake Charlevoix and Lake Michigan. The town is centered around a quaint main street, with a bridge across a canal on one end and a town green on the other. The grass slopes gently toward the water; plunked in the middle is a white bandstand, where the locals put on evening concerts. The next morning we drove to meet the relatives and were quickly engulfed in hugs from various cousins, whose names and relationships came at me so fast, I had trouble keeping them straight. Over the next three days we swam in a social soup. We were fussed over and given "Grandma D's" recipes for scones and chocolate cake. We poured over family trees and documents tracing the Darnton lineage back to the thirteenth century to the town of Darlington, near England's North Yorkshire border. We followed them through the centuries as they married and propagated and crossed the ocean. Robert, my great-grandfather, came to this country and moved to Adrian as a machinist for the railroad. A tubercular young man, he was married to one Mary Lanchester. I learned that my grandfather, also named Robert, had been a printer and foreman at the Adrian *Times and Expositor,* then a clerk and sales manager for a wire-manufacturing company. A Republican and an Elk and a member of the order of the Knights of the Maccabees, he became a respected town father. He moved into a solid three-story Queen Anne house on a corner lot on Comstock Street. He was president of the school board, captain of the Adrian National Guard, head of the Liberty Loan drive for World War I, and, finally, after getting the top score on a civil service exam, postmaster, a position equivalent in prominence to mayor.

The Darnton facility for mathematics and engineering showed itself in my father's siblings. A number of my uncles and cousins occupied important positions at General Motors. When I heard this, I thought of my mother's prediction that I would become an engineer.

One afternoon we were taken sailing on Lake Charlevoix by Darntons in their forties. One of them, a handsome man, who kept one hand on the tiller, said that his father's generation had set a negative example. They had worked too hard and spent too many hours at the auto plants. The implication was that they had missed out on life's pleasures. "We never saw them in the evenings. They had no family life and no social life. That's one mistake we all made sure we're not going to make."

We got quick capsule biographies of relatives who previously had been only names to me. Even though I was a stranger, because I was close in blood I was offered remarkable intimacies and confessions. My father, I learned, was not the only one to have been struck by wanderlust. His older brother, Clifford, had disappeared for years on end. He rode the rails, crisscrossing the country, picking up odd jobs in fields and factories. He spent so many hours close to the pounding pistons and wheels that he very nearly went deaf. Once, while picking apples in Washington State, he decided to visit his brother Robert, who was working as a machinist in a steel mill in Monessen, Pennsylvania. "He came across country in a boxcar full of apples," recounted one of Robert's sons. "For three or four days, the only food he had was apples. He got there dressed in nothing more than a jacket and summer clothes. The landlord called up the stairway, 'There's a man here who wants to see you. He says he's your brother.' Cliff stood there, cold and shivering. He said he'd like to go to work. Dad told him it was possible they could put on another machinist in the mill. He'd talk to the foreman the next morning. He left Cliff in bed. It was all arranged—he was to turn up at the employment office at eight or nine o'clock. Cliff never showed up. He left a note that he had taken Dad's only overcoat. He couldn't take the cold and hoped to send the coat back by parcel post. He never did."

Charles, another brother, also rode the rails. One day, as family lore has it, he jumped off a train on the outskirts of Ames, Iowa, and made his way to a hobo camp. A bunch of bedraggled men were cooking cans of stew over an open fire, and sitting there with them was Clifford. He and Charles fell into each other's arms and vowed to stick together and find work at a local cement mill. They got the jobs but didn't keep them very long. In hearing these stories, I didn't tell my cousins that I, too, had picked apples in Washington or that during my hitchhiking days I had once been held overnight in a jail in Ames.

The stories about Barney were tales seen through the eyes of children. They described how he loved to play with them and how he was quick to invent games. One recalled a Christmas day when he was five and his family had been summoned to Adrian because his maternal grandmother was dying. Barney, fifteen, spent the day with him, dressed up as Santa Claus, sack and all. "It was a sad day for my parents, but he wanted to make sure it was a traditional day for a young believer. He was the only one in the family who expressed his feelings to me in terms I could relate to." Another cousin remembered an occasion when his younger brother, Paul, suffered from mumps: "Uncle Barney came for a visit and sat across from him on a davenport, and every once in a while he'd make a funny face, and each time it'd make little Paul smile and every time he smiled, it hurt. I think my mother was not genuinely pleased with your father's humor, but I know Paul was." He told how the family was plagued by a hornet's nest just above the back door, until Barney took a baseball bat to swat it down, then dropped the bat and ran for his life, just making it back indoors.

I came upon a letter written twenty years ago by my deceased cousin Robert. It was filled with recollections about Barney. He remembered seeing him train with National Guard troops in an Adrian park in 1917 and then, one morning, being awakened by his grandmother to watch them march from the armory to the railroad station for the trip to Camp Custer, near Grand Rapids. "That was the last time I saw your father until after the war in 1919," he wrote. The armory was where the town's citizenry had convened in the spring to unanimously elect Barney's father president of the Patriotic League, an organization that raised money for the war and took on the isolationists. I imagine that a son coming of fighting age at this time must have felt incredible pressure to enlist.

I recalled a piece my father had written in 1939, on the eve of World War II, entitled "Letter to an Imaginary Son." It described war in a no-nonsense way and what it was like being an infantryman. He wrote about overcoming the fear of cowardice, contending with exhaustion and boredom, and dealing with incompetent officers who made life-and-death decisions. He told how disillusionment and dehumanization settled in and how soon the man on the front lines felt alienated from civilians, even family, who wrote determinedly optimistic letters. At one point, he described for his imaginary nineteen-year-old son a mass meeting in the local opera house; he attended it as a buck private in the National Guard, along with his brother Tom, due to report to the navy. It was to approve a resolution for the draft. "All the town's public figures spoke at that mass meeting—the mayor, the editor of the paper, the county judge, and your grandfather. Nobody on the stage was under fifty years old. There were some rousing speeches (I can still hear old Judge MacIntosh, his bony finger pointing aloft, shout: 'As long as there is a God in Heaven we will spend our lives and our treasure that the right may triumph!'). The draft resolution was adopted unanimously. Afterwards Tom turned to me and said: 'Did you notice that they didn't ask for any remarks from the guys that are going to be drafted?' On our way home we talked long and seriously about the fact that old men decided there were to be wars, and young men fought the wars. We didn't come to any satisfactory answer."

Barney was sent to Camp MacArthur in Waco, Texas, and then in January 1918, the 32nd Division sailed for France. He saw plenty of tough fighting—the Red Arrow was the first to break through the Hindenburg Line, the major German fortified defensive zone. In six months, the divison had only ten days of rest and suffered more than fourteen thousand casualties. Among those from Adrian alone, seventy young men did not come back.

I discovered letters that Barney wrote home to his brother Robert. His youthful script seems to make light of the hardships of battle. He used vague terms to describe the fighting, like "the excitement" or "our licks against the Boche" or "another shot at it." He asked his brother to calm his mother's fears. "It's only once in a while that one gets the sensation of the backseat occupant of a car going sixty miles per hour over a rough road, you know." But he did write one sentence that spoke volumes about conditions at the front: "I have not yet got accustomed to sleeping with rats playing around in my hair and on my face and I'm afraid I never will." War, he wrote, was impossible to describe. "You can hear stories from thousands of chaps who have been there, but I don't think human imagination can conceive the thing. One has to see it. Bob, the thrill and glory is sadly lacking from the real thing. That stuff is all supplied between the battlefield and the printing press."

After the war, Uncle Bob wrote, Barney enrolled in the University of Michigan and had top grades in his freshman year. In the summer of 1919, he went to Flint to live with Bob's family while working a night shift at the Buick plant. He drove finished cars from the assembly line to the yard's shipping station. Barney's father had been given a Buick coupe that Easter as a reward for his war-bond drive, and his son taught him how to drive. There was, however, a hidden motive: After the lessons Barney used the car on dates, disconnecting the odometer to cover his tracks. In his sophomore year, he joined a fraternity off campus, stopped studying, and watched his grades plummet. He dropped out. "My own assessment," Bob wrote, "would be that he was older than his peers and his war experience had begun to influence his life."

He joined the *Port Huron Times Herald* and within a year became its legislative reporter. In the state capitol building at Lansing he had an encounter with a black man who had grown up across the street from him and who had been a close friend. Now the man was a barber—a dead-end job that was the best he could expect—and he was bitter and estranged. That encounter helped to make Barney a lifelong advocate of racial integration. I recalled a letter that Robert Sherrod, the *Time* correspondent in the Pacific, wrote to the *Times*. Describing my father's grave site, he noted that he was buried near "an American Negro and a native named Wotia of the Papuan Infantry Batallion." He added, "That would have pleased Barney. He had firm convictions that all men would one day be brothers, or they would be slaves."

Once Barney moved east he lost touch somewhat with his family, especially after his father died in 1925. He did not take his first wife to Michigan for a visit, and his letters to his brother Robert crossed a political divide that was widening. Robert, like his father, was a died-in-the-wool Republican and Catholic. Barney had distanced himself from both the party and the church. Once, after interviewing Eleanor Roosevelt, he predicted in a letter to Robert that one day historians would conclude that FDR had rescued capitalism, a thought his older brother could not abide. Still, Robert wrote to my brother, Bob, "If you thought your father's family had labeled him with 'black sheep' tendencies, you may correct those impressions. I think most were quite aware of the life style of some members of the press but were not passing any judgment."

I found myself asking one of Uncle Robert's sons whether he thought his father had been a bit straitlaced. He began to answer; then his throat tightened and tears came to his eyes and he said, "This is a little hard. . . . I'll try to pick it up later." For a few minutes we talked about other things; then he cleared his throat and resumed. "Let me see if I can put into words what I was trying to say before. My father was a long ways from being a saint. And . . . he had a relationship which I doubt if my kids know about, and I don't know that I ever told them. He had a relationship with a woman who worked in the Buick plant that he worked in, and it got to be a serious bone of contention. And my mother in her wisdom said, Let's have this out. I'm putting it in words that she never said to me, but I'm suspecting what might have happened. Let's have this out. If you want a divorce, I'll be reasonable and give it to you with one understanding. And that is, there are two little boys left in this family—that's my brother and myself. She said, They go with you. And if you're going to have another relationship, whoever is in that relationship is going to have to raise those kids. I've already raised three for you and that's all I'm going to do. And so . . . I have no idea why we did this . . . but my brother and I were dressed up in our best Sunday school clothes and we went three or four blocks, up Patterson Street to east Patterson—we lived in west Patterson—and we went into a sitting room and we were told to sit there. And soon a door opened and this woman came out and she looked at us for a while, looked us up and down and then went back out. And she was the woman my father was having a relationship with. She looked at us and she . . . didn't want to take us. And so he had to break the relationship off."

The following morning Nina and I left and drove south along the lake shore and then down toward Adrian. I wanted to see the house on Comstock Street where my father had grown up. We crossed southern Michigan. The road was straight as a razor's edge and the corn on both sides was five feet high, waving slightly in the breeze. The sky was lead gray, but with a softer gray light on the horizon. A storm seemed to be brewing, but it never arrived. When we entered Adrian, we could see the place had fallen on hard times. Some stores were boarded up and the streets were pretty much deserted at one o'clock in the afternoon. We ate at one of the two diners, Mr. Ed's, the only customers.

We found the house at 526 Comstock Street without any trouble. The porch had been closed in and a room had been added on in the back and the roof crest had disappeared, but it was recognizable as the house that Robert Darnton built in 1902, replacing a smaller house, which was moved to the back of the property. I had seen the earlier house in a family photo from 1919 in which the entire Darnton brood posed before the steps, twenty-six in all, counting spouses and children and a lone spinster aunt—the women seated demurely on chairs, the men in their jackets and ties standing stiffly behind. They seemed handsome and healthy as they stared out at the camera, all of them lean and tall. Barney, the handsomest of the lot, was standing on the left end, his temples prematurely gray.

I took photos of the house. A man from across the street wandered over to ask what I was doing—the sign of a good neighborhood, I thought. I explained that my father had grown up there many years before and we talked for a while, until he lost interest and left. The house appeared empty, but I didn't knock on the door. Later, dropping by the imposing Romanesque castle of the Lenawee County Historical Museum, I learned that the house on Comstock was occupied by the president of the historical society, Jan Richardi. That was a stroke of luck. We got in touch and she bombarded me with material from Adrian. She mailed old clips about Robert Darnton's family from the local papers, the *Times* and the *Daily Telegram*. They conjured up visions of a time and place when news reckonings were of a smaller caliber: a blaze coursing down the wiring of a chandelier stem in the Darnton dining room—"the daughter had the presence of mind to turn off the switch and the trouble was over"; a prowler on the back porch while Miss Darnton, the same daughter, was home alone—he lingered for five minutes and left moments before the police arrived; a lengthy front-page lead story on the death of Robert Darnton, accompanied by a fulsome editorial on his accomplishments.

Jan also sent on booklets that resurrected Adrian's prosperous days in the early twentieth century. Located where the industrialized East met the boundless prairies of the West, it was a young city of eight thousand. Every year, it seemed, a new building was going up—a city hall, a school, an opera house. Close to a dozen factories produced wire fence, an industry that made Adrian "the fence capital of the world." (The Page Woven Wire Fence Company, where my grandfather worked, had sold some 625,000 miles by 1916, "enough to encircle the earth *more than twenty-four times*," noted one pamphlet.) Great hopes were placed in the nascent auto industry, in particular the home-produced luxury "Lion Car," which had a collapsible canvas top. A young man named Thomas Edison, sixteen years old, worked at the local telegraph office.

In reading this material, I found it amazing to think that my father's life and mine, touching three centuries, occupied such different worlds. He was born in November 1897, and I have lived into the twenty-first century. I've seen jet planes and the moon landing and the rise of computers—none of which he could have imagined. Our lives had spanned the golden age of newspapers: his when Adolph Ochs bought the *Times,* mine before newspapers fell into decline.

When Barney was young the packed-dirt roads of downtown Adrian were ruled by horse and buggy. Outhouses sat in every backyard, so that the smell was oppressive, especially in summer. As a child he saw electricity come in, as well as telephones and running water. I imagine him riding horses to the outlying farms and in the winter trudging through two-foot snowdrifts to school. The high school yearbook, the *Sickle,* carried a darkly brooding photo of him in 1913, when he was president of the freshman class. A bit of doggerel recalled that he rallied his classmates to fend off the "disdain and contempt" of sophomores.

> *They soon intrusted the class*
> *To Byron Darnton as leader*
> *And learned to hold high their heads.*
> *So that when by the enemy challenged,*
> *They valiantly conquered their foe,*
> *And made those impertinent Sophmores*
> *To experience misery and woe.*

I went to my father's grave in Oakwood Cemetery, a short walk from Comstock Street. It was in a family plot not far from the gate of the main entrance, a prominent position, perhaps due to his father's status. Barney had a small headstone—with only his name and dates. It was located to one side of his father's and mother's, which seemed fitting, since I had been told he was his father's favorite child. Luckily, his father died before he did; I don't know how the old man would have stood the pain.

I stared at the tombstone. I felt the shock of seeing his name, and then a double shock because his name in full, Francis Byron Darnton, was different from the one I carried in my head. I knew the grave site intimately, the slight slope of the ground, the presence of trees off to the right side, the slant of the sky. I recalled these details from the funeral I attended when I was a small boy. Then it had been crowded with people and covered over by some sort of canopy, and my attention had been taken up by the firing of the guns. Still, knowing that something was sacred about the ceremony and the place, I had reduced the landscape to its essentials and absorbed them.

Returning there, I imagined the casket underground, long gone, and my father's bones, long disappeared. Then I tried to stop thinking of that and instead made an effort to imagine what my father had been like before died. This was easier to do than it would have been five years earlier. When I began this project, I wrote down all the facts I knew about him and found they covered barely half a page. Since then I've talked to some of his contemporaries and, thanks to my brother, read interviews with some of those who are now dead.

I've been able to connect some dots and fill in some blank spaces. I've picked up some traces—a humorous crack here and there, an image of him in the trenches during World War I, the knowledge that he dressed well, that he was attractive to women, a sense of his enthusiasm for adventure and for drink. I have a feeling of his calmness and his integrity. But I still don't know the whole man, what motivated him or why he made the decisions he did. I've been looking at an empty room—the occupant having long since fled. How paltry are the traces left behind by a life, even one concentrated around those supposed things of permanence called words. We spend our time upon the earth and then disappear, and only one one-thousandth of what we were lasts. We send all those bottles out into the ocean and so few wash up onshore.

One thing that I had achieved in Michigan was an evocation of the life I might have lived had he not died. It was in the resort town of Charlevoix where we would have come for visits. I would have learned to sail and gone water-skiing and listened to concerts on the town green, and maybe explored the Upper Peninsula on camping trips. My mother would have enjoyed drinks during the summer evenings and probably would have gotten tipsy, but she wouldn't have become a drunk. I would have had a whole second family and been more secure and less lonely.

On impulse, after visiting the grave, I found a phone booth and called my cousin Bill, who had welcomed us so warmly at his cottage in Charlevoix. He seemed glad to hear from me. I thanked him for his hospitality and then stammered out the one question I had forgotten to ask: When I came for a visit at the age of thirteen, had they been aware that Mom was an alcoholic? He answered quickly. "No, I had no knowledge of that. I don't remember anyone ever saying that to me. It's a question that never came up." He paused, seeming to search for the right words to say what he wanted. "I can't tell you enough," he said slowly and solemnly, "that your feeling that you were the only Darntons in the world was not true. Please know that you have family here. We're always here and the latch is always open for you."

I thanked him again. I knew the sentiment behind the words was genuine but that I would not take him up on the offer.

CHAPTER 20

I decided to track down Hub Cobb, the man who had lived with us when I was young and who suddenly, and inexplicably, dropped out of our lives. I wanted to learn more about my parents. Hub had come from their world and had been romantically involved with my mother. I figured he had to know a lot. I traced him to a small Connecticut town called Deep River. I wrote him, then called. A stepson who was visiting at the moment said Hub, now eighty-eight, was frail and in a nursing home but would be happy to see me.

During the two-hour drive from New York three days later, I pulled off the road twice to jot down questions. I listed them on the last page of my notebook, where it'd be easy to scan them, an old reporting habit, and the list grew to cover two pages. I took along a small tape recorder, which I had tested twice. As I pulled into the parking lot of the Saybrook Convalescent Hospital precisely at noon—the agreed-upon time—I felt unaccountably nervous.

The lobby had a stomach-wrenching odor, a mix of disinfectant and bedpans. I gave the receptionist my name and said I had come to see Mr. Cobb. A flickering of shadow crossed her brow. There seemed to be a problem. She disappeared into a back office, and I began to worry. Maybe I needed an appointment. Maybe Hub had changed his mind about seeing me. When she returned, her expression suggested the problem was indeed serious. Mr. Cobb, she said, had collapsed a little over an hour ago and been rushed away in an ambulance. I must have turned ashen, because she seemed to transfer her concern to me. She quickly provided the name of the hospital. In the car, I berated myself. More than half a century had passed since I had last seen Cobb. At any time over the last five, ten, or twenty years I could have called him up, but now it turned out I had missed out by only one hour!

I sped to the Middlesex Hospital in Essex and rushed into the emergency room. I asked a nurse if Mr. Cobb had been admitted. She checked a short list and nodded. "You let family members in, don't you?" I inquired. (I was not, technically, claiming to be one.) She said the patient was waiting admission to a room and then led the way through two doors to a small, crowded corridor. There, strapped to a gurney, was Hub. He had an oxygen tube under his nose and electrodes pasted to his forehead. He appeared shrunken. I found it hard to believe that this could be the man from my childhood—Van Johnson in a leather jacket—but the more I scrutinized him, the more his features seemed to merge into an almost-forgotten face.

He looked at me, bewildered. I explained who I was. He stared, perhaps a little less confused. "Hub," I said, "you remember we were supposed to meet. I know this probably isn't a good time . . . but I wonder if I might ask you a couple of questions." He nodded weakly. I said that I remembered him fondly, as did my brother, and that we had talked of him over the years. A doctor began hovering nearby. I thought I had time for only a single question. It popped into my brain. I looked down at him. "Do you happen to know . . . did my mother ever tell you . . . why she and my father never married?"

His face twitched a bit. He seemed to be summoning up energy. His voice came out slowly, in a croak. "No," he said. He paused, then seemed to feel it necessary to elaborate. "She never told me that. Or if she did, I didn't pay it any attention." An aide came and pushed his gurney away.

On the way home, I mused over the fact that of all the questions scribbled in my notebook, *that* was the one I had most wanted to ask. It was, I realized, a question that had rankled more as time went on. (I did manage to interview Hub two weeks later, when he returned to the nursing home, but his memory was so impaired, he could provide no information.)

The thought of my parents living "in sin" wasn't upsetting as a moral issue. But insofar as it raised questions about their commitment to each other, it tore at the foundation of the myth that my mother had cultivated throughout our childhood. If their love had been as unbounded and eternal as she'd made out, why not consecrate it in the eyes of society? My mother, a romantic, would surely have wanted a wedding. She would have loved everything about it: the ceremony, the bridal dress, the prospect of friends making witty toasts, a theatrical moment in the public gaze. And she had not been one to flout social convention lightly. Why else would they have pretended to be married and gone through the charade of picking an anniversary date?

One possible answer, of course, was that one or the other had been unable to secure a divorce. But that seemed unlikely. I remembered how vividly my mother had described winning her freedom from her first husband on the grounds of adultery, how she'd had to pretend to catch him in flagrante with another woman, a prostitute, and her contempt for him when he'd insisted on actually having sexual intercourse to get his money's worth. And as for my father—his second wife, Pollie, had insisted to my brother that she had rushed through her divorce so he could remarry. I reread Bob's notes from his interview with her. She had provided various details, including the fact that she had hired a cousin to represent her, a young lawyer who served up mountains of legal background to the irritation of the judge, who kept saying, "I know, I know."

I was skeptical about some of Pollie's information because she was bitter—she was, after all, the woman Barney had spurned. Still, she didn't seem to be the type to lie outright and say something had happened if it hadn't. She was convinced that our parents had gotten married, and had even suggested that Mom had been lying when she said they hadn't. In the interview Bob had pressed the point. Maybe, he ventured, having undergone two divorces, Barney rejected marriage as a "bourgeois" institution. She fixed him with a hard stare. "But Barney *was* bourgeois," she insisted. "He was very conventional." What he wanted was an old-fashioned kind of wife who would stay home and cook and raise kids. "And when he got Tootie, he got what he wanted."

I suddenly remembered something Pollie had said. At one point, an FBI agent had called on her, posing questions about Mom, who had, apparently, been applying for a government job. After beating around the bush, the agent asked what he wanted to know: Why had Tootie left her first husband, Clarkson Hill? Pollie answered the question with a question: "Have you ever *met* Clarkson Hill?" Her implication was clear: The man was a twerp. The agent couldn't help but laugh.

Invoking the Freedom of Information Act, I wrote the FBI, requesting any information on file about my mother. I didn't hear back for months, and then to my surprise, in November 2006, a thick envelope arrived. It was part of a dossier covering some sixty-seven pages, initiated in April 1951, in connection with her application to work for the State Department's Voice of America. Since the position dealt with news and propaganda, it was clearly a sensitive one. The investigation into her background, a cover form stated, was "to be assigned immediately" and completed within two weeks. FBI offices in New York, Washington, and New Haven were mobilized for the task. The first reports from agents interviewing neighbors and colleagues were entirely positive: " . . . all advised that they consider her to be an individual of high moral character, excellent reputation, and loyal American citizen." She had no police record and her credit rating—other than late payment of a bill amounting to $30.05 to a department store—was unblemished.

Then, one day before the deadline, a snag arose. "Unfavorable information requires additional investigation," a handwritten note said. Apparently the Bureau had stumbled onto the fact that my mother had been previously married. An internal Teletype message referred to her as "Eleanor Darnton, née Choate, aka Mrs. Clarkson Hill," and suggested checking divorce records in Trenton, New Jersey (where she had lived with her first husband), adding, BUREAU ADVISED MATURE EXPERIENCED AGENTS TO BE UTILIZED THIS INVESTIGATION. The Newark FBI office compiled comprehensive records on both Mr. and Mrs. Hill during their three years in New Jersey but could find no record of divorce proceedings. Obviously, the State Department was not eager to hire a bigamist. In Philadelphia agents fanned out to conduct more interviews in Philadelphia, Jenkintown, Moylan, Media, Chester, Washington, and New York. They didn't turn up any dirt. On the contrary, their reports extolled her qualities in a litany that sounded like the Boy Scout oath: She was capable, efficient, intelligent, loyal, morally upright, and altogether worthy of hire. "She associates with reputable citizens whose loyalty is unquestioned," concluded a nine-page report in mid-May.

But then came a report from the New York office that sent the Bureau into high alert. It was based on an interview with the publisher of YOU magazine, already defunct, where my mother had worked as the editor from 1937 until April 1939. The publisher said she was very capable, but he questioned her "moral character." He noted that when she was hired, she was Mrs. Clarkson Hill, and then she became acquainted with Byron Darnton, also married. The report went on:

He said that the HILL family and the DARNTONS were very close friends and apparently had known each other socially for several years. However, he stated that toward the latter part of Mrs. Hill's employment with "YOU" magazine, Mrs. HILL left her husband and Mr. Darnton left his wife and the two established a residence in Connecticut without benefit of divorce from their respective spouses. [Name redacted] advised that this created quite a scandal and caused considerable gossip among persons who were acquainted with the two families. He said that as he recalled the incident, when Mrs. HILL advised her husband that she was leaving him, her husband refused to give her a divorce in spite of which she left to live with Mr. DARNTON. He further stated that shortly before her termination with "YOU" magazine, Mrs. HILL became pregnant by Mr. DARNTON, which forced her to resign her position.

For good measure, the publisher asserted that the immoral Mrs. Hill hung out with a group of people who were, in his opinion, "somewhat sympathetic to the Communist cause," though he did not go so far as to say that anyone in the group joined un-American organizations or took antigovernment stands on any ideological issues. He declined to furnish a signed statement or appear before a government hearing board. No one else, among dozens questioned, cast any aspersions on her loyalty or politics.

The FBI investigation flew into top gear. Internal messages were sent off to various bureaus, signed with a single name: Hoover. (Maybe all messages were sent out in his name. I can't believe that the director would have interested himself in my mother's background check—but who knows?) The case—number 123–6451— had become urgent. One such Teletype notice commanded:

VERIFY MARRIAGE OF APPLICANT AND BYRON DARNTON BY PUBLIC
RECORDS. ASCERTAIN BIRTH DATA RE APPLICANTS CHILDREN BY
RECORDS. BVS. SUBMIT ON AMENDED PAGES TO REPORT OF JUNE
TWENTY. EXPEDITE.

HOOVER

Special agents in Hartford, New Haven, Bridgeport, and New York swung into action, looking for a certificate to prove my parents had gotten married. They couldn't find it. One of the agents noticed that *Who's Who* listed their marriage date as April 23, 1938. Another noted that their address at the time was in Westport and suggested looking there. A special agent interviewed a source in the Westport town clerk's office and came away empty-handed. In Hartford, the agents poured through all the marriage records between 1937 and 1939. Nothing turned up.

My mother's divorce decree from Clarkson Hill was finally located in New York County Supreme Court. But where was my father's divorce decree? Hoover—either the individual or the generic—must have been apoplectic. Then came information that Byron Darnton had been divorced in Philadelphia. Hoover fired off another Teletype message:

INFO RECEIVED . . . BYRON DARNTON DIVORCED PHILADELPHIA,
APRIL THIRTYNINE. DARNTON THEREAFTER MARRIED APPLICANT.
REVIEW COURT RECORDS PERTAINING TO ABOVE DIVORCE FOR

DATE THEREOF, DATE OF MARRIAGE SAID DIVORCE DISSOLVED, FULL NAMES OF LITIGANTS, GROUNDS, ETC. BEAR IN MIND FOR PURPOSES OF CLARITY IN YOUR REPORT THAT APPLICANT AND POLLACK BOTH HAVE GIVEN NAMES ELEANOR. EXPEDITE.

HOOVER

But the Philadelphia office came up empty-handed. To be certain, the agent culled through the files for an eight-year period and found no record of Barney's divorce, no record of his marriage to my mother. Then an agent in Washington turned up a possibly significant discrepancy in my mother's passport applications. In one she said she had been married on April 29; in another she gave the date as April 28.

At this point, the written record petered out. Needless to say, my mother didn't get the job. The reason was provided in a box that was checked, indicating that the applicant had been turned down "as a result of suitability determination." When I saw this, I cast my mind back to that period. I remembered that Mom had been hopeful of landing a government job. A neighbor in Washington told her that the FBI had been asking questions, which made her very anxious. I suspect that she was fearful that word would get out that she had a drinking problem and that this would be made part of some permanent record. I recall her saying that it was horrible that the government could pry into a citizen's private life. I held her FBI file in my hand, assessing its weight. She had little idea, I thought, of just how much prying the government had done and just how thick her dossier had become.

I succeeded where the FBI had failed—that is, I was able to dig up my father's divorce decree, as well as my mother's. Equipped with the index numbers from the Department of Records, I went to the County Clerk's office in the Surrogate's Court in lower Manhattan. It was just north of City Hall, where I used to work. The building, a seven-story Beaux-Arts masterpiece with an ornate granite façade of thirty-six-foot-high Corinthian columns, had been built one hundred years ago to impress. As I entered the cavernous lobby under skylights several floors up, facing a grand staircase inspired by the Paris opera house, I was impressed—though I had no idea why divorce records would be kept there. I was directed to the seventh floor, where I followed a corridor lined with shelves stacked to the thirty-foot ceiling, packed with yellowing folders. Inside the cluttered gloom of a vast chamber, a man was asleep in a chair near a desk fan that, rotating slowly, mussed his hair. A young clerk fielded my inquiry. I explained what I wanted. There was a problem, he indicated.

"What year did you say?" he asked.

"Nineteen thirty-eight."

"Divorce records are sealed for one hundred years."

"*One hundred years*—you must be joking."

"Nope. You need a court order to unlock them."

As we talked, a grizzled old man shuffled by, carrying an armful of folders. He was about seventy, dressed in a blue smock and wearing glasses with thick lenses. He put the folders on a dolly and disappeared behind a stack of shelves. I paid him little mind. I assumed he was probably a filing clerk placed in a dead-end job by some Democratic party boss.

"Isn't there anything I can do?" I asked the young man.

He shook his head, doubtful. "Not much. Talk to Bruce."

"Who's Bruce?"

"He'll be back."

I chatted with the young man some more and then with another clerk who wandered over. We talked about the magnificence of the building, which was, the clerk said, built in 1907. Together with the Municipal Building across the street, it was the centerpiece of the City Beautiful Movement, which emphasized grandeur in civic architecture. It was certainly grand, I agreed, and as we talked, I felt the gaze of a pair of eyes upon me from the other side of the stacks. After some minutes, the old man in the smock returned.

"That's Bruce," said the clerk.

Bruce, it turned out, had been eavesdropping, so it wasn't necessary to repeat my request. He took down the index number to run a check on whether the divorce decrees had "been weeded out," and he disappeared again. Most decrees between 1910 and 1958, explained the clerk, had been tossed out. Bruce returned. I was warming to him and I was in luck. The records were intact. He directed me to go to the basement of the state supreme court building at 60 Centre Street. I was to ask for Mickey Ruiz. "Don't ask for anyone else," he cautioned, "except maybe for Erlon or Kevin. And whatever you do, don't tell them it's about a divorce."

A few blocks away I mounted the steps of the state supreme court building, familiar to millions of fans of *Law and Order*. I went through a metal detector, crossed a marble lobby, and descended to room 103 in the basement. It was crowded with doughty-looking people, whom I took to be gofers and researchers for divorce lawyers. They seemed familiar with the setup. I filled out two requisition slips and went to the counter. Mickey wasn't there—maybe out to lunch, I was informed. I handed in the slips anyway and a clerk told me to return in two or three days. There was no mention of a hundred-year exclusion rule. I had no idea if that requirement was a fiction or if I had luckily slipped through a crack in the bureaucracy.

When I did return, the records were waiting for me, two thick stacks in closed envelopes. I carried them to a long table and sat down. I decided to look at my mother's file first. Among the papers was a soft-focus photo of Clarkson Hill. I stared at it, this relic from my mother's prior life—he looked like a dandy with a pencil-thin mustache, swept-back hair, and a weak chin. He had the louche air of someone who belonged on the wrong end of a divorce action. There were affidavits and legal summonses and transcripts, all signed and stamped and properly recorded. In the legalistic folderol of the era, in which men of honor were supposed to sacrifice themselves before the altar of the court, my mother was the plaintiff and Hill was the defendant. So the very first words of the case were a lie. An affidavit from a certain Helen Rafshoon established that she had served "a man known to her to be Mr. Hill" with the summons on June 9, 1938, at the Hotel Astor. He didn't turn up in court—"the Defendant has not answered," the record stated ominously—but my mother did. She provided basic information: names, addresses, length of marriage. Then an architect named Charles Du Bose took the stand. He swore that he was with his wife and Mrs. Hill at the Hotel President on May 4 at seven o'clock in the evening.

QUESTION: What did you do?

ANSWER: I went to the desk clerk and asked if Mr. Hill was registered and I found out that he was. I was told he was in room 1423 and I rejoined Mrs. Hill and Mrs. Du Bose.

QUESTION: What did you do then?

ANSWER: We took the elevator to the 14th floor and I knocked at the door. . . . I heard Mr. Hill's voice from within the room. He said: "Just a minute." He opened the door. . . . I pushed against it. I saw him with a woman. She had on a dressing gown. His legs were bare. He had no shirt or undershirt on. She was part sitting, part lying on the bed. She was wearing some sort of negligee and attempted to pull the cover over herself.

QUESTION: Had they been drinking?

ANSWER: Yes. The bed was in disarray.

Adultery. An open-and-shut case. Interlocutory judgment was entered October 17, 1938. A ruling was made October 25. Three months later, it became official. As a result, according to the law of that time, it was "not lawful for the defendant to marry any person other than the plaintiff during the lifetime of the plaintiff except by express permission of the court"—a punishing requirement. New York State made adultery the only grounds for divorce in 1787, just after the Revolution, and, incredible as it seems, that outdated stipulation remained law until 1967.

My father's case was a bit more intriguing, if that's the word. He, too, was being divorced because of adultery, but in this instance, he was actually the guilty party. He didn't appear in court, but his ghost seemed to hover over the proceedings. The summons was served on him on November 23, 1938, and the person who served it, in Grand Central Station no less, was Cedric Worth. *Cedric Worth!* That was a name I had encountered before—in fact, twice. He was Barney's buddy from the *New York Evening Post* and the fellow quoted in *The Dictionary of Misinformation*, the one who remembered my father's crack, "Anybody who hates children and dogs can't be all bad." Worth, according to Bill MacKaye, the son of my father's best friend, was the very same man who had been courting my mother shortly before Barney won her hand in not-quite marriage. (I later checked Worth's obit. After his newspaper days he became a screenwriter and went on to ignominy as a central figure in a phony scandal about the B-36 procurement program.)

I imagined that Worth had served the papers on Barney as a friendly act, maybe even a truce offering. In any case, there was certainly an overlapping array of characters in this drama—and no small amount of playacting in this divorce, too.

Pollie took the stand. She said they had been separated about fourteen months, that they had had no children, and that she wanted no alimony. There followed a couple of witnesses who testified to my father's licentious behavior while he lived at a residential hotel, the Hotel Murray, at 66 Park Avenue. A room-service waiter, one James A. Iver, was shown a photo of Barney and identified him as the man who lived in 5A, a two-room apartment with a kitchenette. He also identified six room-service checks for breakfast that Barney had signed (cost: one dollar for two people). "I gave him the pencil to sign it," testified the bellhop. The defendant was "in the company of a woman who was not Mrs. Darnton." He was, according to Iver, dressed in pajamas and a bathrobe and the woman was in a negligee. Looking off to the left, the bellhop saw a bedroom with twin beds that "had been slept in." A night elevator operator, one George Geehan, testified that he had seen the couple, too, taking them up to the room but not down.

But one exchange with the bellboy gave me pause:

QUESTION: How many different women who were not Mrs. Darnton did you serve breakfast to?

ANSWER: At least two.

That stopped me. *At least two different women.* Given the time period, from November 1937 to February 1938, one of them could well have been Mrs. Hill, who four years later would become my mother. But there was another woman as well—perhaps more than one. I looked at the room chits with my father's signature and then at his photo, a studio portrait, airbrushed so that the background looked like a spray of mist. He was gazing at the camera, deadpan. I thought back to my mother's letters to him, the one in which she said she had to learn to trust him all over again. Had she found out that he was sleeping around? I remembered one other tidbit that Pollie had given my brother—that after my mother, Clarkson Hill had remarried, unaware that Barney had seduced *his* fiancée. So Barney had betrayed him twice—with his wife and with his wife to be. All this jumping in and out of bed: What had my father been looking for? Pollie had claimed he was "a deeply unhappy man," someone who reached out for the nearest woman after a couple of drinks. I looked at the photo again. I wouldn't have called it the face of a contented man. I wondered if he would have settled down with my mother and us two boys after he returned from the war, and whether he would have been content to live a conventional, reasonably circumscribed life in a house in the suburbs.

The divorce records did help to fill in one blank. My father's decree was filed February 15, 1939. It thus became final three months later, or on May 15. That was five days *after* my brother was born, on May 10 of that year. So my mother's explanation of why they'd never married was probably true. It was against the law for my father to wed again in New York State. Their wounds from the legal disentanglement of two divorces were still raw. They could have run off to some place like Maryland, but Bob had already been born. It would have been embarrassing for her to stand before a justice of the peace if that came out. And perhaps some reporter would have filed an item on it. Then the scandal, only now beginning to fade, might rise up again. Or at least this is probably what they told themselves, living in the hothouse atmosphere of the New York City press. They probably just let it slide. Hell, they were practically married. They told everyone they were married. They *felt* married.

That's one version. They fell in love and had to be together, to hell with the outside world. The other—for anything is possible when it comes to filling in a blank space—is what Pollie had hinted at but never stated outright: that Mom snared Barney, that she got herself pregnant, and that he had little choice but to marry her. Eventually, according to this version, he came around, accommodating himself to the facts. In truth, he had always wanted children. Pollie couldn't produce any. But it took a while for him to arrive at this decision and that's why he postponed getting a divorce until the last-possible minute.

Needless to say, I found this version most depressing. It was the antithesis of my mother's romantic fairy tale.

I decided to reread their letters.

There are more of hers to him than his to her. The dates are uncertain. A slip of paper falls out of the stack, reading in Mom's handwriting "1937–38," but which letters it refers to is not clear. They are dated only by days of the week.

The early ones, from his time visiting his family in Michigan, are loving. In one, he provided her with family news—glimpses from that confusing group of brothers, cousins, nieces, and nephews—and ended, "Have I told you this trip that I love you? Why must I always be telling you that? Don't you know? . . . If by this time you don't know it you are indeed Mrs. Choate's little dullard. Darling, I'm happy!" Another ended:

> *Long ago I talked to you about our having a little area in time in which we might learn to love each other naturally, without outside pressures of any kind. This separation is providing me with that quiet, and I have learned to love you very much indeed. Oh, very much indeed, Darling.*
>
> *Goodnight, my Sweet.*

She replied:

> *Darling, darling, darling, darling—*
> *I got two letters this morning! Two whole beautiful letters. And all my days are so mixed up—they all run into each other backwards and forwards in such a lovely flow—that I can't for the life of me keep straight what letters of mine you have now—or had when you called or will have or will have had or what I will have had—you see what a lovely mix-up it can be.*

The next batch of letters were written much later, after Bob was born and while Barney was traveling around the country. In November 1939, he covered California's "Ham and Eggs" elections, a controversial proposition to establish a thirty-dollar-a-week old-age pension, which had inspired a thunderous populist movement. (It was defeated.) Barney returned to the West to do a seven-part series on the plight of migrant workers the following year, the same year that John Steinbeck won the Pulitzer Prize for *The Grapes of Wrath*.

These letters are very different. Barney's are businesslike, casual, and affectionate. He told her he was having a problem with a tooth and filled her in on minor complaints about work—that it was hard to get around Los Angeles, that he'd come cold onto a story right on deadline and that he'd filed "a very late and very lousy piece." He hastened to add, "All this sounds like a tale of woe. It isn't. I'm having a swell time, although it is nothing but work."

Mom's letters are chatty and supportive. She wrote to encourage him, told him his stories were terrific but that he shouldn't get his hopes up for a Pulitzer. She kept him posted on developments at home, especially Bob's every smile and gesture and ounce of weight gained. She seemed genuinely taken with watching her son grow. She bragged about how well she was coping—renewing license plates, paying bills, and cooking food in the fireplace during an ice storm. Her underlying theme: I'm keeping the home fires burning while you're off in the big world doing important things. She was content with being a "newspaper wife," she said. She was trying hard not to be demanding but wanted him to know that when he was away, there was a hole in her life. At one point, she asked, "Is Orion over the orange groves?"

Their letters restored me. I believed that their love was the real deal.

When I read hers, in that same handwriting I had come to know so well from her flood of letters to me at boarding school, I couldn't help but conjure up her younger self. There was a flame to her of which I later saw only the embers. She was trying so hard for happiness. I felt sad for my mother, her hope and energy, her youthful optimism as she tried to finally connect with the right person. I lingered over her long sentences, the dashes that she poured on in a gush of expression to capture what she wanted to say. I felt compassion for her belief in the future, for her experiencing the exquisite joy of a teenager at the age of thirty-two, and for her missing her beloved, giving up her job, and relinquishing herself to another for the first time.

And I felt sad for my unknown father—he did indeed have a way with words, a casual wit, an ability to bare his soul if need be—and I felt sad for myself and the fact that I would never know him. My mother used to say during her down times, "If only you had known him—you especially, you're so much like him—the two of you would have gotten on so." And finally I mourned for the whole dream they had concocted together, the cozy house in the country and the Tom Collins under the tree and the jeep to drive to the railroad station, the loss of it all, so unimaginable at the time of their writing the letters. A piece of shrapnel comes screaming out of the sky, and irreversibly it overturns lives, reducing four to three, changing everything, ending joy and dreams.

CHAPTER 21

In March 2009, I was flying from New York to Michigan and reading a book called *Weller's War*, a collection of the war dispatches of George Weller, a correspondent for the *Chicago Daily News*. Weller won the Pulitzer Prize in 1943 for a story about an emergency appendectomy performed on a nineteen-year-old seaman with no operating room, no anesthesiologist, and no surgeon—in a submarine in enemy waters. It's a story of Yankee improvisation with a happy outcome (the patient survived).

There I was, not deep in the ocean but high in the sky, turning pages, when I came upon a dispatch that knocked me back in my seat. It was headlined WRITER MOURNS DARNTON, KILLED IN NEW GUINEA. It said:

> *"Barney" Darnton of* The New York Times, *buried yesterday in New Guinea, was among the best-loved, as well as most respected, of war correspondents in the Pacific area. His plump but debonair figure, his large head with the slightly graying hair of 44 years and his gentle and sensitive voice were the accouterments of a spirit well equipped for his task.*

Barney Darnton had the searching eye of the reporter, without being cynical. Making no excuses for himself and working without stint, Barney was nevertheless always the first to excuse shortcomings in others. His principles as a correspondent were high; he was always ready to strip the story to its skeleton in order to keep a strict truth. His work was balanced, flexible and honest without ever being dull.

What this correspondent loved best in Barney after knowing him nearly ten years was his slow, dry wit which was completely untainted with Manhattan smartness but had, rather, a warm, fatherly quality. . . . He was one of the few members of the profession with whom one could be silent and yet know the silence was unwasted. Barney lies today in New Guinea's thick soil. This last silence will be endless.

That brief description captured Barney better than anything else I had read. It struck me as another visitation, another note in a bottle washed ashore from that "undiscover'd country." These unlooked-for nuggets of information began falling into my lap once I had decided to find out more about my father's time in the Pacific and the bombing of the *King John* and the *Timoshenko*.

One nugget came from Robert Sherrod, the *Time* correspondent. He had roomed with Barney in Melbourne for a period. After his seventy-fifth birthday he wrote a letter and enclosed a photo of Barney, himself, and other correspondents posing in a slit trench. He had combed through his diary to tell my brother and me about those days, when the correspondents were desperate for stories and sharing a general sense of gloom that history was being made elsewhere and "there wasn't going to be much war in the Southwest Pacific for a while."

The correspondence continued, and over time Sherrod provided more intimate details. There was, for example, no small amount of sex. "We early arrivals in Australia after Pearl Harbor were astonished by the females. They were an uncommonly handsome lot, probably because they spent so much time outdoors in healthful pursuits. And they had no compunction about jumping in bed, or waiting in the lobby of the Australia Hotel in Sydney ('the passion pit') for an invitation to jump. I remember an Army lieutenant's reaction: 'We went upstairs, and I turned to close the door. By the time I looked around—jee-pers—she had her damn clothes off.' " Sherrod added, "But I never knew Barney Darnton to participate in the plucking of this luscious fruit."

Another source was Lewis B. Sebring, Jr., of the *New York Herald Tribune*. After the war, he wrote three drafts of a book never published, "MacArthur's Circus," a splenetic account of the general at a time when "MacArthur for President" clubs were springing up. I found it on microfilm in the archives of the Wisconsin Historical Society on the Madison campus of the university, my alma mater. After filling out forms I was given a pair of white gloves in case the material included photographs. An assistant emerged from the stacks pushing a cart piled with boxes. Luckily, Sebring turned out to be something of a pack rat, having saved everything from postcards to pictures of my father's burial.

He described the wrestling matches with the censors at great length, especially Barney's angry attempts to deal with them. MacArthur himself he seemed to regard as a scheming, ego-driven popinjay. "He was heartily disliked, ridiculed and even hated under the wartime shroud of censorship," he wrote.

MacArthur's announcement of my father's death had called it "accidental," a vague description conjuring up a range of possibilities, most having little to do with combat.

Mom knew early on that Barney had been killed by friendly fire—that insidious oxymoron—and she learned some of the details about what had happened from correspondents who either wrote her or visited our house in Westport. Barney was the first of their cohort to die in the Pacific (and one of the first of a total of sixty-eight or so killed anywhere throughout the war). Uncovering the truth about the circumstances was compelling for them. But gradually her desire for more information gave way to a kind of fatalism and a belief that one must make concessions to the military's need for secrecy. What good would finger-pointing do? She noted in one of her long-ago letters that she didn't even want to learn the name of the pilot, only that she desired him to "be comforted and to realize that mistakes are as much a hazard of war as direct enemy action."

I wanted to carry the research further. I knew that there had been

a fateful error in communications—that the pilot hadn't been noti-
fied to expect friendly vessels in what had come to be seen as enemy
waters—but I wanted to know more about the engagement itself.
Had the plane's crew tried to identify the ships? Had the soldiers
known the plane was American? Which had fired first, the ship or
the plane? I wasn't intent on establishing blame—at least I think
I wasn't—as much as simply trying to find out whatever could be
found out. It seemed a sacred obligation to go back and fill out the
record. So I accumulated reams of material: stacks of letters, diaries, and journals, interviews with soldiers from the 32nd Division,
and enough books on the war in the Pacific and the bloody Battle
of Buna, piled on the windowsill of my New York study, to block
out the sunlight.

The bombing occurred in the run-up to Buna, when the army was
transporting men and equipment from the south of the island to the
north. The buildup, involving the first major airlifting of troops,
was to be kept secret, since MacArthur was determined to keep
the impending American attack under wraps. Col. Lloyd A. Lehr-
bas, a former AP man who had become an aide to MacArthur, set
down that explanation in a letter to my mother, written five months
after the bombing. Recounting just the bare bones, he added, "I
realize there are questions you might wish to ask and we can now
add some details. At the time the Japs didn't know our troops had
crossed to New Guinea and we, regretfully, could not permit the
factual account to be made public." He didn't mention that the
Japanese had pretty good intelligence anyway. They had the loyalty of some of the indigenous northern tribes, who presumably
would have passed on information about American landings, and
they also used spotter aircraft to monitor Allied troop movements.

An alternate explanation for the secrecy is that the episode was
embarrassing to the army and to the publicity-conscious MacArthur,
especially coming at the start of his long-awaited island-hopping
campaign. The general had a notorious proclivity for suppressing
news that might reflect badly on him or his organization, and his
staff justified this on the grounds that not to do so might be harmful
to the war effort.

Just how important MacArthur's reputation was to him emerged
in the course of my own research. Documents turned up that

showed that MacArthur had been worried about certain papers that were found among my father's personal effects and that he'd ordered them destroyed.

This odd fact surfaced twice in the last few decades. Once was in December 1975, when Robert Sherrod wrote to Seymour Topping, then the *Times'* assistant managing editor, bringing the episode to the paper's attention. Perhaps he thought it worth a news story. In any event, the *Times* didn't write one, and Topping sent the letter to me. Then a few years ago, Philip Weiss, a writer researching a novel, found the documents at the MacArthur Memorial Archives and Library in Norfolk, Virginia, and mentioned them in an article in the *New York Observer*.

The documents are an exchange of letters. One was to General MacArthur in Melbourne from George W. Cocheu, a colonel who had been his roommate at West Point. Cocheu, in charge of the Army Effects Bureau in Kansas City, Missouri, said he was "puzzled" as to what to do with two documents found in Barney Darnton's possessions after his death. He warned, "I appreciate that these papers, if they fell into the hands of somebody not too friendly to you, might be used to your very great personal disadvantage. If you will let me have your views and what you want done with them, I will be governed accordingly." MacArthur replied quickly, saying, "I . . . suggest that the documents because of their nature be destroyed."

The exchange stirred my blood. Had I come across some long-buried scandal that had caused the pilfering of papers from my father's personal effects? Alas, that proved not to be the case. The papers in question turned out to be two cablegrams from the *Times* directing Barney to approach the MacArthurs and offer them a substantial amount of money for their memoirs once the war was over. My father told the *Times* to submit the proposals through channels, directly to MacArthur's aide, Colonel Diller. There's no record if the *Times* did so, and in any case, the general didn't accept such an offer. In his letter he struck a dignified posture, saying that he had referred all such offers—including a "dazzling" one of $500,000—to Colonel Diller with instructions to decline them. As was often the case, MacArthur's truth was no one else's. Mr. Sherrod contacted Diller in 1975, and Diller said that MacArthur had never instructed him to reject the offers.

The documents turned out not to be earthshaking, but they do provide a glimpse into the personality of the Pacific commander and his sensitivity about press coverage. The mere fact that such an offer from a newspaper could prove embarrassing shows how much the spirit of public service has changed in today's military, in which generals serve a year or two in Iraq and then trot out their memoirs.

That story was not the only one about my father that the *Times* decided not to run. In 2006 I found an unpublished story from long ago stashed away in the *Times* archives. The story was written by Anthony Leviero, a *Times* reporter who had served as an intelligence officer in the war. The piece was datelined "Washington, March 9" and was filed, according to a handwritten scribble at the top, in 1947. The lead paragraph said:

Washington, March 9—Byron Darnton, war correspondent of The New York Times, *was killed in a pitched battle between American ground and Air Forces late in 1942 in perhaps the first of a number of tragic incidents during the war in which American aircraft mistakenly attacked our own troops.*

The story was based largely on an interview with Sheridan Fahnestock, the brother of Bruce, the lieutenant killed alongside Barney. Sheridan had investigated the attack in a visit to Pongani two days after it happened. The story blamed "a group of B25's from General George V. Kenney's Fifth Air Force," saying that the ground forces had indeed informed the air forces of the troop movement—an assertion that the air forces denied—and also that the soldiers on the ship fired only *after* the first bomb had been dropped. Far from being an incidental minor accident, the bombing was part of a full-fledged battle between friendly forces that "got intense for a few minutes as the planes repeated their attack." Leviero's account was wrong in some respects—its assertion that more than one plane had been involved, for example—but it advanced the story of my father's death. Without it, as far as any reader of the newspaper of record would know, he had simply perished in an accident. I asked myself why Leviero's story never ran. The explanation came in a note from the managing editor, James: "The story was not used on the ground it would not do any good," he wrote. Even with the war long over, instances of friendly fire remained controversial. As I was to see occasionally in my own career, when it comes to suppressing information, self-censorship by editors and reporters can top official censorship.

Interestingly, historical reconstructions seem to turn up an interconnectedness among people and events that was not apparent at the time. When Gen. Robert L. Eichelberger, who had taken command when American forces bogged down at Buna, sought a collaborator to write his war memoirs, *Our Jungle Road to Tokyo,* he turned to Milton MacKaye, Barney's best friend. MacKaye ensured that Barney received his due. In one section Eichelberger recalled a session with reporters who briefed him when he first arrived in Australia.

> *Byron Darnton, a great reporter from* The New York Times, *was the unofficial but acknowledged dean of the American correspondents, and "Barney" arranged that unusual conference. I went to dinner at the press house which the correspondents shared. After a little preliminary wassail and an excellent meal, coffee was brought in, and tunics were loosed at the neck. Barney acted as an informal chairman, wise, balanced, humorous, as I began the cross-examination of my hosts. . . . No military textbook with which I am familiar suggests the questioning of correspondents as a method by which a commander may inform himself. But around the dinner table that night—with everything off the record and no holds barred—I received from a group of intelligent newspapermen a first-rate orientation course. When they finished I had a pretty clear idea about the currents of the waters in which it was my unchosen destiny to swim.*
>
> *Already, so early in the war, my friend Barney Darnton was gone. Many gallant newspapermen died subsequently in posts of danger, and many people forget—because the newspapermen were not soldiers—that all of them came to posts of danger voluntarily.*

At the same time, a top aide to Harding, the general whom Eichelberger replaced, was E. J. Kahn, Jr., a young writer for *The New Yorker*. He wrote an article for *The Saturday Evening Post* about war correspondents, called "The Men Behind the By-Lines." He began it:

> *Ask almost any war correspondent stationed in the Southwest Pacific whom he regards as tops in his field, and he will tell you that the man was Byron Darnton of* The New York Times. *Barney Darnton isn't top man any more because he was killed last fall when a bomb fragment struck him in the head. . . . If so irreverent a corps of foreign representatives as the foreign correspondents in Australia and New Guinea could be said to have had a dean, Darnton was it. He could not only beat most of his colleagues at English billiards but he was unanimously accepted by them as the unofficial leader of their lively gang. People who knew him were inclined to the belief that he might have been the inspiration for the old story of the butler who, announcing seven journalistic callers to his mistress, said, "Madame, there are six reporters here and a gentleman from the* Times.*"*

In an attempt to find accounts of the bombing, I cast a wide net. I managed to get notices in a newsletter put out by an organization called the American WWII Orphans Network and in the *Red Arrow News* of the 32nd Division. I also wrote an article for the *Smithsonian* magazine that mentioned my research. That brought a message from a retired seventy-five-year-old surgeon, David C. Marshall. He said that his father and my father were on the same troopship to the Pacific. He mentioned that he had some diaries and photos to share with me, so I drove down to visit him and his wife, Helen, in their redbrick Federal house on a winding suburban street in Pennington, New Jersey. They gave me a friendly welcome. A quiet-spoken, refined man, he explained that he was on "a quest" to document and write about the wartime exploits of his father, also a surgeon, Lt. Col. John Hugh Marshall. Colonel Marshall had set up the giant 153rd Station Hospital in Queensland and then moved up to Port Moresby to open a field hospital. The small frontline hospitals were the forerunners of the MASH units in the Korean War.

Dr. Marshall had converted his second-floor study into a World War II research library. He told me that his father was killed in a train wreck. In November 1951, the surgeon was returning from a meeting of the American College of Surgeons in San Francisco when his train stalled in a blizzard in the Rockies and was struck from behind by another train. "I began to realize he'd been through an awful lot of things in the war I wanted to know about." Years later, visiting his mother in Ohio, he learned there was a footlocker in the attic. "I went up there one afternoon in winter. It was cold. When I opened the trunk, I couldn't believe it. Old photographs, diaries, movies. I sat up there cross-legged, freezing, looking at all this stuff. I read it all over the next few days. Everything I had wondered about was there." But it was not enough. So he made a pilgrimage to Australia and New Guinea, looking for the hospitals, which had disappeared. He walked through the Bomana War Cemetery, twelve miles north of Port Moresby, the one where my father had been temporarily buried, and he described his feelings on seeing the rows upon rows of white crosses and other markers. "It looked to me like most of the interred were Australian, mostly airmen," he said haltingly. "The two native guides I had with me were very good. . . . They'd stop and point. . . ." His throat tightened and he could not go on. Helen walked over and put an arm around his shoulders. We talked some more and had lunch and then I left, carrying with me a copy of his father's wartime diary.

The first entry was the day before Pearl Harbor. I read Dr. Marshall's small, neat handwriting and followed him through the early stages of the war. My heart raced as I came to October. He recounted bombing raids in Moresby, chitchat, details of daily life. Then, on Monday, October 19, he stopped off at the small hillside hospital called Koki. "I had the first *shock* of the war. My good friend Mr. Darnton of *The New York Times,* a former classmate in Ann Arbor lit school and correspondent who came over on the transport with me, was here dead, killed by the Japs at Buna." Fahnestock's corpse was there, too. "I viewed the bodies. Within an hour we received 8 more wounded by plane."

Early on, one of my first questions was what kind of protective gear had my father worn. I had come across an old article in *Newsweek,* written after his death, that said, "Darnton was the type of reporter who always turned up where things were hottest," and described a telling incident.

His friends like to tell about the time a newly arrived photographer wanted to photograph a Port Moresby airdrome the Japs had been bombing with clocklike regularity. All the reporters had shunned the spot for weeks, but Darnton took the greenhorn in tow. They arrived simultaneously with a squadron of Jap bombers, whose bombs hit as if aimed for the pair. The camera in the photographer's hands was smashed, his tin hat torn by flaying metal. Darnton, without a tin hat because he disliked them, was unscratched.

Dr. Marshall's diary answered my question. He wrote, "I have Barney Darnton's helmet with the bullet hole through the filler. I am afraid he did not have on his steel helmet." The surgeon's supposition was wrong in one respect—the hole he saw was not caused by a bullet, but by a piece of shrapnel. Yet his account was the first confirmation of something I had suspected—that when my father stood at the wheelhouse door, guiding the pilot to avoid the plumes where the bombs were falling, his head was unprotected. He was wearing only the sun-resistant cellulose lining.

In addition to the diary, I brought home from that visit copies of films the doctor had taken while stationed in Australia and New Guinea. And there, after shaky views of pitched tents, scrub brush, and dirt roads, was the only film footage of my father I'd ever seen. A group of correspondents are standing around a jeep. Suddenly, Barney appears in a close-up, leaning against the jeep, smiling under his mustache, his eyes twinkling. His head is bare, his widow's peak clearly visible. He has apparently just made a joke of some kind. The camera focuses on him for less than two seconds, but it took my breath away. I recognized him instantly. The next holiday, my brother and his family and my family gathered around the TV and I put the tape in. There was a collective gasp. A niece muttered, "My God!" I looked over at my brother. His eyes misted over and, for what seemed like quite a while, he couldn't speak.

CHAPTER 22

After the deaths of their husbands, my mother became friends with Bruce Fahnestock's widow. Mom sent her a telegram saying, "Because they were together I feel we are close now. I know you must feel as deeply as I do that it is important to take up the future with the same spirit and purpose that was theirs."

I don't know if my mother ever learned what I was to find out years later—that the two adventurous brothers were more than naturalists and ethnographers. They were American spies. They were using their maritime expedition to collect important information for the U.S. military, at the behest of President Roosevelt. Because of their knowledge of the Pacific, they were well equipped for an undercover role. The sons of an inventor and boat designer, they grew up sailing on Long Island Sound. Sheridan, age twenty-one, yearned to undertake an expedition to the South Seas and enlisted his older brother Bruce. They salvaged and renovated a sixty-five-foot schooner, *Director*, assembled a crew of four other young men, and set sail in 1935. Their mother joined them in Panama. The expedition lasted three years. They collected flora and fauna and three chestloads of artifacts for the American Museum of

Natural History, wrote books, and gave lectures about their adventures with kava-drinking island chiefs, grass-skirted native women, twenty-foot-long sharks, and feasts of roasted pig.

The voyage was so successful the family wanted an encore. In 1940 they set their sights on the Dutch East Indies, specifically to help preserve rapidly disappearing native music. A Manhattan socialite donated a three-masted schooner, *Director II,* which was loaded with elaborate devices for recording music and birds. But anthropological and ornithological pursuits were not the only mission. FDR had called the Fahnestock brothers to the White House for a chat. He listened to their starry-eyed ambitions and then asked if they would be willing to engage in a little espionage. He wanted them to report on a number of developments in the South Pacific, particularly on Japanese infiltration and defense preparedness in the Dutch colony. The brothers readily agreed and, at the suggestion of the Office of Naval Intelligence, decided to keep their cover as civilians. Privately, they called themselves "the President's men." As Sheridan wrote in a later letter to Roosevelt, "So, we went to the Indies as two young men whose only purpose was to collect primitive music and enjoy life."

The brothers were also supposed to reconnoiter harbors. "We had a Piper Cub in a crate on board and we were supposed to fly along the coasts and take photographs," recalled Philip Farley, aged eighty-nine, sipping a vodka tonic at a Lexington Avenue bar nearly seven decades later. He had been the ship's navigator. "From the air, you could spot the natural channels between the coral reefs. That way, we'd locate the entry to the harbors for refuge. We were on our way to Tahiti when Paris fell, and the Vichy government there made us take the plane off." Farley sailed with the Fahnestocks for eight months and left the *Director II* shortly before the yacht ran aground and sank in an unmarked channel on the Great Barrier Reef off the coast of Queensland, Australia.

In the spring of 1942, the Fahnestocks returned to the Pacific as part of an operation called "Mission X," a group of specialists in logistics and communications. In Australia, their job was to scour the ports and requisition small craft for troops and supplies. The fleet eventually became known as the U.S. Army Small Ships Section. Again, Philip Farley was part of the group. "One of the first ships I found was the *King John*—she was a big old trawler with a problem in reverse gear," he said. "I remember panicking because I had to shut off engines in midstream—I was just floating, at the mercy of the current—until I could shift it and go backward." Farley got to know the Fahnestock brothers well, rubbing elbows in tight shipboard quarters. He seemed more impressed with Sheridan than with Bruce. "Sher was bright, hardworking, steady. He was the reliable one. Bruce, the older, was excitable. He was a wild character." My ears picked up. I had an image of Bruce leaping up and manning the machine gun, and I wondered if he had been the one to fire first.

I asked: "*Wild* how?"

Farley didn't skip a beat. "He's the type of guy who'd jump up and fire a machine gun."

"Is that what you think happened?"

"Sure. We all thought it."

I remembered an account of the bombing in a letter my mother had written to one of Barney's brothers. I went home and dug it out. She described the plane flying over Pongani and then returning "for another look." To the pilot and crew the ships must have looked Japanese, she wrote. "Now evidently Bruce Fahnestock opened fire—the correspondents were bitter about this and I never told his mother. They thought it was stupid and fed the pilot's distrust. At any rate, he began to drop bombs. Barney, standing by the captain, called the way they were dropping and the captain zigzagged out of their way."

I found a letter to Mom from Bruce's mother, Mary Fahnestock, in the same file. She was grateful that Mom had supplied her with information about the attack because it "cleared up" so many things. "I feared Bruce had been struck in the face and had suffered. Also, the plane at 3,000 feet clears another point. I thought all along (from your silence on that point) that Bruce had manned the gun (also he was a marvelous shot) and now I know that no one could know the identity of the other at that distance and neither could take the chance to wait. He died as he lived, finished every job he started in a big way! . . . I would like [his child] to know that his daddy died behind a gun."

Mom had similar concerns. One was whether Barney had suffered before dying. Another was whether he had been disfigured. Almost all accounts of the attack went out of their way to reassure her on both points. General Harding, the officer who had given him permission to go, wrote to her ten days afterward: "I think you may take some comfort from the knowledge that there was no suffering and disfiguring mutilation. He died instantly, after being wounded in the back of the head."

I found reason to question his assertion. Through the U.S. Army Center of Military History at Fort McNair, I obtained an after-action report of the attack, filed by the fleet commander, Lt. Col. Laurence McKenny. It presented an account seen from the vantage point of the ships. He described the unidentified bomber flying overhead and "not requesting identification of motor launches flying flags of the United States." The first bomb was dropped and the ships' machine gunners opened fire—whether before, simultaneously, or after is unclear—and the plane left and then returned to drop more. Among the list of those killed and injured, Byron Darnton was first. The notation said he "died in rowboat of head wounds." So his death had not been instantaneous. When I first read this sentence, it felt like a blow to my gut. My reconstruction of his last moments was turned upside down. I wondered, Was he at all conscious? Did he understand what was happening? Did he have time to think of anything—of us?

I became obsessed with compiling a minute-by-minute account. I obtained a list of survivors from the 128th Infantry, mostly those who had attended 32nd Division reunions, and I tracked them down. I managed to find half a dozen soldiers still alive who had been on one of the two ships. Not surprisingly, their recollections had eroded over the decades. Their stories often didn't tally as to the time of the attack or even the day—another lesson in how easily history slips away. But the bombing itself was seared into their memories—partly because it was their first time under fire and partly because many realized they were being targeted by an American plane. "You don't forget something like that," said Joseph Meicher of Madison, Wisconsin, who was eighteen when he joined the service in 1940. Seated in his wood-lined study, amid war memorabilia, he continued: "We knew it was our plane. We could see the star on it. We zigzagged, tried to get away. The bombs kept coming down. We had a bunch of barrels on board and every time a bomb went off, I ducked between the barrels. Later I found out they were filled with gasoline." He laughed dismissively. "Imagine if one of those had gone off."

"It was about eight o'clock in the morning," recalled Earl R. Beecher, then ninety-one and, like Meicher, now deceased. "We were going to make a beachhead. We watched some planes go over—there were two or three of them—and then this sucker comes along and . . . I don't know what got into him. He opened the bomb doors and the lieutenant on board got onto the machine gun—a fifty-caliber—and started firing. Then the plane dropped bombs. They were daisy cutters. They went off just above the water and cut down everything around them. The other boat got a chance to get out in open water. The lieutenant, who knew a lot about boats, wanted us to get out in open water so we could maneuver away from the bombs, but the major on board, who outranked him, thought we should try to make it to shore. He was wrong. That's the army for you."

Beecher was wounded in the head—he lost part of his nose and was blinded in one eye—and was hospitalized for five months. He had had debilitating headaches into old age. "The shrapnel showered the boat. It went everywhere. We could see that the plane was American. I don't know why they couldn't see our American flag. It was flying high. They were eager to get a Jap boat. From what we heard, if they hit a Jap boat, they'd get some rest and a case of scotch. If I could have caught that pilot, I would have killed him." That was his feeling back then. And now? He paused, then grunted. "It's water over the dam, so you just have to forget it."

Ernest Gerber, eighty-five years old, and a retired career officer living in Sun Prairie, Wisconsin, was on the *Timoshenko* and recalls the attack vividly. "We got to Pongani and anchored offshore in preparation to go in. We heard this plane. It went overhead; then it returned. Of course, everyone looked to see what it was. And we spotted a bomber. It was quite high. As it came closer, we could see the bomb-bay doors open. And a bomb dropped out—actually, two of them. We had officers with field glasses and they recognized the plane as American. They saw that star. When it started dropping bombs on us, our people manned fifty-caliber machine guns and opened fire. They dropped two more bombs. They never directly hit either boat that was there. But the shrapnel was what caused the damage. It injured a couple of people on our ship. We were told that people on the other ship were killed. After the plane took off, the natives came out in their outriggers and we paddled to shore, and we made the first beach landing of World War II.

"We were disgusted with the air force. I did hear from somebody in our regiment—he ended up in a hospital, either in Port Moresby or Australia, and happened to be in the same ward as a crew member of that plane that bombed us. The story that the crew member told our infantrymen was that they were told when they started out on their mission there were no American ships in the area and anything they saw they should bomb."

I began a search for a "mission report" from the U.S. Army Air Forces. I figured I had accounts of the attack as seen from the ships and now I wanted an account from the air. A report from the aircraft commander might settle the question of who had fired first and clear up other discrepancies. Mostly, I wanted to learn the pilot's identity. It seemed a significant piece of the puzzle. I remembered a vague story that the pilot had gone to see my mother to beg forgiveness—a story that clearly never happened, given that she said in her letter that she had never learned his name. But in the same letter she said that a Darnton family friend from Adrian, an infantry major named George C. Bond, who had lost a leg in battle, reported that during his hospital stay a man in the neighboring bed turned out to be the pilot and had suffered a collapse. Perhaps I had somehow conflated the two stories. Or in my childhood fantasies I persuaded myself that any man who had committed such a heinous act deserved to suffer a nervous breakdown, like the stricken aviator in the movie *Twelve O'Clock High*. Once again, history had erased its solid lines and left behind only tantalizing traces.

Finding the pilot's name was no easy task. I enlisted the aid of a young researcher named Edward Rogers, who was compiling a history of the Fifth Air Force's 3rd Bomb Group and contacted me after reading my notice in the Orphans Network newsletter. After several months, he had narrowed the search to the group's 13th Squadron, but the squadron's records for March through December 1942 had been lost in a plane crash the following January. Incidents of friendly fire were rarely if ever recorded—unless the plane was on the receiving end.

Finally, out of the blue, Rogers sent me a message: "Found It!" He had located the pilot's name by checking the personal diary of another pilot, Harry Mangan. An entry for October 19 read: " . . . New Guinea goes well tho Dave Conley bombed our own landing party below Buna the other day—the simple dogs at Moresby didn't warn him and on his reco he bombed a boat not knowing it was ours. I understand that there were casualties." At last! The pilot was David M. Conley. The plane itself was named *Baby Blitz,* and I was able, with Edward's help, to obtain a photo of it resting on a landing strip, the flight and ground crew posing in front of it.

I was also able to track down Conley's last known address, a residence in Leisure World, a retirement community in Mesa, Arizona, and got a phone number. Before I even had a chance to think of what to say, I dialed, holding my breath while I waited for the connection. But the number was no longer in service. Later, to my dismay—but also, strangely, to my relief—I learned that Conley had died in May 2001.

I found out that he had a son named Wilder Conley. I called the management of Leisure World, in hopes of securing a forwarding address, but there was none. Internet search programs failed to turn up a contact. So I hired a private detective. The detective came up with a cell-phone number for Wilder in Jacksonville Beach, Florida. I practiced my pitch—the delicate question of whether his father had ever expressed remorse for killing my father would require some tact. I reached him at work—he was a phone solicitor—and we made a date to talk the following day. We chatted for well over an hour. Wilder Conley was accommodating. He filled me in on his father's thirty-year career with the air force and said he would send on numerous photos and clippings.

On the critical issue—the incident of friendly fire—he said his father had never mentioned it. In fact, he hadn't talked much about his war experiences at all, at least not at home. He might have with other pilots.

In a week's time, a carton arrived containing a scrapbook, photos of shirtless crew members posing before B-25s, and yellowed news clippings from Topeka, Kansas, Conley's hometown. He was the son of a veteran of the Spanish-American War. One clipping dated back to the day he became a cadet; it showed him with ten other young men, standing in the front row and looking serious, his right hand raised to take the oath. I examined all the photos. Conley was a handsome devil, curly-haired, with strong cheekbones and classic midwestern looks. There were articles about his numerous awards (the Air Medal for twenty-five operational missions, the Distinguished Flying Cross, the Silver Star, the Purple Heart, and oak-leaf clusters). There was his certificate of training from flight school, pay stubs, lists of equipment, V-mail letters home, and even flight records, including one for October 18, listing it as a reconnaissance mission.

Some items gave a sense of the man. An article in a U.S. Air Force museum magazine written six years ago by a fellow pilot, Hal Maull, described what Conley was like as a copilot. It said he "made one insufferable pun after another." When the two spotted land returning from a mission, Maull would put the plane on autopilot and they'd play cribbage: "It may seem insane but it was one of the things that removed us from the insanity of war." One time they were forced to make a crash landing on a reef and were stranded in the jungle for a month; short of food, they came upon a wild steer and drove it onto a beach, where Conley was supposed to shoot it. He couldn't bring himself to do it—"it was a case of *buck fever*"—and Maull had to grab the rifle to dispatch the beast.

Conley was wounded in the Japanese attack on the Philippines on the first day of the war. He was rescued from a hidden American base during Gen. Ralph Royce's daring long-distance raid in April—the very mission that my father wrote about when he and Carleton Kent hitched a ride to Charters Towers and interviewed the pilots, getting a scoop that was then delayed by MacArthur's censors. I wondered if Barney had seen Conley there or even talked to him.

All in all, the items in the box presented a glamorous record of an aviator's exploits. After the war, his life appeared much less exciting and even anticlimactic and a little sad. He was employed at an air force desk job, then for NORAD as an operations officer, and finally as an installation repairs manager for Sears Roebuck. In old age he had a series of transient strokes and was taken to his son's house in Jacksonville Beach to die.

In all the clippings, documents, and snatches of conversations with his son, there was not one hint that anything untoward had happened on October 18, 1942. It seemed unlikely that Conley had suffered a nervous breakdown, and if the deaths he'd caused that morning upset him, he kept it bottled up. As I looked over the small box of official documents and personal remnants of his life, it was almost as if the attack over Pongani had never happened.

But at least one of his few surviving buddies recalled it. "The friendly fire incident—I remember it well," said Vernon J. Main, a crew chief in the 13th Squadron, who also served as flight engineer on combat missions and had earlier evacuated Conley from the Philippines during Royce's raid. Main flew off in a different direction from Conley that morning. "There were two missions that day and we split the force and went to different places. I think we went to Finschhafen and they went to Buna. That's where it happened. We were staging out of Moresby and we found out when we came back. We felt terrible." He pointed out there had been no procedure for identifying a friendly vessel. "We had no protocol for that." Couldn't Conley, spotting two unidentified vessels, have radioed his base to see if they were ours? I asked. "You wouldn't have been able to transmit from Buna to Moresby because the mountains were in the way."

The same point—the difficulty in knowing who was who—was made in the article written by Hal Maull. "At this early stage of the war there were no such things as aircraft and warship identification courses," he wrote. "I doubt that we could have told the difference between a US or Japanese vessel unless we could have seen the flag on the stern." The *King John*, however, *had* been flying a U.S. flag, and so had the *Timoshenko*. And there was a recognition procedure for a friendly plane coming in to Moresby—circling the shipwreck in the harbor counterclockwise at five hundred feet. Apparently, things were different above contested waters, where pilots were loath to take unnecessary risks. "There was no protocol or anything to check on the identity of a ship," noted Harry Mangan, the pilot in the 13th Squadron who had kept the diary. In a phone interview he said, "It'd be too dangerous. You wouldn't risk flying

low or dipping a wing or anything like that. We didn't go sticking our noses in someplace that was hot. We got in and got out as
quickly as we could." Though he had referred to the incident in his
diary, Mangan said he no longer remembered it.

Recently, Vernon Main was a docent at the National World
War II Museum in New Orleans. He made a point of telling visitors
how primitive flying was in those days. "We had some pretty crude
instruments. We were using *National Geographic* maps of New
Guinea and the Pacific Ocean dated 1930. They didn't have any
charts for that part of the world." He said pilots often didn't know
who was below them, on ground or on sea. "The thing I remember
coming out of the war," he added, "was don't ever, ever fly over a
vessel in the water, because they're going to shoot your ass down if
they're friendly or not. You always have to fly parallel to a ship."

In the end, I was not able to locate the U.S. Army Air Forces report.
A search of records at the Air Force Historical Research Agency
at Maxwell Air Force Base turned up nothing. Nor did a trip to
the chaotic National Archives in College Park, Maryland. After a
frustrating day acquiring entry credentials, fighting through crowds
of researchers, applying for records that were distributed only at
certain times—a bewildering process called "pulls"—I came away
empty-handed. The volume covering the 3rd Bomb Group for that
specific period was missing, the only blank space in a long stately
row of thick bound books. So I never did succeed in finding an
account of the bombing from the air. But I was able to find something even more valuable—a description from an eyewitness on
land.

I was led to it by a retired Australian soldier living in Mooloolaba,
Queensland, named Alan Hooper. As a young man, Hooper went
to Papua with the Queensland militia shortly before the war. He
transferred to the Papuan Infantry Battalion, which was made up
of natives called "Fuzzy Wuzzies" because of their distinctive hair.
When the Japanese invaded, he stayed on north of the Owen Stanley Mountains, leading patrols. He also wrote many letters home to
his wife, and these, together with his diary and his reminiscences,
made for an arresting book, *Love, War and Letters*. After reading

it, I contacted Hooper. In the course of our correspondence he sent along a manuscript written by another Australian, Tom Grahamslaw, a leader of a military outfit called the Australian New Guinea Administrative Unit (ANGAU). Grahamslaw was a legend. Operating in enemy-controlled territory, he gathered intelligence, provided native carriers (the "Fuzzy Wuzzy Angels") to transport wounded soldiers to safety, and was part of the network of heroic "spotters" who peered through binoculars and reported enemy movements by ham radio. The reminiscences of Grahamslaw, now dead, were partially published in a magazine, *Pacific Islands Monthly,* in 1971. The part that was not published included a thorough, presumably neutral description of what actually occurred.

On 18 October, shortly after I had returned from a patrol, some of my native police sighted two ships approaching from the direction of Tufi. They dropped anchor off Pongani, where they were in clear view of us.

The ships were crowded with troops wearing jungle green uniforms. When I left Port Moresby our troops were still wearing khaki, and as far as I knew, the Japs were the only ones garbed in jungle green. Furthermore, the headgear of the new arrivals looked much the same as that worn by Jap troops.

While we were somewhat uneasily speculating as to the identity of the new arrivals we sighted an American medium bomber, with its markings clearly visible, flying over the ships and obviously trying to identify them. The ships immediately opened fire on the aircraft, which responded by dropping several bombs, after which it made one strafing run and then departed.

All this made me believe the ships were Japanese, and I thereupon informed New Guinea Force by signal, after which I transferred the communication set to a more secluded place several miles inland. On resuming contact with H.Q. I learned that the ships were American.

Accompanied by Wilkinson and several police I made a beeline through the bush to Pongani, where we were accosted by an American patrol. These troops believed they were in enemy occupied territory and they regarded us with suspicion.

However, I was able to establish our bona fides when I met their commanding officer, Colonel McKinney. He had been informed that an ANGAU reconnaissance party was somewhere in the area.

I learned from McKinney that two members of his force had been killed and fifteen wounded by the bombs dropped by the aircraft. One of the dead men was a U.S. war correspondent named Brian Darnton (I'm depending on memory for his name), and the other was Lieut. Bruce Fahnestock, who was C.O. of American Small Ships at Milne Bay. I gathered it was Fahnestock who gave the order for the ships to fire.

So I ended up with a narrative that made sense and, to my mind at least, settled the matter. Conley had spotted the two ships and overflown them without noticing the American flags. He'd turned around and come back with the bomb-bay doors open. Seeing this, or maybe fearing it, Fahnestock had opened fire with the machine gun, which confirmed the pilot's conviction that they were enemy ships. In short, my father's death resulted from a tragic series of blunders both in the air and on water.

One frustrating aspect of my interviews with the aging vets from the *King John* was that none of them remembered my father—that is, until June 2006, when I received a letter from Plainview, Texas, written in a shaky hand. Its contents made me want to fly right down there to talk to the writer, Robert L. Owens. But I then received a message from his daughter that he was hospitalized with a lung infection, and so I put off my visit for a month, until he was better. I flew to Amarillo and drove down the Panhandle, across pool table–flat country. The land was treeless and windswept, with not much to see, just wooden telephone poles leaning toward the dusty ground and an occasional silo. The radio played three things: preachers, country music, and heavy metal. I was in the middle of nowhere.

I found Owens's house easily, a low-slung white ranch on a street of modest homes called Zephyr Road. An old Buick with a Purple Heart license plate was in the driveway. A wheelchair ramp led up to the front door, which was open. The handrail was decorated with carved figures of small animals. Owens himself was waiting for me right inside, sitting in an easy chair in the living room. He rose to greet me—a large man, over six feet, with a broad, open face, wire-rim glasses, and a head of healthy white hair. He had a slight stoop and a friendly manner but seemed unsure on his feet and sat down again quickly. I saw that he was dressed in a good plaid shirt and slacks, as if in anticipation of my visit. His daughter, Sherita Hatch, was there, too.

We talked for a while and then they showed me around. The living room was decorated with paintings of flowers. Lifelike replicas of birds hung from the pull chord of a fan and perched on a table lamp's shade. Dolls were positioned on the couch. Above the purple carpet, supported by plaster angels, was a long coffee table, and on it were two Bibles and a crucifix. War memorabilia occupied his small study. There were plenty of photos. In them the young Owens looked capable, handy with a gun, the kind of man you'd want on patrol with you. I looked at his wedding picture. He was as skinny as a string bean and gawky, tilting his head up at the camera, the way people do who are not used to being photographed. His wife had died many years before.

We sat back down to talk with the air-conditioning running and the TV on mute. He told of his early years in Comanche territory in Oklahoma. At the age of twenty-one, he was inducted into the army and went to Fort Ord in California, where he joined the 32nd. He went to Australia aboard the *Monterey*, the same ship that had carried my father three months before. On his way to Camp Cable outside Brisbane, the brass lectured them. "I remember them telling us, 'Now you're the foreigners. Don't start popping off your mouth about them driving on the wrong side of the road.' In Brisbane, they were glad to see us at first, but boy, going out with their girls and everything, they was ready to run us out before it was over with." He got word his outfit was going to New Guinea. "The evening we shipped out, we were in such a hurry and we had to dye our fatigues green. I burned some holes in mine and they were still wet when we put them on." They were airlifted in a Flying Fortress to Port Moresby and then later to the northern coast. There they boarded the trawlers for the journey up the coast.

"There were two ships. The one I was on—the *Saint John* or something like that, your dad was on it and I got to talk to him for a while. I don't remember the conversation now, probably just little things. We were going to make a beach landing—that was the purpose of it—and your dad being there with us as a reporter, I wondered what in the world he was doing on the ship. We had a pretty good little trip there on the water. I'm sure we probably talked about the excitement of going to a beach landing for the first time. Then that B-25 came over and started bombing us."

Owens stretched his long legs out before him, and when he got nervous, he rubbed the sides of his shoes together and they made a squeaking sound. He did that now. I asked him a question about something he had put in his letter, but he seemed not to hear me and repeated again that he wished he could remember what they had talked about. "It was so long ago, I really don't remember." He resumed the story and said his ship was carrying ammo and the other ship was carrying canned goods. I asked him again about what he had written, and again he seemed not to hear. Instead, he described how the ships tried to maneuver out of the way, one going closer to shore, the other out to deeper water. He looked away from me and continued. "After they dropped the bombs, the natives that came to meet us out at the ship—some of them were educated in Australia and they were trained . . . so they had those canoes with the . . . I never know what to call them; they had a little bamboo platform and a floating thing on the side, to carry supplies on. . . ." His voice trailed off and he paused for what seemed like a long time. Then he went on. "Well, that's when I helped your father off the ship onto, onto that. It would have taken him to the beach." He had finished the story, but he hadn't been able to bring himself to talk about the thing he had written to me.

We talked some more and I reminded him of what he had put in the letter and he said he was sorry he'd written it. "I thought afterward, Well, I shouldn't put that down." He didn't want to talk about it again. I told him that it was all right, that he shouldn't worry about my feelings, that I was only eleven months old when my father died and had no memory of him and so whatever he had to say wouldn't hurt me. He looked over quickly and then away again. "Well," he began slowly, "as I wrote you, I was the one who picked up your father's body. I wrapped him in a blanket—you know, we had these blankets with us; we called them 'G.I. blankets.' So I wrapped him in one and put him on one of those native canoes and he was taken to shore."

Owens stopped talking for a bit, then resumed and again went off on a tangent. "And there was a second lieutenant there—he had a small shrapnel wound and he raised so much Cain, our company commander, Captain Florey, said, 'When you get back on that ship, I don't want no part of you. If you raise so much Cain over such a small wound.' " He paused, looked over at me, then resumed his narrative. "So then we got off the ship. When we did, when we got your father down there on the beach, there was a native hut there. It started to rain. We thought, well, we'd have a little shelter. But there were sand fleas there; they'd just eat you up. You couldn't sit in it. Then later, a native came running up that had been a captive of the Japanese and he had escaped. Of course, we couldn't understand what he was saying, but the other natives there understood and they told us. He said the Japanese were just a short distance from us and we didn't have time to dig in or do anything ourselves, you know, so we signaled the ships that were still in the bay and they came closer and the natives in those canoes got us back out on the ship and we were out of there."

We talked about other things for a while, including what life was like in New Guinea. "The women run around in grass skirts. Their breasts—one would be normal; the other be hanging way down, 'cause they used it to feed the pigs. These little pigs be following after them. When we first got there, the Japanese had raped the women, so the women hid." He had vivid memories of the Battle of Buna. "One night out on patrol, three of us got trapped. We had to spend the night in the water, under barbed wire, so close to the Japanese that we could hear them talking. Finally we found a communication wire in the morning and followed it back to our company. When I come off the front lines, the seat of my pants was out, the knees was out, my underwear was long rotted off, my shoes were off. Nature itself was as bad as the enemy, the mosquitoes and the swamps. You could be sitting there on guard duty at night, you know, out in those swamps, and you hear something come into the water and it gets closer and closer and you click the safety off your M-1, ready, you know, and about that time it be a squeal, it'd be a swamp rat. And just stuff like that. The Japanese had a twenty-five-caliber with an exploding shell and they fire it at a distance and it hit a tree and it would explode like it was fired right at you. And there's a bird that would holler, 'Hey, hey,' and you think somebody was calling you until you found out that was a bird. You had to get used to it. And occasionally some of the boys would just absolutely lose it. We had one boy in our squad who lost it and he was behind me and he yells, 'There's one, there's one,' and he starts firing. And the leader yells, 'Owen, you all right?' and he knocked that kid's rifle down. There's very few in our company that wasn't killed or wounded or had malaria. I remember one, just slightly wounded, but he didn't make it. I guess his heart just gave out."

At one point, he told a joke to show how big the mosquitoes were: "They used to say you could pump gasoline into them, thinking they was an Airacobra." I realized with a start that this was the very same joke my father had recounted in a dispatch.

Owens was wounded at Buna. He was standing in a river, up to his neck in water, when a mortar round landed nearby. A log in front of him stopped most of the shrapnel, but one piece flew up his nose, and he spent several weeks in a field hospital. One memory that still bothers him is of an insect. "I remember one night a bug got in my ear, all night long. I couldn't get it out. I poured water in it. It went on fluttering. It was like to run me crazy. Funny, a thing like that, it sounds small—I think back on it and it gives me the shudders."

Each time I eased the talk back to the raid on the *King John* and each time he told me a little more about the attack, how the bombs sent plumes of water high into the air, and more about my father. He said he didn't remember my father's wound but that he knew it was in the back of his head or his neck and he was sure he died quickly. He said he and one other soldier laid my father's body on the platform of an outrigger. "Then we went to the beach and laid him on the shore back aways. And handling him . . . there was blood. The blood seeped through my trousers. . . . And . . . that's what I shouldn't have told you—that later, when it came time to eat, I looked down at the blood on my pants and I couldn't do it. I was too upset. It was my first time. His blood was all over me."

He rubbed his legs so that his shoes were squeaking and he stopped talking.

He looked relieved that he had said it. He said that of all the war memories—standing in water up to his neck, being alone in the swamps, being hit by shrapnel—that moment was the worst: sitting on the beach, his rations open before him, the sand fleas biting him, the blood on his pants. When I left, he shook my hand strongly and wished me well. I thanked him for everything.

CHAPTER 23

The nine-seater Cessna Caravan took off from the Port Moresby airport at dawn and by first light we were over the Owen Stanley Mountains. I stared down at the terrain, an uninterrupted blanket of knotty green, and recalled the forbidding descriptions I had read of what lay below. Nina and I were on our way to Pongani. I had come on a mission. It had become important, essential, to see the place where my father was killed. I wondered if any villagers who had witnessed the bombing might still be alive, though I realized this was a long shot, since sixty-five years had passed and life expectancy on the island back then was well under forty.

I pulled out a map of New Guinea. Various writers have tried to conjure up a beast whose shape best conforms to the island. William Manchester in his book on MacArthur, *American Caesar*, described it as a dragon. Karl Shapiro, the poet who served as a medical corps clerk there in 1942, thought it looked more like a sprawling bird. In his recollection of the war years, *The Younger Son*, Shapiro tells of rain so voluminous that "it was more like a shipment of solid water with no space between the drops," of clouds of mosquitoes that fell on the soldiers, bats that were more like flying foxes, and the stench of "God knows what vegetation [that] made it impossible to breathe." He remembered a remark by Aldous Huxley that if Wordsworth had visited the tropics, he would have deserted nature forever or at least "thought twice about the countryside kindliness of things." He summed up: "Nobody had ever called New Guinea the isles of the blest, and nobody ever would. It was the island of the damned, and they were in it."

Turning from the map to the landmass below, I thought the beast it most resembled was a hideous-looking giant iguana I had seen in the Galápagos. A hump of land poking northwest into Indonesia looked like the beak-shaped head. The hills rose like folds around the unsightly neck, while the mountains formed the spiny crests along the upper back. The eastern peninsula dangled toward Australia like a leg. Even the dark green colors and the open patches of dark brown seemed right. I remembered how repellent the actual giant lizard had appeared, sitting still for hours on black volcanic rock, absorbing the sun's heat into its cold-blooded veins.

Before flying into Port Moresby on a plane sparsely filled with glum businessmen, aid workers, and other Third World adventurers, Nina and I had spent three weeks in Australia and New Zealand. I was struck by the people's continuing involvement in World War II, as if the war had ended, say, twenty years earlier, instead of more than sixty years ago. On ANZAC Day, the equivalent of our Memorial Day, hundreds of thousands turn up at dawn for commemorative services.

In Papua New Guinea—or PNG, as everyone calls it—the war has left a different legacy. There's no national celebration—national *any-thing* seems out of the question, since the population of six million–plus is splintered into remote, virtually inaccessible villages. The people eek out subsistence livelihoods, living in thatched huts, growing yams and vegetables, and hunting wild pigs. They speak some 850 languages and owe allegiance to local clans, not some distant abstraction of government. The insular system of local allegiances and obligations is called *wantok,* after the pidgin expression "one talk," which refers to those who share a language. In short, their lives seem untouched by the twenty-first century.

But they *were* touched by the great conflagration of the last century. During the war Papuans were pressed into service by both sides, by these strange outsiders who were either small and yellow or large and white and were fighting each other to the death. The locals were used mostly to haul supplies and evacuate the wounded. The landscape is still littered with the ancient relics of war—old landing strips, bombed-out planes, and sunken submarines. Jeeps and tanks rust in the forests, having been left behind when the troops moved on, like a stage set deserted by the actors. So many soldiers died—including thousands of Japanese never accounted for—that even today, after heavy rains, villagers report an occasional skeleton rising up in the mangrove swamps like a mummy in a horror movie.

In Australia, Nina and I noticed that when we told people that we were going next to New Guinea, their faces would cloud over. More often than not, they gave a warning; they had known someone, a friend, a neighbor, a young backpacker, who had gone there and not returned. The stories were often the same: The person had been robbed and killed in town or had ventured into some distant village and been drawn into a dispute that turned deadly. Many of these arguments seemed to revolve around land; the Papuans held their ancestral territory sacred and many visitors didn't understand that to trespass upon it without permission, and without payment, was a serious affront. Port Moresby and some regional capitals, like Popondetta, in Oro Province, where we were bound, were among the most crime-ridden places anywhere. Gangs of young toughs from the provinces roamed the streets. They were called by the pidgin name "rascals," which, when we first heard it, endowed them with an innocence they didn't deserve.

In Moresby we were taken in hand by Erik Andersen, a young lawyer originally from New Zealand, and his gorgeous wife, Mary-Anne. I had met this couple through a complicated chain of e-mails and we had hosted them in New York. They met us at Jacksons International Airport. It was mercilessly hot—the heat slapped us in the face the moment we stepped off the plane. We hopped into their Land Rover for a tour of the capital. The roads were crowded, less with cars than people walking on the shoulders and dashing across the roundabouts. Women sold stacks of coconuts by the roadside, children swarmed everywhere, and fires in dusty market stalls sent up plumes of smoke. Young men lounged about, sitting on curbs and leaning against buildings. These were the legions of unemployed. They gave the place an ominous feel, as if the calm could be broken at any moment by an explosion.

The Andersens' hilltop villa, where we were given a room, did not ignore sensible precautions. There was a ten-foot-high fence with a gate at the bottom of a steep driveway, a fierce-looking guard from a clan notorious for using poisoned darts, two large dogs, and a "rape gate" to seal off the bedrooms at night. As the hot night fell with tropical speed, we sipped gin and tonics on their veranda, which overlooked the harbor far below, where dots of light gleamed from an industrial wharf. Sounds of frogs and insects came from all directions. Then it was back into the Land Rover, out the guarded gate, a quick trip through town to another ten-foot-high fence topped by concertina wire, through another gate, to a large clubhouse filled with hard-drinking expatriates. After dinner, the process was repeated in reverse.

In the morning we were up at 4:30 a.m. There was a muggy haze and we drove through empty streets to the airport. Our bags were weighed in and more people showed up to join our contingent. In addition to Erik, who wanted to come along to see how this trip would play out, there was a translator I had enlisted from a local newspaper, the *Post-Courier*. His name was Barnabas Orere, and he said to call him "Barney"—which I took as a good omen. Barney was dressed in a flaming red Adidas T-shirt. He was an engaging type with a quick smile. His mother came from a village near Pongani, so he was fluent in the local language. He seemed to have a quick explanation for everything that we encountered. Erik, meanwhile, who had long dreamed of starting an indigenous film company, had arranged for a camera crew to accompany us. He was hoping to produce a three-part series on PNG and the war. The crew consisted of a cameraman, Carl, a cheerful young Papuan who had studied at the university, and a soundman, Samu, a quiet chain-smoker with Rastafarian curls, who came from a nearby island, where his grandfather had been a headhunter. I wasn't crazy about the idea of a camera dogging my steps, but that seemed to be the price in order to split the cost of the chartered plane. Besides, the two looked to be good company. The pilot, Ian Smith, loaded the bags, carefully checking the balance, and we were off.

Looking down from the Cessna, I saw Port Moresby rapidly disappear. The snaking brown roads ended, then the last swatch of tin roofs. We passed over a muddy brown river, lowlands, and forested hills that rose rapidly to the mountains. Occasionally there were clusters of tiny huts nestled in the valleys, and then all signs of human habitation dropped away. Our companions pointed out the sights, at first hard to distinguish in the undulating green landscape. There were the Goldie River and a crocodile farm, and Owers Corner, the beginning of the Kokoda Trail. There were Mount Victory, where the Japanese were pushed back; the swampy Lake Myola, where the Allies dropped supplies; and Iora Creek, where the Australians and the Japanese took turns spilling blood on the ground for the right of ownership. Finally, wrapped in a veil of swirling mists, was the most mysterious landmark of all, dubbed "Ghost Mountain" by the American soldiers who encountered it. MacArthur had ordered them to cross the mountains on a native trail, the Kapa Kapa, even more treacherous than the Kokoda. It took them alongside the supernatural-looking 9,500-foot peak. The trees and vines were shrouded in glowing moss and phosphorescent fungus, so that everything shimmered in the constant darkness, and they could hear but not see subterranean rivers. Many American soldiers agreed with the natives that the place was haunted. After forty-two exhausting days, they arrived at their destination on the coast, meeting up with troops that had flown there in thirty-five minutes.

These tales were well known to Carl and Samu. It was hard to say whether they were reciting them for my benefit or simply because they enjoyed them. The stories clearly formed a pivotal chapter in their island's history, the dramatic appearance of the outsiders, whose "cargo," a term encompassing everything from wristwatches to jeeps, transformed New Guinea. Coming after the missionaries, the arrival of foreigners uprooted centuries of village life, triggered a migration to the cities, and, after independence from Australia in 1975, brought the era of international exploitation. Now precious timber and minerals were being carted away by the shipload to China and elsewhere.

In what seemed like no time, the plane passed over the mist-shrouded summit and began its descent on the other side of the mountains. We reached the savanna lowlands and then the coastal mangrove swamp. Our destination was a bare strip outside Popondetta. Flying over it, I saw half a dozen puzzling constructions, large horseshoe-shaped earthen mounds positioned around the strip like opened claws. Erik explained that they were revetments built over sixty years ago to shelter American fighter planes from aerial bombardment. The Cessna put down gently and we climbed out onto the strip. Thirty feet away, off to one side, was the blacked carcass of a B-25 Mitchell bomber. The scars of the long-gone war were everywhere.

Waiting for us was Dale McCarthy, a beefy Australian in a safari jacket, dark glasses, and a duck-billed cap. McCarthy was in charge of trucking palm oil along a desolate stretch of highway frequented by bandits and getting the barrels to sea. He was our host and guide. I had reached him through another e-mail contact, an Australian colonel who knew that part of the coast. It was immediately clear Dale was the right man for the job. He exuded a sense of command. As a seemingly self-appointed "police chief" of the area—a designation attested to by the block-letter print on a blue cap and a revolver in the glove compartment of his truck—he knew how to negotiate with the local clans. He also ran a small fishing lodge called Bendoroda, where we would stay as we ventured out to Pongani. Even in the best of times, Pongani was difficult to reach, a long trip down the coastal road and then a three-hour trek by foot. But because a bridge on that route was washed out, the only way to get there now was by boat along the shore.

Five minutes down the road, as Dale was extolling the fish that fall all over themselves for the privilege of being caught in the waters around his lodge, the sky opened up and discharged a rain the likes of which I had never seen. As the poet Karl Shapiro had prepared me, it was as if a gigantic bucket in the heavens had overturned. The windshield wipers on the truck were black streaks across an uninterrupted flood wash of water—we felt we were looking through the portal of a washing machine. Eventually, we reached Dale's boatyard on Oro Bay, pulled over, and jumped across exploding puddles to the shelter of a large metal hangar. Inside we had to yell above the noise—it sounded as if a dozen drummers were pounding on the roof with clubs and chains. Dale stood at the open door and stared at the solid wall of water. When I walked over to him, he frowned.

"Keeps up like this, we won't be able to get there today."

"So we could wait—go tomorrow," I ventured hopefully.

"Oh no," he replied. "It's been set up for today. I sent a runner in from Popondetta. You can't change it." He shrugged. "Around here, you don't just wander into a village without advance word."

He walked deeper into the hangar, leaving me to wonder about the improvident turns fortune could take in this part of the world. My throat tightened. I suddenly thought that the whole expedition might come to nothing. I realized how much I wanted to reach Pongani, how much I was counting on getting there. I wandered back inside, sat down on a crate, and brooded anxiously.

Luckily, the rain lasted only a few hours. When it let up, Dale used a crank to launch his twenty-one-foot center-console outboard, the *Kekeni,* down the rails and into the water, and we climbed aboard. Around us rainwater was evaporating in bursts of steam. Across the bay a wooded hill sloped to the water; in the center was a forty-foot-wide gash in the earth, the path for bringing down the magnificent logs of cedar, mahogany, and rosewood from the higher forests. Looking behind us, I could now see Mount Lamington rising out of the clouds. It looked calm enough at the moment, but in 1951 it had rained down fire and superheated gases, killing about three thousand people. A comparable eruption today would probably kill more, I figured.

We set out along the coast, moving south. Over the drumming of the motor, Dale talked about his dream of establishing ecotourism—a steady stream of adventurous types who wanted to fish and to slash their way through the jungle discovering the hidden war relics. "They're scattered everywhere. This was the training ground for the U.S. soldiers all through the campaign to retake the Philippines. I've come across jeeps and motorbikes and trailers. Back there in the bush, there are thirty-two amphibious DUKVs, a P-38 on blocks, and the Japanese sandman (the nickname for a particular P-38). In 1986, an American airman who had eight kills came all the way back to visit his downed aircraft."

The trip to Bendoroda took an hour. On the way, we passed

by Pongani and swerved toward shore so that the villagers would know we were still planning to come. I felt a throb of excitement. I could see some rusty metal roofs and thatched huts, but no people or signs of life. We sped on and about fifteen minutes later arrived at Bendoroda, a village on the mouth of the Bendoroda River. It was home to about two hundred people, who were accustomed to foreigners. Dale, in partnership with Augustin Begasi, a son of the chief, had set up his lodge here. Small groups of fishermen from around the world had come to snag black bass and black snapper in a catch-and-release program.

We were greeted with a "sing-sing" by the chief and half a dozen others, who chanted and banged drums as they led us through an archway of palm fronds stuck into the sand. Children scattered at our approach but then followed us around, not timidly. They were used to arrivals like ours. Like most of the adults, they wore cast-off Western clothes—shorts and T-shirts emblazoned mostly with the names of sports franchises and American universities. The welcoming ceremony was dramatic and seemed heartfelt enough, though I had to admit that, having seen the same ceremony on a video made by an Australian TV network, I had the nagging sense that this performance was something of a ritual done for tourists. It reminded me of those times in Kenya when we would hand over shillings to spear-carrying Masai warriors so that our girls could pose next to them—something, we were to discover later, that our children detested.

The lodge itself was basic, erected on stilts, with walls and ceilings made of woven sago leaves. There was an open-air veranda at the front for eating and drinking; connected to this was a covered walkway that led to six small rooms. There was a generator for electricity, a belowground compost heap for a toilet, a makeshift shower fed by a bucket of water, and mosquito netting free of holes. Our lunch, prawns and salad, was surprisingly good. Afterward, we got back in the boat and set out for Pongani.

As the boat hurtled away from shore, my excitement began to mount. The sun was out now and the wind whipped against my face. I felt my senses come alive and my mind focus. Carl trained the camera on me for a minute or so and then, seemingly out of respect for my privacy, swerved away to shoot the shoreline. Nina reached over and placed her hand on mine. It struck me that I was following the same route my father had taken in the *King John* that fateful morning. Our boat was using a depth sounder to avoid reefs, while his boat had used human spotters lowering lead lines from the bow, but the path was the same. The mountains in the distance, now clearly visible, with rings of mist around the lower slopes, were the same mountains he had seen. The empty expanse of the sky, the choppy water—both were the same. We rounded a promontory, entered a wide bay, and drew closer to shore. The tree line, the listing coconut palms, and the pale yellow beaches were the same. The odd thing was that it all looked ghostly familiar. I felt I had seen it somewhere before. In fact, I undoubtedly had—in my mind's eye. Perhaps I was extrapolating from old black-and-white photos I had seen, photos that showed GIs unloading supplies from boats, wading ashore through waist-deep water with crates on their shoulders or carrying wounded men on stretchers. I could have picked the spot out from a thousand similar spots in an instant.

We passed the mouth of a river, the Songada, and drew closer to Pongani. Now I could make out the thatched huts—there appeared to be about a dozen of them—and people. They were crowded close to the water's edge, small dark shapes seemingly looking at us. I felt my heart race. We were less than half a mile from shore, approaching fast. It occurred to me that perhaps we were not far from where *he* had been when the *King John* lifted anchor and moved toward the beach. In another five minutes, we drew closer and I was actually *there*, right where *he* had been when he was taking notes—his last notes. I looked up at the sky, still cloudless, as blue as it had been on that morning long ago. I sought out the southeast, where the plane had come from. Now I was certain I was at the very spot where the bombs had dropped, where the two ships had frantically tried to outmaneuver them, where Fahnestock had leapt up to man the .50-caliber machine gun . . . where my father had been killed.

Odd thoughts occurred, odd sensations. I remembered touching the rock in Jerusalem where Muhammad was said to have ascended, and entering the tomb where Christ's body had been placed, and walking beside the funeral pyres of the Ganges in India. I remembered viewing the battlefields of Gettysburg and Vicksburg, the graves of Normandy with their white crosses and Stars of David extending as far as the eye can see, and the gaping cavity where the World Trade Center towers once stood. Was it so unthinkable that these places released something into the ether, some form of energy, a cosmic hiccup at the moment of so significant a transfiguration? After all, my mother had insisted that she, on the other side of the world, knew of our father's death the instant it occurred. Hardly credible, I had often thought. But what if? What if his spirit *had* vaulted into another life through a tear in the sky? If that was so, then I was at that very portal. I felt an overwhelming awe. The light from the sky seemed too strong, the wind too sonorous, my skin too sensitive. I could feel the hairs on my arms bending in the hot breeze.

The translator interrupted my thoughts, telling me to look toward the figures onshore. They were leaping up and down. Pongani is not Bendoroda, he said. The clan here was unaccustomed to visitors. Perhaps some of them had never encountered white people. At that moment I noticed that the movement on shore was coordinated; the natives wearing ceremonial dress were swaying in a slow, undulating dance. From a distance all I could see were brilliant colors, brown bodies with splashes of red and white. I heard the sound of drums and chants. "I will tell you what to do at every step," the translator said. "And, oh—there might be a spear charge. If they charge at you, do not flinch. Don't worry—they won't hurt you." I hoped it would happen.

We came closer still and I could make out the village more clearly. I counted a dozen huts, three with tin roofs. Freshly cut palm fronds were sticking above the water to form a channel for our boat, and Dale carefully steered through them. The chants and drumming became louder. Ten young men danced along the shore, moving gracefully forward and backward in time to the drums as the waves lapped at their ankles. They were in full native regalia and carried spears decorated with feathers. Beaded headbands on their foreheads held brilliant red-and-white plumes, plucked from birds of paradise. The plumes cascaded around their faces. Their foreheads and cheeks were streaked with white paint. Necklaces of shells and tusks swayed on their chests, and brown capes—made from pounded tree bark called tapa—swung from their shoulders. Around their midriffs they wore brown skirts made from the same material, with boldly painted black designs. Bracelets of woven grass adorned their arms and ankles. The impression they made was overwhelming—a welcoming ceremony that implied acceptance but carried just a hint of menace. It seemed to say, You can come onto our land, but at our sufferance. And you must behave while you're here.

Behind the dancers, men and women swayed to the drums, many also in native dress. Some of the women were bare-breasted and had red hibiscus blossoms in their hair. A number of the men wore Western T-shirts and shorts. They were solemn, not smiling. Weaving through the crowd were the drummers, pounding on thin, hollowed logs covered with animal skins. The rhythm was steady, accentuated every so often by a piercing sound—a man blowing into a conch shell. The crowd was shouting something over and over again. *"Oro! Oro!"* they repeated—words that meant, our translator told us, "You are welcome." He said we should yell it back, and we did.

The shouts increased as we stepped off the boat and the crowd became even more excited. The dancers became more frantic; they ran up and down the beach faster and faster, until they turned and came at me full speed with spears drawn. I stood my ground and they passed within inches. The crowd yelled even louder. *"Oro! Oro!"* We yelled back. The charges were repeated two or three times. Finally, the dancers stopped. We were guided up the beach, through a passageway of palm fronds decorated with red and white flowers. Around us the villagers pressed close, a jumble of children and men and women whose teeth were missing or blackened or red from chewing betel nuts. They stared at us fixedly, especially the children. I felt something else underlying the boisterous welcome; it was difficult to pin down—a communal sense of expectation, perhaps, or some indefinable tension.

A trio of women held up flowered leis and we bowed to have them placed around our necks. They smiled, crying, *"Oro! Oro!"* A woven mat suddenly appeared before us and our translator told us to step onto it. We did. Another mat appeared in front of us. We took two steps onto that one and the one behind us was quickly whisked away and placed ahead. The process was repeated and we moved like this, from one mat to another, advancing slowly up the beach. I saw ahead of us a long open hut and the mats guided us toward it. When we reached it, our translator caught up with us.

"The chief is there," he whispered to me. "Go inside and greet him, but do not touch him."

I did as instructed, clamoring up one side to enter the hut. Nina followed me, and the others in our group followed her. Men and women from the village crowded in after us, and still more stood outside, pressing their faces close. The drummers still played, and from time to time someone would cry *"Oro! Oro!"* and then everyone would shout it for a minute or so. It would die down and then someone would start the chant all over again. The chief was sitting cross-legged near the entrance, dressed in black shorts and a blue-and-white short-sleeved sports shirt. His hair was gray and his back stooped. He thrust his hand out, and after a moment's hesitation, disregarding the translator's instruction, I shook it. He then shook hands with Nina and everyone else in our group. He smiled kindly and we all sat down. I glanced over at him again, trying to size him up. He had large ears, heavy wrinkles, and a band of tattoo dots across his cheeks and the bridge of his nose. Through the translator I asked, "Are you old enough to have any memories of the war?" His answer was hard to make out over the din and the continuing shouts of *"Oro!"* which still resounded every so often. The chief seemed somewhat confused, but I couldn't be sure that this wasn't from some error in the translation from English to Motu and back again. Our translator suggested that the chief was "too elderly" to understand.

The longhouse was about twenty feet in length, with a thatched roof and open sides, built on a frame of thick logs and mounted on stilts about four feet off the ground. Bits of raffia hung down on the sides, swaying in the ocean breeze. It was clearly a public space—I was told afterward that it was used for village meetings to discuss important matters, like setting up a school, and on those occasions when a candidate for parliament came to solicit votes. As visitors, we were given privileged places around the sides, so that we formed a rough circle. About thirty villagers crowded in around us while the others watched from the outside, clinging to the logs, a solid wall of people with men at the top and wide-eyed children at the bottom.

It was time for introductions. The chief's name, we were told, was Cyprian Oiroembo. A procession of villagers filed by, stopping before each of us to shake hands and give their names. First came the women, after them the girls, then the boys, and finally the men. I was surprised that each had a Christian first name—Grace, Margaret, Elizabeth, Henry, James—and sometimes even English surnames—Hutchinson, Robinson, Braithwaite—until I realized that they had been baptized by missionaries. The reach of Westerners had not entirely passed over Pongani. The last in line was the son of the chief, Donald Cleland, who spoke in a high-pitched, excitable voice, interspersing his remarks with whoops and shouts of *"Oro!"* Dressed only in a scant loincloth, he was bedecked with necklaces of boars' tusks and had tucked tufts of grass into his headband. His cheeks were fiercely painted in red and white stripes and he presented a frightening mien.

A bouquet of flowers was in a pot on the floor, propped upright by a slice of watermelon rind. Next to it was a pile of coconuts. A man with a machete picked up one, whacked it deftly three times to knock the top off, and handed it to me. I smiled, nodded thanks, and drank. The milk tasted sweetly sour. He picked up another coconut, opened it for Nina, then did the same for everyone in our group.

The discussion began. I was prepared for this—villages in this part of PNG are known for democracy, sometimes an excess of democracy; everyone has a say and takes as much time as he wants saying it. A man stood and delivered a lengthy speech of welcome, which was translated in bits and pieces. Then our translator recounted the reason for my visit. As he introduced the others in our group, each was applauded. Another man stood and spoke and then our translator prepared to speak again. "I've briefed the chief," he explained in an aside to me, "and now I have to brief the community." He stood up, rubbing his red Adidas shirt with one hand as he launched into a lengthy explanation of my purpose. Afterward, another man stood and welcomed us. Then Donald, the chief's son, leapt up and began a lengthy discourse. He spoke in rapid bursts, interspersed with translations. "You have come a long distance. You are welcome. Thank you for making it your business to come here." Speaking of the war, he said, "Your people came here and our place was disturbed. You came to see that, so I thank you very much. . . . Many people here who saw the war have died. They were children when the war arrived and they saw the war with their own eyes and they fled into the bushes in fear. Our people were terrified—they saw the guns fire and so they ran to escape. So tell me now why you have come—because for these people, the war is still with them, and no one has talked to them." Donald's voice rose in excitement and spittle flew from his mouth. "My father was sixteen years old when the war arrived. He walked four times on Kokoda and went all the way to Milne Bay. Those white men who came from overseas returned home and were well looked after. But look at my father"—here he gestured toward the chief—"he is forgotten."

I rose and I thanked them for the gracious welcome and their hospitality. I told them that I had wanted to see the place where my father died and said that my mother had always thought his spirit had been released here. I added that many people had suffered in the war, on all sides, and that Americans were very grateful for the assistance the Papuans had rendered and in particular for the aid they'd given the wounded. Now I wanted to know if anyone remembered my father and what had happened on that morning long ago.

After I sat down, I realized that we should offer to make a donation, but I wasn't quite sure whether this should be done in public. I asked our translator quietly and he said, "No, not now."

Another man, who had come with us from Bendoroda, made a speech. The translator only passed along a bit of it, in which he said, "I've been dealing with tourists for a while. I don't want you to blame me later if you miss out on some opportunities."

The discussion went on for quite a while and now many people were talking at once. The crowd was getting restless. A clutch of elderly women to my left seemed disapproving. Whether they were angry at me or at their own speakers wasn't clear, but they seemed upset. Some of the men peering in from the outside were whispering to one another. Finally, Donald took to the floor again, sounding exasperated. He spoke for quite a while and ended by saying, "When you get their stories, will those people benefit or no? When the white men returned home from the war, they were looked after, but for our people, no one bothered to help them."

I suggested to our translator that it was time to offer money, but he shook his head. So I made another speech, saying that if I could talk to people, I would write their stories and the outside world would learn about them and perhaps then they would get some benefit. As this was translated, I could see that Donald looked dubious. The stalemate continued and everyone fell silent for a while. I began to feel frustrated and unaccountably anxious. I had come all this way, only to see my chance to talk to the village elders slipping away. The more I thought about it, the more I wanted it. I was beginning to despair.

Then Dale McCarthy came to my rescue. He roused himself and stood and walked over to the translator. "We're talking money now?" he inquired. The translator nodded. Dale raised both hands and addressed the crowd. "It may not be the right place to do this," he said, his voice loud, "but I'll make a contribution. I'll donate five hundred kina [the equivalent of about two hundred dollars]. But I won't give it to any one person. It'll go to the school."

There was a general murmur of approval. A man jumped up and said, "How about the clinic?" The remark was quickly translated. "Okay," replied Dale. "I'll give two hundred and fifty kina to the school and two hundred and fifty to the clinic." That settled it. The negotiations were over. Everyone started talking at once; people came over to shake my hand. I looked over at the elderly women, who now seemed pleased. Trays of food appeared—yams, pineapple, watermelon, and various other delicacies, which I could not identify. Dale appeared at my elbow and quietly told Nina and me which ones to avoid. Donald leapt up, saying, "Now you may collect the stories. We have someone here who can talk about the war."

I was led to a corner where an elderly man was sitting with his legs crossed. His age was difficult to judge, but deep wrinkles creased his face. He looked kind and intelligent. His skin was a dark bronze color and his teeth were dyed red from betel nuts. He was wearing a light brown shirt and two necklaces made of nuts and small circular pieces of pink and white shells. He said his name was Alexander Girewo and that he was born in 1936. I did a quick calculation: He would have been six years old at the time of my father's death. I turned on my tape recorder and pulled out my notebook as he softly began telling his story. He paused every so often to allow the translator to catch up. He said he had been very young when war came to the village, seemingly out of nowhere and without warning. His first memory of it was the sight of two planes being chased by two other planes. They zoomed low in the sky right over the beach and he had no idea of what they were until his elders told him that the first planes were American and the pursuers were Japanese. They were fighting each other—the people inside the planes—and one would win and the other would die. "We were terrified. We fled into the bushes." He said shortly after that, the older boys, including his brother, the chief, went off to become carriers in the war.

I could bear the suspense no longer. "Did you see the attack that killed my father?"

He nodded yes. He answered slowly, as if striving for precision. I stopped writing in my notebook.

"I was in the village. The boat with your father on it was out in the water, at the mouth of a river, when it was bombed." It was, he said, early in the morning. "I was on my way to school. We all heard it. People ran to investigate and I ran along with the people."

He sat, looking thoughtful while this was translated. Then he resumed. "The white men came in from the boats. They brought the dead and injured and laid them on the beach. I went to look. There were two men dead and a third badly injured. They were all dressed in military clothes."

He did not have much more to say. "Only the older people could get close to the bodies. We small children weren't allowed to go near." He added, "I was appalled and saddened by what I saw." He waved his hands in the air, a gesture of resignation. "But what could I do? It had happened."

He reached over and touched me. Then I talked to the chief himself, who had been sixteen when the war started. But he was not able to answer any questions and his recollections were dim. "It was a bad time," he repeated more than once.

When everyone finished eating, another elder clapped for attention. A villager entered the longhouse, carrying something in both hands. He approached me and unwrapped the bundle. Inside was a handsome necklace threaded with shells and wild banana seeds, with two curved tusks of wild boar rising up like crescent moons in the center. Looking very serious, he held it before him. I heard the son of the chief say something quietly and the translator whispered, "This man goes everywhere with this thing and now he's about to part with it." The man placed the necklace around my neck. Then the chief lifted another necklace, this one made of nuts, with a large half-shell pendant. The chief gently placed this one around my neck, too, and I was told to hold the shell between my teeth. I did, with the shell facing toward my chest. Everyone laughed. I was told to turn it around, and I did, biting it so that the bowl of the shell faced the crowd. They applauded vigorously. The first man took the floor. "These two things are very important to us. When our son or daughter gets married, they cover the price. They are like money or in place of a pig. When we don't have a pig or money, we give these instead. So they are very important. They are what make people married. Today, John got two uncles. These two uncles got married to John. So take these, and when you go back to your home, you put them on the wall, and when you look at them, you will think of your two uncles who saw your father die."

I was too overcome to speak. I finally managed to say how honored I was to have my new uncles. Then we stepped down from the longhouse. I had brought a Polaroid camera and I took photos of the villagers, who clustered around to see the dark negatives and broke into smiles and laughter when their images gradually materialized. I was besieged on all sides: Everyone wanted a photo, and soon I ran out of film.

I felt a tug on my shirt and turned. It was Alexander, the old man who had witnessed the bombing. He gestured for me to follow and we walked down the beach until he stopped. He pointed to a spot in the sand. We did not have a translator—and besides, there was nothing to say—so we just looked in silence for a long while at the place where my father's body had lain.

It was time to leave. We waded back out to the boat and climbed aboard. The entire village gathered at the water's edge to see us off. They sang and danced and waved as the boat pulled away. We waved back and continued waving until they were tiny figures way off in the distance. I took off the two necklaces and wrapped them in a spare shirt and put them on a shelf in the boat where they would be safe. We sped away, heading toward Bendoroda.

My father's death seemed suddenly real to me. Maybe it was having spoken to someone who had seen his body. Maybe it was looking at the spot on the sand where he had lain. Maybe it was the dislocating sense of returning to a place I had only visited in my imagination. But my father's death hit home in a way it never had before. It was not catharsis; it was revelation. I felt decades of illusion drop away and turn to anger—pure white-hot anger. What a senseless, tragic death! What a difference that one little sliver of shrapnel meant to our lives—my mother's life, my brother's, mine. How it had changed everything that followed. Why had he gone on the *King John*? Why hadn't he worn his helmet? Why had he been standing by the pilothouse? Why did all those little decisions conspire to put him at the wrong place at precisely the wrong time? I felt the depth of the loss. I felt his absence, and I felt as if I were mourning him for the first time.

We spent the night in the fisherman's lodge in Bendoroda. It was our last day there and we had been told to get up at dawn and meet the elders. I awoke early. Lying in bed, with only thin walls of leaves between us and the outside, I heard the village stirring around me. I was immersed in the sounds of it—I could hear chickens scratching underneath our floor, the yapping of dogs running around, a baby crying somewhere, pots being put on outside fires, women talking softly. After Nina and I went outside, we had yet another surprise. We were told solemnly to undress—and put on the clan's regalia. I was handed a loincloth, a huge headdress, and a thick club. Nina was decked out in tapa cloth and beads. We were officially inducted into the tribe, which was related by marriage to the Pongani tribe. The villagers here did not want to be outdone by their friendly rivals up the coast.

The ceremony took several hours, which turned out to be a problem. For all that time, I was half naked, and in my excitement I had neglected to put on insect repellent. I suddenly felt faint. When I went to my room, I realized I had been bitten by sand fleas. Hundreds of welts rose up. Nina counted them—more than four hundred on my back, chest, thighs, legs, and arms. I took a heavy dose of Benadryl and we prepared to leave in the boat. Nina hugged the chief's wife, who said they were now sisters.

Dale ferried us down the coast to a comfortable diving resort called Tufi, where I recovered in a cabana with air-conditioning and scotch. Some of the bites were suppurating. Nina insisted that I take an antibiotic we had with us. She also found a local man on the beach, who gave her a plant, instructing her to squeeze the juice and apply it to my skin. It didn't seem to work—nor did the creams we had with us. I felt feverish and weak. Lying on the bed, under a spinning fan, the compulsion to scratch the bites was strong. I was struck by the thought that I was enduring only one-thousandth, one-millionth of what our soldiers had endured there six decades earlier. I had come away with an appropriate souvenir from the beach where my father had died. The next day, we returned to Port Moresby, and after that, we flew to New Zealand and then home.

In New York, I hold a small wooden box, ancient-looking and fragile. On the top, a label is torn, but the heading can be made out: ON HIS MAJESTY'S SERVICE. And below that, faded almost into invisibility, are the words: "This package contains personal effects [of] the late BYRON DARNTON, war correspondent." The top, held by a single nail on one side, swings open.

First there is a small notebook with my father's familiar scrawl. He'd labeled it: "Mainly personal accounts—fliers. One conference—Diller." Then there are the shoulder patches: "Correspondent U.S. Army" in tight-knit yellow print, two chevrons, and two more of the famous 32nd, a red arrow bursting through a solid line. Below that is his passport, the old green kind, valid only for Australia and five other countries in the Pacific for "newspaper work." His photo is inside a raised round seal of the State Department, making him look like a target. He is wearing a jacket and vest, his tie slightly askew, and he is smiling but also frowning slightly, a combination that appears both hopeful and worried. His thumbprint holds the photo in place in the upper right corner. Below that is a pair of broken glasses in a case. Then there's a small golden booklet, an alumni list from the Adrian public schools from 1857 to 1930. I see he's drawn arrows to mark friends and family members. Why did he have that along? Did he use it to establish connections with the soldiers he was interviewing? Near the bottom I find a brass insignia for the collar: war correspondent. Then I come upon a faded checkbook from the Commonwealth Bank of Australia; after the last check, for rent, he'd written a balance of fifty-four pounds, eleven shillings, and three pence. Then I see his dog tag with his name and several Japanese characters and on the reverse side the number 2314338.

Finally, I lift out his war correspondent's credential and identification card, and when I open it, I see a small collection of photos. There's one of Mom, cut into an oval—it must have been extracted from a tiny frame—looking so young, with large, dancing eyes. I've never seen her looking so beautiful. Then there's one of Bob, sitting in a sandbox, looking serious. Something else falls out—a tiny photo, less than an inch long, half an inch wide. It's of a baby, who's being held up in the air by the hands of an unseen adult. The baby looks familiar. I stare at it. Surprise! It's me. My father kept my photo in his ID card, carried it around with him, always.

I sit back in my chair and imagine him. I see him taking it out and showing it to his colleagues, who look at it out of a sense of camaraderie and mumble something pleasant. I see him pulling out his credentials and showing them to an officer to talk his way onto some air force base. The photo slips out and flutters to the ground, just as it has done with me, and he stoops over to collect it, a bit embarrassed. I see him looking at it before he goes to sleep in the correspondent's hut after searching the night sky for Orion, the constellation that connects him to our mother.

I also see him that last morning on the *King John*. It is that quiet time, with dawn just breaking and the mountains taking shape in the far distance. The soldiers around him are coming to life, stretching their legs after a sleepless night, talking quietly. Grenades are passed around. The men are nervous. Some of them catch fish for breakfast. Now there's nothing to do but wait for the order to launch the boat. It looks like it will be a magnificent day; the sky is blue. I imagine my father is excited by thoughts of what might lie ahead, and a bit nervous, too. But he's been through it all before, seen much worse in the trenches. He's older. It's up to him to project an air of calm for the younger men. And he does feel calm. He pats his notebook in his breast pocket to make sure it's there. He touches his side pocket. There are the usual accoutrements: his glasses, his passport, his identification card.

He takes out the card, opens it. There are the photos he's seen dozens of times. He looks at the one of his wife, with her strong brown eyes, and then at the photo of his elder son, looking serious and handsome—it's been so long since he's seen him. And then he holds up the little postage stamp–size photo, his younger son. He doesn't know him yet, not at all, really. But he will . . . he will.

ACKNOWLEDGMENTS

The recollections of my parents' contemporaries and the research of documents would have been prohibitively daunting without the assistance of dozens of people. Many helped me from the best of motives: curiosity and a highly developed spirit of the hunt. Foremost among them is my brother, Bob, who provided guidance and turned over notes of interviews he conducted in the 1980s and an article he wrote for *Raritan*. Others who helped reconstruct those days were Bill MacKaye and Shane Riorden, sons of two of my father's closest friends, and Janice Pollock, daughter-in-law of the author of *Ex-Wife*.

In writing about *The New York Times*, I am indebted to Lester Bernstein for re-creating the newsroom on the day of Pearl Harbor; Florence Segal for providing information on the News of the Week in Review section; Henry Stern for details about the Women's National News Service; Linda Amster and Jeff Roth for retrieving material from the *Times* morgue; Mary Hardiman for her expertise in tracking down photos; and Edith Evans Ashbury, Harold and Doris Faber, Ed Ranzal, and Lester Bromberg for their reminiscences.

ACKNOWLEDGMENTS

In writing about my family, I'm grateful to Louis Dunn and the Darnton family for their hospitality and readiness to share anecdotes; to Jan Richardi for invaluable historical research; and to Elaine Choate for stories about my mother. In Australia and New Guinea, I thank John Stackhouse for stimulating my interest in PNG; Erik and Mary-Anne Andersen for being gracious hosts and engaging companions; Dale McCarthy for getting me to Pongani; Barnabas Embogo Orere for helping me understand what villagers there were saying; Calextus Simeon for taking photographs of the visit; and Linda Honey of the Tufi resort for providing luxurious surroundings to recover from sand flea bites.

In writing about the war, I extend my deep appreciation to Edward Rogers for coming up with all kinds of historical nuggets, including the identity of the pilot who bombed the *King John*. Robert Owens, with the help of his daughter, Sherita Hatch, granted an interview in the course of which he revisited some painful memories. I'm also grateful to Wilder Conley, who shared recollections and scrapbooks of his father; David C. Marshall, who provided his father's journal and film; and Sheridan Fahnestock, who made available a box load of newspaper clippings, files, and letters about his father. Others who helped out with the Australian and New Guinea side of the story include: Geoff Reading, Alan Hooper, James Cumes, Paul Cool, Justin Taylan, Frank Kunz, and Dave Gore. The letters of Carleton "Bill" Kent and Robert Sherrod and the journal and manuscript of Lewis B. Sebring, and the dispatches of George Weller were also indispensable. So was information provided by Philip Weiss, veterans of the 32nd Division and the 3rd Bomb Group, and the surviving stalwarts of the small ships fleet, including Philip Farley, Jack Savage, and Ern Flint. Joe Larkin contributed a photograph of my father soaking his boots in a tub of water. Bill Evanoff gave permission to use a photo of the plane *Baby Blitz*, taken by his father, Alexander Evanoff, and Neil Sandery allowed me to use photos taken of troops aboard the *Timoshenko*.

I am also grateful to the institutions that aided my search: the Wisconsin Historical Society, the Franklin D. Roosevelt Library, the Veterans History Project, the Australian War Memorial, the Air Force Historical Research Agency, the American World War II Orphans Network, the 32nd *Red Arrow News*, the Australian

National Maritime Museum, and the U.S. Army Center of Military History at Fort Lesley J. McNair. The Hertog Research Assistantships at Columbia University provided the services of an excellent researcher, Stacy Cook. Sally Holm, editor of the *Andover Bulletin,* fielded numerous queries. I thank Susan Lee for research and fact-checking and Catherine Talese for tracking down photographs.

I am also indebted to numerous books and magazine articles for background, facts, and color. E. J. Kahn's profile of General Harding in *The New Yorker* mentioned that the officer tucked Kipling poems inside his army manual. Kahn also noted, in a magazine piece in *The Saturday Evening Post* ("The Men Behind the By-Lines") that a guileless neighbor of the War Correspondents' Convalescent Home in Brisbane offered the reporters a gift of calf's-foot jelly. For the description of the *King John* and the *Timoshenko,* including the anonymous general's line "Goddamned war's gone all old-fashioned on us!" I am beholden to Lida Mayo's valuable book, *Bloody Buna.* The book also described the scene aboard the *King John* the day and night before the bombing, the change in orders for Lt. Col. Laurence McKenny, and the attack itself, along with General MacArthur's memorable jeep foray to the start of the Kokoda Trail and his meeting with "Gestapo Gus." *Forgotten Fleet* by Bill Lunney and Frank Finch and *Raggle-Taggle Fleet* by Ladislaw Reday provided material on the assembly of the small ships fleet, on "Mission X," and on the bombing. William Manchester's *American Caesar* provided essential background on General MacArthur, a portrait that was rounded out, as described in the text, by Lewis B. Sebring Jr.'s unpublished *MacArthur's Circus,* found on microfilm at the Wisconsin Historical Society. It gives an almost blow-by-blow account of military censorship. Also helpful were *War Diary 1942* by George Johnson and *Pacific Microphone* by William J. Dunn. Information on the sacred rite of the Ajumawi Native Americans comes partly from Richard Cohen's new book, *Chasing the Sun.*

Finally, I'd like to thank Sonny Mehta of Knopf and my editor, Phyllis Grann, for their advice, patience, and guidance, and my agent, Kathy Robbins, and her husband, Richard Cohen, for their substantive suggestions. Others who read the manuscript and improved it were Felicity Bryan, Peter Osnos, David Grann, and my niece, Kate Darnton. I am thankful to Jackie Montalvo and Maria Massey of Random House and David Halpern, Katie Hut, and Mike Gillespie of the Robbins Office. And closer to home, I am deeply grateful to my wife, Nina, and our three children, Kyra, Liza, and Jamie. They encouraged me every step of the way and read every word, multiple times.

A NOTE ON THE TYPE

The text of this book was set in Sabon, a typeface designed by Jan Tschichold (1902–1974), the well-known German typographer. Based loosely on the original designs by Claude Garamond (ca. 1480–1561), Sabon is unique in that it was explicitly designed for hot metal composition on both the Monotype and Linotype machines as well as for film setting. Designed in 1966 in Frankfurt, Sabon was named for the famous Lyons punch cutter Jacques Sabon, who is thought to have brought some of Garamond's matrices to Frankfurt.

Composed by
North Market Street Graphics, Lancaster, Pennsylvania

Printed and bound by
Berryville Graphics, Berryville, Virginia

Designed by
Maggie Hinders